always up to date

The law changes, but Nolo is always on top of it! We offer several ways to make sure you and your Nolo products are always up to date:

1 **Nolo's Legal Updater**

We'll send you an email whenever a new edition of your book is published! Sign up at **www.nolo.com/legalupdater**.

2 **Updates @ Nolo.com**

Check **www.nolo.com/update** to find recent changes in the law that affect the current edition of your book.

3 **Nolo Customer Service**

To make sure that this edition of the book is the most recent one, call us at **800-728-3555** and ask one of our friendly customer service representatives. Or find out at **www.nolo.com**.

please note

We believe accurate and current legal information should help you solve many of your own legal problems on a cost-efficient basis. But this text is not a substitute for personalized advice from a knowledgeable lawyer. If you want the help of a trained professional, consult an attorney licensed to practice in your state.

2nd edition

The Complete Guide to Selling a Business

By Attorney Fred. S. Steingold

NOLO

Second Edition	OCTOBER 2005
Editor	EMILY DOSKOW
Cover Design	SUSAN PUTNEY
Book Design	TERRI HEARSH
Proofreading	JOE SADUSKY
Index	THÉRÈSE SHERE
Printing	CONSOLIDATED PRINTERS, INC.

Steingold, Fred
    The complete guide to seling a small business / by Fred Steingold.--2nd ed.
      p. cm.
    ISBN 1-4133-0362-5
    1. Sale of business enterprises--Law and legislation--United States--Popular works. I
Steingold, Fred. Sell your business. II. Title.

    KF1355.Z9S74 2005
    346.73'065--dc22

                                               2005047752

Quanity sales: For information on bulk purchases or corporate premium sales, please contact the Special Sales Department. For academic sales or textbook adoptions, ask for Academic Sales. 800-955-4775, Nolo, 950 Parker Street, Berkeley, CA 94710.

Acknowledgments

I wish to thank Emily Doskow for her superb editing.

Thanks also to:

Marcia Stewart for building a strong foundation for this book in its first edition

Jake Warner for his many helpful contributions and unflagging encouragement

Mark Hartley, CPA, for his analysis of tax issues

Glen J. Cooper for his insights regarding business brokers

Terri Hearsh for her production magic

Andre Zivkovich and the Applications Development Department for creating the CD-ROM, and

Susan Putney for designing the great cover.

About the Author

Attorney Fred S. Steingold is an expert on business law, advising entrepreneurs on how to start, buy, run, and sell businesses. He is the author of Nolo's *Complete Guide to Buying a Business, Legal Guide for Starting and Running a Small Business*, and *The Employer's Legal Handbook*. His monthly column, The Legal Advisor, is carried by trade publications around the country.

Table of Contents

Introduction: Using This Book to Sell Your Business

Part 1: Overview of the Process

1 Deciding Whether—And When—To Sell

2 The Key Steps in Selling Your Business

3 The Key Legal Issues in Selling Your Business

4 Tax Considerations When Selling Your Business

8 Finding the Right Buyer

9 Structuring the Sale

10 The Investigation Stage: How Sellers and Buyers Check Each Other Out

11 Drafting a Letter of Intent

Part 3: Preparing a Sales Agreement

12 Preparing the Sales Agreement and Other Legal Documents

13 Who's Selling, Who's Buying—And What's Being Sold

14 The Sales Price and Terms of Payment

Part 4: **Preparing the Promissory Note and Other Sales Documents**

19 Promissory Notes and Other Installment Payment Documents

20 Bill of Sale, Lease Assignment, and Other Documents for Transferring Your Business

21 Documents for Noncompete and Future Work Commitments

Part 5: Closing the Deal

22 Preparing for a Smooth Closing

Appendixes

A How to Use the CD-ROM

B Sample Sales Agreements

Index

Using This Book to Sell Your Business

Through hard work, ingenuity, and possibly a bit of good luck, you've built a viable business. Now, you're ready to sell—or at least you're thinking about it. But the process may seem intimidating, and you probably have lots of legal and financial questions. Whether you want to handle the whole sale yourself or work with lawyers, accountants, and other professionals, this book can help. It provides step-by-step guidance to do it right—from marketing and positioning your company in preparation for the sale to negotiating the best deal.

Each year, some 750,000 American businesses change ownership. Most of these are small and mid-sized businesses: retail stores, beauty salons, quick-print shops, restaurants, tax preparation services, landscapers, electrical contracting firms, and modest manufacturing operations—to mention just a few. Keep in mind that no matter what kind of business you own—a professional services company, a neighborhood bagel shop, or a home-based website that sells imported garden tools—there's likely to be a buyer out there looking for a business like yours. But finding the right buyer and selling the business on favorable terms will require both planning and hard work. This book will help you get the job done with a minimum of hassles, worries, and expenses. It provides step-by-step guidance, checklists, and all the forms you need, from the day you first consider selling to the closing. Using this book, you can sell your business to a reliable buyer at a favorable price—and protect yourself legally and financially.

A. Is This Book for You?

This book focuses on the sale of small to mid-sized businesses. Though much of what you learn here will also be applicable to selling larger enterprises, this book definitely is not concerned with the sorts of mergers and acquisitions that you read about in The *Wall Street Journal*. It can help you if you fit this profile:

- You have a business that might sell for tens of thousands of dollars or even several hundred thousand dollars, but probably not more than $2 million.
- You own the business yourself or with one, two, or a handful of others.
- Your business is set up as a sole proprietorship, partnership, corporation, or limited liability company (LLC).
- You want to sell your business—not merge with the buyer's business and keep a long-term role in its management (although you may work as a consultant for a short transition period).

Does this sound like your business? If it does, then this book has exactly the information you need to move forward with a smooth and profitable sale.

B. How This Book Can Help

Unlike other big transactions in your life, such as selling or buying a house, a business sale doesn't follow a paint-by-numbers routine controlled by an established market and common practices and procedures. Instead, each business sale is somewhat unique; there are no standard procedures to follow. This means that you and the buyer must work out the answers to a number of important questions. This book explains the territory—from legal and financial terms and how deals are structured to the nitty-gritty of what goes into a sales agreement and what happens at a closing.

To make it easy to find what you need, the book is organized into five sections with an appendix and a CD-ROM so that you can tailor the sales agreement and other legal documents to fit your particular sale. Here's a brief overview.

1. Overview of the Process

The first six chapters explain the entire sale process, so you'll know what to expect. You'll learn how to:

- decide whether or not to sell
- time your sale
- prepare for the practical and legal steps involved in successfully selling your business
- analyze the tax consequences of selling your business

- set a realistic price range for your business, and
- choose and work with lawyers, accountants, and other professionals.

2. Getting Ready to Sell

Part 2 (Chapter 7-11) helps you get started with the actual steps you'll need to take in order to sell your business, and explains how to:

- prepare your business for sale— which commonly takes more time and elbow grease than you might think
- create a marketing plan designed to attract financially sound buyers
- negotiate for the best possible price and terms
- legally structure your sale
- put legal protections in place to help assure that you get paid in full
- investigate the buyer's credentials, and
- draft a letter of intent.

3. Preparing a Sales Agreement

Parts 3 and 4 are the heart of the book. They show how to tailor your own sales agreement and the other legal documents that you'll need to transfer your business to its new owner. These are not cookie-cutter documents. They must be fine-tuned to fit the needs of your transaction—and these chapters show you how to do that.

Part 3 (Chapter 12-18) focuses on the sales agreement: the crucial document that you prepare and sign after you and the buyer agree on the price, terms, and legal structure of the sale. The sales agreement ties together all the sale terms. Whoever prepares the first draft—you, the buyer, or a lawyer—you need to understand the legal consequences of every clause. The seven chapters in Part 3 show you how to put together a sales agreement that's clear, complete, and legally binding. The agreement will cover such important issues as:

- how the buyer will pay for the business—one lump sum or install-ment payments
- which business liabilities you'll be responsible for
- your promise (if any) not to compete after the sale, and
- employment and consulting deals.

4. Preparing the Promissory Note and Other Important Sales Documents

Part 4 (Chapter 19-21) of the book shows you how to put together the other documents and papers you'll need to complete the sale of your business, including:

- the bill of sale
- the promissory note
- the security agreement, and
- the covenant not to compete.

These documents help assure that there will be no slip-ups or delays when the time comes to turn over the business to the buyer.

5. Closing the Deal

Finally, you'll be ready to take the final step in your journey: actually transferring the business to the buyer at closing. In Part 5 of this book (Chapter 22), you'll learn how to construct a comprehensive closing checklist so that the closing goes as smoothly as possible.

C. Working Efficiently With Lawyers, Accountants, and Other Professionals

Selling a business for top dollar may not seem like a job you want to tackle all on your own. But, fortunately, the process can be broken down into small pieces, each of which you can understand and master. With this book, you should be able to handle much of the work yourself. And if you call in a lawyer, accountant, appraiser, or business broker as needed, you'll be able to explain just what you need and why.

This book will alert you to specific situations in which you're likely to benefit from professional help. For example, because your business and the deal you strike with the buyer are unique, it's a good idea to have a lawyer review your sales agreement before you sign it. Similarly, although this book provides a lot of information about the tax laws, analyzing your individual tax exposure is a task best left to an experienced expert such as a CPA after you've reviewed the tax material here.

By doing much of the work yourself, the fees you pay for professional services should be far lower than what you'd pay if you used experts to handle the entire sale of your business. In fact, you stand to save thousands of dollars. Once you firmly grasp every step of the sale process, you can act as a knowledgeable general contractor, with your professional advisers serving as your cost-efficient subcontractors. This book will help you along that path.

Icons Used in This Book

 Warning: This icon cautions you to slow down and consider potential problems.

 See an expert: This icon lets you know when to seek the advice of a lawyer, accountant, or other expert.

 Fast track: This icon indicates that you may be able to skip certain material that may not be relevant to your situation.

 Recommended reading: This icon is used to make note of other books or resources for more information about a particular issue or topic.

 Tip: This icon signals a special suggestion that will help make your sale go smoothly—or will assure that legal requirements are met.

 CD-ROM: This icon means that the form discussed in the text is on the CD-ROM included in this book.

Part 1

Overview of the Process

Deciding Whether—And When—To Sell

If you've already decided to sell your business, you're probably anxious to get on with the job. That's fine. Skim or skip this chapter and move on to Chapter 2.

Like many other entrepreneurs, you may be ambivalent about giving up your business. For a variety of family, economic, and emotional reasons, you may be trying to sort out whether it makes more sense to sell now or to soldier on for a few years and sell later. Hopefully, by explaining exactly what's involved in the sales process, this book will help you decide.

When planning to sell a business, it almost always pays to pace yourself. Few businesses are sold overnight, and when they are, they're commonly sold for too little. In fact, the process of preparing and selling a business for top dollar to a reliable buyer may take two or three years to complete. It follows that even if you decide not to pull the sales trigger for a few years yet, you may be wise to begin now to get your business ready for a possible sale later.

A. Deciding Whether or Not to Sell Can Be Agonizing

You're not alone if you start out believing that the decision to sell or keep your business is strictly a matter of dollars and cents. Many other business owners have shared this belief. So as you go through the decision-making process, you may be surprised to discover that in addition to monetary concerns, selling a business almost always involves an array of personal considerations as well. It's perfectly normal if part of you wants to sell while another part is not so sure. And, of course, there may be other decision makers in the picture: Co-owners, family members, investors, and key employees may also weigh in on whether it's a good time to sell. For example, if your long-time co-owner is moving to Barcelona and wants to sell now, you may have little choice but to agree. Or poor health may dictate that you find a buyer as soon as possible.

But let's assume for a moment that your sale is largely discretionary. Even if selling your business now makes excellent sense based on a purely economic analysis, emotional ties to your work may gently nudge you in the direction of holding on. Despite the many headaches and frustrations that go with owning a business over any period of time, chances are you'll have personally identified with the business in profound ways that can make you hesitate when you consider life without it.

Think of it this way: For years, you've been creatively solving problems in a world filled with action. On good days, running your business is stimulating and, on the best days, you experience a heady rush of adrenaline. You'd be less than human if you didn't wonder sometimes

Sometimes It's Not All or Nothing

Although this book focuses on the sale of an entire business, that's not the only way to get a large chunk of cash out of the business you've built. Sometimes it's possible to sell a part of a business and keep the rest. That's particularly feasible when a business has multiple functions. Then, you can continue to enjoy the action but direct your time and energies to the part of the business that you enjoy most—or that you believe is the most profitable. The key to executing this strategy is usually to divide your business in a way that potential buyers are attracted to the bits you plan to sell, while at the same time you retain at least the seeds of a successful new enterprise. And, of course, you need to convince the buyer that you won't use the portion of the business you keep as a springboard from which to re-create a business that directly competes with the one you sold.

EXAMPLE: Joe owns Today's Kitchen Inc., an upscale shop that sells and installs stylish imported kitchen cabinetry. His company also creates custom kitchen plans—including recommendations for elegant counter tops and top-of-the-line appliances. And if the customer wishes, Today's Kitchen will provide a skilled construction crew to install everything. As the business and his profits have grown, Joe has become increasingly disenchanted with the installation part of the business. Not only can some customers be impossibly nitpicky, but the day-to-day hassles of installation take Joe away from his real love, drawing kitchen layout plans and building the fine custom cabinetry to fit them. As a result, he decides to sell the installation part of the business to Lyle, a master carpenter who enjoys working on site with homeowners (even fussy ones). They arrange for Lyle to have an office and shop within Joe's business space so that Joe can handily refer customers to a skillful and reliable contractor, and Lyle can count on a steady stream of referral business. Lyle agrees to pay Joe $30,000 for the installation business (payable in installments over a three-year period), plus 10% of Lyle's net profits for each of the next three years. Lyle also agrees to pay a modest monthly rent to Joe for the office and shop space he'll occupy. As part of the deal, Lyle gets to take over (and earn money from) several installations currently in progress and 10 that are about to begin. Joe agrees that he'll be available to consult with Lyle about any on-the-job design issues that arise. Finally, the two agree that for three years Joe will not reenter the installation business.

about whether, after selling your business, you'll mourn the loss of these exciting feelings and not know how to replace them. If you're contemplating retirement, your ambivalence may be especially pronounced.

If you start by accepting that your mixed feelings are common and under-standable, it will be easier to work through them. If you haven't already done so, it often helps to explore these issues with a spouse, partner, friend, or relative—especially one who has small business experience. But choose your advisers well; sometimes those closest to you may (unknown to themselves) have a vested interest in either maintaining the status quo or pushing for change. So, in some instances, it may make the most sense to explore the issues with a knowledgeable outsider—such as a successful and re-spected entrepreneur in your area—who can offer more objective insight.

And even if you conclude that it's best for you and your family to move on, you may still face the problem of actually letting go. Although you may know that your health, age, or changing interests mean it's time to sell, the fear of stepping into something new can lead you to experience considerable anxiety and may even cause you to pull back when it would be wiser to move ahead. In a sense, creating and growing your business is a little like nurturing a child to maturity. If you've successfully helped your children spread their wings and fly

off on their own, perhaps it will be easier for you to similarly shed your business.

But just as the prospect of freeing yourself from business worries can be enticing, you'd be typical if you also had lingering doubts:

- Am I doing the right thing to sell now?
- Will I get enough money to justify all my hard work?
- What if the buyer doesn't pay future installments?
- What will I do next?
- Will I really be improving my financial or personal situation?

By giving you a solid understanding of the tasks involved in selling a business, this book can make it easier to make decisions about what's best in your situation.

B. Do You Have a Saleable Business?

Poorly performing businesses are of-ten easy to part with. Especially if your enterprise has been a financial disappoint-ment—or requires horrendously long hours—you may be anxious to say adios. But obviously, when a business does poorly—often through no fault of its own-er—selling it can be difficult or impos-sible. This, of course, raises the question of whether it's wiser to try to improve a poorly performing business enough to make it saleable or to simply walk away.

It's hard to fix a failing business, especially one you no longer want to own. After all, if a quick fix was possible, chances are you'd have already done so. It often makes more sense to simply close a sagging operation, face up to your feelings of failure and possibly even guilt, and accept the fact that no one is likely to be naïve enough to buy your ailing business.

This means that before you spend the time and effort of trying to sell your business, you need to determine whether, realistically, you have something to sell. Fortunately, in many instances, there are steps you can take to make a borderline business saleable. In later chapters (especially Chapter 7) you'll find practical suggestions for doing this. In the meantime, here's a list of factors that can help or hurt your chances of selling your business.

1. Factors That Make a Business Saleable

Typically, to have a saleable business, you'll need to be able to offer a buyer one of more of the following elements:

- **A solid profits history.** In most instances, a buyer will want to see that the business has made money—not lost it—for at least the past two to three years. And if the buyer will be working in the business (which is very common for small business owners), the business should also produce enough income to generously reward the owner's day-to-day

efforts. Sure, there are a few exceptions to this "no profits, no sale" rule, as might be the case where a potentially lucrative business is still in its start-up phase or some outside event suddenly changes the fortunes of a poorly performing operation. But if your profits are bad, your story must be good.

- **A good location that can be taken over by the buyer.** This is particularly important when location is essential to the success of the business—for example, a pharmacy that's located close to a number of doctors' offices, or a restaurant in the heart of your town's theater district. If you're leasing the space that your business occupies, you need to make sure the new owner can continue to use the space. If so, prospective buyers will be especially impressed if your lease has locked in a favorable long-term rent or options to renew. Similarly, it can help make your business saleable if you own the building that the business occupies. Again, the buyer knows that the location is secure— and, if you're willing to sell the building, the chance for the buyer to own it may itself be an attractive feature. Of course, if you have a service business in which customers rarely have to come to your business place, location isn't as important.

- **Premises and equipment that are in good repair.** An efficiently equipped and smoothly running operation is a huge plus, since it means that the buyer can build on success, not have to create it. By contrast, a sensible buyer will likely be turned off by a business—profitable or not—that looks shabby and whose equipment is either broken or in obviously fragile condition.

- **An attractive inventory of goods.** It helps to have a stock of fresh, good-looking items that are available to sell the moment the buyer takes over. By contrast, half a store full of stale inventory that's obviously turning over slowly and includes obsolete, out-of-favor, or over-priced items will turn away knowledgeable buyers. Obviously, inventory is primarily a factor in selling a retail business—and not terribly significant if yours is a service business.
- **An exclusive distributorship that can be taken over by the buyer.** If your business has the exclusive right to sell attractive merchandise or services in a desirable area, the buyer will be protected from local competitors that otherwise might be selling the same brand or offering the same branded service. For example, a catering business that is one of four operations approved to cater functions at the most popular wedding venue in town is sure to attract buyers.
- **A loyal group of customers or clients.** A ready-made roster of repeat

customers means the buyer can hit the ground running. If your local service business enjoys a good reputation, chances are you've built a solid customer base. For example, a plumber who has built the best business in the area over a 30-year period really has something to sell.

- **Lucrative long-term contracts with customers or clients.** Buyers will be impressed if you've already booked future business that they can take over. For example, if ABC Landscaping has just signed favorable long-term contracts with several highly solvent hotels, there's money to be made from day one.
- **Limited competition.** If you can't have a monopoly, being in business where there are few competitors is the next best thing. For example, if yours is only one of three companies equipped to clean the outside of large buildings in a mid-sized city, a buyer might see your business as a fantastic opportunity.
- **Trade secrets, copyrights, patents, or trademarks that are hard or impossible to replicate.** If your little company publishes the best local guides for Northern New England or a best-selling employment book, the buyer is able to acquire money-making intangibles that no one else has or can easily replicate. Similarly, for many businesses, a clever, well-known, and highly respected

business name or trademark is a highly attractive attribute.

- **Accounts receivable that are relatively easy to collect.** When solid sales are already on your books, the buyer knows that cash will flow in almost immediately.

- **A specialized and highly competent workforce.** Assuming that the workers will stay on when the new owner takes over, the buyer doesn't have to do the often-difficult work of assembling a talented staff. Of course, if your workforce consists of counter clerks or other minimally skilled workers, your workforce won't be a factor in a sale, because a buyer can find replacements with very little effort.

- **A business that complements the buyer's existing business.** Synergy is a hugely efficient way for a business to build up its bottom line. A deli, for example, may find that your bakery will fit well with its existing business. Similarly, a dry cleaning business may see a benefit in acquiring your shirt laundry. And when the business being acquired is a direct competitor whose market clout has forced the acquirer to keep prices low, the strategic attractiveness of combining the business is further enhanced.

Of course, this is only a partial list. The point is that many small businesses do have a lot of value to offer a prospective buyer. Hopefully, in analyzing your own business, you'll be able to identify at least several attributes that will be of particular interest.

2. Factors That Make a Business Hard to Sell

There are some businesses that for one reason or another are unlikely to be snapped up by a buyer. Realistically, you can expect to have trouble finding any takers if your business includes some of the following elements:

- **Business loses money.** Face it, if your balance sheet is consistently written in red ink, it will be tough to get to first base with a buyer. Yes, you may have a story about how your business is really a diamond in the rough, but a typical buyer is likely to conclude that were this really true, you would have long since polished it.

- **Sales have been declining.** If your sales have gone down significantly over the past several years, it will be very hard to generate much interest in buying your business. True, you may be able to show that you've learned to run the business more efficiently, so that even though your gross income has declined, your profits have increased. But a prospective buyer will realize that this can't last forever, meaning you'll need a convincing plan to reignite growth.

- **Profits don't exceed the value of your labor.** Even if your business shows a modest profit, it may not be sufficient to make your business saleable. For example, a buyer may not see much advantage in working 60 hours a week to earn $40,000 a year—especially if the buyer can earn the same amount for working a normal 40-hour week as an employee for someone else and not have the headaches of running a business.

- **No longer part of a popular trend.** Millions of business start-ups try to cash in on a hot trend. For example, frozen yogurt, video rental, pet food, and nail care shops all have had their moment as the latest, greatest thing. But today, if the hot action in your area is in coffee houses or gourmet sandwich shops, it may be hard to sell a frozen yogurt business, even one that makes a small profit. The point is that when a once-trendy business goes out of fashion, you'll need strong profits and a good business plan to hook a buyer.

- **Lawsuits and other disputes.** A pending lawsuit can definitely put a damper on the sale of a business. Ditto for unresolved claims that haven't hit the courts yet and administrative proceedings or investigations that seriously affect your business. Even though you might offer to take full legal and financial responsibility for any negative consequences, many potential buyers will pull back, fearing the unknown—including how lawsuits and other disputes may affect the public image of the business. In short, if you can't reach settlements before you start to market your business, the saleability of even a well-run, profitable business may be negatively impacted.

- **Large debts.** Debts tend to send the message that your business doesn't produce enough cash to keep current on bills—or, equally harmful, that the cash flow is wildly unpredictable. True, if your business is still in its start-up phase—or has recently expanded or made an acquisition—a relatively high debt burden may be explainable. And you can also offer to remain responsible for payment of existing debts as part of the sale. But none of this is likely to be enough to convince a buyer to sign on the dotted line unless your business has the robust cash flow and profits necessary for long-term success.

- **Deep-pocket competition.** Buyers will likely be scarce if your market niche is under obvious assault by big-money competitors. For example, your bicycle sales and repair shop may bring in a tidy profit, but if a well-heeled national chain of similar shops is coming soon to a shopping plaza near you, watch out. Potential buyers may (rightfully) imagine that your business is about to be steam-rollered.

- **Rapidly declining neighborhood.** Some businesses (an export-import operation, for example) are immune to negative changes in their environs because they're not closely identified with or dependent on that area in the first place, or can easily move. But you'll almost surely be in a leaky sales boat if a fast-declining location is important to your business.
- **No long-term lease.** Businesses that are location-sensitive are likely to face problems finding a buyer if the prospective new owner can't be assured of a long-term lease. If your lease is about to expire and the landlord has other uses for the space, you can expect prospective buyers to back off once the implications sink in.
- **Business can be duplicated at very little cost by a prospective buyer.** Some businesses are so easy to start that prospective buyers may see little or even no advantage to buying one that's already in operation—unless, of course, there's great name recognition, contracts for ongoing work, or a super lease that assures an ideal location. Why buy a run-of-the-mill home fix-it business or house-cleaning service if all you need to start a similar operation is a good tool kit or a vacuum cleaner? After all, why should someone spend $25,000 or even just $10,000 to buy

your business when they can start a similar one for far less? In short, unless you can come up with a compelling reason that your business is especially valuable, you may need to face the fact that it's simply too small or easy to replicate to be sold.

Even if your business has very little going for it, don't get discouraged. It's often possible to improve the prospects of a business that at first seems to be a lost cause.

EXAMPLE: Jane runs a sole proprietorship called Jane's Janitorial Service, specializing in cleaning small office buildings. Jane runs the business from her home, storing the necessary equipment (vacuum cleaner, brooms, pails, and mops) and cleaning supplies in her basement. Occasionally, Jane hires a helper or two to work with her. She has no long-term contracts but currently cleans two buildings whose owners seem satisfied with her work. Jane is planning to move to another city and would like to sell her business to a new owner, but she quickly finds out she has no takers.

But Jane doesn't give up on the idea of selling over the next six months and is able to sign three-year cleaning contracts with her two existing business customers plus win a bid process to clean a good-sized new professional building. Now, with profitable contracts in hand, Jane is able to find a buyer.

C. Working Out Problems With Your Co-Owners

In the best-case scenario, when you want to sell, your co-owners will agree with your decision and you can efficiently divvy up the tasks of selling. But if they don't agree, or have different ideas on how to proceed or what price to put on the business, you've obviously got a serious problem—one that can jeopardize your chances of getting the best price or even scuttle the sale.

This section will suggest ways to head off or resolve problems with your co-owners.

1. The Value of Buy-Sell Agreements

Fortunately, not all co-owner disagreements turn into a sale-damaging problem. In the best-case scenario, you and your co-owners anticipated the possible sale of the business someday and agreed—well in advance—on a method for moving forward. You may have worked out how, whether, and when a sale can be made under the terms of a buy-sell agreement when you set up the business. Or perhaps the subject of a possible sale was covered in another document such as a partnership agreement, a shareholders agreement, or an LLC operating agreement. Often these documents provide that if one owner wants to leave the business, the others can buy out the departing owner's

interest, based on a fixed price, a clear-cut formula, or an appraisal. Or these documents may simply provide that if one co-owner wants out, that's enough to trigger a sale. If your co-owned business has such a buy-sell or other agreement in place, it will govern your sale options, and it's unlikely that current differences of opinion among co-owners will affect your decision.

But even if you haven't had the fore-sight to sign a buy-sell or other similar agreement, and a possible sale is still a few years off, it's not too late. You can approach your co-owners with the sensible suggestion that you plan ahead for a peaceful transition by signing such an agreement now. Even co-owners who may at first be reluctant to do this should quickly see that risking a serious spat with other owners is a sure way to destroy a business's value.

Recommended reading on buy-sell agreements. By far the best source of self-help information on how to proceed is *Business Buyout Agreements: A Step-by-Step Guide for Co-Owners*, by Anthony Mancuso and Bethany K. Laurence (Nolo).

2. How Mediation Can Help Resolve Disputes With Co-Owners

Now, let's assume that you don't have a buy-sell agreement and that you want to sell—but for any one of a dozen reasons your co-owners aren't convinced it's the right move. You might point out to them that unless you can all agree on a future course of action, under the laws of your state, you may be able to simply petition a court to dissolve the business, resulting in a liquidation of its assets. This will probably be seen as an empty threat, as your co-owners will quickly see that liquidating the business would almost surely destroy most of its value.

Especially if you're selling the business because there are underlying differences among the owners that make it hard for all of you to continue to work together, you'll all need to lay aside your animosities and work cooperatively during the sales process or risk disaster. Sometimes it's possible to reduce short-term friction by agreeing on a general plan of action and then delegating one person—such as an outsider or nonowner CEO—to carry it out. Another solution is a buyout. One contending faction can buy the other out and then prepare the business for sale to an outsider.

If the disagreements among the co-owners or with an unrealistic heir of a deceased owner run so deep that you can't even rationally and civilly discuss a realistic sales scenario, it's often time to bring in a mediator—a neutral third party who's been trained to help people come to voluntary solutions to seemingly intractable problems. Especially if the mediator has experience in the field of small business ownership disputes, a creative idea may emerge that you and your co-owners hadn't previously considered. Let's say, for instance, that you're the part owner of an electrical business that does electrical contracting and also runs a lighting store. Maybe, with the help of a mediator, you can work out a deal where you keep the lighting store and the other owners keep the contracting business. Then, you'll be free to apply your ideas to build the profitability of the store, with the idea of selling it within the next two years. This would neatly sidestep the unsavory prospect of trying to sell a business over the objections of reluctant co-owners. Or suppose you and the wife of your recently divorced co-owner (who, thanks to a divorce settlement, now owns half the business) can't agree on a sales price. The mediator may help the two of you agree on several commonly accepted business valuation methods. (See Chapter 5 for advice on how to value a business.)

Recommended reading on mediation. For top-notch guidance on the mediation process, read *Mediate, Don't Litigate: Strategies for Successful Mediation,* by Peter Lovenheim and Lisa Guerin (Nolo). One key to a successful mediation is to select a knowledgeable mediator who all the owners feel is both competent and neutral.

D. Choosing the Best Time to Sell

Once you've taken the steps to polish your business for sale (as discussed in detail in Chapter 7), you're ready to start the process of looking for a buyer (the focus of Chapter 8). In a perfect world, the exact time you'll want to list your business for sale will depend as much on the temperature of the market as on personal needs. If selling is urgent because, for example, you have serious health problems or are moving away from the area to take a well-paying job, you'll be under pressure to act as quickly as reasonably possible to try to find a buyer. But in instances where you're not under extreme pressure to sell, you'll have more discretion over timing. Consider the following factors—business cycles, changes in the neighborhood, interest rates, industry trends, and the health of your business—in weighing the pros and cons of acting now or waiting awhile.

1. Business Cycles

As you know, business cycles wax and wane, as do the fortunes of particular business segments. (For example, the market for men's suits and sport coats languished when chinos and polo shirts became the workplace norm.) Obviously, you'd like to sell your business when market demand is high, not low. And occasionally, when some event results in

skyrocketing profits, this can mean acting at warp speed to prepare your business for sale before the updraft dies. By contrast, it's also true that if your geographical area or business sector is experiencing a recession, you may want to wait until things improve. Especially if you believe that time is on your side—for example, if your men's store specializes in traditional workplace attire and you believe that the fashion pendulum will soon swing back in your direction—waiting a year or two can add significantly to your sale price.

But figuring out the best time to sell is not always intuitive. True, when business conditions are great and buyers are plentiful, deciding to sell may not require a Ph.D. in business psychology. But even in less-certain times, there may be eager buyers. For example, when there's a recession and midlevel managers are being laid off by the droves, a number of these liberated ex-wage slaves—some of whom may even have received a generous severance package—may decide to abandon the job market entirely and either start or buy a business. And when they do, they may even be attracted to a bad-luck (and possibly low-cost) business segment with good prospects to eventually rebound.

2. Changes in the Neighborhood

If your business derives much of its sales locally, the physical conditions in the surrounding area can and often should influence your timing. For example, assume that your business is in a congested urban setting with limited parking, and that this is costing you customers unwilling to deal with the hassles of reaching you. If the city is about to break ground on a long-awaited parking structure nearby that will solve much of the problem, you may want to wait until the structure is done before you start marketing your business.

Or suppose you have a retail business in a more remote area but know that several large condo complexes are scheduled to be built in your area soon. It might pay to wait until the new construction is well along so that potential buyers can see for themselves the possibility of increased customer traffic, making a purchase attractive at a higher price than you'd get now.

3. Interest Rates

Unlike the housing market, bank interest rates usually don't play a decisive role in determining whether the market for small businesses is strong or not. The reason: Most small business purchases are financed by the seller rather than by a bank. But some buyers may need a bank line of credit for purchasing equipment and supplies or for making renovations, so it can be easier to sell some businesses when interest rates are low. Of course, if rates are rock bottom, it probably means the entire economy is tanking, and unless your business is counter-cyclical, you'll want to wait for at least a small upturn.

4. Industry Trends

You may conclude that the future is bleak for your entire industry—or at least for the little guy in your industry. If so, you may decide that now's the time to bail out, even if it's too late to get top dollar. For example, in many areas, traditional neighborhood hardware stores are being squeezed out by large, warehouse-style home improvement centers. Similarly, independent stationery stores and bookstores are increasingly finding it hard to compete with huge outlets that offer football field-sized displays of merchandise. In short, if your business is in an industry facing similar consolidation, you have a choice: Try to fight the trend, or sell before you get steamrollered.

And, of course, competition from mega-competitors isn't the only danger facing a small business. Other enterprises may be imperiled by technological change or shifting consumer priorities. Look what happened to once-profitable TV repair shops as TVs became so reasonably priced and reliable that millions found that it made more sense to buy a new TV rather than to fix the old one. Or consider what happened to travel agencies when the Internet made it a snap for savvy travelers to self-book reservations: Airlines were able to cut or eliminate the commissions formerly paid to travel agencies.

If your industry is likely for any reason to face a calamitous profits breakdown, there's usually ample warning, as there was in all the examples above. So, if you spot a highly disadvantageous business reality bearing down on you, you'll need to either reposition your business or move to sell it as quickly as possible.

5. The Health of Your Business

If your business is solidly profitable and likely to be more so in the future, chances are it will be reasonably easy to sell whenever you decide to make the move. And this is especially likely to be true if yours is in a growing field in which small enterprises are expected to continue to thrive. But if you believe one-time factors such as the bankruptcy of a key competitor have helped your business crest a profits wave, you'll probably want to consider putting it on the market sooner rather than later. Similarly, you'll want to hold off on selling if for any reason— whether from a natural disaster such as wildfire or unexpectedly poor market conditions—your business is currently doing worse than it probably will be doing a year or two from now.

!   **Be prepared to pull back in the face of adversity.** Even if you believe your business sale's stars are all in the right alignment—the economy, your profits picture, and business trends are ideal for putting your business on the market—you need to be ready to pull back and bide your time if market conditions suddenly turn dicey. Because psychologically it can

be extra tough to do this if you've already promised your spouse a new house and made a down payment on a boat, my advice is to never plan to spend a dollar from a business sale until the deal has closed and it's firmly in your grasp. For example, if you start to market your profitable family restaurant, located smack dab in the center of a booming high-tech district, and overnight the business falls on hard times because of a bad economy, you need to be willing to delay the sale. Instead, you might consider pulling your restaurant off the market and eking out a small profit for a few years until the technology sector revives and your bistro again has a line out the door.

E. If You Need to Leave the Business, But the Time Isn't Right to Sell

In some situations, you may realize that your wish to sell your business quickly is in conflict with your wish to sell for top dollar. When that's the case, anything you can do to relieve yourself of the pressure to sell in a hurry will be worthwhile. In some cases this can mean looking for a creative way to delay the sale while still meeting at least some of your personal needs.

Suppose you've reached a time of life when you simply don't want to work any more. And let's say, because of a health problem, this conclusion hits you hard just at a time when economic conditions are less than ideal for selling your business. If you go ahead anyway and sell your business based on your strong need to retire, you'll almost surely have to resign yourself to accepting a relatively meager sale price. But maybe selling now is not the only way to reconcile your personal needs with marketplace realities. One excellent approach might be to arrange for someone to run the business for the duration of your illness, and then put your business on the market when conditions are more favorable. Or if your health conditions are more serious, you might find and hire a manager—perhaps promote a key employee—to carry on the business until economic conditions improve.

EXAMPLE: Phyllis has owned and personally managed a thriving flower shop for some 30 years. Recently, she decided it's time get out of the business and do some traveling. Unfortunately, she has also concluded that, for a variety of reasons including the fact that her part of the country has been hit hard by a cyclical downturn, now's not the best time to market her business. In fact, Phyllis realizes that if she had sold just two years previously, she probably would have received twice as much as she can expect to get today. Believing that business conditions will be better in a year or two and prices for flower shops such as hers will take a corresponding bounce, Phyllis decides to turn day-to-day decision making over to her experienced and reliable manager. For a generous bump in pay, her manager agrees to run the shop until Phyllis is ready to sell. In the meantime, Phyllis will take some shorter, but still exciting, trips and continue to work part time until the time is right to sell.

F. Staying Involved With Your Business

You may feel completely comfortable in selling your business and never looking back. That's fine. But it's also possible that for financial and emotional reasons, you won't want to walk away from your business entirely. For example, if you own a well-known real estate brokerage firm and are thinking about retirement, you may prefer a gradual transition from work to retirement. Keeping some—albeit less—involvement with the enterprise you've built so that you're able to do productive work and interact with colleagues may be more attractive to you than immediately abandoning all of your ties to the business.

If staying connected to the business— at least for some months or years—is important to you, you'll want to build this arrangement into the terms of your sale from the start. Although your desire to stay active in your business may dampen the ardor of some potential suitors, it may excite others.

1. The Buyer May Want You to Stay

A big reason why sellers can stay involved with their businesses after a sale is that many buyers prefer it that way. For example, the buyer of Maria's Ristorante Italiana may be very anxious to have the familiar founder Maria stay involved, at least for a year or two. Not only does Maria know how to run a successful kitchen, but a fair portion of the business's value may be wrapped up with her charisma.

Similarly, in your own business, the buyer may want you to stay on to help create a feeling of genuine continuity with employees, customers, and suppliers. Although from the buyer's point of view it can sometimes be difficult to deal with an egotistical or overbearing former owner, it can be far worse to cope with a suddenly failing business.

2. There Are Many Legal Routes to Staying Involved

To accommodate your needs and desires to maintain a role in your business—as well as to accommodate the wishes of the buyer—you'll want to propose and be ready to negotiate contractual terms. It can be a simple consulting (independent contractor) arrangement in which you provide assistance, as needed, for a period of three or six months after the sale. Or it can be an ongoing employment relationship in which you agree to work for the buyer for several months or even years. And, of course, there are other possibilities. The key thing to understand is that this type of arrangement is common and can be fine-tuned to fit your and the buyer's situation and needs.

Chapter 21 provides information on how to put together employment agreements and consulting agreements.

> **EXAMPLE:** Angela owns Creative Cloth Associates LLC, a company that sells innovative upholstery fabrics that she designs. After several years of owning and running this successful firm, Angela decides to sell the business so she can spend more time with her grandchildren. Angela has to admit to herself that even though she's become weary with the hassles of running a business, she still thoroughly enjoys sitting in her studio and doing the design work that makes her fabrics so special. Fortunately, Drew, an experienced fabric sales executive and prospective buyer of the business, recognizes his need for Angela's design expertise. They agree that after Drew buys the business, Angela will continue to work part time as a consultant for at least two years, working with Drew and others to create the designs that are so important to the company's

success. This will give Drew time to plan an orderly transition to the time when he and other talented designers will completely take over.

G. Protecting Your Future Ability to Earn a Living

It's also possible that for all sorts of personal reasons you *won't* want to remain involved in the business that you're selling. Or even if you do, you may wind up with a buyer who's willing to pay a highly attractive price for your business but wants you completely out of the picture—and for good measure, wants you to agree not to be a competitive threat.

If you're willing to sell your business and sever all ties with it, you'll probably be asked to sign a covenant not to compete, sometimes called a noncompete agreement. Typically, this covenant will list the types of work and business ownership you are prohibited from engaging in for at least a few years.

Sometimes, you'll only have to agree not to compete within a narrowly defined geographic area (Bergen County, New Jersey, for example). But if your business has a national following, as would be true if you sell a specialized type of kites on the Internet, it may be a 50-state or even a worldwide prohibition. From your point of view, a noncompete agreement will work fine if you're retiring or planning to move into a completely unrelated line of work. But if you plan to stay active in the same broad industry, you'll need to carefully think through the implications of agreeing to any noncompetition agreement. The reality is that you may still need to earn a living and you may not want to give up completely the opportunity to earn money doing what you do best. For suggestions on how to protect yourself and a sample noncompete agreement, see Chapter 21.

☑ Checklist for Thinking About Selling

- ☐ Accept the fact that you may have unexpected emotional ties to your business.

- ☐ Determine whether your business is saleable (most are).

- ☐ See if there are steps you can take to make a poorly performing business more attractive to potential buyers.

- ☐ Resolve any problems with co-owners that may threaten the sale.

- ☐ Gauge whether this is the best time to sell.

- ☐ Explore ways to stay attached to your business if you so choose—at least for the short term.

- ☐ Think about how you'll earn a living after the sale so that a noncompete agreement won't sideline you.

Chapter 2

The Key Steps in Selling Your Business

To sell your business on optimal terms, you must attend to many practical and financial details. You must, for example, determine a realistic price for your business, prepare your business for a sale, find the right buyer, and negotiate a sales agreement. If you've never sold a business before, the multitude of tasks may feel a bit overwhelming. But don't worry: Each will be explained in detail in the chapters that lie ahead. Still, it helps to have the big picture so that you can understand how the pieces fit together. This chapter will provide that big picture and give you a context for the individual steps.

It's crucial for you to learn how to build appropriate legal protections into your sale. To that end, this book will emphasize the legal measures you can take to protect your financial interests throughout the sales process. For example, if you sell your business on an installment basis, you'll want to craft a sales agreement and other legal documents that reasonably assure that you'll receive all remaining payments from the buyer and that you can take back the business if the buyer stops paying you. Likewise, you'll want to make sure you don't get stuck with liability for business debts that the buyer incurs. These and other key legal issues are introduced in Chapter 3. You'll find clause-by-clause details of a sales agreement in Chapters 12 through 18 and examples of other necessary legal documents in Chapters 19 through 21.

A. Figuring Out What Your Business Is Worth

Before you go through the effort of preparing your business for sale, you'll undoubtedly want to have a good idea of how much it's worth. For example, in 1901, when Andrew Carnegie offered to sell his huge steel operations to J. P. Morgan, Morgan immediately asked, "How much?" Carnegie promptly picked up a napkin and wrote "$480 million" (perhaps $10 billion in today's dollars). Morgan said yes and the sale was made.

Just from talking to others in your industry or from articles you read in trade publications, you may already have a pretty good ballpark idea of what a business like yours is worth. But your seat-of-the-pants notion of your business's value may also be wide of the mark. At the very least, you'll want to refine it based on a convincing method that you can later use to motivate a skeptical buyer to pay your price.

And, of course, there are other reasons why it's crucial to estimate your business's value accurately. If you set your price too high, you may be disappointed to find that potential buyers are scared off, with the result that word gets around that your enterprise is of little interest. By the same token, if you set the price too low, a savvy buyer may try to snap up your business at your bargain basement discount. And this means that unless you suddenly try to raise the price mid-negotiation—something that can be tough to do—you'll end up selling your business for less than it's worth.

Pricing a business is both an art and a science. As you'll learn in Chapter 5, there are several methods you can use: valuing the assets, basing your price on comparable sales, calculating return on investment, or using an industry formula based on sales or units. Whatever valuation approach you employ, you'll probably end up with a range of values rather than one absolute number. And always bear in mind that while it's essential to set and be able to defend a price for your business, in the last analysis, the number you name won't be nearly as meaningful as the one a willing buyer agrees to pay.

B. Preparing Your Business for Sale

If you were planning to sell your car, you would probably do a number of things to make it more appealing to buyers. Especially if you were determined to get top dollar, you'd want to tune the engine, tap out the dents, replace the worn floor mats, give the car a good wash, and wax it.

You'll want to go through an analogous process in preparing to sell your business—but the task inevitably will be more complex and prolonged. In addition to making sure the physical assets of the business are clean and attractive, you'll need to attend to less-tangible matters, such as the financial picture you'll present to buyers. In the time you have before you put your business on the market, this will typically mean taking sensible steps to reduce expenses while also doing all you can to increase gross and net income.

Chapter 7 provides extensive advice on preparing your business for sale, including how to get financial statements and other paperwork in order. You'll also almost surely want to recast your balance sheet to legitimately present the most favorable profits picture. For example, let's say that you've been taking some legitimate tax write-offs such as the cost of attending business conventions at attractive locations, in part because these trips have been enjoyable for you. Before you put your business up for sale, the fact that these and other similar expenses reduce your profits is fine with you, because they also reduce your taxes. But once you place a business-for-sale sign in the window, these same expenses can become a problem, since they make your business look less profitable than you'd wish. That's why it usually makes sense to create an alternate balance sheet showing that eliminating the trips would yield significantly more profit—an important point for a buyer who initially may be more interested in staying home and pumping up the bottom line than in touring Bermuda.

In addition, depending on your business, you'll likely have a long list of other presale priorities. You may, for example, need to address an environmental clean-up issue, get rid of outdated inventory, or renew your lease (assuming, of course, you occupy a good location on favorable terms). These topics and more are covered in Chapter 7.

C. Creating a Plan for the Future

Another potent sales tool—one worth thinking about creatively and developing carefully—is a business plan that looks ahead for the next three or five years. The plan you create should be a credible and convincing document that helps the buyer envision future growth and profits. But in addition to painting a rosy picture of the next several years, your plan must contain the details needed to convince a skeptical buyer that you aren't blowing smoke. Think of your plan as a roadmap showing the buyer how to actually take your current business into new and exciting profits territory. Let's say, for example, that you own a business that repairs and maintains swimming pools. Your business plan might describe in detail a strategy for expanding into the servicing of hot tubs and backyard spas, using the same work crew and trucks. A prospective buyer who's keen on growth may be swept along by your vision and move quickly toward a purchase.

But creating a convincing business plan isn't only a sales tool. It can also be a huge help in convincing a buyer not to find a reason to withdraw from the transaction. Think of it this way: Since no business is sold in a day, or even a week, there will be plenty of time for a nervous buyer to develop cold feet and seek to back out of the deal. If your plan does nothing more than counter this natural tendency, it will more than pay for the time and energy you invest in creating it.

Chapter 7 will give you some useful resources for putting together a solid business plan.

D. Marketing Your Business

Once you've priced your business, prepared it for a sale, and developed a long-term business plan, it will be time to drum up prospective buyers. That's the focus of Chapter 8. As discussed in detail in Chapter 8, it's possible that someone close to you—an employee, a relative, a friend, a supplier, or a customer—may be an interested and logical prospect. Or if your business is well known and popular—and especially if Lady Luck has taken a chair in a corner of your office— word that your business is for sale may be enough to bring prospective buyers to your doorstep.

But finding a qualified buyer isn't that easy for most small business owners. Chances are that to make a desirable sale, you'll need to reach out to a bigger audience of potential buyers. This often includes putting ads in newspapers, in trade publications, and on websites that list businesses for sale. In addition, you may want to consider engaging a business broker to help locate an additional pool of potential buyers—although you will, of course, have to pay a substantial commission if you go that route.

In some instances, your best strategy will be to start your sales process by broadcasting the availability of your business. The idea here is simple: The more people who know about your desire to sell, the more the word will spread ("Did you hear that Edna plans to sell the Whale Point Bed and Breakfast?"), making it more likely the news will reach a serious buyer. But don't just assume that announcing far and wide that your business is available is always the best strategy. In some instances, discretion, if not secrecy, is a better approach—especially if you fear that premature disclosure of your plans might cause key employees to defect, customers to look elsewhere, or suppliers to tighten your credit. In fact, if your situation dictates keeping your intentions mum, your main concern may be to avoid prematurely spreading word of your plans. And in a world where competitors are always watching, sometimes doing this can be harder than you might imagine. For example, let's say you own a security firm that installs alarm systems and monitors the automated calls that come in if someone sets off an alarm. If, after years of maintaining a stable pricing

policy, you suddenly hold an aggressive sale and substantially increase your advertising budget with an eye towards impressing a buyer with the fact that you've signed up a large number of new accounts, you may inadvertently telegraph your intention to sell.

E. Negotiating the Deal: Key Sale Issues

A prospective buyer may express interest in your business, but rarely will you be able to emulate Andrew Carnegie and strike a deal instantly. And even if you do come to a quick and enthusiastic handshake agreement, there will be plenty of chances for the deal to fall apart as the details are worked out. For one thing, the buyer will inevitably want to dig deeper into your business and learn more about the dozens of nitty-gritty operating issues. And because the sale price will probably be paid in installments, you'll want to make sure the buyer is creditworthy and has the necessary entrepreneurial skills and personal attributes to make a success of the purchase. Obviously, it will take time to complete these other steps—such as designing a prudent security agreement in case the buyer later defaults. In addition, there will be many other legal and practical details to be worked out, including the following:

- **Structure of the sale.** Will you be selling your entire business entity (your partnership, corporation, or LLC), or just its assets?

- **Assets being transferred.** Will you keep some assets (accounts receivable, for example, or a laptop computer) that are currently part of the business?

- **Payment terms.** Will the buyer pay full cash up front (relatively rare)? If not, how big a down payment will you insist on? And what payment terms and interest rate will the buyer commit to?

- **Seller protection.** If the seller fails to make a required payment, what legal recourse will you have to unwind the deal or recover your money from other sources? For example, will you receive a security interest in the buyer's house as well as an interest in the business's assets?

- **Seller warranties.** What, if any, warranties will you make about the condition of the business or its assets? For example, are you willing to guarantee that no environmental hazards lurk within the business premises and, if they do, are you prepared to pay the cost of the clean-up?

- **Buyer warranties.** In addition to providing security in case of nonpayment, what, if any, other warranties will the buyer make? For example, until you've been paid off, will the buyer agree to keep the business equipment in good shape, maintain the inventory at presale levels, and

continue to operate from the current location?

- **Liabilities.** How will you and the buyer handle current business debts? Will responsibility for some current debts and threatened lawsuits be transferred to the buyer? Or will you agree to stay liable for all presale obligations? And on the other side of the coin, will you be adequately protected from future debts and lawsuits?

- **Ongoing connection to the business.** Will you and the buyer agree that you'll perform future services for the business? If so, for how long, and how will you be compensated?

- **Ability to compete.** Will you be able to immediately invest in, own, or work for a similar business? If you'll be restricted, how confining and long term will the restrictions be?

Later chapters provide the information and forms you need to negotiate the deal. Chapter 3 provides an overview of the legal issues. Chapters 9 ("Structuring the Sale"), 10 ("The Investigation Stage"), and 11 ("Drafting a Letter of Intent") will help you work towards a sales agreement.

F. Signing a Sales Agreement

The chief legal document used in the sale of your business is called a sales agreement. This legal contract captures the details of the sale as outlined in

Section E, above. Its purpose is to spell out your rights and obligations and those of the buyer in plain, easy-to-understand language. If it's drawn up thoughtfully and carefully, the sales agreement should allow you to transfer your business entity or its assets to the buyer smoothly on a specified date (called the closing). And if a dispute arises before or after the closing, the clear terms of your sales agreement will be the first place you'll look in an effort to resolve it.

Because the sales agreement is so crucial in the sale of your business, Part 3 of this book—Chapters 12 through 18—is devoted to a clause-by-clause analysis. Part 4 (Chapters 19 through 21) covers other important sales documents, including a promissory note. But before you draft and sign a sales agreement and related documents, it's essential that you carefully read the intervening chapters so that you understand the legal and practical import of every term and are sure that nothing significant has been left out.

G. Closing Your Sale

After signing the sales agreement, there's one more step before the business is actually transferred to the new owner. This takes place at a meeting (called the closing) at which the buyer pays you the sale price, or at least the agreed-upon down payment, and typically signs documents such as a promissory note and security agreement. In exchange, you sign stock certificates or LLC documents (if an entity sale), or a bill of sale for the business assets, plus all the necessary paperwork to turn ownership over to the buyer. The last chapter of this book (Chapter 22) provides details on the closing, including how to prepare for it and handle any last-minute problems that may occur.

☑ **Checklist of Steps in Selling Your Business**

☐ Determine a reasonable price range.

☐ Prepare your business for sale.

☐ Market your business to prospective buyers.

☐ Negotiate a deal.

☐ Create and sign a sales agreement.

☐ Get ready for closing.

Chapter 3

The Key Legal Issues in Selling Your Business

In addition to understanding and mastering the key practical steps involved in selling your business, you need to pay close attention to a whole slew of legal issues. Failing to do so means you're at risk of receiving far less money (and far more misery) than you bargained for. For example, let's say the buyer agrees to purchase your business on an installment basis—a very common arrangement—and after a year or so simply stops making payments. If you didn't anticipate and address this possibility in your sales documents, your only recourse may be to sue the buyer, who may have become insolvent. As you'll learn in this chapter, there are a number of techniques you can use in putting together your deal to help avoid this grim outcome. For example, you can retain a security interest in the business, which will at least let you take back the business even though it may have declined in value under the buyer's ownership. Or you can retain a security interest in the buyer's home or other real estate through a mortgage or deed of trust so that you'll have an additional resource to tap into if the buyer stops paying you.

If, as part of your sale, the buyer assumes the legal obligation to pay past business liabilities and shield you from them, you'll want to include wording in the sales agreement that makes the buyer's commitment as clear—and as legally binding—as possible. This is especially important if your business is a sole proprietorship or partnership, since in these cases you're personally liable for business debts.

The sales documents must also cover your relationship to the business after the closing. This can include spelling out the kinds of services you'll provide to the new owner as a consultant or independent contractor. And if you'll be severing your relationship to the business you're selling, but may someday want to work in a field related to that business, you need to make sure that a noncompete clause doesn't unreasonably tie your hands.

This chapter presents an overview of the important legal issues normally involved in selling a business. Later chapters will go into detail on all the topics raised here and explain how to include the necessary language in your sales agreement and prepare other key documents, such as a promissory note, to give yourself the maximum legal protection.

 This book shows you how you to handle many of the tasks yourself. But especially when lots of money is involved, it often makes sense to have a lawyer review your handiwork. In addition, the book will alert you to legally fraught or tricky situations in which professional help is especially important. For an overview of specific ways that lawyers can help with legal issues, see Chapter 6.

A. Take Presale Legal Protections

In the process of selling your business, you may have preliminary discussions with a number of prospective buyers, including employees, investors, and possibly even competitors. During this exploratory stage, you'll probably be asked to provide some financial and other details about your business. Knowing what information you can sensibly release and how best to do it requires thought, tact, and protective legal language. And even with all these, the process is never completely risk-free.

You need to exercise appropriate caution because, no matter how excited a potential buyer appears about the chance to buy your business, it's always possible that the deal will fall through. If so, you don't want to wind up in a worse competitive position. This would occur, for example, if a competitor were to back out of a deal to purchase your business after learning valuable proprietary information about your operations. That's why, even if a potential buyer seems absolutely trustworthy, it's essential that before you share key financial, customer, or operational information, you insist on both a confidentiality and a nondisclosure agreement that commits the buyer to use the information solely for the investigation of your business. That makes it much easier to obtain an injunction and perhaps an award of monetary damages if, for example, the potential buyer improperly uses or discloses your trade secrets or sensitive financial information. These types of agreements and related issues you face in the early investigation stage of selling a business are covered in Chapter 10.

⚠ Even the best of legal documents can only go so far in safeguarding confidential information. Confidentiality and nondisclosure agreements should never be your sole means of protection. These documents can only support a good disclosure strategy—not replace it. So you'll also want to follow the sensible plan of not disclosing highly sensitive information at the earliest stages of your negotiations.

B. Understand the Differences Between Selling the Business Entity or Just Its Assets

Your business may be organized now as a sole proprietorship, a partnership, a corporation, or a limited liability company (LLC). Sole proprietors and partners don't need to focus much on the question of whether it's better to structure the deal as an asset sale or an entity sale. That's because with a sole proprietorship, there's no separate legal entity to sell; by definition, you, as the sole proprietor, will be selling just business assets. And although it's theoretically possible to sell a partnership by substituting new partners for old, a sale of a partnership is also almost always structured as an asset sale.

But if your business is legally organized as a corporation or LLC, there are, broadly speaking, two principal ways to structure the sale. The first method is to sell the corporate or LLC entity. The second method is to hold on to the entity and, instead, sell all or most of its assets.

The importance of understanding the differences between asset and entity sales will come up repeatedly as you proceed through this book. It affects everything from how you write off the sale price on your tax return, to liability issues and how ownership will be transferred. So although this material is seriously short on sex appeal, you'll want to master it. Here's a preview of what you can expect:

- In Chapter 4, you'll see that the way you and the buyer structure the sale can greatly affect the income tax you'll owe on the gain you realize from the sale—and how quickly the buyer can start seeing tax benefits.
- In Chapter 9, you'll understand buyer and seller perspectives on asset and entity sales and important liability issues related to the type of sale.
- In Chapters 12 through 18, you'll learn that several sales agreement clauses will vary depending on whether you have an asset sale or an entity sale.
- In Chapters 19 through 21, you'll see how the documents used to transfer

ownership of the business will differ based on how the sale is structured.

1. How an Entity Sale Works

Let's assume that your business is either a corporation called Protobiz Inc., or an LLC called Old Stuff LLC. Here's how an entity sale would work:

- **Selling the corporation.** You (and your fellow shareholders, if any) can sell all your stock in Protobiz Inc. to the buyer, in which case the buyer will become Protobiz's owner and will have the right to control all the assets the corporation owns: furniture, fixtures, equipment, inventory, intellectual property, and so on. The corporation, under its new ownership, will remain responsible for the debts and other liabilities of the business.
- **Selling the LLC.** You (and your fellow members, if any) can sell your membership interests in Old Stuff LLC to the buyer, making the buyer the owner of the LLC itself—again, with the right to control all its assets. The LLC, under its new ownership, will remain responsible for the debts and other liabilities of the business.

This is not to say that all entity sales are the same, as some details may differ. For example, in selling a corporation or an LLC as an entity, you and the buyer may agree that some assets will be transferred to you before the closing. You and the buyer may also agree that you'll assume personal responsibility for some of the existing debts of the business.

2. How an Asset Sale Works

Assuming that your business is either a corporation called Protobiz Inc., or an LLC called Old Stuff LLC, here's how an assets sale would work:

- **Selling the assets of the corporation.** You (and your fellow shareholders, if any) can arrange to have Protobiz Inc. sell all or most Protobiz Inc. assets to the buyer, in which case you'll continue to own what amounts to nothing more than the Protobiz corporate shell. After the sale, Protobiz will still exist but will have no (or few) assets other than a promissory note from the buyer for the balance of the purchase price. The assets that Protobiz Inc. sells aren't limited to physical property. The buyer can acquire Protobiz Inc.'s intangible assets as well, such as the company's goodwill and its trademark. When the assets of the corporation are sold, the buyer won't automatically become responsible for the debts and other liabilities of the business but may agree to assume liability for at least some of them.
- **Selling the assets of the LLC.** You (and your fellow members, if any) can contract to have Old Stuff LLC sell all or most of the assets to the buyer. If so, you and the other original Old Stuff LLC members will continue to own the LLC shell. If your LLC sells all of its assets to the buyer, its only remaining asset may be a promissory note from the buyer. When the assets of the LLC are sold, the buyer won't automatically become responsible for the debts and other liabilities of the business but may agree to assume liability for at least some of them.

3. Why Sellers Usually Prefer Entity Sales, and Buyers Asset Sales

Why is the legal distinction between an asset or an entity sale important if the result under either approach is that the buyer ends up owning your business? One important reason is that how your transaction is structured can affect how the proceeds of the sale are taxed and how the buyer writes off the purchase price. As you'll see in Chapter 4, buyers typically are able to begin getting depreciation benefits sooner if they acquire the assets rather than if they buy the corporation or LLC. The flip side is that you, the seller, will usually fare better from a tax standpoint if you sell the entity rather than its assets, because you will pay tax at the low long-term capital gain rate. By contrast, in an asset sale, part of your tax bill may be computed at the ordinary income tax rate, which is higher. And you'll probably feel especially skittish about using an asset sale for a C corporation, since you'll face the distasteful risk of double taxation.

Incidentally, this tax benefits issue is often resolved by a compromise by the seller and the buyer that's reflected in the sale price or the terms of payment. For example, if you sell your business on an asset basis in which the buyer will be saving money on taxes, you have a legitimate case for seeking a higher sale price or terms a bit more favorable to you.

Another reason why buyers typically prefer an asset sale is that it gives them a better opportunity to pick and choose among the assets they'll acquire and omit less-desirable ones. In addition, in an asset sale, buyers recognize that in most cases, they're not going to be responsible for existing debts of the business unless they agree to accept responsibility. By contrast, in an entity sale, it's assumed that all the liabilities go along with the sale—though to make the deal happen, the shareholders or LLC members who are selling may agree to be responsible for some specified liabilities.

As mentioned above, what's best for the buyer probably won't be best for you. In an ideal world, you, as the seller, will usually find it most advantageous to transfer your entire corporation or LLC entity to the buyer. That way, you not only get favorable tax treatment but also are less likely to have to keep any undesirable assets of the business, and are less likely

as well to have to worry about paying existing business debts. In the real world, however, buyers sometimes have more clout than sellers when it comes to setting the terms of the deal, meaning that many sales of small businesses turn out to be asset sales.

Still, a buyer may be well motivated to buy your entity rather than its assets. This can happen, for example, if your business is highly sought after, putting you in a very strong bargaining position. Similarly, you may be able to insist on an entity sale if your corporation or LLC has a valuable lease for the space where you do business, and the lease can't be assigned to the buyer. By buying your corporation or LLC, the entity continues to be the tenant, so the buyer gets the benefit of the lease. (This won't always work; some landlords state in the lease that a change in ownership of your entity will be treated as a forbidden transfer of the lease.) You'll learn more on this subject in Chapter 7. For now, just be aware that you may sometimes have good ammunition for persuading a buyer that an entity transfer will benefit both of you.

 Not all entity sales are exactly the same. Important details may differ. For example, in buying a corporation or an LLC as an entity, you and the buyer may agree that some assets will be transferred to you before the closing. You may also agree to assume personal responsibility for some of the existing debts of the business.

C. Be Clear on What You'll Sell and What You'll Keep

If you and the buyer have agreed to an asset sale, you'll want the sales agreement to clearly list all of the assets you're selling. This may seem obvious, but a surprising number of sales agreements simply say the seller is selling, and the buyer is buying, "all the assets of the XYZ business." Including a list in the sales agreement is good common sense even if you plan to transfer all assets of the business to the buyer. But a list is especially important if you decide to keep some of the assets, such as cash, accounts receivable, and perhaps even a desk and chair you've grown attached to. Or maybe you're going to license, not sell, some item of intellectual property like a proprietary formula copyright or patent. Again, the point is that to avoid future arguments about exactly which assets you're selling and which you're retaining, you need to be very specific in the sales agreement about what's being sold and what's not. Otherwise, you may get into a legal fight later over whether something as seemingly trivial as the business's phone number or trade name belongs to you or the buyer.

Now if yours is not an asset sale but, instead, you're selling your corporate or LLC entity, you usually don't have to worry about specifying in the sales agreement the assets being sold. By definition, everything the corporation or LLC owns will be transferred as part of the sale. But occasionally there are some corporate assets that you'd like to delete from the sale. For example, the corporation may own the computer you use, which is loaded with programs and data which you'd like to keep. If you sell the corporate stock to the buyer, the computer will automatically be transferred as part of the sale. To prevent that from happening, you'll need to transfer the computer and, in some instances, the software and information it contains, from the corporation to yourself before the closing of the sale. And to be sure the buyer is clearly on notice as to your plan, you'll want to make it clear in the sales agreement that the computer—and any other items you are keeping—won't be owned by the corporation when the stock is transferred. Otherwise, if the buyer thinks that the computer is part of the deal and later discovers that it's missing, you might find yourself accused of fraud.

Likewise, you need to be careful to exclude from any entity sale items you personally own that are present on the business premises. Since personal items were never owned by your business entity in the first place, you may at first think that doing this is unnecessary. But when you realize that the buyer may not know that the original Jackson Pollock painting on your office wall and the handsome Oriental rug in the conference room are your personal treasures and not owned by the business, the wisdom of this approach becomes apparent. To avoid a possible misunderstanding, mention these items in your discussions with the buyer, and make sure they're specifically called out as exclusions in any listing of the property the company owns.

 Chapter 13 helps you craft appropriate language in your sales agreement that clearly spells out what's being sold and what's not.

D. Understand the Transfer of Intellectual Property

A substantial number of small businesses own intellectual property—a legal term that covers copyrights, trademarks, patents, and trade secrets. Although fundamentally different from physical assets like machines and buildings, your intellectual property can be the most valuable asset that the business owns. For example, if you've built a solid reputation for the high quality of your services or goods, then your business or product name will have positive associations among existing customers. Someone looking to buy your business will certainly want to get the benefit of that reservoir of goodwill, knowing it will help ensure not only that current customers return, but also that they will recommend the products and services to others.

On the financial side, you want to be sure that you don't overlook the worth of intellectual property when you negotiate the sale price. On the legal side, you need to be aware of exactly what legal rights you own. In some cases, before offering your business for sale, you may need

to protect your rights through federal or state registration or by getting a release from some other person or business who may claim full or partial ownership of the intellectual property.

Then, in preparing the sales agreement, you need to be clear about which intellectual property the buyer will be acquiring and which you'll be retaining. In some cases, it may be appropriate to retain legal ownership of intellectual property but license the buyer to use it. In other situations, the reverse may be the way to go: You transfer the intellectual property to the buyer but receive back a license to use it. Chapters 7 and 10 have more information about your business's intellectual property, including how to get your paperwork in order for the buyer.

Intellectual property law is a legal specialty. Relatively few business lawyers have extensive training and experience in this field. If your business has highly valuable intellectual property, you should consider consulting an intellectual property specialist for advice.

E. Build in Legal Protections If the Buyer Stops Paying

In your dealings with the buyer, your negotiations about what's being sold, and the price and terms of the sale, are primarily business, and not legal, matters. By contrast, legal considerations come into play when you start to put your deal in writing. You'll want to try to build in protections to make it as likely as possible that you'll get the full amount the buyer promises to pay—especially in an installment sale.

When most small businesses are sold, the seller doesn't receive the purchase price in one lump sum, although, of course, cash deals do occur—especially where the buyer is a larger corporation or can get third-party financing. But more typically, the buyer makes a down payment and gives the seller a promissory note for the balance. The promissory note usually sets up a schedule of payments to be made over a period of time, such as three or five years, with the buyer also agreeing to pay interest on the unpaid balance.

If your business is a healthy one and if the buyer has a good management and credit record, you'll probably get your payments on time and eventually get every dollar that's owed you. Obviously, with a shakier underlying business or purchaser, the risk of buyer default increases. But no matter what the condition of the business or the buyer, the reality is that whenever you receive a promissory note for part of the sale price, there's at least some risk the buyer won't make all the required payments. Maybe the guy you sell to will turn out to be a compulsive gambler who blows all his money on gambling debts. Or, for some reason not apparent when you agree to the sale, the woman who buys your business may decide to open late and close early, bringing her

cash flow to a screeching halt. In short, in these and a plethora of other similarly unhappy eventualities, that check you're counting on getting each month may not arrive.

It's essential that you consider and adopt a number of practical and legal means to protect yourself should the purchaser default. Here are some common techniques you'll want to consider (later chapters provide specific details on how to protect yourself in these ways):

- Carefully investigate the buyer, and only sell to someone who is financially strong and has a good credit record.

- Insist on selling to a buyer who has a proven record of entrepreneurial competence, preferably in the same field you're in.

- Get a substantial down payment. A buyer with a good chunk of money already invested in the business has an obvious incentive to keep the business alive and thriving and to pay off the promissory note.

- Have the promissory note cosigned by the buyer's spouse and, if possible, guaranteed by a parent, friend, or investor who's clearly financially solvent. When a second (hopefully wealthier) person is standing behind the buyer's promise to pay, it's much more likely that you'll eventually receive the full sale price for your business.

- Get the buyer to give you a first or, more likely, a second mortgage or deed of trust on real estate the buyer owns that has enough equity to cover the amount outstanding on the promissory note.

- Have the buyer sign a security agreement allowing you to take back the business assets if payments aren't made.
- If the business operates from rented space, seek the right to take back the lease as well so you can get back into business if necessary at the same location.

F. Assure Your Ability to Earn a Living Later: Guidelines for Noncompete Agreements

Unless you're elderly, seriously ill, or subject to other circumstances that make it clear your entrepreneurial days are over, someone who's buying a business will be worried that you may start a competing business or go to work for a competitor. That's a legitimate concern. After all, no one wants to write a big check for a business only to learn that the former owner has opened up across the street and is pursuing the same pool of customers or clients. Buyers typically try to make sure this doesn't occur by asking sellers to sign a covenant not to compete (also called a noncompete agreement) for a period of years. Depending on the type of business, the covenant may limit your competitive

activity only in a certain geographic area. But in other instances—a publishing venture or Internet-based business, for example—the covenant not to compete may prevent you from engaging in a similar business anywhere in the United States or, in rare instances, even worldwide.

Don't be surprised if the person who buys your business asks you to sign a covenant not to compete, either as part of the sales agreement or separately. If you're retiring or are going into a completely different line of work, you won't care much about how broadly the covenant not to compete is written. You're not planning to do that kind of work anyway. By contrast, if it's possible that you may want to do something in the same or a closely related field in the future, you do need to pay close attention to how you limit your "competitive" activities. For example, even if you never plan to set foot in another bagel shop after yours is sold, you will need to be alert to the noncompete language if you might want to invest in some other food-related business, start a restaurant, or open a catering firm.

Here are some ways to make sure you can still earn a living in the line of work you know best.

Carefully limit and define the types of activities that will be off limits. If you're selling your bagel shop, but after taking a year off you may be interested in opening a sit-down restaurant that will serve breakfast and lunch, including the occasional bagel, be sure this activity isn't ruled out.

Specify things you reserve the right to do. For example, if you're selling a court reporting business but plan to use your skills to do closed captioning and other services for TV news programs, you'll want to be sure that you have the right to use your stenographic skills in this way.

If possible, limit any noncompete agreement to a geographic area—like a five-mile radius from the business being sold or, if appropriate, the same county or state. (In some businesses, especially those carried out partly online, the buyer may not be satisfied with a geographic limit, since the business may effectively be nationwide or worldwide. In that case, you'll need to focus on what you can do in the future rather than where you can do it.)

Limit the number of months or years the noncompete clause will be in force. Often two or three years are plenty for the purchaser to get established.

Consider specifying certain customers or clients who are off limits, with everyone else fair game. In some types of service or manufacturing businesses, this is the most effective way to craft a noncompete agreement.

 Covenants not to compete are discussed in greater detail later in this book. Chapter 16 includes appropriate sales agreement language and Chapter 21 includes the form itself.

G. Limit Your Legal Liabilities to Third Parties Once the Business Changes Hands

Obviously, you'd like to be able to sell your business for a good price and, at the same time, shed all liabilities associated with the business. The extent to which you're able to do this will depend, in large part, on how your business is organized and the language you put in your sales agreement. This section looks at your potential liability to third parties following the closing. The next section (Section H) covers the possibility of unintended liability to the buyer. Liability issues are addressed in various parts of the sales agreement, most particularly in Chapter 15.

1. Corporations and LLCs

Your corporation or LLC may have liabilities that will continue to exist after the closing. In thinking about who will be responsible for these ongoing liabilities, it's important to remember that corporations and LLCs are legal entities that are separate from their owners (shareholders and members, respectively). You need to distinguish between whether you'll personally be liable for debts, lawsuits, and other business liabilities and whether the business entity itself will be liable once the business is sold.

a. Does It Matter Whether It's an Entity Sale or an Asset Sale?

Normally, when your business is a corporation or an LLC, you won't be personally responsible in the future for its business debts. This is true regardless of whether you sell the entity or just its assets. The main exception is if you've previously guaranteed payment of a business debt—for example, by signing a personal guarantee to pay a promissory note for money a bank has lent to the business. In that case, you'll continue to be personally liable to the third party after the sale. And if, in an entity sale, you agree with the buyer that you'll personally pay off a certain debt, you'll have personal liability for making good on that promise. (See Section H, below, for more on your exposure to personal liability.)

Now that you understand the usual extent of your personal liability when selling a corporate or LLC business, let's look at whether you should be concerned about the fact that the entity itself has ongoing liabilities. Here, whether the sale is an entity sale or an asset sale does make a difference.

If you sell your corporation or LLC as an entity, its liabilities will no longer be your concern (unless, as noted above, you previously guaranteed payment of a business debt—such as a promissory note—or have agreed with the buyer that you'll be personally responsible for certain liabilities). Those liabilities remain with the entity and are its sole responsibility.

If your corporation or LLC simply sells its assets, however, you'll still own the corporate or LLC shell, and the liabilities of the company will continue to exist. If they're not paid, a creditor may sue the company and get a judgment against it. Chances are your company will be receiving installment payments from the buyer at that time, which you had hoped would trickle down to you. But if a creditor seizes that money to satisfy the judgment, you won't get the money. So in a sale of your corporation's or LLC's assets, even though you may not be personally liable for ongoing business debts, there can still be financial consequences for you.

It's clearly in your best interest to consider what liabilities may be hanging out there. Then, you'll need a clear statement in the sales contract of what existing liabilities the buyer will be responsible for and an agreement that the buyer will indemnify your company from any court-issued judgment resulting from those liabilities. (As with the indemnification for personal liability, it's only as good as the financial stability of the buyer.)

Be aware that your contract with the buyer making the buyer responsible for certain past debts doesn't take your company off the hook with the creditor—sometimes called a third party. The creditor can still sue your company, which is the reason you need a commitment from the buyer to handle the defense of the lawsuit and pay any judgment that's awarded.

b. Your Personal Liability to Third Parties

If your business is a corporation or an LLC, you'll rarely have to worry about being personally liable to third parties (people other than the buyer) for debts or other claims associated with the business. This means that normally, even after you've sold your entity or its assets, no third party can get a judgment against you for business debts and then seize your personal bank accounts, your home, your car, or your paycheck to satisfy the debt. The main exceptions to the general rule—that is, situations in which your personal assets may be at risk—are these:

- **You've personally guaranteed a business obligation.** Example: You've signed a document assuring the bank that you'll be responsible for a business loan if the corporation or LLC doesn't pay it.
- **You've personally committed a tort (civil wrong) while running the corporation or LLC.** Example: You caused a personal injury to a customer, or you lied about (defamed) a former employee, with the result she failed to find another job.
- **You've had authority to direct which bills your corporation or LLC would pay, and you failed to make sure**

that employment taxes were paid. Example: While you were in charge, the company didn't send the IRS the income taxes and Social Security and Medicare assessments that the business withheld from employee paychecks.

- **You've been careless in observing corporate or LLC formalities.** Example: You've mixed personal funds with business funds, signed contracts without making it clear you were acting only as an agent of the company, and otherwise blurred the line between you and the business entity.

In each of these situations, your personal assets may be at risk for existing debts even after the business is sold, regardless of whether you've sold the entity or only its assets. You'll need to review your situation carefully to see if you may have exposure under any of these legal theories. If so, you may still be able to do something about it. If you've guaranteed a bank loan, for example, and the balance is small, maybe the bank will be willing to release your guarantee—especially if the loan can be secured by a lien on valuable business assets. Or if you face a personal injury, defamation, or other tort claim, maybe your business liability insurance coverage will take care of it. Failing that, maybe you can settle now for a reasonable sum so the liability is no longer hanging over your head.

In some cases, the buyer may be willing to protect you from personal liability for some or all business debts or claims that arose while you were associated with the business. To do so, the buyer would need to promise in the sales contract to indemnify, defend, and save you harmless from specified claims. This means the buyer will pay for a lawyer to defend you in a lawsuit and will pay any judgment against you—kind of like an insurance policy. The key is that you must be convinced that the buyer has sufficiently deep pockets to make good on this promise.

2. Sole Proprietorships and Partnerships

By now you should clearly understand that if you run your business as a sole proprietorship, you're personally responsible for all business debts, and the same goes for each partner in a general partnership. Unlike a corporation or LLC, the law makes no distinction between the owners and the business when it's run as a sole proprietorship or a general partnership. As an owner, you're on the hook for all business obligations.

Knowing this and knowing that your personal assets are at risk if business liabilities are not paid, you need to carefully analyze what debts your business owes and what potential claims may pop up after closing. For example, if a hot-headed customer has been bitterly complaining that your repair shop ruined the engine of her vintage motorcycle, is

there the chance of an expensive lawsuit down the road? If there is, you can bet that the customer's lawyer will name you in the lawsuit, given that you owned the business when the alleged damage was done—and may also name the new owner for good measure. If the customer wins in court, it's almost certain that the judgment will at least go against you, even though you've sold the business. And if your sales agreement doesn't cover how you and the buyer will handle such a judgment, you'll likely wind up having to pay the whole award.

Depending on the negotiations over the sale price and other terms, the buyer may agree to take responsibility for some or all of the past debts and possible future legal claims such as the motorcycle lawsuit described above. Again, whatever debts the buyer agrees to take over, make sure your sales contract contains a well-drafted indemnification clause—and that you feel comfortable that the buyer will have the wherewithal to pay off the debts when the creditors come knocking on the door.

3. Dividing Legal Liability by Contract—A Simple Solution to a Complicated Problem

Obviously, whether you're selling the assets of a business organized as a corporation, an LLC, a partnership, or a sole proprietorship (or a corporate or LLC entity), handling the many types of business debts and other potential liabilities can be complicated. Fortunately, there's a legal way to simplify all of this. This consists of your agreeing to remain legally responsible for debts and obligations that arose before the closing, and the buyer agreeing to be responsible for all debts and obligations that arise afterwards. These commitments can be accompanied by indemnification language in which, for example, you agree to handle any lawsuit for past debts, and the buyer agrees to handle any lawsuit for future liabilities. At this point you may be wondering why this language is even necessary. After all, wouldn't someone initiating a lawsuit two years from now just sue the new owner? Not necessarily. Creditors tend to sue any-one and everyone who could conceivably be liable.

If the seller or buyer is a corporation or LLC, you need to consider, too, whether the individual owners (old or new) as well as the business entity are personally agreeing to protect the other party from liability. Remember the general principle that a corporation or LLC is legally sepa-rate from the people who own it. An indemnification signed by a corporation or LLC doesn't personally bind the owners of the entity. The owners themselves must sign if they're to be held liable.

EXAMPLE: Evelyn, a sole proprietor who owns a pet supply business called The Pet Stop, sells her business to Household Friends LLC, a limited liability company in which Bill and Marvin are the members. In the sales contract, Evelyn agrees that she will indemnify, defend, and save Household Friends LLC harmless from and against any debts or claims arising in the period before the closing of the sale. Similarly, the LLC agrees that it will indemnify, defend, and save Evelyn harmless from any debts or claims that arise after the closing. Wisely, Evelyn insists that Bill and Marvin personally join in the indemnification so that she has another place to turn for protection if the LLC becomes insolvent.

Sometimes, the simple formula needs to be tweaked slightly to fit the situation. In the pet supply example, suppose that Evelyn is expecting a bill for $7,500 from a company that sells pet food to her store. If the parties have agreed that the buyer will be responsible for paying that bill, the sales contract will need to refer specifically to that bill as an exception to Evelyn's duty to pay all past expenses.

H. Protect Yourself Against Unintended Liability to the Buyer

In addition to being concerned about your personal liability to third parties for business obligations, you need to be alert to the possibility that you may face unexpected and unintended liability to the buyer—and do your best to avoid or limit it. Sometimes, of course, your continuing liability to the buyer is intentional. This happens when, in your sales agreement, you expressly say that you'll remain obligated to pay off certain business debts such as the balance on the business's Visa account or that you'll be responsible for other stated liabilities. That's all right because, obviously, you have control over which business obligations you're agreeing to take care of. But there are other, less-obvious sources of liability to the buyer that you should be aware of.

1. Liability for Inadequate or Misleading Disclosures

After the closing, the buyer may become disenchanted with the business and may claim that in negotiating the sale, you withheld crucial information about your business or that you distorted the information you did provide. Especially if the business does poorly in the future, the buyer may concoct a claim that you failed to provide full and accurate information and use this issue as an excuse to sue you for damages or withhold installment payments. This means you need to be very careful to tell the prospective buyer the truth and nothing but the truth so no cover-up claims come back to haunt you. See Chapter 10 for a discussion of why full and truthful disclosures are essential.

2. Liability Based on Your Warranties

In addition to the quality and extent of the data you give the seller, there are the warranties you may have to provide in the sales agreement. For example, you may be asked to warrant (guarantee) that there are no environmental problems at the business location. That's fine if you're sure it's true. But if it later turns out that there's a leaky underground storage tank or that the soil behind the loading dock is contaminated with heavy metals, you may get socked with the cost of a required clean-up. If you're unsure about any of the facts that you're asked to warrant, step one is to find out. Only then can you sensibly use caution and plan to protect yourself. Another less-protective approach—but one that may be necessary where an investigation would be expensive—is to provide a warranty that's based only on your actual knowledge. For example, if you don't know whether there's an underground storage tank on the ten-acre parcel you are selling, you might want to say in the sales agreement: "Seller warrants that to the best of seller's knowledge there are no environmental problems." That may be a subtle distinction, but it can save you tens of thousands of dollars later on. See Chapter 15 for more on why you need to pay close attention to how you phrase warranties and representations.

I. Comply With State and Local Laws That May Affect Your Sale

The sale of a business is not heavily regulated by state statutes or local ordinances. For the most part, the sale is governed by traditional contract law as created over the years by the published decisions of courts. Basically, within very broad limits, the courts will hold you and the buyer to whatever deal you mutually agree to. But even though contract law predominates in business sales, you may encounter some state statutes or local ordinances. Here are the major areas of possible concern and the chapters where these are discussed:

- **Usury statutes (Chapter 9).** These are laws that limit the amount of interest that a lender can charge a borrower—or anyone to whom credit is being extended. If your buyer will be signing a promissory note for the balance of the sale price, the interest you charge will be regulated by the usury statute in your state.
- **Bulk sales statutes (Chapter 20).** These laws—on the books in a small and diminishing number of states—set out procedures for notifying creditors when a business that has an inventory of goods is sold.
- **UCC-1 Financing Statement (Chapter 19).** This form is signed by a buyer who has agreed to give the seller a security interest in assets of the business. You'll need to file this form with a designated state office—typically the Secretary of State's office.
- **Transfer of vehicles (Chapter 20).** In an asset sale, you may be transferring one or more vehicles to the buyer. Usually this can be accomplished by completing forms provided by your state's motor vehicle department.
- **Transfer of real estate (Chapter 20).** Occasionally, the sale of a business includes the sale of real estate. Typically, this involves your signing a deed which the buyer then files with the land registry office in the county where the land is located. But there are precise technicalities to be followed, so you or the buyer will generally want a lawyer's help. To learn more about the process, you can check with the land registry clerk or a knowledgeable person at a local title company.
- **Licenses (Chapter 10).** There's wide variation from state to state and from business to business about what licenses are required—and what needs to be done when a business changes hands. First, make a list of all the state and local licenses and permits currently held by your business. Then contact each office that issued a license or permit and inquire about what, if anything, needs to be done when the business is sold.

- **Taxes (Chapter 4).** Check with your state revenue office to find out about any state forms you need to file and taxes you need to pay when you sell a business. Also check with your county and city tax offices about local tax filings.

- **Entity matters (Chapter 20).** If your business is a corporation or an LLC, check with the state office—often the Secretary of State's office—where you filed the original corporate or LLC documents. Depending on the shape of your deal, you may need to file papers for a change of registered agent or to change or cancel an entity name. The clerk will also be able to tell you about any other documents you need to file. With a partnership or a sole proprietorship that uses an assumed or fictitious name, you can inquire at the county office where such businesses are registered.

How to do your own legal research. If you have a specific legal question not covered in this book—for example, the cap on promissory note interest in your state—you may want to do some legal research on your own before calling your lawyer. To get started, check out Nolo's free online legal research center at www. nolo.com/statute/index.cfm. In addition to general background information on a wide variety of legal topics, you can access statutes of all 50 states, plus federal laws, at Nolo's legal research center. In addition to Nolo's website, check out the official website of your state for links to relevant business and tax agencies, such as your state department of revenue. To find your state website, see www.statelocalgov.net.

Finally, if you still need help, we recommend *Legal Research: How to Find & Understand the Law*, by Steve Elias and Susan Levinkind (Nolo). This nontechnical book gives easy-to-use, step-by-step instructions on how to find legal information.

☑ Checklist of Key Legal Issues When Selling Your Business

☐ Protect your confidential information.

☐ Understand the differences between an asset sale and an entity sale.

☐ Be clear on which assets will be transferred and which you'll keep.

☐ See that intellectual property is treated as the valuable asset it often is.

☐ Have a secure position if the buyer stops making payments on an installment plan.

☐ Don't sign too broad a noncompete agreement.

☐ Limit your liability to third parties.

☐ Pay close attention to your representations and warranties.

☐ Learn about and comply with local and state laws that affect your sale.

Chapter 4

Tax Considerations When Selling Your Business

To intelligently negotiate a sale of your business, you need a reasonably accurate idea of how much federal income tax you'll owe. Your tax bill may be quite substantial if you've owned your business for a while and it has increased in value over the years. This chapter summarizes the federal income tax principles that apply to a business sale. Your own tax adviser can help you apply these rules to your specific situation— something that this book obviously can't attempt.

The rules for computing the tax on the sale of a business can be extremely complex, often creating a far bigger headache than you've experienced in preparing your typical Form 1040 tax return each year. So seek good tax advice early in the sale process. If you wait until after you reach an agreement with a buyer, you risk missing out on tax-saving opportunities—or selling at a price that turns out to be disappointingly low because it doesn't adequately reflect your tax liability. Be sure to read Chapter 6, which covers how to work with accountants when selling your business. Fees for accounting services relating to your business or its sale are generally tax-deductible.

A. An Overview of Key Tax Issues

A number of factors will influence how much federal income tax you'll pay on the sale of your business. These factors are covered in greater detail later in this chapter. Here is a brief overview of the main ones:

- **The type of legal entity you've chosen for your business.** You've most likely set up your business as a C corporation, an S corporation, a single-member limited liability company (LLC), a multimember LLC, a partnership, or a sole proprietorship. There are differences in how the tax laws apply to each of these business entities. For that reason, each entity is addressed separately in the sections that follow.

- **How your sale is structured.** The big issue here is whether you sell your business as an entity or you sell its assets. Depending on which route you and the buyer agree to, there can be widely different tax consequences. This can be especially significant if you own a C corporation, because a sale of corporation assets (as opposed to the sale of the corporation itself) exposes the sale proceeds to the possibility of double taxation (once at the corporate level and again on your personal return), as discussed in Section E, below. (See Chapters 3 and 9 for a discussion of the legal differences between an asset and an entity sale.)

- **Whether the sale price is paid in one lump sum or is spread over a number of years.** If you receive full payment

Resources on Federal Tax Law

The federal tax code contains thousands of pages of fine print—and it changes often. So, in many cases, going straight to a tax expert is your best bet. But if you'd like to see IRS forms and official instructions, or if you have a specific tax question you'd like to research yourself, here are some useful resources on the federal tax consequences of selling a business:

- The IRS website, www.irs.gov, is a good starting point. You'll find tax forms, instructions, and numerous publications that explain tax law— although in gray areas on tax law, the information reflects only the IRS perspective. The following publications are especially helpful in the sale of a business: IRS Publication 537, *Installment Sales*; IRS Publication 544, *Sales and Other Dispositions of Assets*; and IRS Publication 551, *Basis of Assets*.

- *CCH Standard Federal Tax Reporter*, published by Commerce Clearing House, www.tax.cchgroup.com. This multivolume work is the gold standard for tax research but may be more than you need.
- *Tax Guide for Buying and Selling a Business*, by Stanley Hagendorf, published by Knowles Publishing Inc., www.knowlespublishing.com. This is a focused treatment of the tax complexities and perhaps your best bet for learning about this subject in depth.
- *Guide to Buying and Selling Small Businesses*, published by Practitioners Publishing Company, www.ppc.thomson.com. This book is written primarily for accountants and has excellent coverage of the tax issues.

when you sell your business, your gain will be taxed all at once on your next tax return. By contrast, if you sell your business on an install-ment payment basis, your immediate tax liability will be limited, because you'll only receive a portion of the sale price during the current tax year and will be taxed now only on that portion. You'll pay tax on future installments in later years as pay-ments are received. If you receive those installments in years when your overall income is less than it is now—often the situation if you're retiring—you'll pay tax in a lower tax bracket, meaning you'll keep a larger percentage of the sale price.

- **Capital gains vs. ordinary income.** When you sell your business through an asset sale (as opposed to an entity sale), you'll need to allocate the sale price among the different categories of assets established by the IRS. How you allocate the sale price can have a major effect on your tax liability. The gain on some assets will be taxed at ordinary income rates; the gain on other assets will be taxed at the lower long-term capital gain rates. Obviously, for tax reasons, you'll want more of the sale price to be allocated to assets taxed under the latter rate. The ordinary income rate for individuals can be as high as 35%. By contrast, for individuals, the highest tax rate for long-term capital gain is 15%, unless you're selling real estate, in which case some of the capital gain may be taxed at 25%. Long-term means that the asset was held for more than one year. Short-term—as in the phrase "short-term capital gain"—means that the asset was held for one year or less; the gain on such an asset is taxed at the ordinary income rate.

- **Whether you'll receive compensation in future years for work you do for the buyer after the closing.** You may agree to continue working for the business after the sale, either as an employee or an independent contractor. If so, you may be willing to agree to a lower sale price if you're confident that you'll be earning generous compensation in the years ahead. This may result in your paying lower taxes overall—especially if you'll be in a lower tax bracket in the years when you receive the compensation. Offsetting this potential advantage, however, is the fact that work-related earnings are taxed at ordinary income rates, not capital gain rates. Keep in mind, too, that if you go work for the buyer as either an independent contractor or an employee, there will be other taxes to pay: self-employment tax (for Social Security and Medicare) if you're a consultant, and similar levies if you're an employee, though the employer will bear part of the load.

Check Your State's Tax Rules

In addition to the federal income tax consequences of selling your business, you need to understand the state tax consequences of the sale. While many states follow the federal tax pattern, some do not. For example, some states charge a business transfer tax in addition to an income tax. A good starting point for learning about the tax system in your state is *All States Tax Handbook*, published by Thomson/RIA, www.riahome.com. Your state's department of revenue can provide further specific guidance. To find yours, go to your state's home page (see www.statelocalgov.net).

⚠️ **Be careful when selling your business to a family member.** If you sell your business at an artificially low price—as sometimes happens in a family deal—the IRS stands to lose revenue, so family transactions are scrutinized closely by the agency. You'll need to consult a tax adviser for help in putting together a family deal so that it's not successfully challenged by the IRS.

B. Understanding the Federal Tax Rate That Applies to Your Sale

To figure out the federal tax consequences of selling your business, you will, of course, need to know the tax rate that will apply to the sale proceeds. This can be more difficult than you might imagine. As many as four separate tax rates may apply to the proceeds of your sale. Here is a brief overview of the applicable tax rates:

- **Ordinary income rates.** This is the tax rate you pay on personal income, such as your salary. The rate can be as high as 35%. You're probably aware, however, that the ordinary income rates are applied in brackets. The first taxable dollars you receive are taxed at a much lower rate, so that even if you're in the 35% bracket, only part of your income is taxed at that rate.
- **Long-term capital gain rates.** These rates apply to the gain on capital assets that were held for more than

one year before being sold. The rate generally is 15%, but for individuals in the lowest tax brackets, it's only 5%. Gain on capital assets held less than a year (short-term capital gain) is taxed at ordinary income rates.

- **Real estate depreciation recapture rate.** You'll be concerned with this rate only if your business owns real estate and you're selling it. You'll need to pay tax at the 25% rate on the depreciation that you've already taken on the real estate.
- **C corporation income rates.** The gain that a C corporation receives when it sells its assets is taxed at the corporate income tax rate ranging from 15% to 39%, as explained in Section E, below. In addition, the owner pays individual income tax when the cash is distributed to him or her. Hence, there's a double tax when a C corporation sells appreciated assets and distributes the proceeds to its shareholders. If, instead, you sell your corporate stock (an entity sale) and you've owned the stock for more than a year, you'll pay tax at the long-term capital gain rate. This is one level of tax rather than two; the corporation doesn't pay income tax when its stock is sold. The C corporation income rate also applies to the gain received in an asset sale by an LLC or a partnership that has elected to be taxed as a C corporation—two extremely rare scenarios.

Given all these considerations, it's easy to see that tax planning can be a thorny subject in the sale of any business. That's compounded by the fact that the best tax strategy for the seller may not be the one that's best for the buyer. For instance, in a sale that requires the allocation of the sale price by asset classes, the allocation will affect how much of the sale proceeds are subject to taxation at ordinary income rates and how much at long-term capital gain rates. As the seller, you'll prefer to have as much of the price as possible allocated to assets that will lead to long-term capital gain treatment, because the tax rates are lower. But your strategy will reduce the buyer's opportunity to take large expense or depreciation deductions in the year or years immediately following the sale. This translates into higher tax bills for the buyer.

Another potential source of conflict is your desire to reduce the amount of "recaptured" depreciation. Suppose you've already fully depreciated (written off for tax purposes) business equipment that's part of the sale. The buyer will have the opportunity to depreciate it all over again. But the tax law is designed to prevent the same depreciation being taken twice, so you'll need to report (recapture, in tax parlance) as ordinary income the depreciation you've taken. With that tax law quirk in mind, you'll normally want to assign a low value to the already-depreciated equipment so that you'll have less depreciation to recapture

and therefore less income to be reported and taxed. But the buyer will want to assign a high value to it so as to be able to depreciate or write off a larger amount in the future.

To reconcile differences like these, you and the buyer may have to adjust the sale price up or down to reflect who takes the tax hit.

C. Tax Issues When Selling the Business Entity

For tax purposes, the distinction between an asset sale and an entity sale is significant for some businesses but not for others. (Again, see Chapter 9 if you don't firmly grasp what these terms mean.) The key is what type of business organization you've chosen to use.

- **Sole proprietorships and single-member LLCs.** If you're a sole proprietor, your business is *never* treated as a legal or taxable entity separate from yourself for federal tax purposes. This means when you sell the business, the sale is always treated as if you sold its individual items of property (that is, it's treated as an asset sale). So if you own a sole-proprietorship business, you may choose to skip most of this section and go directly to the discussion of asset sales in Section D, below. The same is true if you're the sole member of an LLC and pay taxes as an individual, which is the case if you haven't filed the form electing to be taxed as a corporation. Because your LLC isn't treated as a separate taxable entity by the IRS, the sale will always be treated as an asset sale for federal tax purposes.

- **Corporations, multimember LLCs, and partnerships.** If your business is a corporation, a multimember LLC, or a partnership, selling your entity can lead to significantly different tax consequences than if your entity sells its assets. The rest of this section summarizes the federal tax highlights of an entity sale. Asset sales are covered later in the chapter.

1. The Mechanics of Entity and Asset Sales

Chapter 3 introduced you to the concept of entity and assets sales (a subject that's covered in more detail in Chapter 9). Because understanding this distinction is so crucial, let's briefly review the basics. Assuming your business is organized as a corporation, you can accomplish an entity sale by selling your shares of corporate stock to the buyer. In that case, all the business's assets (furniture, equipment, accounts receivable, real estate, inventory, and so on) continue to be owned by the corporation, which is now owned by the buyer.

Alternatively, you can have an asset sale in which your corporation sells its assets to the buyer, and you continue to

hold onto your stock; this means that you still own the corporation, though it may be nothing more than an empty legal shell.

Many buyers prefer an asset sale for tax reasons or because they're concerned about being stuck with the business's liabilities. (See Chapters 9 and 15 for details on liability issues.) On the tax side—which is the focus of this chapter—buyers may prefer an asset sale, because this allows them to establish a tax basis in an asset equal to the sale price allocated to that asset. The buyer can then begin to depreciate or otherwise write off the asset right away, using a write-off period of three, five, or seven years, depending on the applicable IRS rules. (Goodwill and other intangible assets must be amortized over a 15-year period.) This helps to reduce the buyer's current taxable income.

By contrast, if the buyer acquires the stock of your corporation or the membership interests in your multimember LLC, these large tax-lowering subtractions from current income are not available. The entity can't begin again to depreciate its older assets over a relatively short period. Someday, maybe many years in the future, the buyer may sell the stock. At that point, the buyer will be able to deduct the stock cost (the buyer's basis) from the new sale price, paying capital gains tax on the difference. Buyers who strongly desire to receive their tax benefits sooner rather than later will prefer to acquire your assets rather than your entity.

But other economic factors may be more important to the buyer so that they outweigh these tax concerns.

The rest of this section covers in more detail the chief tax considerations when you sell the entity rather than the assets. The sale of assets is covered in Sections D through I, below.

2. Selling a Corporation

For tax purposes, there are two kinds of corporations: C corporations and S corporations. Your corporation is a C corporation unless you and your fellow shareholders filed Form 2553 with the IRS, in which you elected to be taxed as an S corporation. The main difference between the two types of corporations is that a C corporation files a separate tax return and pays taxes on its income as a corporate entity, while the income of an S corporation is passed through the corporation to the shareholders, who are taxed on their respective shares at their individual income tax rates. In other words, with an S corporation you're taxed as if you had a partnership rather than a corporation. (Similarly, if you have a single-owner S corporation, you're personally taxed for the business profits.) This difference in taxation between a C corporation and an S corporation becomes especially important when an asset sale is involved, as explained in Section E, below.

The sale of corporate stock in either a C corporation or an S corporation is treated as the sale of a capital asset. As a shareholder, you'll pay tax on the profit you make on your investment at the ordinary income rate or the long-term capital gains rate, depending on whether you've held your corporate stock for longer than a year. The corporation doesn't pay a tax since it has sold nothing.

EXAMPLE: Arnold forms a corporation called Arnco Inc. He invests $20,000 in the company in return for 20,000 shares of stock. Five years later, Arnold sells his shares of Arnco stock for $100,000. He has realized a gain of $80,000. Since Arnold owned the stock for more than one year, his gain is taxed at the long-term capital gain rate. Arnco itself pays no tax on the transaction.

So far, this discussion has assumed that you're going to receive a taxable gain from the sale of your stock. But, of course, it's also possible that for tax purposes, you'll experience a loss. In that case, you'd like the loss to be treated as an ordinary loss (rather than a capital loss) so that the loss can offset ordinary income, which is taxed at a higher rate than capital income. Ordinary-loss treatment is available for up to $50,000 of loss ($100,000 if you and your spouse file jointly) if the stock you're selling was issued as Section 1244 stock.

A Tax Break for Certain Corporations

A person selling the stock of a C corporation that's a Qualified Small Business Corporation (QSBC) is entitled to a tax break—though that break seems less significant now that the long-term capital gain rate is only 15%. Figuring out whether your C corporation meets the IRS definition of a QSBC will take some doing. You'll probably need an accountant to sort out all the technical requirements for you. Or you may prefer to check one of the reference books mentioned in "Resources on Federal Tax Law," above.

If you and your C corporation do meet all of the IRS tests for a QSBC, you can exclude from taxation 50% of your gain on the sale of your corporate stock if you held the stock more than five years and received the stock after August 10, 1993. The remaining gain is taxed at a 28% rate.

The taxable gain in the Arnco Inc. example above would be $40,000 (not $80,000) if Arnco turned out to be a QSBC.

Here are some of the technical criteria from the tax law:

- Your corporation must have been a C corporation at all times.
- Your C corporation won't qualify as a QSBC if it's engaged in one of a number of service fields including, for example, health, engineering, architecture, or consulting.
- Your C corporation needs to use at least 80% of its assets in the active conduct of a business.

To figure out whether or not you own Section 1244 stock, look back to when your corporation first issued the stock. Check your corporate record book for a director's resolution stating that your stock was issued as Section 1244 stock. (Often you'll find this in the minutes of the first meeting.) Assuming you find that your stock is Section 1244 stock, you must also make sure all the following rules are met:

- The stock was issued to you for money or property—and not for services.
- The stock was issued to you as an individual—and not to a partnership or other corporation.
- No more than half of the corporation's gross receipts for the past five years (or life of the corporation if it's less than five years old) came from passive income like royalties, dividends, or rent. Income from sales of products or the providing of services would be okay, because that's not considered to be passive income.
- The total amount the corporation received for all Section 1244 stock it issued didn't exceed $1 million.
- The corporation is a U.S. company.
- You're the original purchaser of the stock.

3. Selling a Sole Proprietorship or a Single-Member LLC

If you're the sole owner of your business and it's not a corporation, you most likely have organized it as either a sole proprietorship or a single-member LLC. For reasons explained below, this means your sale will almost always be taxed as an asset sale, no matter how it's structured in the sales contract. The exception is a single-member LLC that has used IRS Form 8832 to elect to be taxed as a C corporation. As you would expect, this rare bird will be taxed like a C corporation, applying the tax principles summarized in Section 2, just above.

Let's begin with the sole proprietorship. A sole proprietorship has no separate legal or taxable status, so it follows that it can't be sold as an entity. This means the sale is always treated as an asset sale, and you are taxed personally on the gain. (See Section G, below.) The tax rate will be determined by looking at how the sale price was allocated among the assets of the business. For some assets you'll pay tax at the ordinary income rate; for others, you'll be taxed at the long-term capital gain rate if the assets were held for more than one year. For example, the gain on inventory will be taxed at the ordinary income rate. The gain on equipment and vehicles held for more than one year will be taxed at the long-term capital gain rate.

The tax situation for an LLC is similar. From the standpoint of personal legal liability, an LLC—even a single-member LLC—is an entity separate from its member or members. But for tax purposes, your single-member LLC, which has not elected

to be taxed as a C corporation using IRS Form 8832, will be disregarded and you personally will pay tax just as if you sold the assets of a sole proprietorship. Again, tax rates will depend on how the sale price is allocated among the assets sold, as explained in Section I, below.

4. Selling a Partnership or a Multimember LLC

If you own part of a multiowner business that's not incorporated, you probably have organized it as either a partnership or a multimember LLC. If you sell the business as an entity, your partnership or LLC will pay no tax (unless you have elected corporate tax status using IRS Form 8832). You and the other owners will be treated as if you've sold a capital interest similar in some ways to the sale of corporate stock. You start with your basis in your partnership interest or your LLC. Then you subtract your basis from the sale price. The resulting number is your gain. It will generally be taxed as a long-term capital gain if you owned your partnership or membership interest for more than a year.

D. Selling the Assets of a Business

As discussed above in Section C and throughout this book, if your business is a legal entity—a corporation, an LLC, or a partnership—you have a choice of either selling the entity or arranging for the entity to sell its assets, which can lead to different tax consequences. However, the sale of a business operated as a single-member LLC, whether structured as an asset sale or an entity sale, will almost always be treated for tax purposes as a sale of assets, meaning that the principles discussed in this section rather than in Section C will apply. And if you're a sole proprietor, you don't have a choice: Your sale will always be an asset sale—both legally and tax-wise.

You'll need to be cautious if you have a C corporation and are considering an asset sale. As you'll see in Section E, below, such a sale raises the unhappy prospect of paying federal tax twice: once at the corporate tax rate and then again at your individual rate. (Fortunately, that problem can sometimes be managed to avoid some negative tax consequences.)

If you sell the assets of your business—not the entity—the process of figuring out the federal tax consequences can become quite complex. First, you need to look at each asset (or asset group) included in the sale and then properly assign it to one of several classifications for tax purposes. Second, you must decide how much of the purchase price should be allocated to each asset group. For example, if you sell your greeting card store for $200,000 and the assets of the business include an inventory of goods, equipment, and business goodwill, you need to assign a

portion of the $200,000 to each of these three categories. Similarly, if you own an appliance repair business that owns the building where the business is conducted, you'll need to attribute part of the sale price to equipment and supplies, part to the real estate, and the rest to goodwill. (You'll learn more about the allocation process in Section I, below.) Finally, you must determine the gain (or loss) on the sale of each asset or asset group.

 The tax rules governing the process of selling the assets of your business are exceptionally intricate. After reading this overview, consult a tax adviser for help in applying the rules to your specific tax situation.

Generally speaking, in a business sale, assets will fall into one of the three broad categories of capital and noncapital assets described below. But as you'll see in Section I, below, for tax reporting purposes, the IRS has further broken down these categories, so you'll eventually need to assign the assets to seven categories, as follows.

1. Capital Assets

For income tax purposes, many assets of a small business are classified as capital assets. When the assets are sold, the gain will be taxed to the seller at the long-term capital gain rate if the assets were owned by the business for more than a year, except for any depreciation recapture, which will be taxed at higher rates. (Different rules apply to assets sold by a C corporation; see Section E, below.)

In general terms, capital assets are assets that last a while, including such things as depreciable equipment (tools, furniture, manufacturing machines, computers, and vehicles, for example) and real estate, as well as goodwill and some intellectual property such as copyrights. The main exceptions—assets that are not treated as capital assets—are inventory and trade receivables (amounts that customers owe to the business, commonly known as accounts receivable). Section 3, below, covers noncapital assets.

EXAMPLE: Digital Data LLC, a small software development business, is being sold. The sale price is allocated among capital assets and noncapital assets as follows.

Capital Assets
- computers, CD burners, scanners, printers, phone system, photocopiers, fax machines, and other office equipment
- furniture
- vehicles
- land and building owned by the LLC, and
- copyrights.

Noncapital Assets
- inventory of unsold CD kits, and
- accounts receivable.

In addition, the two members of the LLC (Anita and Hal) are each giving the buyer a covenant not to compete. The money they receive for the covenants is taxed at ordinary income rates.

The tax rate on the sale of capital assets is determined in part by looking at the type of legal entity making the sale. If your business is organized as a C corporation, the tax on the gain realized in the corporation's sale of its capital assets will generally be computed at C corporation income tax rates. Then, unfortunately, you and the other owners will be taxed again when the corporation distributes the net proceeds to you. This same tax scheme applies to the rare LLC or partnership that's elected to be taxed as a C corporation. But it's often possible to limit or even eliminate the burden of double taxation. (See Section E, below, for more on asset sales by a C corporation.)

By contrast, if you have a sole proprietorship, partnership, S corporation, or typical LLC (one that has not elected corporate tax treatment), you and the other owners, if any, will pay tax on the gain on your personal income tax return using Form 1040. Your business entity will pay no income tax—though your partnership, S corporation, or multimember LLC will need to file an information return with the IRS. In other words, there's no double taxation on the gain from the sale.

However, it's important to understand that not all the gain you receive on the sale of capital assets will be taxed at the capital gain rate. If you claimed depreciation in earlier years on property such as business equipment and furniture, the amount of this depreciation must be calculated ("recaptured") and will be taxed at ordinary income rates. (See Section 2b, below.)

As noted earlier, gains or losses on capital assets are treated as long term if the assets are held for more than a year. You compute your net capital gain by subtracting capital losses from capital gains. In most instances, this means any remaining gain is taxed at a comparatively favorable 15% rate. If you end up with a net capital loss—either long term or short term—you can subtract that loss from ordinary income to the extent of $3,000 a year, or $1,500 if you're married and you and your spouse file separate tax returns. If your losses exceed these limits, you can apply the unused part to offset ordinary income in future years until the net capital loss has been used up.

2. Section 1231 "Capital" Assets

Capital assets (see definition earlier in this section) that can be depreciated are called Section 1231 assets. IRS depreciation rules usually affect the taxes you pay when you sell the Section 1231 assets of your business.

Section 1231 assets consist mainly of:

- business real estate
- furniture, fixtures, and equipment that your business has held for more than a year, and
- intangible personal property (including some covenants not to compete) that can be amortized under Section 197 of the tax code.

a. Seller's Viewpoint on Section 1231 Assets

Suppose you sell all or most of the assets of your business at a gain. And further imagine that some of these nonreal property assets have been depreciated under Section 1231. The depreciation you've previously taken must now be recaptured and treated as ordinary income in the year of sale. (This is true even if you sell the assets on the installment basis.) To understand how this works, let's say that you sell your business for $400,000 and that $25,000 of the sale price is allocated to a commercial sound system that your restaurant bought for $50,000. And let's say that over the years, you took $45,000 in depreciation for the sound system, which means you now have a tax basis of $5,000 ($50,000 − $45,000 = $5,000). The $20,000 difference between your basis ($5,000) and the sale price of the system ($25,000) must be treated as depreciation recapture, meaning it's taxed as ordinary income in the year of the sale. Even trickier rules apply when the depreciated asset that is sold is real estate. Basically, any accelerated depreciation that's been taken for real estate must be recaptured at ordinary income rates. Other depreciation that's been taken (nonaccelerated depreciation) is taxed at a 25% capital gain rate.

b. Buyer's Viewpoint on Section 1231 Assets

The buyer who acquires Section 1231 personal property assets, such as machinery or furniture, can start over and depreciate (write off) these assets following depreciation or amortization periods prescribed by the IRS. For example, a buyer who acquires computers from you may be able to write off the cost over a five-year period and may be able to write off the cost of office furniture over a seven-year period.

3. Noncapital Assets

Some assets are not classified as regular capital assets or 1231 capital assets. Gains or losses on these items are treated as ordinary income or loss. This category can include such assets as:

- inventory
- promissory notes given to your business
- accounts receivable, and
- real estate or other depreciable trade or business property held for less than a year (even though it would have been Section 1231 property if it had been held by the business for more than a year).

E. Asset Sale by a C Corporation

If your business is incorporated, the first question to ask is whether it's a C corporation or an S corporation. It's a C corporation unless you and the other shareholders filed Form 2553 with the IRS electing to be an S corporation. As you probably know, a C corporation pays tax on its income as a separate tax entity, and then the shareholders pay tax on any dividends that are distributed to them. Obviously, this is a form of double taxation but, during the life of the corporation, this isn't a problem and may even be advantageous. For example, if the owners work as employees of a company and the company pays all its annual profit to them by way of tax-deductible salaries, bonuses, and perks, the corporation has no net income and is therefore not taxed. In other situations, small business owners prefer to operate as a C corporation because they plan to retain earnings in the corporation for future expansion (and not pay them out to owners). In this situation, the retained earnings up to $50,000 are taxed at the favorable corporate income tax rate of 15% (an additional $25,000 is taxed at 25%).

Recommended reading on C corporations. For more information on why some owners choose to do business through a C corporation, see *Legal Guide for Starting & Running a Small Business,* by Fred S. Steingold (Nolo).

By contrast, an S corporation is a pass-through tax entity, meaning that business income is taxed as if you're a sole proprietor or partner. The corporation pays no tax, but you—as an owner of S corporation stock—are taxed on your share of the profits whether or not they're distributed to you. The effect of this is that when your S corporation sells its assets, there will be just one level of taxation (unless your company was a C corporation in earlier years). But as with any sale of assets, the tax rates you'll actually pay will depend on how the sale price is allocated among the assets (for example, among capital or noncapital assets) and whether depreciation taken in the past is being recaptured.

The tax rules are far more complex when a C corporation sells its assets. First the corporation pays federal tax on the gain from the sale at a C corporation's ordinary income tax rates, which are as follows:

First $50,000 of taxable income	15%
Next $25,000 of taxable income	25%
Next $25,000 of taxable income	34%
Over $100,000 of taxable income	34% to 39%

Then, when the corporation distributes the proceeds of the sale to you and the other shareholders, you're taxed on what you receive at the dividend tax rate—usually 15%, but 5% if you're in a low tax bracket. In short, when a C corporation sells its assets, it can result in double taxation. Consequently, whenever possible, owners of a C corporation will prefer to sell their entity, not its assets.

Fortunately, there are effective ways to soften or, in some instances, even eliminate this harsh tax result, as described in Sections 1 and 2, below. And if these methods don't solve the double taxation problem for you, you may be able to encourage the buyer to go along with a stock sale rather than an asset sale. (See Section 3, below.)

1. Try to Have Some of the Purchase Price Paid Directly to You

As just explained, when a C corporation receives the purchase price and then distributes money to you and any other owners, there are taxes due at both the corporate and the shareholder level. But there's no corporate tax on sums you get directly from the buyer for a legitimate reason, such as your agreeing to sign a covenant not to compete in the future. You're not asking the seller to pay you for any assets owned by the corporation (a no-no, since the corporation, not you, owns these assets), but simply arranging for a reasonable part of the overall payment package to come directly to you in exchange for a personal promise.

EXAMPLE 1: Bonnie, the sole shareholder of Bonco Inc.—a C corporation—sells the business to Max. Max pays Bonco $500,000 for Bonco's assets. Bonco pays income tax at the C corporation income rate on the gains it receives in the sale. Bonnie pays income tax at the capital gain rate on the proceeds of the sale that are distributed to her as a dividend. All of the sales price is exposed to the possibility of double taxation.

EXAMPLE 2: Conrad, the sole shareholder of Conco Inc.—a C corporation—negotiates with Paula for the sale of the business. They agree that $500,000 will change hands, as follows:

- Paula will pay Conco $250,000 for its assets.
- Paula will pay Conrad $100,000 for his covenant not to compete for three years.
- Paula will pay Conrad $150,000 for consulting services over a two-year period

Conco pays income tax at the C corporation income rate on its gain from the $250,000 it receives. Conrad pays income tax at the capital gain rate on the proceeds that he receives from Conco ($250,000 less the taxes Conco paid). This means there's double taxation on this part of the $500,000. But Conco pays no tax on the $100,000 that Conrad gets for his covenant not to compete or for the $150,000 he gets for consulting

services, with the result that this money is only taxed once.

In Example 2, although part of the burden of double taxation is avoided, Conrad will still owe income tax at ordinary rates on the money he receives for his covenant not to compete and for his services. And on the part he gets for his services, he'll also owe self-employment tax (which goes to the IRS for Social Security and Medicare). Still, Conrad's overall tax outcome is probably better using this strategy.

2. Pay Yourself a Bonus

Another effective and popular way to reduce or even get rid of the burden of double taxation in a C corporation's sale of its assets is to pay yourself some or all of the income as a bonus—assuming that you've been working as an employee of your business. The corporation can deduct the payment to you, meaning that that money won't be taxed to the corporation. You, however, will be taxed at ordinary income rates on the money you receive. This strategy for avoiding double taxation can pass IRS muster only as long as the compensation you receive is reasonable. For example, if you've been receiving $100,000 a year in salary from your C corporation and then, following a sale of the assets, you receive a $750,000 bonus, the IRS may treat some of that amount as a dividend, which will result in double taxation. However, the IRS would probably go along with a $150,000 bonus, especially if you could show that your overall compensation was reasonable in your industry.

3. Try to Convince the Buyer to Go Along With a Stock Sale

For liability and tax reasons, a buyer may be reluctant to go along with a sale of the corporate stock. Sometimes, however, you can provide an incentive for the buyer to do so. Chapter 9 explains why in some circumstances a buyer who might normally prefer an asset sale may nevertheless be eager to buy the stock—for example, to take advantage of a very favorable lease that the corporation has on the space it occupies.

But unless the ability to take over a lease or favorable contract trumps all other financial considerations, a buyer may be concerned that buying your corporate stock will mean inheriting the business's tax basis for assets that have already been heavily depreciated. In that case, the buyer will lose the opportunity for substantial tax deductions through depreciation. By contrast, by buying the company's assets, the buyer can up the basis to the actual sale price of those assets—and get the tax benefits of depreciating them from that higher starting point. One way you may nevertheless make a stock sale more palatable

is to advocate allocating a substantial part of the sale price to a consulting agreement, which the buyer can deduct promptly as a business expense.

F. Asset Sale by an S Corporation

If your business is organized as an S corporation and it sells its assets, there's no double taxation at the federal level. As explained in Section D, above, an S corporation pays no tax on income; gains and losses are passed through to the shareholders.

There are two special issues to consider when your S corporation sells its assets.

1. S Corporations Face Double Taxation in Some States

While most states follow the federal scheme and tax S corporations at the shareholder level only, the District of Columbia and the following states don't go along:

California	Michigan	New York
Connecticut	New Hampshire	Tennessee
Louisiana	New Jersey	Vermont

This means that S corporations located in one of those places will face a state (or D.C.) income tax at the corporate level when the business sells its assets—and then a tax on the shareholders when distributions are made. This won't be a big deal if the income tax rate in your state is low but, unfortunately, that isn't always the case.

2. Converted Corporations May Owe a Built-In Gains Tax

If your S corporation was converted from a C corporation in the past, it may have to pay a special tax called a built-in gains tax, which is computed at the highest corporate rate. (If you've had an S corporation right from the beginning, you don't have to worry about this tax.) Generally speaking, the tax will apply if your corporation converted to S corporation status after 1986 and owned built-in gain assets (ones with a fair market value greater than their tax basis) when it switched over to an S corporation. Assets that the corporation acquired after the switch-over aren't subject to this special tax. There's a 10-year recognition period for the built-in gain. After the 10 years, there's normally no built-in gain to the S corporation.

You'll very likely need accounting help to sort this out. For now, just be aware that the corporation will owe this tax. The impact of the double taxation is moderated somewhat by the fact that the amount of the taxable gain passed through to you and the other shareholders is reduced by the tax the corporation pays.

G. Asset Sale by a Sole Proprietorship or Single-Member LLC

If yours is an unincorporated one-owner business, you're almost certainly operating as a sole proprietorship or a single-member LLC. Selling a sole proprietorship business is treated as the sale of a collection of assets. Depending on how the sale price is allocated among the different asset classes (see Section I, below), the income tax you pay may be at ordinary rates for some assets and at long-term capital gain rates for others. The same is true for virtually all single-member LLCs; there's no tax on the LLC itself—only on the gain received by the member. The exception is if you've filed IRC Form 8832 to elect to have your LLC taxed as a corporation, in which case your sale will be taxed as if you had a C corporation that sold its assets (as described in Section E, above).

H. Asset Sale by a Partnership or Multimember LLC

If you have a multiowner business and it's not set up as a corporation, you're almost certainly operating as a partnership or a multimember LLC. These are pass-through tax entities (unless your LLC has elected to be taxed as a C corporation—see Section E, above), meaning that the business itself doesn't pay an income tax, but the partners or members do. The tax may be computed at either the ordinary income tax rates or at the long-term capital gain rate, depending on how the sale price is allocated among the different classes of assets.

> **EXAMPLE:** Vintage Advantage, a partnership, sells its assets for $65,000. It allocates $15,000 of the sale price to equipment and $50,000 to goodwill. The partnership has already fully depreciated the equipment. The partnership has $15,000 of ordinary income (depreciation recapture) on the equipment and $50,000 of capital gain on the goodwill. The ordinary income and capital gain are passed through to the partners and taxed on their individual tax returns.

I. Allocation of the Purchase Price

When you sell your business, you'll need to allocate the sale price among the seven categories of assets established by the IRS—though again, this isn't necessary if you sell your corporate stock. (See Section C, above.) To reduce the chance of IRS complications, it's best if you and the buyer agree on the allocation and put it in the sales contract. The IRS doesn't have to accept your joint allocation, but normally it will if the allocation is reasonable. There's also IRS Form 8594

(*Asset Acquisition Statement*) that you'll need to file with the IRS. The buyer will have to file a Form 8594, too. The tax laws don't require that the two forms match, but if they don't, it's a red flag inviting an IRS review. If that happens, the IRS may decide to not accept your numbers or the buyer's numbers but may make its own allocation instead. Again, to avoid the trouble and unpredictability of this type of hassle, you and the buyer will want, as part of your sales process, to agree on the allocation to be reported to the IRS so that your Forms 8594 are consistent. The form and applicable instructions are on the CD-ROM at the back of this book.

Where to find the forms. You'll find copies of IRS Form 8594, *Asset Acquisition Statement,* and instructions on the CD-ROM at the back of this book.

The allocation of the sale price is important to you, because it's used to figure out your gain or loss on each asset you've sold. Obviously, you'd like to assign as much of the sale price as possible to items that will result—tax-wise—in a long-term capital gain rather than ordinary income. To do this, you'll want to assign relatively high values to certain items such as buildings and goodwill. The buyer, however, will be motivated by tax considerations to lump assets into categories that can be written off or depreciated quickly. This helps reduce the buyer's tax burden in the early

| Form **8594**
(Rev. October 2002)
Department of the Treasury
Internal Revenue Service | **Asset Acquisition Statement**
Under Section 1060
▶ **Attach to your income tax return.** ▶ **See separate instructions.** | OMB No. 1545-1021

Attachment
Sequence No. **61** |

| Name as shown on return | Identifying number as shown on return |

Check the box that identifies you:
☐ Purchaser   ☐ Seller

Part I   General Information

| 1 Name of other party to the transaction | Other party's identifying number |

Address (number, street, and room or suite no.)

City or town, state, and ZIP code

| 2 Date of sale | 3 Total sales price (consideration) |

Part II   Assets Transferred—All filers of an original statement must complete.

4 Assets	Aggregate fair market value (actual amount for Class I)	Allocation of sales price
Class I	$	$
Class II	$	$
Class III	$	$
Class IV	$	$
Class V	$	$
Class VI and VII	$	$
Total	$	$

5   Did the purchaser and seller provide for an allocation of the sales price in the sales contract or in another written document signed by both parties? . . . . ☐ Yes ☐ No

If "Yes," are the aggregate fair market values (FMV) listed for each of asset Classes I, II, III, IV, V, VI, and VII the amounts agreed upon in your sales contract or in a separate written document?. . . . . . . ☐ Yes ☐ No

6   In the purchase of the group of assets (or stock), did the purchaser also purchase a license or a covenant not to compete, or enter into a lease agreement, employment contract, management contract, or similar arrangement with the seller (or managers, directors, owners, or employees of the seller)? . . . . . . ☐ Yes ☐ No

If "Yes," attach a schedule that specifies **(a)** the type of agreement and **(b)** the maximum amount of consideration (not including interest) paid or to be paid under the agreement. See instructions.

For Paperwork Reduction Act Notice, see separate instructions.   Cat. No. 63768Z   Form **8594** (Rev. 10-2002)

Form 8594 (Rev. 10-2002)   Page **2**

| **Part III** | Supplemental Statement- Complete only if amending an original statement or previously filed supplemental statement because of an increase or decrease in consideration. |

7 Tax year and tax return form number with which the original Form 8594 and any supplemental statements were filed.

8 Assets	Allocation of sales price as previously reported	Increase or (decrease)	Redetermined allocation of sales price
Class I	$	$	$
Class II	$	$	$
Class III	$	$	$
Class IV	$	$	$
Class V	$	$	$
Class VI and VII	$	$	$
Total	$		$

9 Reason(s) for increase or decrease. Attach additional sheets if more space is needed.

Form **8594** (Rev. 10-2002)

years of ownership, speeding up the buyer's return on investment. The chart at the end of Section 1, below, shows which assets sellers and buyers usually prefer to value relatively high and which they usually prefer to value relatively low. Possibly with the help of tax professionals, you and the buyer should be able to arrive at an allocation you can both live with. (Allocation of the sale price in the sales agreement is covered in Chapter 14.)

1. The IRS Allocation Categories

The IRS rules establish seven asset classes for the allocation of the sale price.

Class I: Cash and Cash-Like Assets

Cash and cash-like assets include:
- money, such as cash on hand, and
- bank and money market accounts.

You'll probably be keeping the money, in which case there will be nothing to allocate to this class.

Class II: Securities

This category includes:
- certificates of deposit
- U.S. government securities
- readily marketable stock or securities, and
- foreign currency.

Again, it's unlikely that you'll be including items such as these in the sale of your business.

Class III: Accounts Receivable

This category includes the amounts your customers owe the business. The accounts receivable are allocated here if they're included in the sale—which may or may not be the case. Selling the accounts receivable typically shifts the burden of collection to the buyer but, as you know, buyers often are hesitant to acquire accounts receivable because of possible collection problems. However, in exchange for the buyer taking over these accounts, you can assign a discounted value to them so as to allow in advance for those that may not be collectible.

Class IV: Inventory

This category consists primarily of the goods you keep on hand for sale to customers. But remember that any goods that you're holding on consignment from others are not considered to be part of your inventory.

Class V: Other Tangible Property

You can think of tangible as meaning anything you can touch. Since inventory (one type of tangible property) is already covered by Class IV, this category typically includes:
- land and buildings
- furniture
- equipment, and
- fixtures (improvements that are permanently attached to buildings).

For land, buildings, and valuable equipment, it may be useful to get and

General Guidelines for Allocating the Sale Price to Keep Taxes Low

Your tax adviser can analyze your assets and propose a plan to allocate the sale price among those assets to keep your tax bill low. The following chart provides general guidance on how sellers and buyers typically approach asset-allocation issues— whether they prefer to allocate a low or high amount to a particular asset class or have no preference.

IRS Asset Class	Seller's Preference	Buyer's Preference
Class I: Cash and Cash-Like Assets	No preference	No preference
Class II: Securities	No preference	No preference
Class III: Accounts Receivable	No preference	No preference
Class IV: Inventory	Relatively low amount	Relatively high amount
Class V: Other Tangible Property	*Personal property:* Relatively low amount *Real estate:* Relatively high amount	*Personal property:* Relatively high amount *Real estate:* Relatively low amount
Class VI: Covenants Not to Compete and Other Intangible Property	*Covenant not to compete:* Depends on type of business; see note below *Other intangible property:* Relatively high amount	*Covenant not to compete:* Relatively low amount *Other intangible property:* Relatively low amount
Class VII: Goodwill and Going-Concern Value	Relatively high amount	Relatively low amount

***Note regarding covenants not to compete:** When an individual (such as a shareholder) rather than an entity (such as a corporation) is paid for a covenant not to compete related to the sale of a business, the individual usually will prefer to assign a relatively low value to the covenant; this is because the fee received for the covenant will be taxed at ordinary income rates. But different principles will apply in an asset sale by a C corporation. In that situation, the shareholder will want to reduce the burden of double taxation and, for that reason, will prefer to assign a relatively high portion of the total payment package to the covenant and less to the asset being sold.

rely on an appraisal by a respected appraiser to reduce the chances that the IRS will later challenge the value that you and the buyer assign to these items.

Class VI: Covenants Not to Compete and Other Intangible Property

Just as tangible means assets you can touch, intangible means property that you can't touch or physically possess. An intangible is typically a legal right—often recognized in a document. Here are some examples:

- covenant of a selling corporation or LLC that it won't compete with the buyer
- patents, copyrights, and trademarks
- trade secrets
- customer or client lists, and
- licenses or permits granted by the government.

Note that a covenant not to compete given by a sole proprietor, or by a shareholder or an LLC member as an individual, is not treated as an asset in the IRS asset allocation form. Such a covenant, however, must be disclosed separately on line 6 of the form.

Goodwill and going-concern value are also types of intangible assets, but the IRS has given them a category of their own (Class VII). Buyers typically don't like to put much value on intangible assets, since it will take 15 years to fully amortize (write off) these items. Sellers, however, like to have more of the sale price allocated to intangibles, because these are capital assets and, for that reason, are taxed at the capital gain rate.

Class VII: Goodwill and Going-Concern Value

This class is a catch-all for any part of the sale price that doesn't fall into one of the first six classes. It recognizes the fact that a business with a good reputation and many loyal customers who can be expected to patronize the business in the future may be worth more than the sum of its parts—and that this extra value is often reflected in the sale price. As the seller, you'd like to assign a relatively high value to Class VII items, as the proceeds from the sale of these items are taxed at the capital gains rate.

2. Applying the Allocation Rules

Obviously, the allocation of the sale price will vary widely from business to business, but the following example will illustrate how the system works.

> **EXAMPLE:** Steve, a certified personal trainer, has owned a successful exercise club for ten years. He sells it to Barbara for $500,000. Steve also signs a consulting contract under which he will provide consulting services to the business for two years and receive $50,000 for those services. And he agrees not to compete with the business in return for a $5,000 payment from Barbara.

Steve and Barbara agree to allocate the purchase price as shown below.

Because the consulting agreement and noncompete covenant are not assets of the business that Steve is selling, they're not included in the allocation of the sale price. Instead, they're disclosed on Line 6 of the IRS asset allocation form.

Steve will report the consulting and noncompete fees as ordinary income when he receives them. Barbara will deduct the consulting fees as current business expenses when she pays them to Steve, and she'll amortize the noncompete fee over a 15-year period.

Class	Allocation of $500,000 Sale Price	Reason
I. Cash and Cash-Like Assets	$ -0-	Steve will be keeping the money that's on hand.
II. Securities	$ -0-	The business has none.
III. Accounts Receivable	$ 10,000	There is $15,000 owing for club memberships, but collecting the full amount may be a problem for Barbara.
IV. Inventory	$ 2,000	For club T-shirts, power drinks, and pulse monitors on hand for sale to club members.
V. Other Tangible Property	$350,000	For the building and equipment.
VI. Covenants Not to Compete and Other Intangible Items	$ 50,000	For the club's membership list and all rights to Steve's copyrighted fitness manual.
VII. Goodwill and Going-Concern Value	$88,000	The rest of the sale price, reflecting the club's convenient location and its loyal membership base.

☑ Checklist for Tax Consequences

☐ Learn the tax rates that may apply to your sale.

☐ Remember that paying tax at the long-term capital gain rate beats paying at the ordinary income rate.

☐ Understand the tax differences between an asset sale and an entity sale.

☐ Avoid an entity sale for a C corporation.

☐ Carefully allocate the sale price among assets for the best tax results.

☐ Consider the possible tax advantages of an installment sale.

☐ Evaluate all the taxable elements: sale price, covenant not to compete, and payments for post-closing services.

☐ Agree with the buyer on figures for the IRS asset allocation form.

☐ Consult a tax professional early on.

■

Chapter 5

Putting a Price on Your Business

A key task in selling any business is deciding how much it's worth. Price your business too high and you'll scare off potential buyers. Price it too low and you'll leave money on the table. But if you hope for precision in pricing your business, you'll be disappointed. No pricing formula, expert estimate, or clairvoyant can accurately provide a sales figure that's exactly "right." So while you need to price your business sensibly, you won't know how much it's really worth until the day a buyer writes you a check.

Still, even though you can't know in advance exactly what your business will sell for, you can arrive at a reasonable asking price. Start by taking all relevant valuation information into consideration to identify a range of possible sales prices. Depending on your business, the low end of the range will probably be little more than the liquidation value of the physical assets. The high end is likely to be based on income projections and what an enthusiastic buyer might pay for the right to receive (and hopefully increase) those earnings in the future. If you have a healthy business—especially one with a well-established customer base and positive reputation—you'll probably pick an initial asking price towards the top of your range and then, if necessary, be prepared to back off a bit in negotiating the final price. In pricing your business, you'll need to take into account the general economic climate, as well as trends in your industry—whether positive or negative. And, of course, if you have to sell quickly, you may be required to settle for less than you'd receive if you could take your time.

This chapter explains the main factors that influence pricing and suggests ways for you to arrive at a realistic price range. Chapter 7 tells you how to prepare your business for a sale so that it brings a decent price, and Chapter 8 offers suggestions for finding the right buyer.

A. There's No Universal Pricing Formula: Many Factors Affect Price

Like other business owners, you may have a notion that there's a simple, widely accepted formula to determine what your business is worth. You may even expect that when the time comes to sell, you'll plug your numbers into a long-established valuation formula to get a reasonable idea of what the sale price will be. Unfortunately, no such magic formula exists. Instead, there are multiple approaches to figuring out the value of a business—all of which are subject to a myriad of exceptions and caveats relating to factors in and outside your business. For example, the presence of a major new competitor or a lingering economic downturn may make the best formulaic price estimates irrelevant.

Several factors go into pricing a business, including terms of payment, type of buyer, market demand, and your personal needs.

1. Terms of Payment

The price a buyer will agree to pay is often tied directly to the terms of payment. Although it would be terrific if you could get paid in one lump sum, in the real world, chances are that you'll be selling your business on an installment basis in which the buyer pays you over time. It follows that the terms you require, such as the amount of the down payment, the repayment period, and the interest rate, can all affect how much a buyer will agree to pay. And keep in mind that an installment sale may affect your sale price calculation in another important way: You may want to charge more if you'll be paid over five rather than three years, since during the repayment period, you'll be exposed to more risk of buyer default.

Keep in mind that selling on an installment plan can benefit you if the installment payments put you into a lower income tax bracket than would apply if you received the entire sale proceeds in one lump sum.

2. Type of Buyer

The task of setting the price is complicated by the fact that there are different types of buyers. Some buyers are looking to buy a business as an investment to be run by a hired manager. Others may consider your business as a strategic addition to a similar business they already own, in which case, they may be able to reap the benefits of scale; bookkeeping expenses, for example, may increase only slightly when the buyer adds a second location. But an even larger percentage of buyers are looking for a business in which they can work day to day, and these buyers will be sizing up the prospects of your business as a job or career. Especially when the buyer will be relying on the business for a livelihood, the sale price and the terms of payment need to result in cash flow not only sufficient to cover operating expenses and monthly installments, but also enough to pay the buyer a decent salary for the hours that he or she works.

3. Market Demand

A huge fact of life in selling anything of value, including a business, is current demand: what a buyer will pay for what you have to sell. As you probably know from selling a house or other valuable property, timing can be crucial. You may come up with a selling price or range that—based on all available evidence and the best evaluation approach—is unimpeachably fair. In other words, you may feel you've really determined the true value of your business. But market forces beyond your control may have a major impact on the price you get. If a number of similar businesses have just been put on the market or there's been a recent spate of factory closures in your area, there may be no interested buyers at your price or within what you believe is a reasonable range. If that happens, your obvious choices are to lower your expectations and take less or, if your situation allows you do so, to take your business off the market until conditions for a sale improve.

4. Your Personal Needs

Poor health or financial pressures may force you to sell your business within weeks or just a few months. If, for these or other understandable reasons, you need to sell quickly, you'll probably have to take less than the optimal sale price. Similarly, if you're unable or unwilling to work for the buyer—even for a short time after the closing—that fact may diminish the value of the business in the eyes of a prospective buyer. Many buyers prefer to have the seller stay on board during the transition period and feel that it adds value to have such an arrangement.

B. Sales of Comparable Businesses

The closest to an ideal way to set a value on your business is to see what other small enterprises like yours have sold for.

In the real estate business, this is called looking at comparables. But unlike house sales, where it's usually not too difficult to find recent sales of homes more or less like yours, in the business world there may have been few, if any, recent sales of businesses similar to yours. What's more, since small businesses tend to be unique, even if you are able to find a somewhat similar sale in your field or area, the business won't be the same as yours in terms of location, sales volume, number of employees, and a host of other important factors. And even in the unlikely event that you can find the recent sale of a company that very closely resembles yours, you may not be able to get access to accurate numbers. Unlike sales of real estate, which often leave a public paper trail, reliable business sales numbers can be hard to come by— especially because rumor, exaggeration, and just plain blarney often obscure the facts.

⚠ Watch out for incomplete sales information. Go to any event with people in your field—or just attend a service club meeting—and you're sure to hear that so-and-so sold his business for such-and-such dollars. For example, at a Kiwanis lunch, you may learn that Emma got $1 million for her dry-cleaning business. Even assuming this number has some truth to it (and it often may not), you may not be told other important details. For example, the reports of the sale price may not mention that Emma agreed to work for the buyer for three years as part of that price, that the deal included transferring a building and valuable surrounding land to the buyer, and that Emma only got 15% of the purchase price up front with the rest to be paid over five years.

Nevertheless, by collecting information from a number of sources, including trade publications, business brokers, the Internet, and personal contacts, you should be able to come up with a reasonably accurate ballpark estimate for what businesses like yours are selling for.

 Resource on comparable sales. A good place to look online for comparable sales information is the Business Valuation Resource site at www .bvmarketdata.com, where you'll find information on the company's BizComp service.

C. The Income Valuation Approach

The income valuation method assumes that your buyer is looking at a business as just one more type of investment, competing with stocks, bonds, real estate, and other business opportunities. The question then becomes, "What kind of return would a buyer expect from an investment in this business?" Once you arrive at this number, you can work backwards to determine the price you're willing to pay.

This method also assumes that a buyer won't buy a business that doesn't give him or her the desired return on the investment. Rather than determining what the business is worth on some objective level, under this method the buyer determines what the business is worth to him or her, given what the buyer hopes to accomplish by purchasing it. So in this context, you'll need to have some ability to estimate what the buyer is hoping to get out of the business.

Here's how it works: As you know, a buyer seeking a conservative investment might look into U.S. government bonds. The money invested in those bonds is about as safe as you can imagine. In return for that safety, an investor would probably be satisfied with a relatively low interest rate—say, 5%. If an investor puts $10,000 in a 5% government bond, they can be confident that for the duration of the bond, they'll receive $500 each year in interest. When the bond matures, they'll get back the initial $10,000 investment.

But most any business is more risky than U.S. government bonds or other conservative investments. So a buyer looking to buy a business as an investment will reasonably want the expected annual rate of return to be higher—at least 10%-12% for an extremely stable business, but 15%-20% or more for a riskier small enterprise. This is where the income valuation approach comes in.

⚠ **To use the income valuation—or investment—method of determining the right price for your business, you need to be convinced that you can predict the business's profits for the next three to five years with a reasonable degree of accuracy—and you need to be able to predict your buyer's desires with some accuracy as well.** Otherwise, you have nothing solid on which to base your computations—it's all speculation.

Here are a couple of examples of how you can use your prediction of future profits and your desired rate of return to come up with a value for a business.

EXAMPLE 1: Let's say that based on your research, you reasonably expect that your business will produce annual profits of $50,000 for each of the next several years. Let's also say that your business is in a relatively volatile field, so that the investment is somewhat risky. A buyer will probably want a high return on his or her investment, perhaps 20% a year. So how much is the business worth? Let's start with the following formula:

Business Value x Desired Rate of Return = Expected Annual Profits

Here, we know two of the three variables, so we can plug those numbers into the equation:

Business Value x 20% = $50,000

As you'll remember from your high school math classes, another way to state this is:

$$\text{Business Value} = \frac{\$50,000}{20\%}$$

Now, using a calculator, let's divide $50,000 by .20 (the decimal equivalent of 20%). The answer is a value of $250,000.

If everything goes according to plan, you can sell the business for $250,000, offering the buyer the opportunity he or she wants: to receive a return of $50,000 a year.

EXAMPLE 2: Now let's say that if because of the business's long history of profitability you'd be happy with a 15% rate of return. Here's how the formula would play out:

Business Value x 15% = $50,000

Let's restate the equation this way:

$$\text{Business Value} = \frac{\$50,000}{15\%}$$

Now, using a calculator, we'll divide $50,000 by .15 (the decimal equivalent of 15%). The answer is a business value of $333,333. If everything goes according to plan, the buyer will invest $333,333 in the business and receive a return of $50,000 a year.

As you can see, deciding on the rate of return you think a buyer will want to receive is crucial. In these examples, the difference in what the buyer might be willing to pay if you use a 15% return rate rather than a 20% rate is significant. At the 15% rate of return, you'd value the business at $333,333, but if your buyer is counting on a 20% rate of return, you'd value it at only $250,000.

You can't rely solely on this type of income formula to arrive at the value of a business. For one thing, you and the buyer will need to factor in an estimate of how future inflation or deflation might affect the business and its income. Even more important is the fact that the buyer will probably be looking at the business not just as an investment, but also as a way to earn a living. You'll need to demonstrate that the price you set is worth it not only for the rate of return, but also because the cash flow is sufficient to support the buyer.

D. The Asset-Based Approach

Another commonly used approach to putting a price on your business is to tote up the value of the assets, starting with the tangible ones, such as furniture, equipment, and inventory. If the tangible assets are in reasonable shape, there may be a ready market for them. This obviously would be based on your assets' resale value, not how much it would cost to replace them. An appraiser can help you put a value on these tangible assets.

You should normally treat this figure as the smallest amount you'll accept for your business. But if you're trying to sell a money-losing or otherwise troubled business—or are under pressure to quickly sell a tiny business that depends primarily on your efforts—the value of the physical assets may be the most you can hope to get.

EXAMPLE: Carl owns a T-shirt shop in a resort town. He has a month-to-month lease. Lately, Carl's business has barely broken even because other T-shirt shops have opened and because a scare from a large forest fire left the town less popular than it once was. Carl has a chance to take a full-time, year-round job in another city and wants to sell his business to make it possible to do so. He adds up the value of the tangible assets, including the shelving, counters, display cases, furniture, computer, T-shirt printing equipment, and inventory. He arrives at a figure of $22,500, which is probably the most that he'll be able to realize for his business—especially since he needs to sell quickly in order to take the job elsewhere.

But even if your business has been performing poorly of late, don't just assume that it has no worth over and above the value of its tangible assets. By carefully analyzing your business, you may be pleasantly surprised to realize that favorable long-term contracts with customers or suppliers or other intangible assets mean you have more to offer a prospective buyer than is at first apparent. A long-term lease for a good location with below-market rent is one especially valuable intangible asset. You should definitely consider your lease as being valuable no matter the profitability—or lack thereof—of your business. Hopefully, the lease can be transferred to a new owner, as explained in Chapter 7. That's great, because you can treat the lease as an asset and can assign some value to it. Similarly, there may be value in your business name, or in patents, copyrights, or customer lists you own. Your employees are also an important intangible asset. Again, having such assets in the picture can usually justify adding something to the value of the tangible assets.

Just as you shouldn't overlook the value of intangible assets such as a transferable lease, you need to remember that negative factors such as unresolved lawsuits can reduce the value of your business. But business liabilities, whether known or unknown, will only be significant if the buyer will be assuming responsibility for them. If you agree that you'll be solely responsible—and the buyer is convinced that you have the financial resources to follow through—the liabilities are unlikely to affect your asset pricing.

⚠ Don't confuse asset pricing with an asset sale. These two terms are similar but have very different meanings. Throughout this book, you'll see that a sale of a business can be structured as an asset sale (in which a corporation or LLC sells its individual assets to the buyer) or an entity sale (in which the owners sell their entire business in the form of corporate stock or an LLC membership interest to the buyer). The point here is that the asset method of pricing a business can be used no matter whether you sell your corporate or LLC entity or hold onto the entity and sell a laundry list of its key assets. The same, incidentally, is true for all the other methods of valuing a business. In short, the method used to value a business for purposes of a sale doesn't depend on how the sale is structured.

E. Industry Formulas and Rules of Thumb

In some specific fields, valuation formulas often gain credence over time. For example, you might be told that in a certain field, businesses commonly sell for ten times profits or two times sales. Unquestionably, such formulas promise a quick and easy way to price your business. The problem is that these formulas are almost always too simplistic to serve as anything more than a very rough guide for the sale of real businesses, which have quirks and characteristics that must be factored in and that cause deviations from standard formulas.

1. Formulas Based on Sales or Earnings

In some businesses, it is often said that you can arrive at a sales value by multiplying either gross sales or net earnings by an accepted number. So in some niches of the publishing business, you may read in a trade journal that profitable companies commonly change hands at from 1.2 to 1.5 times annual sales. In theory, these formulas are derived from industry experience over a number of years, as represented by data covering lots of previous sales. In reality, such formulas may be based on little more than industry lore and may not accurately reflect current market conditions or the particular business niche you're in. Thus, in the real world of book publishing, textbook publishers tend to sell for a higher multiple of sales than the industry average (because the textbook backlist tends to have more value and discounts are lower). By comparison, publishers that concentrate on popular fiction must settle for a lower multiple (because even a long string of bestsellers is no guarantee of future success).

If you're considering buying a business in a field where formulas like this are part of the culture, go ahead and look at what the figure would be using that formula. But then make sure you carefully consider all of the factors that might cause the sale price to deviate from the number you reach with that calculation. And be prepared for the seller to do the same.

2. Formulas Based on Units

In some industries, there are also pricing formulas based on the number of customer contracts in place or the number of machines in operation. For example, you may read that a company that sells and monitors security alarm systems can be priced based on a widely recognized sum for each customer currently under contract for alarm monitoring services. Similarly, it may be claimed that a food and beverage vending machine business may be priced based on a sum for each vending machine currently owned by the business and in operation at a money-making location. Again, at best, formulaic approaches like these are extremely rough guides. Because in any real sale there are so many other variables to be accounted for—from competition and location to consumer trends and general economic conditions—it's a poor idea to apply a formula uncritically to your situation. Still, almost everyone tosses these numbers around, and they may have some utility in determining whether your price is within a normally accepted range. If you're way off the mark, it may be a sign that you should take a second look at your calculations and assumptions.

F. How Appraisers and Other Experts Can Help You Set the Price

This chapter covers the general principles of business valuation, but it can't deal with the dozens of often complex and conflicting factors that go into pricing a particular business. Unless you already have some specialized knowledge or experience valuing businesses, it often makes sense to pay a reasonable amount for the opinion of a small business accountant, experienced business broker, or appraiser.

1. Accountants

An accountant can help organize and evaluate your financial data and then apply whatever pricing formulas might be available. Also, the accountant can help you present the pricing information in a format that will make sense to a prospective buyer—and, equally important—to the buyer's own accountant. See Chapter 6 for advice on finding and working with accountants.

2. Brokers

A broker can help by tracking down elusive information about sales of comparable businesses and then tailoring that information to current market conditions in your community. If you'll

be handling most of the sale yourself, including finding a buyer, make it clear at the outset that you just want the broker's opinion on pricing the business. Be particularly careful if the broker replies with a free opinion suggesting an unrealistically high value, since this may be the first salvo in a campaign designed to get you to change your mind and retain the broker on a commission basis. If that happens—and the estimate later turns out to be fantasy—"free" will get expensive very quickly. See Chapter 6 for advice on finding and working with brokers.

3. Appraisers

In general terms, an appraiser is someone who routinely puts a value on things such as real estate, equipment, and businesses. Some appraisers are—or started out as—accountants. Others are—or were—real estate agents. And still others have simply attended some seminars on appraising. If you decide to hire an appraiser, you must be very careful to choose the right one. Historically, appraisers have excelled in assigning a value to tangible property such as land, buildings, and equipment. However, in most cases, a business is worth more than the sum of its assets, so you need to pick an appraiser who understands and has had experience in including the nontangible factors, such as a favorable lease or excellent goodwill.

A banker or real estate broker may be able to suggest a good local appraiser. You can also find appraisers through such organizations as the American Society of Appraisers (www.appraisers.org) and the Institute of Business Appraisers (www.instbusapp.org). But before you sign on with someone, make sure that he or she has training and experience in appraising small businesses—ideally in the same industry as yours. Ask for the names of past clients and then call these references to learn what you can about the appraiser's competence and communication skills.

Once hired, a careful appraiser will insist on seeing a whole raft of information, including tax returns, financial statements, asset lists, and leases and other contracts. The appraiser will use this information to write a comprehensive report explaining how he or she reached an opinion as to value. Expect to pay several thousand dollars at a minimum for a thorough appraisal and an informative written report. Assuming that the appraiser has good credentials, you can use the appraisal report to help convince the buyer that you've set a reasonable price on the business.

A credible appraisal report can be useful in convincing buyers that you have a solid basis for your proposed price. An experienced appraiser may also be able to point out shortcomings in your business and suggest changes you can make that can justify a higher sale price.

4. Books and Seminars on Valuing a Business

Another excellent option for tapping into expertise is to read up on the subject in greater detail. Specialized books offer much more information on the various pricing methods and provide ample examples of how the theories can be applied to actual businesses. You might start with *Valuing Small Businesses and Professional Practices,* by Shannon P. Pratt (McGraw-Hill), which is the clearest and most comprehensive treatment that you're likely to find.

Other less-expensive choices include *What Every Business Owner Should Know About Valuing Their Business*, by Stanley J. Feldman, Timothy G. Sullivan, and Roger M. Winsby (McGraw-Hill), and *The Small Business Valuation Book,* by Lawrence W. Tuller (Adams Media).

Occasionally, business brokers or appraisers present seminars on valuation methods, and a community college or business school in your area may offer a short course on the subject. Your local Chamber of Commerce may have information about such offerings.

G. Putting It All Together to Price Your Business

This chapter offers just a brief introduction to an enormously important and complex subject. Obviously, to feel anywhere near comfortable with your conclusions about the price range for your business, you'll need to tap into other resources such as professionals, books, and seminars. You'll quickly discover that most accountants, business brokers, and other experts prefer to blend the results of several methods to arrive at a range of values for a business.

But no price you attach to your business will mean much if it doesn't make sense to the buyer, who, after all, is just as interested in attaining a good deal as you are. And remember that because full-cash buyers are scarce, you'll probably have to work out an installment payment plan. That's why the ability of an installment-payment buyer to pay you the full sale price over the long run should be more important to you than whether the buyer agrees to the highest possible price. To repeat a crucial point: During the years the buyer is making payments and also probably working in the business, the business must produce enough income to pay the buyer a decent salary in addition to covering the monthly payments to you.

If you doubt for a moment how important it is to pay attention to the buyer's cash flow and profits situation, remember, your sale won't be complete until the buyer has paid you all the money you've agreed upon, typically in three to five years. Much can go wrong in the meantime, and even the best security arrangements may not guarantee that you'll readily get all that you're owed. For example, if two years after the closing you take back the business because the buyer can't keep up the installment payments, you may have a much-deteriorated business on your hands that isn't worth what's still owed on the buyer's promissory note. To make matters worse, you'll be forced to run the business again until you can find another buyer. And while the sale price will be only one of many factors that will determine the buyer's success, setting too high a price will clearly make it more likely that the buyer will fail.

So even though you'd like the sale price to be as high as possible, you need to be sure that the overall deal—price and payment terms—is realistic. You need to feel reasonably certain that the buyer is unlikely to falter and that the odds are that in three or five years, the buyer will make the final payment. Then, and only then, will the sale be complete.

☑ Checklist for Pricing a Business

- ☐ List and value your assets—both tangible (such as equipment) and intangible (such as your company's goodwill).

- ☐ Learn all you can about the sale prices of comparable businesses.

- ☐ Evaluate the current business climate in your community.

- ☐ Estimate the rate of return an investment-type buyer would expect.

- ☐ Consider whether the sale price and installment payment terms would let a buyer earn a decent living by working in the business.

- ☐ Learn the formulas and rules of thumb used in your industry.

- ☐ Read books and attend seminars on business valuation.

- ☐ Get professional help as needed from your accountant, or hire a business broker or appraiser.

Chapter 6

Working With Lawyers, Accountants, and Brokers

As you start the process of putting your business on the market, you'll need to decide how much of the work you're prepared to do yourself and how much you'll delegate to others. If the sale will be fairly straightforward and you want to limit your expenses, you may decide to perform many routine tasks yourself, using occasional expert help as needed from a lawyer, an accountant, or perhaps a business broker. Armed with the information in this book, many sellers will find that to be a feasible arrangement. Not only will you have the legal and practical information necessary to competently handle your own sale, but you should also be able to save considerable money in professional fees. But to make this approach work, you'll need to find professionals who are willing to offer advice, serve as objective sounding boards, and do some technical chores without trying to take over the whole job.

This chapter discusses your relationships with the main professionals you're likely to hire in the process of selling your business. See Chapter 5 for information about working with an appraiser to help you determine an appropriate sale price for your business.

You May Need More Than Occasional Professional Help

The subcontracting-coaching model of working with lawyers, accountants, and other professionals suggested in this book may not be optimal for everyone. Here are some situations when you may decide to rely much more heavily on professional assistance, doing little if anything yourself:

- You're seriously ill.
- You have recently inherited an enterprise but have little or no business experience.
- You need to immediately leave the area or are otherwise pressed for time.
- You're selling your business to a large company that's aided by a team of seasoned professionals.
- You anticipate that there will be unusual legal or financial complexities.
- Your deal involves a substantial amount of money.
- You're in a dispute with a co-owner or going through a divorce.

Even if you decide to rely heavily on outside professional help, do take the time to read this book carefully. By doing so, you'll better understand all that needs to be done and will have the information you need to effectively supervise the people who will do it.

A. Lawyers

Since you're already in business, you've probably hired a lawyer from time to time to help with legal tasks. Your attorney may have helped or advised you in the creation of your partnership, corporation, or LLC. And perhaps your lawyer reviewed your lease, drafted a contract between you and an independent contractor, or represented you in a lawsuit or at an arbitration hearing. If so, you're already familiar with the kinds of things an attorney can do for a small business.

But if this is the first time that you're selling a business, you may not know the many places in the transaction where a lawyer can assist you.

1. How a Lawyer Can Help

Here are some of the tasks for which the help or coaching of an experienced small business lawyer can be valuable. (See the chapters listed in parentheses for more information about each of these tasks.)

- making sure your partnership, corporation, or LLC documents are complete and up to date (Chapter 7)
- determining what kind of consents to sell you may need from any co-owners of the business and possibly their spouses (Chapter 18)
- figuring out whether or not your lease and other contracts can be readily transferred to a buyer (Chapter 20)
- identifying relevant state and local laws that apply to your sale, such as bulk sales laws (Chapter 3)
- analyzing the other pros and cons of selling your assets versus selling the entity (Chapter 9)
- reviewing the listing agreement with a broker if you're thinking of working with one (Section C of this chapter)
- negotiating terms of the sale (Chapter 9)
- preparing a nonbinding letter of intent summarizing the deal terms (Chapter 11)
- developing a strategy for making sure you get paid the full sale price (Chapter 5)
- determining the scope and wording of your disclosures (Chapter 7)
- drafting or reviewing a sales agreement, including important clauses on the allocation of responsibility for liabilities (Chapters 12-18)
- drafting or reviewing other important documents such as assignment of your intellectual property rights (Chapter 20) or an employment contract you sign with the new buyer (Chapter 21)
- making sure that your consulting agreement or noncompete agreement protects you adequately (Chapter 21)
- preparing or reviewing the necessary transfer documents if you're selling a building or land (Chapter 20)

- creating your closing checklist and otherwise preparing paperwork for the closing (Chapter 22), and
- conducting a smooth and thorough closing (Chapter 22).

In addition, a lawyer with tax expertise can advise you on the tax consequences of your sale.

The key point here is not necessarily that your lawyer should do everything; it's that you should understand that your lawyer can help you with the important steps in the selling process on an as-needed basis. Just how much legal help you buy is your call. Especially if a lot of money is involved, and for that reason you're less worried that professional fees will gobble too big a percentage of your proceeds, you may find it cost-efficient to ask your lawyer to do much of this work. By contrast, if you're counting every penny, you'll be inclined to do the lion's share yourself.

EXAMPLE: Tom has been negotiating with Lori and Toni, two young entrepreneurs who want to buy Tom's food supplement and vitamin shop business. They agree on major terms, and Tom tries his hand at preparing a sales agreement. With the help of this book, Tom understands most of what he's doing but gets hung up on exactly how to word the sections of the agreement dealing with who's liable if a disaffected former employee sues. He also has questions as to how to draft some of the terms of his own one-year employment contract. To get help, Tom takes the sales agreement and employment contract to his business lawyer, Sheila. They talk for 45 minutes. After they part, Sheila spends an hour and a half revising the two agreements. They talk again for 15 minutes and then jointly make the final changes. Tom thanks Sheila and makes sure she'll be available to look over the closing documents later on. Sheila bills Tom for $700 for three and one-half hours of her time. Given the value of the help he received, Tom considers this to be a bargain.

As you read this book, you can prepare a running list of legal tasks for which you'd like a lawyer's help. By doing this, you reduce the chances that you'll omit any needed legal coaching or services. An experienced business lawyer should be able to deal with most aspects of a small business sale, but you may need more specialized legal help in some cases—for example, if there are intellectual property or environmental issues.

2. Finding or Selecting a Lawyer

You may already have an ongoing professional relationship with a business lawyer, or at least have a lawyer you've occasionally consulted in the past. If you're happy with that person's services

Special Business Situations Which Require a Lawyer's Help

Section A describes the many different ways a lawyer can help in your sale. In addition, here are three special situations when consulting a lawyer is almost always necessary:

- **You own a franchise.** The procedures for selling a franchised business are considerably more complicated than those for selling an independently owned and operated business. Your franchise agreement almost certainly will limit your freedom to negotiate the terms of a sale in a number of significant ways, all of which must be allowed for. A lawyer can help make sure that your sale will be consistent with the terms of your franchise agreement.

- **Your business owns a building.** If you're selling the building along with the business itself, you'll need state-specific information on how to transfer ownership. This book doesn't go into depth on the mechanics of transferring ownership in all 50 states. For a lawyer, preparing real estate documents correctly is a routine task.

- **Your business needs a license or permit issued by a state or local regulatory agency.** The procedure for transferring a license or permit to a new owner differs from locale to locale. So while this book explains the role of licenses and permits in some detail, you'll need additional information or help to transfer them. If you have trouble navigating the bureaucracy on your own, a lawyer may be able to cut through the red tape.

and the fee arrangements, you're in a good position to get legal help on the sale of your business. But if you've gotten by without a lawyer's assistance, or feel that the lawyer you know best doesn't have the right experience to help you with your sale, you'll need to do some searching. Finding a good lawyer to assist you in the sale of your business may take a bit of doing, but it's important to persist until you find the right person to help you.

Begin your search by compiling a list of lawyers who are already expert in the field. The last thing you want is someone who will use your sale to learn the ropes while charging you. The best place to start is to seek out recommendations from people who have successfully sold businesses—ideally businesses similar to yours. Also, check with people in your community who own or operate high-quality independent businesses, even if they're not the same type you're selling. These people obviously understand quality in other ways, so why not in lawyers?

People who provide services to the business community can also help you identify lawyers to consider. For example, it can often make sense to speak to a banker, accountant, insurance agent, or real estate broker you respect and trust. Because these business-savvy people frequently come into contact with lawyers who represent businesses, they're in a prime position to make informed judgments. Friends, relatives, and business associates can also provide names of possible lawyers. But ask them specifically for the names of lawyers who've had experience working for business clients—not just any lawyer who handles routine personal services, such as estate planning.

If you want to expand your search, the director of your local chamber of commerce may be able to provide a list of likely prospects. Or you may achieve good results by asking a local law librarian to give you a list of lawyers who have written books or articles on your state's business law and practices. And the director of a trade association may point you in the direction of a lawyer in your locale who has experience working with businesses in your industry.

Checking Out Lawyers

For more information about the lawyers on your preliminary list, check out the *Martindale-Hubbell Law Directory*, available at most law libraries and some local public libraries. You can also reach *Martindale-Hubbell* online at www .martindale.com. This resource contains biographical sketches of most practicing lawyers and information about their experience, specialties, education, and the professional organizations they belong to. Another source of information about lawyers is *West Legal Directory* at www.findlaw.com.

3. Interviewing Prospects

After you've narrowed your list, take the time to talk to your top prospects. Especially if a fair amount of legal work may be involved, many lawyers will be very open to talking to you about your needs as part of an initial consultation— either for free or for an agreed nominal fee. Call each lawyer on your list and try to set up a short meeting at which you can explain your business needs, assess the prospect's experience, and evaluate how the two of you get along—your personal rapport. Also try to judge how accessible the lawyer will be when you have questions. Trust your instincts in deciding if the lawyer's personality and business sense are compatible with yours. And be sure the lawyer is comfortable with working at least to some degree as your coach while you take care of important aspects of the sale yourself. If a lawyer seems more inclined to take charge of every aspect of your sale, look elsewhere, unless that's clearly what you want and need.

4. Understanding Lawyer Fees

Most likely, the lawyers you speak to will charge by the hour—often in the range of $200 to $300 an hour or more, depending on where you live and how experienced the lawyer is. Cheaper isn't always better, as more-experienced lawyers who charge higher rates may

be more efficient and cost you less in the long run. Based on what you want the lawyer to do, try to get an estimate of what the total legal fees will likely be for the services you need. But realize that most lawyers will be reluctant to commit to a firm price, because the hours of services you'll ultimately use are inherently unpredictable. The time spent will depend on how much help you need and how quickly your sale comes together—and whether there are any big glitches in the course of the sale. Still, a ballpark estimate is better than nothing.

To keep your legal costs under control, be well organized. Gather all important documents before you meet with your lawyer, and come prepared with a written list of questions and discussion items. Also, insist that you be given an itemized bill each month. If for any reason your initial bill is for more than you expected, don't just bite your tongue and pay it; call the lawyer and discuss your concerns.

 For more on finding and working with a business lawyer, see *Legal Guide for Starting & Running a Small Business*, by Fred S. Steingold (Nolo).

B. Accountants

You know, of course, that accountants deal in numbers and are steeped in the mysteries of the tax laws (although some business lawyers may also have considerable depth in the tax area). If you're already using an accountant in your business—for example, to prepare your tax returns and financial statements—you have some idea of what he or she can do for you. But if you've never sold a business before, you may not be fully aware of how an accountant can participate at this stage of the game. An accountant may be able to help you in carrying out the following important tasks (see the chapters in parentheses for more details on each task):

- making sure that all your business and personal tax returns have been filed and that you have no outstanding disputes with the IRS or state taxing authorities (Chapter 7)
- organizing your past financial records into orderly annual and perhaps monthly statements that give potential buyers a clear picture of how your business has performed (Chapter 7)
- allocating the sale price among the various assets being sold (Chapter 14) and completing IRS form 8594, *Asset Acquisition Statement* (Chapter 4)
- recasting your income tax statements to highlight the economic benefits of the business that might get obscured by the tax returns themselves (Chapter 7)
- reviewing the financial aspects of your business plan so that it convincingly shows how the business not only will continue to make money in the future, but can also tap into additional profit-making opportunities (Chapter 7)
- estimating the federal and state tax consequences to you of selling your business under varying scenarios, such as whether you're selling your assets only or your entire entity, whether you'll be paid in one lump sum versus installments over time, and whether your estate plan should also be a consideration (Chapter 4)
- reviewing documents that show the buyer's financial status (Chapter 10)
- determining a reasonable range of prices for your business (Chapter 5)
- developing sensible interest and payment terms for the promissory note the buyer will sign (Chapter 20), and
- preparing tax returns associated with the sale, such as the income tax return of a corporation that sells its assets, or the tax return of an individual who sells his or her shares or corporate stock (Chapter 4).

Your best source of accounting help is likely to be a Certified Public Accountant (CPA) because of the rigorous requirements for earning that designation. But a word of caution: Not all CPAs are sufficiently qualified to provide all of the small business sale services suggested above. That's because many CPAs specialize in preparing individual tax returns but don't routinely assist in business sales. It follows that you'll need to probe a bit to see whether the CPA who you're considering has depth in the kind of work you need help with. And especially if you're looking for a CPA to help in setting a price for your business, find out whether the CPA is a Certified Valuation Analyst. A CPA with this certification is more likely to have the price-setting skills you're looking for than one who lacks that certification. (To learn more about these specialists, check the website of the National Association of Certified Valuation Analysts, www.nacva.com.)

You may already have a good working relationship with an accountant qualified to help with your sale. If not, you'll have to do some searching. The process of finding the right CPA is roughly parallel to that of finding a suitable business lawyer. (See Section A, above.) Your best bet is to compile a list of prospects by talking to other business owners—especially ones who've had a CPA's help in selling a business. And lawyers, bankers, real estate brokers, and insurance agents can often provide good leads as well.

CPAs are listed in the yellow pages under "Accountants." You can also use the Internet in your search, starting with the site of the American Institute of Certified Public Accountants at www. aicpa.com and www.cpadirectory.com.

Interviewing your short list of accountant prospects will help you size up the likelihood that you work well with one of them. But for obvious reasons, when checking out a CPA, try to avoid the weeks just before April 15.

Just as it does when you are working with a lawyer, it pays to develop a collaborative relationship with your CPA so that you can decide the exact level of services you want or need. If you have a reasonable facility with numbers, you can certainly save money by doing a lot of the work yourself. But even if you're very good with numbers, you may want to turn to your accountant for help with the tax aspects of your sale.

Like lawyers, accountants typically charge for their services on an hourly basis, as illustrated in the example below.

EXAMPLE: Marian wants to sell her computer repair business. She gets her financial records in order, develops a realistic plan for future growth, and finds a hardworking potential buyer who can make a reasonable down payment. She's ready to offer the buyer a contract calling for the balance of the purchase price to be paid in 36 equal monthly installments. But before doing so, Marian wants to be 100% sure that she's correctly interpreted the federal tax rules that will apply to her sale. To this end, she schedules a one-hour conference with Mark, an experienced CPA, at which Marian fills Mark in on the background of the sale and how she hopes to be paid. After the conference, Mark reviews the draft sales agreement and promissory note that Marian has left with him. When they meet again the following week, Mark explains precisely what Marian's tax liability will be. He also shows Marian how she can reorganize her profit-and-loss statement to make it even more attractive to the potential buyer—and justify a higher sale price. And he recommends a way to allocate the sale price among the business's assets so that her tax burden is reduced. Mark charges Marian $150 an hour for two and a half hours of his professional time. The total bill ($375) is well worth it. Realizing what a big help Mark has been, Marian also hires him to prepare her business and personal tax returns for the year of the sale, since she knows she'll be facing some complex and unfamiliar tax issues.

C. Business Brokers

With this book and appropriate coaching and assistance from your lawyer and accountant, you may not need any other professional help with your sale. But, if your business is highly specialized or might otherwise be difficult to market or sell, or you need to sell quickly, you can also use a business broker help you market it.

One approach is to retain a broker to take over the whole process of marketing and selling your business. In exchange, you pay the broker a tidy commission, often in the range of 10% to 12% of the sale price for a business that sells for $1 million or less. Brokers typically use a sliding scale in which the percentage figure goes down as the sale price increases. So, for example, the broker may propose a commission of 12% on the first $500,000, a commission of 10% on the next $500,000, and perhaps 6% on amounts over $1 million. This can add up to a large sum—for example, $85,000 on a business that sells for $750,000. While obviously this is a huge chunk of change to skim off the sale price, it may be well worth it if the broker can reel in that needle-in-a-haystack buyer who wants your specialized business and is willing to pay top dollar for it.

Chapter 8 provides more details on how a broker can help market your business. Here are some pointers to keep in mind if you decide to hire a broker to handle your sale for you:

- **Find out exactly how the broker plans to market your business.** You'd like to hook up with someone who has creative, aggressive ideas for getting the attention of the perfect buyer.

- **See if you can negotiate a lower commission rate.** If the rate proposed by the broker seems uncomfortably high, it's possible that the broker will agree to a lower rate—especially if the broker is convinced that your business can be sold quickly and easily.

- **Be prepared to pay the broker an upfront fee.** This can range from a few thousand dollars to considerably more. Typically, this fee is non-refundable, so you want to keep it as low as possible. And make sure it will be applied against the commission if the broker is successful in selling your business.
- **Try to retain the right to sell the business yourself.** If you find the buyer, it's not fair for the broker to demand the entire commission. Make sure your contract with the broker eliminates—or at least reduces—the commission if you come up with the buyer. Under this type of nonexclusive agreement, you owe the full fee only if you sell your business through the broker's efforts.
- **Don't get lured into a long-term listing.** Most brokers hope to tie you up for six months or more. Something closer to three months might be more reasonable. See what you can negotiate. You'd hate to lose valuable time if it turns out that your broker is not as effective as you'd hoped.
- **Pay close attention to when the commission is due.** Many brokers want the full payment at closing—even if the buyer is paying you on an installment basis. The commission can equal or even exceed the down payment you get from an installment buyer. From your standpoint, a better arrangement is to pay the broker's commission as you get paid—for example, 10% of each payment you receive from the buyer.
- **Have a clear understanding with the broker about the level of confidentiality you expect.** If keeping a low profile is important (and frequently it is), make sure the broker is willing to be discreet in marketing your business. To make sure that you and the broker are on the same wavelength, capture your understanding about confidentiality in a written memorandum that both of you sign.
- **Be aware that you can wind up with a buyer you don't like.** A broker earns a commission by producing a buyer who is "ready, willing, and able" to buy your business—whether or not you think the person is inappropriate. Ordinarily, if you veto the proposed buyer, you still owe the commission. Most brokers won't yield on this point.
- **Because of potential pitfalls, consider consulting with a lawyer before signing a listing agreement with a broker.** The draft the broker asks you to sign probably won't protect your interests. Your lawyer can help tweak the agreement to make it fairer.

Working with a broker doesn't automatically require that you turn over the entire sale of your business to the broker and pay a hefty commission. You may choose to go off in a different direction. A viable alternative is to do much of the marketing yourself, retaining a broker only to provide specific services for an hourly fee. For example, a broker can suggest places to look for buyers and can then act as an intermediary with those who express interest. A broker who's willing to sell his or her expertise on a piecemeal basis can also help you set a price range for selling your business. Such a broker may agree to charge you a fixed fee or bill you by the hour.

EXAMPLE: Todd (an insurance agent) and Elaine (a school teacher) inherit from their father a small company that manufactures a highly specialized type of machine tool. They feel the most likely buyer will be one of a handful of firms that manufacture similar tools, but they have little experience in how the industry works or how to approach these companies. Deciding that they need help to find an appropriate buyer and structure a deal, Todd and Elaine contact Carol, a business broker who has built a solid reputation for her work in brokering the sale of small manufacturing companies. Carol normally charges sellers a 10% commission for selling a business of this size. After learning that Todd and Elaine plan to do most of the work themselves, Carol agrees to serve as a consultant.

For a $2,500 fee, she'll review their marketing materials and give them a list of the 15 firms she thinks are the most promising potential buyers. Carol also agrees to consult further with Todd and Elaine, as needed, for $150 an hour. Finally, they agree that if the business is sold to a company on Carol's list, she'll receive a commission of 4% of the sale price. Since Todd and Elaine are convinced that the business is worth $1 million or even more, they feel that the fees will be money well spent.

Finding a qualified business broker can be more difficult than finding a qualified lawyer or accountant. That's because, unlike lawyers and CPAs, there are no minimum educational requirements for business brokers, and, generally, they're not required to be licensed—though some have real estate licenses. In addition to your legitimate concerns about a business broker's professional competence, you need to feel comfortable that the broker will respect your understandable wish for confidentiality. A blabbermouth broker can effectively nix your chances of getting a good price for your business and can wreak havoc in your relationships with customers, suppliers, and employees.

Look for a broker who's been in business five to ten years and, if possible, specializes in your type of business (for example, a landscaping service or clothing store). Especially if you're going to hire a business broker on a commission basis, ask for at least three references from satisfied customers you can talk to. Basically, you're looking for a broker who's intelligent, hardworking, creative, and, as already mentioned, discreet. And look carefully at the listing agreement. Typically, you'll be on the hook for the commission even if you sell the business on your own during the listing period. Finally, stay miles away from any broker who proposes to represent both you and the buyer. This is no time for neutrality. You want a broker who is solidly in your corner, looking after your interests and your interests alone.

Your lawyer or accountant may be able to suggest a reliable broker. Also, real estate agents who deal in commercial property may be able to give you valuable leads. Or try locating a broker on the Internet. Visit the site of the International Business Brokers Association (www.ibba.org) or Brokers Network Group (www.bbn-net.com).

Check Your Own Backyard Before Hiring a Broker

If your primary motive in hiring a broker is to find potential buyers, be sure to read Chapter 8 first; a broker may not be needed. As you'll see, there may be many potential buyers within arm's reach (for example, friends, employees, business competitors, and even customers), meaning that you can easily approach the most likely candidates on your own and at no additional expense. And even if, to find likely buyers, you'll have to cast a bigger net, there are ways to do this yourself as explained in Chapter 8. Just like selling your own house, this can be hard and exacting work. But, just like representing yourself in a real estate sale, you can save significant dollars by not paying a business broker's commission.

Checklist for Working With Lawyers, Accountants, and Brokers

☐ Read this whole book, so that you're clear on the legal, financial, and marketing tasks involved in selling a business.

☐ Keep a running list of tasks you feel comfortable handling yourself and those that may require professional help.

☐ Identify possible lawyers, accountants, and brokers to help with the sale based on your own personal contacts and recommendations of other businesspeople.

☐ Interview prospects and select ones you want to work with after checking references and agreeing on fees.

☐ Remember that many well-qualified professionals are willing to work on a piecemeal basis and to coach you on the tasks that you can largely handle yourself.

☐ Keep careful track of your expenses for professional services, since these costs are almost always tax-deductible.

Part 2

Getting Ready to Sell

Preparing Your Business for Sale

If you hope to sell your business for a great price (and who doesn't), it's usually best to allow ample time. There are two big reasons. First, there are almost always many tasks you'll want to accomplish before you're ready to begin talking to prospective buyers, such as getting rid of outdated inventory and sprucing up your business premises. Completing some of these presale tasks will take weeks, others will take months and, in some instances, getting your business well-positioned for sale will take a year or more. The second reason is that you'll need to find the right buyer—something that's far easier to do if you're relaxed and not pressured to make a fast sale.

True, sometimes you don't have the luxury of a long lead-in period. For example, if you need to sell because of a sudden illness, the imperative need to relocate your family, the death of your partner, or some other pressing reason, you may have to take some shortcuts, doing the best you can to present a marketable product in a hurry. And occasionally some highly positive market factor may occur that convinces you that you can obtain the best price by selling quickly—for example, the styles you offer in your niche boutique have suddenly become the hottest trend. But more typically, you'll want time to deliberately and thoughtfully prepare your business for sale without urgent pressure so that you can put it on the market at an advantageous time.

This chapter deals with the "getting ready" stage of the selling process—the methodical work you can and should do to put your business in optimum shape for a sale at the best price. This includes developing a convincing plan for the future and getting financial statements, entity records, and other paperwork in shape. Since each business is different, some suggestions in this chapter won't apply to you, and those that are relevant may have to be tailored to your specific situation. But, happily, there's no downside: If you follow many of the actions suggested here, and then for some reason decide you don't want to sell your business after all, your enterprise will likely be in far better shape than it was before you started.

A. Make Your Business Attractive to Buyers

If you bought your business instead of starting it from scratch, you already know a lot about a buyer's perspective. That will be helpful in getting your business positioned for a sale. By contrast, if you built your business from the ground up, you may need to think a bit harder about what a buyer will be looking for.

Here are 16 things you can focus on to make your business attractive to potential buyers. This list may seem overwhelming, but if you give yourself enough time and set priorities, you'll do just fine.

1. Show a Consistent Profit for at Least Two or Three Years

Most buyers will be seeking a business that has a consistent record of profitability. Unfortunately, this means that if three years ago your business had a great year, two years ago you lost money, and last year's profits were only mediocre, a prospective buyer is likely to feel uneasy about what the future holds. In that situation, to position your business for a profitable sale, it may make sense to delay selling it for a year while you work hard to produce solid profits.

Section D, below, provides specific advice on how to improve profitability.

Don't try to fake profits. In the year prior to a sale, many sellers are tempted to do things to inflate profits such as cutting unnecessary expenses. Good. However, there's a fine, but important, line between tightening operations and acting to artificially inflate. For example, a seller might cut expenses by firing key employees, cutting back on customer service, jettisoning the development of new services, and deferring maintenance. Savvy purchasers will be looking for this type of obvious profit-enhancement ploy. Should they find it, they're likely to back off entirely, fearing to trust the seller's other statements.

2. Resolve Outstanding Legal Problems

No potential buyer will want to face the strong possibility of significant lawsuits by unhappy customers or disgruntled employees. Similarly, the fear of having to pay for an environmental clean-up is a huge turnoff. So if you've been receiving demand letters from an angry employee you recently fired or you fear that an inspection will reveal soil-toxicity problems near your loading dock, now is the time to resolve the problem. Be aware that even if you agree in the sales contract to remain responsible for presale claims (a topic discussed in Chapter 15), the buyer still may balk at being anywhere near an ongoing legal entanglement. Section G, below, explains how to clean up existing problems such as pending lawsuits.

3. Demonstrate That Accounts Receivable Can Be Collected

If you want to sell your corporation or LLC entity, including your accounts receivable, you'll need to show that they are almost certainly collectable. You can begin by putting together an aging chart that shows how long the bills have been outstanding—30, 60, or 90 days—and also shows the historical average as a point of comparison. Eliminate any dicey accounts by settling with the slow pays and writing off the deadbeats. (Section G1, below, gives some tips on doing this.)

Ideally, the accounts that remain will have a long record of timely payment. Since the ability to collect a given bill is never a 100% sure thing, the buyer may still expect some discount on the value of the accounts receivable—but if everything is in order, it shouldn't be steep. (Of course, this isn't an issue if, as part of an assets sale, you plan to keep the accounts receivable so that they're not the buyer's problem.) Chapter 14 explains how to deal with accounts receivable in the sales agreement.

4. Clearly Explain Your Business Finances

Your accounting protocols should be clear and consistent from year to year so that income, costs, and cash flow are self-evident. A shoe box full of check stubs and deposit slips won't do the trick—nor will profits manufactured by questionable or overly aggressive accounting tactics, such as suddenly shifting from expensing to capitalizing the costs of developing new services so as to increase short-term revenues. Section B, below, explains how to get your paperwork in order.

5. Provide a Convincing Business Plan for the Future

The buyer will want to build on what you've done in the past and hopefully do it even better. You need to fire the buyer's imagination with specific ideas on where to go from here—a task you can accomplish in large part with a well-written business plan that shows how the profits can be substantially increased. You may have developed a three-year or five-year business plan when you first started out, or maybe you prepared one when you applied for a business loan. If so, you already have a good notion of what goes into making a compelling plan. Now you need one that looks ahead to a time when you're no longer in charge—a plan that the buyer can use as a roadmap for getting from Point A to Point B. And at least as important, a well-drafted business plan can keep the buyer's enthusiasm alive during those nervous days before closing when more than a few buyers get cold feet.

Among other things, your business plan should address trends in your industry, where new customers will come from, how sales to existing customers can be increased, and how your business can become more competitive.

 To learn more about developing a business plan, look at *How to Write a Business Plan,* by Mike McKeever (Nolo). It shows you a good format for business plans, including how to present information about cash flow and profitability. A second excellent resource is the software package *Business Plan Pro* (Palo Alto Software, distributed by Nolo). It offers over 400 sample plans and helps you create charts and tables that look professional.

6. Secure Beneficial Relationships With Suppliers and Customers

In a world in which lots of similar small businesses are often for sale, the existence of good ongoing relationships with customers and suppliers can be a compelling reason why a buyer will prefer one enterprise to another. But unless you can point to solid contracts with customers and suppliers, a buyer is likely to worry that these relationships are personal to the seller and not easily transferable to the buyer. So the more you can do to position the business's success as being independent of you personally, the better price you're likely to get. Especially if your business is a corporation or an LLC, one way to approach this is to try to sign long-term contracts with key customers and suppliers that will remain in effect regardless of who owns the company, as discussed in Section H, below. Another less-formal technique is to introduce the prospective buyer to key customers and suppliers and try to elicit a verbal commitment that past relationships will continue, even if the business comes under new ownership. And, of course, one excellent way to reassure the buyer about continuity is to stay on and work for the new owner for a limited period after the business changes hands. You can work either as an employee or an independent contractor, as discussed in Chapter 9.

EXAMPLE: Lloyd has owned and operated Oak Villa Pharmacy for 25 years and has built a loyal following in his community. Now, as he nears retirement age, Lloyd is negotiating to sell the business to PharmWorld—a national chain of drugstores. To allay PharmWorld's fears that Lloyd's loyal customers will drift away, Lloyd agrees to work for the company dispensing prescriptions three days a week for two years.

7. Provide Assurance That Experienced Employees Will Continue Working for the Business

An able manager can be a strong selling point. If your business is large enough to have an experienced manager or other leader besides you who plans to stick with the business, emphasize this person's talents and potential in your talks with the buyer. Having one or more highly competent people on the scene sends a clear message to the buyer that the success of the business isn't synonymous with you.

Often, the expertise of a strong, committed staff is a powerful reason for a buyer to sign a contract to buy a business. For that reason, in some instances, you may want to sign employment contracts with key people for at least a couple of years. You can also include a covenant not to compete, which should further reassure the buyer that your key employees won't draw away customers by opening or working for a competing business. Properly drafted, noncompete agreements are usually enforceable—but not in California and a few other states.

 Long-term contracts with key employees are not always a good idea. Don't sign long-term contracts with employees unless you're confident the buyer will almost surely want to keep them. If your business has been doing poorly or if you plan to sell to a competing business whose existing employees can do most of the work, the buyer is likely to view the contracts as a detriment rather than as an advantage. In fact, a buyer who doesn't want the people you've contracted with is likely to see the cost of buying them out as a reason to reduce the sale price.

 Recommended reading on noncompete agreements. For in-depth information on noncompete language for employees, consult *How to Create a Noncompete Agreement,* by Shannon Miehle (Nolo). The book clearly explains the legal principles and sometimes tricky rules that affect noncompete agreements and provides step-by-step guidance for developing the legal wording appropriate to your situation.

If you or your key employees are not interested in long-term contracts, you may still want assurance that they'll stick with you through the sale. One way to do this is offer key employees a bonus if they stay for a specified period of time. The new owner can then decide whether to keep these employees on the payroll—and the employees can decide if they want to work for the new owner. The bonus payment will help cushion the disruptions in an employee's life if he or she later moves on to a job at a different company. It's best to put bonus arrangements into a written agreement, which a lawyer can help you prepare.

8. Lock in the Lease

The security of being able to operate the business from its current location (assuming, of course, that the location is a key element of the business and the lease terms are favorable) can be crucial to selling your business. If you lease space for your retail business or for a service business with lots of walk-in traffic, the buyer will almost surely want to lock in a lease for several years, and perhaps have the option to renew beyond that point. So if you rent on a month-to-month basis or your lease is running out soon, it pays to negotiate with the landlord for a long-term lease that will remain in effect even if you sell the business. Section E, below, explains how to make sure your lease helps (and doesn't hurt) your sales effort. Of course, the downside of signing a long-term lease is that if you later have trouble finding a buyer or assigning the lease, you may be personally responsible for the rent payments for a long time.

If you own the building, the buyer may want to buy it from you or sign a favorable lease. Similarly, the continuing availability of parking (whether leased or owned) may be an important consideration for the buyer.

9. Disclose All Relevant Information—Even Negative Facts

A buyer wants to be able to trust you. Any indication that you're less than truthful or that you're not disclosing all pertinent information is likely to be a serious turn-off. Savvy buyers will certainly investigate all aspects of your business, as explained in Chapter 10. It follows that it's a mistake to leave it to the buyer to discover negative facts about your enterprise, especially important issues such as the fact that an exclusive contract with a major supplier is about to end. Even if a fact seems small and unimportant to you in the larger scheme of things (for example, a key manager is pregnant and plans to take a year off), your failure to disclose that information may come back to haunt you. By contrast, presenting negative, as well as positive, information up front helps the buyer see that you can be trusted to tell the truth, even when it's unpalatable.

Chapter 10 provides advice on making full disclosures to potential buyers.

10. Maintain Honest Business Practices

For most buyers, a suggestion that a business occasionally makes windfall profits by playing fast and loose with suppliers or customers will probably kill any chance of a deal. Similarly, if a seller tells the buyer that the business can produce unreported—and thus nontaxed—income, it's likely to cast doubt on the seller's integrity. If a business has boosted profits through shady practices (not paying tax on cash income, for example), the best approach is for the seller to discontinue those practices and delay the sale until the business can show that its profits are legitimately earned.

11. Get the Premises in Shape

When it comes to spiffing up your operation for sale, applying a fresh coat of paint and fixing broken windows and cracked tile are just the beginning. Take a hard look at your workplace from top to bottom and make necessary improvements. Maybe you'll conclude that it's time to install better lighting or signage, replace old carpets, install new bulletin boards, get rid of ten-year-old posters, and buy a couple of new desks. If needed repairs are the landlord's responsibility, insist that the work gets done to your satisfaction. And don't forget the mop and scrub brush: Trying to sell a business that's anything less than squeaky clean outside and in is always a mistake.

12. Make Sure the Premises Are Well Organized and Free of Clutter

No buyer wants to walk into a business that looks like a teenager's bedroom. Having a place for everything and keeping everything in its place sends a powerful message that your business is well run and under control. If this isn't the way you do things now, take the time to make changes. When you finally cash the buyer's check, you'll be glad you did.

Get rid of the Scotch tape. Over the years, the walls of lots of businesses become cluttered with signs, snapshots, phone lists, calendars, Post-it notes, and virtually everything else that can be tacked, clipped, pasted, or nailed into place. Work with your employees to pull it all down. After you repaint the walls, hang some tasteful prints and make small colorful bulletin boards available in employee workspaces so that pictures of children and pets can be corralled into the space. And in hallways and other areas where personnel policies, legal notices, and other information must be displayed, install larger bulletin boards and insist that employees use them.

13. Get Your Inventory in Shape

If yours is a retail or wholesale business, sell off or dump all that stuff you'll never sell for a decent price. It should go without saying that someone who's buying a business doesn't want to pay good money for inventory that can't be sold short of the local flea market. And even though you may be able to explain that the distressed items are only a tiny part of your total inventory, you don't want a pile of unsaleable goods to risk distracting the potential buyer's attention from the current stock that's selling well.

And especially if a buyer has little or no experience in your industry, you'll also want to be prepared to show that there's a good market for virtually everything you do have on hand. For example, maybe you can pull together current ads, catalog copy, and photos from websites displaying similar merchandise at comparable prices. This can help assure a buyer that you're not trying to unload outdated, unsaleable inventory.

EXAMPLE: Duane runs a home entertainment store that sells high-end audio and television equipment. Perhaps surprisingly to a novice, his inventory includes a substantial number of amplifier tubes, cartridges and styluses, turntable motors, and other parts that harken back to the predigital age. To make sure that a prospective buyer of the business realizes that there's still a robust and profitable market for these goods, Duane keeps records showing that loads of well-heeled, die-hard audiophiles still maintain their old analog equipment and rely on Duane's store for replacement parts. In addition, Duane is prepared to demonstrate to someone looking to buy the business that profits on this older equipment are far higher than they are on parts for digital models, which people are as likely to scrap as to fix.

14. Make Sure All Business and Office Equipment Is in Good Working Order

Repair or replace anything that's not performing optimally—especially computer equipment or software that may have become obsolete. When you sit down with the buyer to demonstrate how efficient your whiz-bang technology is, you want it to work the first time, every time. Also, if equipment is obviously old, you want to be able to explain clearly why you are still using it—perhaps because it's sturdily built, rarely needs adjustment, and efficiently gets the job done. Without such an explanation, a buyer may conclude that your profitability depends at least in part on your decision to run old equipment into the ground.

15. Provide a Clear Picture of How You, the Owner, Get Compensated

You may receive a salary, a bonus, fringe benefits—or all these things. Of course, you'll inform buyers about these

forms of compensation. But you can go further, giving them a list of all noncash perks, such as business-related travel and entertainment or a car purchased by the business that may be treated as a tax-deductible business expense. As long as your expenditures are legal and broadly appropriate, this is very helpful information for the buyer, who can decide to keep these expenses or cut them and automatically add a few dollars to the profits number on your balance sheet. For similar reasons, you should also point out any ways that your business benefits family members or others who are close to you. For example (as discussed in Section C, below), maybe your business provides a desirable summer job for your child, or maybe you hire your spouse or other relative and pay them a decent salary. Again, this can be a plus if the buyer is inclined to help his or her own family members or friends—or, in the alternative, concludes that nonrelatives can be hired to provide these services more cheaply.

16. Have a Believable Explanation of Why You're Selling

Few business owners just walk away for no reason from a profitable business that promises a prosperous future. To allay the suspicion that you're trying to unload a business that has hidden warts, you need to convince the buyer you're cashing in your chips now for a good reason, such as retirement, starting a new career, relocating with a spouse who has a new job, or going back to school. And, especially if yours is a somewhat unusual reason to sell (you have decided to run a meals-on-wheels program for low-income shut-ins), be prepared to explain fully and convincingly.

B. Get Your Paperwork in Order

As part of explaining your business to interested buyers—and, later on, when transferring ownership—you'll need to put your hands on a number of financial and legal documents. Starting early to round up and organize this paperwork (or, in some cases, to create it) will help smooth the process of selling your business. Be aware that the buyer will want to see the key paperwork during the investigation stage. See Chapter 10 for details on the buyer's investigation and how to protect the confidentiality of your sensitive business information.

1. Cash Flow Records and Financial Statements

Before making an offer, a sensible buyer will want to see financial records that track your inflow and outflow of money over at least several years. Maybe you've already set up a good system with the help of an accountant or by

using software like Intuit's *Quicken* or *QuickBooks*. Or maybe you recently compiled financial records as part of applying for a line of credit at a bank. If so, you can quickly put your hands on profit and loss statements for the past three years. But if you don't have an orderly system to track your business finances, now's the time to set one up. For maximum effectiveness, you may need to go back a few years and try to re-create this information as accurately as possible.

For a business with relatively simple finances, off-the-shelf software may be all you need to get started. If your business affairs are complex or your computer skills below average, you should seek help from a Certified Public Accountant (CPA). See "The World of Financial Statements," below, for ways a CPA can help organize your financial statement.

 Almost any business can benefit from good accounting advice. Even if your books are well organized and you work with an experienced bookkeeper, it almost always pays to get advice from an accountant with deep small business experience, ideally a CPA. And this is especially true if your planned sale is still several years away. That's because the accounting pro will have time to help you tweak your existing accounting system or install a better one. With your records in solid shape, it will be a simple matter for the accountant to help rearrange the numbers for maximum sales appeal. There's often a bonus to adopting this approach: The accountant is likely to show you legitimate ways to save on your taxes—often in an amount that will more than cover the accountant's fee. And if your small business operates pretty much out of a checkbook, you'll definitely want to do a more professional job in packaging your business for potential buyers.

Many buyers will also ask to see certain financial ratios, depending on the industry you're in. These ratios, where they exist, are a kind of shorthand way to take the temperature of your business and to see if you're doing better or worse than other similar businesses. Commonly used ratios include:

- income per employee
- percentage of payroll devoted to employee costs
- gross profit—or margin—per item sold, and
- the ratio of gross profit to gross income.

In addition, retailers often speak in terms of sales volume per square foot of retail space. But this list only skims the surface. There are a wide range of financial measurements used by America's tens of thousands of different businesses. You need to know how people in your field measure success so that you can use your accounting records to show how you stack up. Trade associations that serve your industry are a good starting point for learning about the applicable

ratios. If your ratios are better than average for your industry, you can justify seeking a price at the high end of the price range. See Chapter 5 for advice on pricing your business.

2. Tax Returns

Buyers will want to see your business tax returns for at least the last three years— and often more. Buyers believe that tax returns are likely to reflect the true income of the business. The thinking is that a business owner, when talking to a buyer, may be inclined to exaggerate the amount of money the business generates, but that the owner is far less likely to resort to blarney with the IRS when the result would be higher taxes. Of course, the flip side, from your perspective as a seller, is that the bottom line on the tax return—the taxable income figure—may not reflect all the financial benefits you get from owning the business. That's because many types of expenses that provide you with a personal benefit are legitimately deducted as business expenses before the bottom line for IRS purposes is tallied. But that shouldn't be a big obstacle: In Section C, below, you'll learn how to properly and legally restate your tax return figures to better show the buyer the true profitability of the business.

The exact tax return that you show the buyer will vary, depending on the type of business entity you have.

The World of Financial Statements

If you turn to a CPA for help in preparing a financial statement, you'll normally have the opportunity to order up—and pay for—one of three types of statements.

Compiled Financial Statement. Here, the CPA simply compiles and organizes data that you provide and does not test it for accuracy. This is the least-expensive way to go. The CPA will undoubtedly put a disclaimer on the work to make it clear that no in-depth review or audit has been performed and that the CPA doesn't vouch for the accuracy of your numbers. While buyers of bigger businesses will demand reviewed or audited financial statements, many buyers of small, easy-to-understand operations will accept any orderly and understandable presentation that they are convinced is honest and accurate. Even with tiny businesses, however, some involvement by an accountant is likely to boost the buyer's confidence that your numbers are accurate.

Reviewed Financial Statement. For a higher fee, the CPA will not only organize your data, but see how it compares to the standards in your industry. And if anything seems out of line, the CPA should dig deeper—for example, if it looks like your restaurant is paying much more for labor than other similar restaurants do. For more-complicated businesses, a buyer may find additional assurance in the fact that your financial data has at least been reviewed by an accountant.

Audited Financial Statement. This is the accounting gold standard—the most thorough and, therefore, costliest type of statement. Here, the CPA evaluates the accuracy of the numbers you present, thus providing the buyer with the highest level of assurance that your financial statements are correct. For example, the CPA's investigation may include visiting a store or warehouse and doing a physical inventory of the merchandise to be sure it's all there. Similarly, in many situations, the CPA will randomly select and review a number of accounts receivable to make sure they're legitimate and represent income that the business is likely to receive.

Type of Business	Type of Tax Return
Sole proprietorship or a single-member LLC	Schedule C from your personal Form 1040 (that's where the business income gets reported and paid)
Partnership or multimember LLC	Form 1065 (your business's information return)
S corporation	Form 1120S
C corporation	Form 1120 or 1120A (corporate income tax return)

 Discuss tax consequences with your tax adviser. The basic tax considerations you face in selling your business are outlined in Chapter 4. But this information is just a start. Unless your business is tiny and its tax position very simple, you'll almost surely benefit from the help of a tax adviser such as a CPA or a lawyer experienced in small business tax issues. The unique tax posture of your business or your personal tax situation can influence many decisions. If you do decide to get tax advice, it's sensible to get that advice earlier rather than later so you can make it part of your planning and preparation. For more on selecting and working with professional advisers, see Chapter 6.

3. Entity Records

If you're selling your business as an entity—which usually means that you and any co-owners are selling all your corporate stock or all the membership interests in an LLC—you'll want to dig out your LLC or corporate records to make sure everything is in good order. At a minimum, the buyer will want to see that your corporation or LLC was properly established and continues to meet other legal requirements, such as filing required yearly statements and paying taxes and fees.

Typically, you may find that in the day-to-day business of running your business, you've been insufficiently attentive to every last legal formality, with the result that you may have skipped annual directors' or shareholders' meetings or failed to pass a necessary board resolution. Fortunately, with a little time and effort, you should be able to easily and inexpensively rectify any problems with your entity records.

Here are the documents and records you'll need to locate (and, in some cases, to create).

a. Documents That You Filed to Create Your Corporation or LLC

At one time, you filed articles of incorporation for your corporation with a designated state agency or you filed articles of organization for your LLC. (Some states may use slightly different names for these papers.) And it's possible you've amended these original filings. Either way, you need to locate these documents, as well as forms you've filed to register a fictitious name or assumed name or trademark. If you've set up an entity records book for your business, all these records should be at your fingertips. Otherwise, you probably have a copy of these documents stored someplace in your business records. But if for any reason you can't put your hands on them, you can almost certainly obtain a copy from the state agency where you originally filed them—usually the secretary of state's office. You'll also want to locate your corporate bylaws or LLC operating agreement—entity-formation documents that are not filed with the state.

b. Legally Required Annual Reports

If you don't have copies of your annual filings or receipts in your records book, call the state office where you're supposed to send these required yearly reports to see whether you've met the requirements. If not, you'll need to file the reports belatedly—perhaps paying some fees and modest penalties.

c. Contractual Agreements With Your Fellow Shareholders or LLC Members

In some instances, these agreements are part of corporate bylaws or LLC membership agreements, which should be in your entity records book. But legally, these contractual agreements can be part of other documents. For example, they can take the form of a separate shareholders' agreement (often called a buy-sell agreement). Either way, these agreements typically spell out the rights and obligations of the owners and often include the agreed-upon procedures for selling business assets, stock, or LLC membership interests.

d. Corporate Stock or LLC Membership Certificates

You'll need these to transfer ownership of the entity. Be aware that while stock certificates are almost always issued to confirm ownership of shares of a corporation, not all LLCs issue similar ownership certificates to their members. Many choose to rely instead on a list of owners set out in the operating agreement as proof of ownership.

It's never too late to issue certificates to corporate shareholders or LLC members. If you did issue such certificates at one time but can't find them now, you'll need to adopt a board or membership resolution to cancel the old ones and create replacements.

e. Promissory Notes for Owners' Loans to or From the Company

Remember, you and the other owners are separate from your corporation or LLC. If you've loaned money to your business, the business should have given you a promissory note stating the terms of repayment. Likewise, if the business has loaned you money, you should have a promissory note. If these documents are missing, you need to create or re-create them.

f. Up-to-Date Records of Meetings

You should have minutes or written agreements signed by directors or shareholders (called written consents) for all meetings mandated by law or required by your bylaws or operating agreement—for example, most corporations require annual shareholders' and directors' meetings. This always is a concern for corporations, since historically they've been required to operate with a high degree of formality. It may or may not be a concern for your LLC. The fact that less formality is legally required means that many LLCs' operating agreements do not require formal annual meetings or written consents. Fortunately, if after reading your bylaws or LLC membership agreement and checking your records, you find that your entity has failed to hold some of the mandated meetings, you can easily remedy this problem by either holding the meeting now or having all co-owners sign consent documents in place of the meetings.

Two essential Nolo books explain every step of the process of whipping your entity records into shape quickly and easily. Both show you how to legally and simply re-create missing records so that your corporate or LLC records are in excellent shape. If you have a corporation, see *The Corporate Records Handbook: Meetings, Minutes & Resolutions,* by Anthony Mancuso (Nolo). If you have an LLC, see *Your Limited Liability Company:*

An Operating Manual, also by Anthony Mancuso (Nolo).

4. Leases, Warranties, and Vehicle Titles

Find the lease for your business space, along with any updates and renewals to it. (Section E, below, explains what to look for in evaluating your lease and how it can help your sale.) If your business has been using leased equipment, locate those leases as well. In the case of equipment that the business owns rather than leases, find any title (ownership) documents such as those relating to cars and trucks, and any warranties that go along with the equipment.

5. Real Estate Ownership Documents

You'll need to locate several documents if you're selling a building or other real estate as part of the deal—but please keep in mind that this book doesn't cover this topic in depth. These documents typically include the deed, the title insurance policy, and any mortgage or deed of trust that encumbers the property. Also, if it's a multiuse property shared by several tenants, you'll need to produce the leases with the other tenants, since the buyer will be stepping into your shoes as the landlord.

6. Important Contracts

Locate all contracts your business has with employees, independent contractors, suppliers, customers, insurance companies, and equipment maintenance firms. If, for some reason, you can't lay your hands on a needed document, contact the other party and get a copy. Contracts can be crucial in a business sale because, depending on the how the sale is structured, the buyer may benefit from them, be burdened by them, or both. This section lists various types of contracts that may be transferred as part of the business and explains how a buyer may view such contracts.

Sections F and H, below, discuss how to make contracts a strong point in your sales pitch. Chapter 10 provides more suggestions for transferring contracts to a new owner.

a. Contracts With Employees and Independent Contractors

Most buyers won't want to be burdened by contracts with lower-echelon employees. This usually isn't a problem, however, since contracts with such employees are rare. By contrast, a buyer who wants to continue and expand your business along existing lines may be pleased that one or more key managers have agreed to work into the future and hopefully (in states where it's allowed) have agreed not to compete with the business.

b. Contracts With Suppliers and Equipment Maintenance Companies

The buyer will be pleased with any contracts that lock in low prices with suppliers and maintenance companies—for example, a good deal with a company that hosts your website. On the other hand, if you've signed long-term contracts at higher-than-current market rates, buyers will see the contracts as a negative factor that discounts the amount they are willing to pay.

c. Contracts With Customers

Contracts that lock in profitable sales with major customers for several years can be a huge incentive for the buyer to offer you an attractive price. Conversely, long-term contracts that are a good deal for the customer but yield little or no profit to you will put a damper on your sale price.

> **EXAMPLE:** Helen's Hideaway, a small hotel in ski country, has signed a contract with a tour outfit in which the owner, Helen, has agreed to provide a number of visitor rooms each season for the next five years. A prospective buyer points out that the room rate is fairly low (not such a great deal for the hotel). But when Helen is able to show that she makes a substantial overall profit because she achieves a fat profit margin on extras, such as the sale of alcohol, food, and souvenirs, the buyer realizes that Helen's business strategy is sound.

7. Licenses and Permits

If your business requires any type of government permit or license, such as might be required for a restaurant or home remodeling firm, be sure to find out the current licensing requirements and whether or not the permit or license can be transferred. Chapter 10 explains how and why to do this.

8. Proof of Intellectual Property Ownership

The term intellectual property normally applies primarily to four important types of intangible property: copyrights, patents, trademarks, and trade secrets. If your business owns any of these assets, you'll want to have appropriate documentation available. Here's a brief overview. Chapter 10 goes into more detail on documents that buyers will want to see on your intellectual property.

a. Copyrights

A copyright is a legal right granted to the creator of a work of authorship, such as a book, poem, or song, or even the ad copy on the side of a cereal box. In theory, all original written material produced by a business is protected by copyright, but most has little value. By contrast, if yours is an information-based business such as a book, magazine, or newsletter publisher; video producer; or corporate training company, your core copyrights

may be your most valuable assets. If so, you probably have a certificate showing that you registered the copyright with the U.S. Copyright Office. Although registration isn't legally required to create a copyright (that's done when the work is created), it is a prerequisite to going to court to enforce your copyright. In addition, prompt registration not only costs far less, but, in the event you register prior to an infringement, you can seek additional statutory charges should you ever have to sue the infringer.

 For complete details on copyright registration, see *The Copyright Handbook: How to Protect & Use Written Works,* by Stephen Fishman (Nolo).

b. Patents

In physical form, a patent is a document issued by the U.S. Patent and Trademark Office (PTO) that grants a monopoly for a limited period of time on the use and development of an invention (utility patent) or on a design for a useful object (design patent).

 Recommended reading on patents. For an introduction to the patent process generally, and to review basic patent law in preparation for a sale, see *Nolo's Patents for Beginners,* by David Pressman & Richard Stim (Nolo).

c. Trademarks and Service Marks

A trademark is a distinctive work, phrase, logo, graphic symbol, or other device that's used to identify the source of a product and to distinguish a manufacturer's or merchant's products from anyone else's—for example, Ford cars and trucks, Dell computers, and Microsoft software. A service mark serves the same function, but for a company's services rather than a particular product—for example, Kinko's photocopying service and Blockbuster video rental service. Trademarks and service marks are often collectively referred to as trademarks.

> **EXAMPLE:** Tom has three pizza shops in two states that he operates under the name of Papa Pepperoni. That name—and a dazzling logo—help Tom's business stand out from a dozen other pizza companies that offer similar menus. Tom registers these marks with the U.S. Patent and Trademark Office so that someone who buys the business will have the utmost legal protection for both the name and the logo.

d. Trade Secrets

These are typically formulas, devices, processes, recipes, and information not generally known by your competitors that give your business a competitive advantage. By definition, there will be no public record of your trade secrets such as a carefully compiled list of repeat customers or a process that gives you a leg up in your industry. Your ability to have a court agree that you own valuable trade secrets depends largely on what you've done to protect the secrecy. Knowing this, the buyer will want to evaluate whether your claimed trade secrets are really valuable. Although employees are bound to maintain your trade secrets, it's a good idea to have key employees—the insiders who know those trade secrets—sign nondisclosure agreements. (Keep in mind that in some states, you must offer an existing employee some additional consideration for executing a nondisclosure agreement. That's not necessary, however, if the employee signs the nondisclosure agreement at the time he or she is hired.) You may also need to demonstrate any other steps you've taken to protect secrecy, such as storing proprietary information in a locked file cabinet.

> **EXAMPLE:** Chester, a master chef, has developed a profitable catering business called Taste of America that specializes in preparing food for banquets and parties based on authentic early American recipes. Tapping into the historical collections of a dozen different libraries, he has found and modified old recipes and menus to allow for cooking techniques not available in colonial times. Chester also has developed a list of customers in his state and three

Have You Got Paper?

If one of the major assets in the sale of a business is the company's intellectual property—for example, the sale of a small software venture or a trade newsletter—the selling company should be prepared to furnish (and the acquiring company should demand) adequate documentation of ownership of the intellectual property. The documentation usually falls into four categories:

- **Registrations, applications, and examples.** If copyright or trademark registrations have been granted or a patent has been issued, a copy of the appropriate document should be available. If an application has been filed, but the registration hasn't yet been granted, then copies of the applications and accompanying paperwork—for example, correspondence from the U.S. Patent Office—should be offered. In the case of trademarks and copyrights, the buyer will also need actual copies of the work or examples of the trademark as used in commerce.

- **Employee contracts.** As a general rule, copyrighted works, trade secrets, and patentable inventions that are created by employees within the course of employment are owned by the employer.

Although a written employment contract expressing that transfer of rights is not required, it is recommended—particularly in the case of employee-created trade secrets and patents. In addition, although employees are bound, without an employment agreement, not to disclose company trade secrets, it is a good idea to include such nondisclosure provisions in company handbooks and employment agreements.

- **Nonemployee contracts.** If you hired an independent contractor to create intellectual property, you should be prepared to provide a written agreement in which the contractor assigns rights. In the case of copyrights, that contract may be an assignment or "work-made-for-hire" agreement; in the case of trade secrets and patents, it should be an assignment.

- **Acquisition agreements.** If your company has purchased intellectual property from another company—for example, you acquired another company's trademarks or copyrights—you should be ready to furnish written copies of the assignment.

adjacent states who share his passion for sampling the food that Americans enjoyed 250 years ago. Recognizing the value of the recipes and the list, Chester adopts several sensible systems to keep both confidential. For example, when hiring key employees who must access this information as part of their work, Chester requires them to sign nondisclosure agreements. Because Chester has treated them as such, these trade secrets are a valuable asset of his business and will play a key role in its sale.

 For guidance on trade secret protection, be sure to consult *Nondisclosure Agreements: Protect Your Trade Secrets & More,* by Richard Stim and Stephen Fishman (Nolo).

 Registration of your business name as a fictitious business name or for use as a corporate or LLC name does not grant you trademark rights. If you registered your business name with local or state authorities as a fictitious name or assumed name, this doesn't mean that you own the trademark rights to the name—that is, the right to exclude others from using a similar name on similar goods or services. If you're unsure whether you have exclusive rights to the use of your business name, consult a trademark attorney before promising that the name is your trademark.

9. Awards, Reviews, and Other Types of Recognition

Depending on the type of business you own, you may have received awards, favorable media comments, or other types of positive recognition. For example, your restaurant or bed and breakfast may have received high praise in a newspaper article or TV feature discussing the best places to stay in your area. Or your landscape business may have won a business-of-the-year award from the local Chamber of Commerce or a design prize from a respected professional group. Recognizing that these discerning folks won't be tooting your horn for you, put your modesty aside and assemble these kind words into a book you can proudly show buyers. For a minimal fee, a graphic artist can help you create a professional presentation through lamination or similar eye-catching techniques. In short, seize the opportunity to put some pizzazz into your sales pitch.

 Although awards can help you pitch your business to a buyer, you might not be able to transfer the awards. For example, if the new owner of a business changes a software product's name or contents, a positive software review awarded to the previous owner's products should not be used without the awarding party's approval. In other cases, the use of a previous award may be a misrepresentation or false advertising—for example, if the new owner of a restaurant changed cuisine and chefs, it would be improper to boast of a five-star review for the previous owner. Finally, some awards are trademarks, themselves—for example, the Good Housekeeping logo—and their use always requires permission from the awarding party. Such permissions usually can't be transferred from one owner to another.

C. Show How Profitable Your Business Really Is: Restate Your Profit and Loss Statement

As explained above in Section B, your tax returns may provide an incomplete picture of just how profitable your business is. Again, that's because the taxable income figure is arrived at after you deduct business expenses and depreciation. As a sensible business owner, you've likely been fairly aggressive—but legal—in taking income-lowering deductions to lower your taxable income. But undoubtedly, many of the items you've deducted—while legitimately tied to business—can also be viewed as personal perks.

Let's take the case of Archie, who owns Jakit, a retail clothing store he runs as a sole proprietorship. On his tax return, Archie deducts several expenses that are an integral part of running his business, such as the rent, utility bills, and the cost of goods sold. But he also deducts the cost of his annual subscription to *The Wall Street Journal,* which he reads for pleasure as well as for business news; the cost of attending several annual industry trade shows often held in desirable locations like San Francisco, Las Vegas, and Orlando; and the cost of club memberships that he holds primarily for entertaining major customers.

In addition, Bev, Archie's wife, is paid a generous—but not legally objectionable—salary to serve as Jakit's bookkeeper, and his children work for the business during the summer. All of these costs are legitimate business deductions—but at least some of them are largely discretionary. Or put another way, the volume of business would probably remain the same if Archie read the local paper, relied on wholesale reps to order new merchandise, and took key customers to dinner at an Applebee's rather than at his club where they also play golf. In addition, Jakit could probably get by with a lower-paid part-time bookkeeper and without hiring teenagers as summer help.

Someone looking to buy Archie's business needs to be shown that these and other similar expenses, such as the lease payment for a business vehicle that's occasionally also used for pleasure, or a legitimate but nevertheless generous store rental payment paid by Jakit to a corporation solely owned by Archie and Bev, in fact amount to owner compensation.

The process of highlighting legitimate tax deductions you have taken for expenses that are not absolutely essential is often called restating or reconstituting the profit and loss statement. The point is, of course, to show the buyer that the profits for Jakit that Archie (in the example above) reports on his tax return don't reflect these other benefits. A potential buyer who sees no need to make some or all of these expenditures can perhaps do the arithmetic necessary to arrive at a higher income number, but it never hurts to point the way. An accountant's help can be invaluable in putting together an accurate and persuasive restatement.

Some of the items you may want to remove from the reconstituted profit and loss statement are these:

- Medical insurance for you and your family. If your business is a C corporation, this may take the form of a medical reimbursement plan.
- Travel and entertainment. Or if some business travel entertainment is absolutely essential—while other trips, meals, and expenses are legitimate, but discretionary—you might want to point out the difference.
- Conventions and trade shows that at least to a degree double as company-paid vacation trips.
- Expensive cars owned or leased by the business. Assuming your business really does need a vehicle, it probably doesn't need a BMW.

- Club memberships. These can be beneficial to a business, but are rarely essential.
- Subscriptions to magazines, newspapers, and electronic services. The new owner may decide to do without.
- Continuing education expenses, including books and videos.
- Legitimate salaries and benefits paid to family members who work in the business. If your spouse does your business's books for a generous salary and your kids earn their college money helping out in the summers, you may be able to show that a new owner could hire strangers for $40,000 less.
- Top-of-the-market rent your corporation or LLC pays you for space in a building that you own. The amount of rent paid for business space typically varies widely, even in the same area. It follows that the IRS normally won't challenge a pricey, but still arguably reasonable, rent. But a buyer who may plan to move to lower-priced space, or perhaps remain in your space but pay less rent, will see that this is a quick way to increase profit.

Also, take a close look at your own compensation—especially if it's relatively hefty. Like the rent, it's a deductible business expense that reduces the bottom line profitability of the business. If the buyer is willing to work for less, it's easy to make an estimate of how much more the business entity will net.

Another big issue to consider is depreciation. You may have used IRS rules to fully and aggressively write off a piece of equipment. The equipment may still have at least several years of useful life, but on the books of your business, the equipment will appear to have no value. To convince a buyer that the value of the fully depreciated equipment is still significant, you may need to get an appraisal. Doing so is definitely worth the cost if you really can demonstrate that the buyer won't have to worry about buying or leasing new equipment for years to come, enabling the business to enjoy very solid profit margins.

 Be prepared for a buyer to be skeptical about your restatement analysis. Especially if the prospective buyer hasn't been in business before, he or she may not understand the routine world of perfectly legal ownership perks and how eliminating them can increase profits. The buyer may even suspect that something sneaky is going on. If you've done your homework and your numbers are as solid as your deductions are legal, simply urge the skeptical buyer to have your books reviewed by a financial adviser who knows the small business ropes. This process will almost surely be reassuring to the buyer. It may even cement the sale.

D. Take Steps to Improve Business Profitability

While it makes sense to crunch and re-crunch your existing numbers to make your business seem as profitable—and therefore as saleable—as possible, it's also key to focus on the business's core or underlying profitability. Especially if you have the luxury of a two- or three-year lead time before you plan your sale, there are many things you can do to legitimately make your business more profitable. Typically, you should be doing these things whether or not you're thinking of selling the business, but the prospect of selling should be a strong motivator to concentrate on increasing income and reducing expenses. Depending on your field, you can get specific ideas on how to increase your business's profitability from many sources, including books, seminars, and professional advisers. But to get you started, here are nine smart ways to improve profitability no matter what type of business you own.

Putting these and other business-improving ideas into practice won't always be easy. And, of course, this will be especially true if you're selling because you're running out of energy or interest. Hang in there. Your creativity and hard work now can often translate into a much higher sale price in the next year or two.

1. Keep Your Workforce Lean

Does your business have too many employees? Having a smaller but hopefully more efficient workforce is a quick way to improve your bottom line. Often this means facing up to the need to replace one or more inefficient people with more-productive workers. One way to evaluate whether your business is overstaffed by people who are underproducing is to check the recommended employee-to-income ratio for your type of business—for example, a small publisher may aim for $225,000 of income per employee. This information is often directly available from industry trade associations or their publications. You'd like to be able to show buyers that your key ratios are well within industry guidelines and, ideally, better than most other companies in the same business as yours.

2. Get the Best Prices for Outside Services

Are you paying too much for maintenance and service contracts? Renewing contracts year after year with satisfactory vendors doesn't take much effort. Unfortunately, following this go-along-and-get-along approach almost always means you're overlooking the chance to get the same work done at far more competitive rates. If you haven't done so in a while, it makes sense to put all significant contracts out to bid. For example, one small business saved $6,000 a year just by soliciting bids for its maintenance contracts, and another reduced its printing costs by over $25,000.

3. Close Down Less-Profitable Locations or Parts of Your Business

Are all your locations pulling their weight? In a multilocation business, it may pay to shut down a less-profitable unit. Let's say, for example, that you have three locations. If two significantly outperform the third, it may make sense to close the third location, especially if you're planning to sell in 18 months or less and don't realistically have much chance of turning it around. This will help improve your profit margin and other indicators of business health.

Similarly, are all parts of your business pulling their weight? If your business does several related but different things, you'll want to make sure that each part is running efficiently and profitably. Perhaps, like many other businesses, you're making most of your money by doing or selling a relatively few things, with the rest essentially treading water. If so, you'll normally want to take steps to quickly improve, cut back, or eliminate the laggards. For example, suppose you have a store that sells and repairs home and car audio systems and also sells a wide range of CDs. Look separately at the profitability of each of these areas. Maybe you'll find that because a big box electronics store has located nearby, you're barely breaking even on your CD sales, even though CDs produce 20% of your gross income. If so, your situation is similar to having a struggling location, as explained above. You'll significantly boost your profit margin—and hence the saleability of your business—if you simply exit the CD business. And you'll have the opportunity to redirect your energy towards growing the profitable parts of your business, perhaps even by getting installation referrals from the large retailer you no longer compete with.

4. Upgrade Your Equipment, Information Systems, and Inventory

Do you have the best equipment and information systems for the job? Maybe it's time to upgrade to newer equipment or software that will do the job better and more reliably. If necessary, you can attend trade shows or talk to colleagues in similar businesses to quickly get up to speed on what's available and how it can help your business. But, of course, don't change unless you're sure the latest and greatest gizmos will either quickly increase your profits or otherwise make your business more saleable.

> **EXAMPLE:** Jenny owns Post Scripts, a bookstore that specializes in remainders—overstocked books that publishers have discontinued.

Her customers appreciate that Post Scripts offers many hard-to-find gems at bargain prices. From her vantage point at the cash register, Jenny has observed that her best customers tend to head directly to particular sections of the store: Biography buffs go to the history section, art lovers make a bee line to the fine arts section, detective fans go to the whodunit section, and so on. To better capitalize on these niche customers, Jenny decides to invest in bar-coding equipment and special software that lets her track her customers' purchases by category. This makes it simple for her to send email announcements and even the occasional postcard to customers when books arrive that may appeal to them. (Fortunately, virtually all Post Script customers consent to being added to Jenny's email lists.) Within a few months, Jenny is pleased to see a 10% increase in sales, more than repaying her for her wise investment.

5. Get Rid of Unnecessary Inventory

Do you have too much inventory? Carrying unnecessary inventory not only takes up expensive space but increases the chance that you'll end up with too many stale goods. Before putting up the for sale sign, it's usually best to have a stock reduction sale or otherwise sell your excess inventory to another business. Not only will this produce the cash you may need to make improvements, but a potential buyer won't be confronted by a stock room or warehouse full of obviously ratty or otherwise hard-to-sell merchandise.

6. Collect, Collect, Collect

Do you have too many slow-paying accounts? No potential buyer will be interested in paying you top dollar for the privilege of chasing deadbeats—and you undoubtedly won't jump with glee if a buyer insists that you keep all seriously past due accounts. In short, if you find yourself in the dicey credit business, it's past time that you adopt corrective strategies such as requiring payment by credit cards from those who don't pay cash. Or, if selling on credit is an integral part of your business, consider tightening up your terms. Continuing to sell to people who pay late is a surefire way both to train them to keep doing so and to make your business less desirable to a savvy buyer.

7. Negotiate the Rent

Is your rent competitive? Rent is a major item for most small businesses. If there's a glut of space in your market, try to renegotiate the rent in exchange for a longer term commitment. Or if you have a month-to-month tenancy or your lease will be up soon, look at the possibility of moving. As explained in Section E, below,

being able to transfer an attractive lease to a buyer can be a key selling point.

8. Stop Theft

Are you losing money because of shoplifting or dishonest employees? A restaurant owner without tight inventory controls is almost sure to have the occasional steak walk out the back door. If the owner has no system at all, a herd may be exiting the freezer without stopping at the cash register. And, of course, other types of businesses that don't protect themselves against theft are almost sure to experience it. Often simple but well-executed security measures are a key part of solving the problem. Read up on good security strategies used in your type of business or, if your situation is unusual, consider seeking help from a consultant.

 For advice on recognizing and preventing employee theft, see *Thieves at Work*, by Ira Michael Shepard and Robert Duston (BNA Books), or *Fraud Examination and Prevention*, by Albrecht & Albrecht (South-Western Educational Publishing). Also, check out http://crimeprevention.rutgers.edu/crimes.htm, the website of the Crime Prevention Service of the School of Criminal Justice at Rutgers. Click on "Employee Theft" for tips and strategies that will help you recognize and prevent employee theft.

Treat employee dishonesty as a wake-up call. If your employees are stealing from your business, it's usually a tip-off that something has gone badly wrong with your employee relationships. Employees who have a grudge against their employers often feel free to help themselves to the goods as a way of getting even. Quickly look at ways to improve employee morale. Workers who like and respect you and your business are far less likely to steal and far more likely to alert you to the occasional bad apple.

9. Market Smarter

Are you getting results for your marketing efforts? To avoid the common practice of wasting your advertising and marketing dollars, track exactly how your customers and clients are finding you. And remember that your highly satisfied customers and clients are usually your best source of additional business. Given the right encouragement and, where appropriate, incentives, they may not only buy more, but may also actively recommend your business to others.

E. Add Value to Your Lease

When to skip ahead. Skip this section if you own your own building or have a month-to-month tenancy—and you're sure the landlord isn't interested in entering into a lease.

When you signed the lease for your business space, you may not have given much thought to selling your business. Now, with a sale firmly on your mind, your lease can become surprisingly important. This is especially so if location is a key element of your business, as would be true if your restaurant is located in a high-traffic part of town, in a desirable shopping complex, or even in an out-of-the-way location you have trained customers to find over many years.

Also, a prospective buyer may well be motivated to buy your business in part because the rent is reasonable compared to other rents locally. Or put another way, in negotiations over the sale price, the fact that you transfer an attractive lease to the buyer can help justify a higher price for the business. But before you can point to your favorable lease to help your sales effort, you have some checking and possibly some negotiating to do with your landlord. Most important, even if your lease has years to run, you need to make sure that it can be transferred to a new owner. Never just assume this is true. Many landlords put a clause in their leases saying that you can't assign the lease to someone else or sublet the space without the landlord's permission. Or if you are more fortunate, the clause may say (or the law of your state may provide) that the landlord can't unreasonably withhold permission for you to assign the lease under its existing terms to a new tenant with sound finances.

Chapter 10 explains the various lease clauses that will concern a potential buyer investigating your business.

But especially if your lease uses the traditional landlord-friendly no-assignment language, you definitely have work to do. Talk to the landlord about changing the lease now through an amendment. Your goal is either to delete the clause entirely or to add wording that requires the landlord to be reasonable in evaluating a creditworthy buyer. If you've been paying your rent on time and have generally been a good tenant, hopefully the landlord will accommodate you—and may even be enthusiastic about helping you use the lease as a selling point so that the business will continue to thrive at the same location. But if the landlord says no or tries to substantially increase the rent—a common ploy if rents in your area have gone up—you'll need to evaluate all your legal options.

Most important, if you run your business as a corporation or an LLC, you may find that your lease was signed in the name of the legal entity—with you possibly signing as a personal guarantor. In this situation, the nonassignment clause probably won't be a legal impediment to a sale if you sell the business entity rather than the assets. That's because the business entity (for example, ProtoBiz Corporation) will still be the tenant after the sale takes place. (The crucial distinction between a sale of an entity and a sale of its assets is explained more fully in Chapter 9 and elsewhere in this book.) Even a buyer who might otherwise prefer to buy only your assets (and not your corporation or LLC) may think again if your favorable lease is only available if the entire entity is purchased.

EXAMPLE: Bill and Jodi—residents of northern Minnesota—form Tropical Tans Inc. for a tanning salon they plan to open. When they find suitable space near where many singles live, Bill and Jodi have Tropical Tans Inc. lease the space for five years, with options to renew for two additional five-year terms—all at what quickly turns out to be a very favorable rate. Tropical Tans opens and from day one shows an enviable profit. Three years later, Bill and Jodi decide to sell the business and move to Hawaii to enjoy real sunshine the year around. Realizing that their excellent location and low rent will be an important part of selling Tropical Tans, Bill and Jodi are disappointed when they study their lease and see that it prohibits transfer without the landlord's permission which, given fast-rising commercial rents, is unlikely to be forthcoming. But when discussing the problem with their lawyer, Bill and Jodi are delighted to hear good news: As long as they sell to a purchaser willing to buy their entire corporate entity—that is, all Bill and Jodi's shares of Tropical

Tans Inc.—their lease will stay in force with no need for a transfer and, therefore, no requirement that their landlord consent to a new tenant.

Sounds great, doesn't it? But you need to read your lease carefully to make sure this strategy will work. Some landlords include language in their leases trying to head off tenants' ability to transfer a lease as part of the sale of a business entity. For example, in the case of a corporate or an LLC tenant, the lease may say that a change in ownership of more than 50% of the business will be treated as an attempted transfer of the lease. If that happens, selling the entity won't automatically give the new owner the benefit of the old lease.

Another aspect of a lease you need to study is its length. Ideally, your lease will continue for several years or give you (and any future owner) the option to renew. By contrast, if your lease will run out in six months and has no renewal option, you'll probably want to negotiate with the landlord to amend the lease so that it lasts long enough to offer a buyer the security of not being booted out shortly after buying the business. To get the landlord to agree, you may have to agree to a somewhat higher rent. And if the lease doesn't already cover the landlord's right to reject unsatisfactory tenants, you may have to accept a lease provision on this. As long as the

rental amount and rejection criteria are reasonable, you'll be well advised to go along with the landlord's request.

If you're unable to work out a long-term lease arrangement in advance of your sale, a prudent buyer may want to make the purchase contingent on being able to sign an acceptable new lease. (Chapter 17 discusses how to deal with these types of contingencies.) This puts your sale at the mercy of the landlord. Possibly this won't prove to be a problem; the new tenant may seem attractive to the landlord, and a lease may be quickly agreed to. But this strategy always comes with a huge downside: The landlord may see the sale of your business as a way to get a new business into the premises. Or the landlord may threaten to say no as a way to blackmail the new tenant into a big rent increase—one that may even be so large it kills the sale.

 Lock up parking and promote it as a valuable feature of your sale. Because customer access is important to lots of businesses, many buyers will be attracted by convenient parking on the premises or nearby. If you enjoy free or low-cost onsite parking, make sure that it's protected by your lease. Or if parking is available nearby, consider taking steps to guarantee that it will continue to exist through a separate lease. Once this is done, pitch parking to potential buyers as a big benefit.

Recommended reading on commercial leases. For more on strategies for negotiating favorable lease terms, see *Negotiate the Best Lease for Your Business,* by Janet Portman and Fred Steingold (Nolo).

F. Communicate With Employees about the Sale

Sooner or later, you'll need to tell employees that a sale of your business is in the works. The question is often, how soon should you do this? If you do it too early—especially if you don't also find a way to reassure them about their futures—you may cause employees needless anxiety about their jobs. Not only is it possible that employee morale and performance may suffer, even worse, some of the best may decide to go work elsewhere, possibly even leaving with crucial information, such as lists of key customers, pricing information, and maybe even your entire strategic plan. But, there can also be a danger in waiting too long to trust employees with the fact that you plan to sell your business, especially when it comes to long-term, loyal employees. Waiting until just before your business changes hands may well be perceived as highly unfair—and in extreme situations, it can even result in some employees' walking out the door, which may also jeopardize the sale.

Realize that as a practical matter, unless yours is a tiny operation and you're personally willing and able to handle every detail of the transaction, it's usually impossible to keep a sale totally secret. For example, if you ask your bookkeeper, sales manager, and marketing chief to pull together profit and loss reports requested by a potential buyer, it won't be long before they guess exactly what's going on.

How and when to disclose information about your plans to sell the business requires careful advance thought. At the early stages, when you're simply preparing to put your business on the market, there's usually no urgent reason to inform all or even most employees. But there are possible exceptions: One is where early on you need the help of a particular employee, such as your head financial person. The other is where word of your plans to sell is likely to leak out from other sources. It's far better for employees to learn about your plans for an orderly transition from you than from outsiders. Sometimes, just informing a few key employees of your plans will be sufficient if you can rely on them to keep the information confidential.

Remember that if you have a corporation or an LLC and are selling the entity, employees with long-term contracts won't have to worry about job security. The entity, under its ownership, will be legally obligated to honor the employment contracts.

G. Clean Up Existing Problems

A buyer's dream of acquiring a problem-free business is often unrealistic, since even most successful businesses will have some unresolved legal or financial issues. But in preparing your business for sale, you obviously want to try to reduce the number or extent of any problems so there will be fewer factors to worry the buyer—each one of which has the potential to either reduce the price or kill the deal. Cleaning up problems is far more crucial when the buyer will be purchasing the entity (corporation or LLC) rather than just the assets of the business. That's because with an entity purchase, the buyer will normally be stuck with all business problems. By contrast, if only the assets of the business are sold, you'll typically remain legally responsible for past problems. And even though, in an entity sale, you may be willing to agree to protect (indemnify) the buyer from future liability for past problems, or even have some money set aside in escrow for a year or more to deal with those problems, it's much better to eliminate the problems before putting your business on the market.

There are several common issues—involving accounts receivable, debts, lawsuits, and environmental hazards—you may need to address in attempting to clean up problems.

1. Questionable Accounts Receivable

If your business extends credit to customers, you probably have a long list of accounts receivable. If you think something like this, "Customers owe me $50,000, so I can add $50,000 to the sale price and let the buyer take over these accounts," you'll want to think again. The buyer isn't going to pay you even close to full value for these accounts without being convinced that 100% of the money will be paid voluntarily and on time. Otherwise, the buyer will expect a large discount—and may even offer to pay nothing for them, preferring to leave the accounts and any collection problems in your hands. To assess how much your accounts receivable are really worth, the buyer will want you to provide an aging report that shows the payment history of each account and how long the current balance has been outstanding.

 Be prepared to educate the buyer about payment practices in your business. In some industries, a bill that's been outstanding for 50 days is way past due. In others, most accounts aren't expected to pay short of 60 days, and many routinely take 90 or 100 days with little risk that they won't pay eventually. So, especially if a buyer isn't thoroughly familiar with the bill-paying culture of your field, you'll need to do a bit of educating.

No matter what your industry's bill-paying practices, the point is that before you can expect the buyer to pay anything like full value for your accounts receivable, you have to clean up any problems. If certain customers or clients are slow-pays or—far worse—potential no-pays, do what you can to resolve their accounts rather than let them continue in an ambiguous state. For example, you might send a series of tougher-than-normal collection letters, combined with personal phone calls when appropriate. And if this fails, the next step may be to couple a threat to sue with an offer of a discount for prompt payment. And there's always the option of turning over the nettlesome accounts to a collection agency or, where larger sums are due, getting a lawyer involved. Many of these approaches take time, so you need to plan ahead. Where the amount owed is relatively small or you're convinced the debtor is a deadbeat or uncollectible, it's usually best to write off the account so that none of your receivables is embarrassingly aged.

2. Business Debts

Your business may owe money to a bank or other lender, or maybe to a number of suppliers. Or you may be paying off a lawsuit judgment or settlement. Even though there often are several feasible ways to pay off debts as part of closing your sale so that they don't burden the buyer, it can also be true that a buyer who sees a business laden with debts may quickly decide to look elsewhere. So, as part of preparing for a sale, you should consider ways to reduce the amount of debt your business owes. This may mean you have to dip into your personal funds or borrow money from a relative, friend, or bank, but it will be more than worth it if, as a result, your business proves easier to sell.

If you're not able to reduce the number of creditors, you may want to propose how your debts will be paid as part of your sale. Some buyers will be willing to assume responsibility for remaining business debts in return for a reduction in the sale price. But another, and usually preferable, option is to propose to the buyer that remaining debts will be paid at closing using some of the money that would otherwise pass from the buyer to you. (Chapter 15 discusses how to do this.)

EXAMPLE: Ron is negotiating to sell his roofing business to Bob. They reach agreement on a sale price of $75,000 with a 20% ($15,000) down payment, and the balance to be paid off over a three-year period. But there's a glitch: Bob doesn't want to be saddled with the $8,000 in debt that Ron owes for equipment. Accordingly, Ron and Bob arrive at a compromise: They agree that Bob will assume only $3,000 of the down payment to pay off the rest. At closing, Bob will write a check for $5,000 to the bank to which the debt is owed and a check for $10,000 to Ron, and will sign agreements to take over the remaining $3,000 of debt.

 IRS or other tax debts are very bad news. No one wants to fight the tax man. It follows that if you have a dispute with the IRS or local tax authorities, you'll want to work toward an early settlement. Even if you're right in principle in resisting the tax liability, an ongoing tax dispute will almost certainly hinder a sale of your business. A buyer who realizes that taxing authorities can seize or tie up assets for taxes believed to be owed is likely to head straight for the exit.

3. Lawsuits and Other Claims

Lawsuits and other claims, whether brought against your business or by it, can take years to resolve. Understandably, a buyer—especially one who's considering buying the entity rather than just the assets—is likely to become apprehensive (maybe even paranoid) if someone has sued your business for a significant amount. The fact that you feel confident that a jury will either find in your favor or will award, at most, a small amount to the plaintiff may not count much. In this situation, trying to reassure the buyer isn't likely to work. In fact, because no buyer wants to face the uncertainty inherent in any court action, selling your version

of events to a prospective purchaser may be a tougher sell than convincing a jury that you're right. So even if you're quite confident that you'll ultimately prevail in court, you're probably better off to seriously consider any reasonable settlement offer. For example, agreeing to pay an extra $5,000 or even $10,000 to a stubborn plaintiff will make especially good financial sense if, by so doing, you're able to sell your business for, say, $250,000 or more.

EXAMPLE: Liz is the owner and president of Jiffy Home Products Inc., a company she hopes to sell in the near future. She recently fired Willie, the company's quality control inspector, because he'd been doing an absolutely terrible job. To her surprise, Liz receives a letter from Willie's lawyer claiming that Willie had been wrongfully discharged. According to the lawyer, Willie suffers from frequent migraine headaches and, under the ADA (Americans With Disabilities Act), he was entitled a reasonable accommodation, which Jiffy failed to provide. The lawyer threatens to sue if Jiffy doesn't pay $75,000 to settle the claim. Liz, knowing Willie's claim to be bogus, would normally say, "Sue me and be damned." But Liz now sees that any pending litigation may hinder a sale. Controlling her anger and using admirable discretion, Liz grits her teeth and negotiates a $12,000 settlement with Willie and his lawyer.

 Try not to let claimants know that your business is up for sale. Upon learning that your business is for sale, your lawsuit adversary is almost sure to hang tough, knowing that prolonged litigation may foul up your deal. Sensing that you're likely to be under greater-than-normal pressure to resolve the dispute, a savvy adversary will likely up the settlement ante, hoping to extract more money than is deserved.

Fortunately, legal claims—even those for which court papers have been filed—can usually be settled without a full-fledged trial. Even if the plaintiff is unreasonably demanding, consider proposing the use of one or more types of alternative dispute resolution (ADR) to move toward an early settlement. The ADR techniques to consider include:

- **Negotiation,** in which you and the other side—either on your own or through lawyers—try to reach a workable compromise. Often it's best for your lawyer to make a preliminary call to let the other side smell the possibility of a settlement. Then it may make sense to slow the process down for a few weeks or months to plant doubt. Then authorize your representative to try and work out an affordable deal.

- **Mediation,** in which an impartial mediator helps both sides explore options that may lead to a voluntary settlement. The dispute gets resolved if—and only if—both sides agree on the terms of a settlement. When both parties sincerely are looking for a way to resolve a dispute, mediation has a very high chance of success. Judges and court administrators have become big fans of mediation, and they often encourage and sometimes require litigants to try mediation before a case goes to trial. Many courts maintain lists of trained and certified mediators, which can ease your job of finding the right person.

- **Arbitration,** in which an arbitrator hears all the facts and then issues a legally binding decision that resolves the matter. Unlike a trial by a judge or jury, an arbitration hearing is conducted in private. In selecting either an arbitrator or a mediator, try to find one who specializes in business claims, or who at least has had some experience with such claims.

Besides being quicker, these techniques are almost always less expensive than a lawsuit and will consume less of your time and energy, so you can concentrate better on running your business and getting it ready to sell.

For a comprehensive and practical discussion of mediation and other methods of resolving disputes, see *Mediate, Don't Litigate: Strategies for Successful Litigation,* by Peter Lovenheim and Lisa Guerin (Nolo). For lists of professional mediators and extensive information on mediation, see the Mediation Information and Resource Center at www.mediate.com. To learn more about arbitration and find an arbitrator, see the American Arbitration Association's website at www.adr.org.

4. Environmental Issues

Buyers today are especially sensitive to environmental issues, because they can become legally responsible for the potentially huge cost of a cleanup even if the problem predates their purchase of the business. Although true horror scenarios are rare, buyers are sensible to be a little paranoid when it comes to worrying about environmental hazards and to demand a full investigation into any possible environmental problems.

It follows that your first job is to assess whether or not you have any environmental hazards. The vast majority of businesses don't, as would be true if, for example, you run a consulting business from a rented space in a new building. But some other businesses, such as dry cleaners and gas stations, may have real environmental concerns, especially those that have been in business for many years. You need to think about environmental issues in situations such as these:

- You own a dry cleaning business that uses drums of volatile cleaning fluids that may have leaked from their containers.
- Your lighting store is located on property you own which years ago was occupied by a gas station and may have tanks buried underground or have soil contamination problems resulting from leaking tanks or midnight dumping.
- Your retail store occupies an older building that you own that may contain asbestos insulation or lead-based paint.
- Your garden supply business repairs power lawn mowers, and the gasoline-oil fuel sometimes drips into soil behind the shop area, meaning that the soil should be tested and maybe even removed if seriously contaminated.
- You suspect that the restaurant you're selling may have toxic mold on the kitchen walls.

In these and many other situations, you'll need to do some further checking and maybe take expensive remedial steps. If you haven't done so already, consult an environmental expert, who may recommend that you obtain a Phase I study to check on possible environmental hazards: air pollution, contaminated soil or water, asbestos, and so forth. In a Phase I study, the consultant will research the history of the site and neighboring sites; this will typically include interviewing people familiar with your area, looking at aerial photos to check on past uses of the site, and reviewing government documents that might disclose hazards. If the findings show a need for further investigation, a Phase II study may be in order, which often involves having engineers and chemists actually test the soil, air, structure, and groundwater for signs of contamination.

Depending on the nature of the problem and how it got started, the cost of a cleanup may be shared by you, the landlord, the government, and perhaps a former building occupant or business owner. Like everything else you do to get ready to market your business, curing the problem up front will benefit you in the long run by making the sale process go more smoothly and increasing the price you're likely to get the buyer to pay.

H. Nail Down Vital Relationships With Customers and Suppliers

Favorable business relationships with customers and suppliers have almost surely contributed to the success of your business. These relationships can be a valuable asset when you sell your business, but much more so if you have written contracts in place. For example, your photography studio may have for years done all the photos for a dozen public and private schools and a number of youth sports leagues. If you've never signed a multiyear contract—relying instead on your good personal contacts to assure future business—now is the time to put something in writing. After seeing that a big chunk of your business is guaranteed by three-year contracts, a hesitant buyer will be much more likely to make a favorable offer for your business, knowing that the stream of income will continue.

Advantageous relationships with suppliers are also valuable—especially if the terms are captured in written contracts. Suppose you've been able to get a good deal on merchandise that you sell at retail or on parts that you use in making repairs. A potential buyer will be reassured if you can show that you have a several-year agreement with the supplier that locks in the favorable prices.

In negotiating contracts with either customers or suppliers, try to include a clause that allows you to transfer the contract to a new owner of the business— although such a clause is far less necessary if you have a corporation or an LLC and you intend to sell the entity rather than its assets. That's because, in most cases, a contract signed by a corporation or an LLC remains in effect even if the ownership of the entity changes hands.

But be aware that if you own a small business that involves a strong element of personal service—for example, a graphic design firm or a land survey company—customers may rightfully be reluctant to sign a long-term contract that may allow some unknown person to provide the services in the future. If you run into resistance, you may be able to overcome it by proposing a clause that allows a buyer to take over the contract as long as you remain involved to some extent in the business.

> **EXAMPLE:** Paula, who owns Metro Services LLC, provides maintenance for municipal buildings so that local cities and counties can reduce their own high-cost staffs. Paula's profitable contract with the City of Fernburg is about to expire, and she is negotiating with the city manager for a new five-year contract. Paula's current contract says that the city can cancel it if Metro Services LLC is sold to a new owner. Paula knows that during that next five years, she will likely sell the business, so she asks that the new contract include language that will keep the contract in force even if she sells the LLC. The city manager balks because, while the city has confidence in Paula (after all, she has a good record of meeting deadlines and doing excellent work), the city is less confident about how well an unknown buyer would

do. Paula proposes—and the city agrees—that the new contract can be transferred as long as Paula remains associated with the business after it's sold and works at least 10 hours a week as a consultant.

I. Prepare a Checklist of Presale Tasks

Below is a checklist of the items covered early in this chapter—the features that buyers look for when they evaluate a business. Spend some time evaluating how your business shapes up. Almost certainly, in some areas, there's a need for improvement. The more you can do to provide an appealing package to prospective buyers, the more likely it will be that you'll get top dollar for your business.

Of course, not all of the items on the list will apply to you. A service business, for example, won't be concerned with inventory issues. But for those items that do apply, take sufficient time to figure out what needs to be done. You can then turn the checklist into an action plan—a blueprint for a successful sale.

 Where to find the forms. You'll find a Checklist of Presale Tasks on the CD-ROM at the back of this book.

☑ Checklist of Presale Tasks

Attributes That Motivate Buyers	Does this apply to your business?	Action Plan
Consistent profit for two or more years	☐ yes ☐ no	
No unresolved legal problems	☐ yes ☐ no	
Proof that accounts receivable can be collected	☐ yes ☐ no	
Clear and consistent accounting protocols	☐ yes ☐ no	
Convincing business plan for the next few years	☐ yes ☐ no	
Solid relationships with suppliers and customers	☐ yes ☐ no	
Commitment of experienced employees to stay with the business	☐ yes ☐ no	
Long-term lease at a favorable rent	☐ yes ☐ no	
Complete disclosure of all relevant information	☐ yes ☐ no	
Honest business practices	☐ yes ☐ no	
Attractive and organized business premises	☐ yes ☐ no	
Current inventory that's in good condition	☐ yes ☐ no	
Business and office equipment that is in good condition	☐ yes ☐ no	
Clear list of noncash perks, such as business-related travel	☐ yes ☐ no	
Sensible or convincing reason for sale	☐ yes ☐ no	
Organized paperwork, including cash flow records, tax returns, leases and important contracts, and documents such as entity records	☐ yes ☐ no	
Other	☐ yes ☐ no	
Other	☐ yes ☐ no	

Chapter 8

Finding the Right Buyer

Over the years, you've learned how to successfully attract customers for your business's goods or services. Sometimes, especially during your business's start-up phase, this may have seemed like a Herculean task. But with hard work and maybe a little good fortune, you did it. Now you face a different, more targeted, but essentially similar challenge: how to find the person or group willing to buy your entire business for a good—hopefully a very good—price.

Obviously, the pool of customers for a business that may be worth as much as $100,000, $500,000, or even $1 million or more is far smaller than the pool of customers who buy your products or use your services. Your task of finding the right buyer for your business is further complicated by the fact that unless you locate a well-funded buyer who wants to add your operation to an already-successful enterprise, chances are you won't find someone who's able and willing to pay for the business all at once. Instead, in a more typical scenario, the buyer will offer to make a down payment and expect you to accept a promissory note for the balance, which may be as much as 80% or even 90% of the sale price. Typically, the note will require the buyer to pay off the balance in installments over two to five years. In short, when you find a potential buyer, there's a good chance you'll be going into the credit business.

Extending tens or even hundreds of thousands of dollars of credit to a purchaser can be a huge problem, and many interested buyers will not prove to be worthy of your trust. The last thing you want to do is sell your business to someone whom you can't count on to make payments. You don't want to have to worry about dunning the purchaser for your money or face the prospect of taking your business back several months or years down the road after it has deteriorated on someone else's watch.

This chapter will help you find good potential buyers—one of whom hopefully will not only sign up to buy your business at an attractive price, but will follow through by making required payments on time, every time. For starters, you'll learn about the different types of buyers who may be the right candidates to buy your business, including some who are hiding in plain sight (Sections A and B). There are probably more good prospects out there than you may have imagined.

Competitors may be serious buyers—or perhaps not. If one of them expresses interest, you need to be cautious. As explained in Section C, you don't want to give out too much sensitive information in the early stages.

Then, in Sections D, E, and F, you'll discover the most effective strategies for reaching buyers and when it may pay to bring in a business broker to help put together a deal. Finally, in Section G, you'll find out how to quickly size up prospects so you don't waste time on tire-kickers and long shots.

Elsewhere in this book, you'll find details on how you can greatly reduce the risks of your sale turning into a financial disaster. For example, Chapter 10 explains the ways you can screen prospective buyers for financial reliability once negotiations are under way. And Chapter 9 describes several techniques you can use to assure that you'll be paid in full—for example, getting personal guarantees from the buyer and other signers and taking a security interest not only in the business assets but in the buyer's home as well.

A. First, Look for Buyers Close to Home

Often the best prospects to buy your business are people you already know—including friends, family, and employees. Finding a buyer close at hand is good news for several reasons. Perhaps the most important reason is that you can then eliminate much of the sweat and angst of a wide search. Another is that because you already know the person, you'll be better positioned to weigh his or her strengths and weaknesses than would be true with a stranger. And third, a prospective buyer who is an employee or otherwise knowledgeable about your enterprise will already know a lot about how to run it. While not every business owner has the good fortune to have an obvious and accessible buyer, it happens more frequently than you might imagine.

Checklist of What to Do Before You Look for Buyers

You'll probably have several tasks to complete before you're ready to seek a buyer. For example, you may need to:

- prepare your business for sale as recommended in Chapter 7, including putting your premises in tip-top shape and getting your financial records in order
- decide whether you prefer an asset sale or an entity sale
- come up with a rough sale price and general terms
- prepare a sale information sheet that describes your business and the major sale terms that you're looking for
- decide whether you want to be involved in the business after the sale and, if so, how much and what type of involvement would be ideal
- draft a confidentiality agreement for prospective buyers to sign, and
- let key employees know that you're putting the business up for sale.

---

1. Employees

Someone already working across the room—especially someone who's worked there for years and knows the good, the bad, and the ugly—may jump at the chance to become the new owner. Or a group of two or three current employees may be interested in forming a partnership, limited liability company, or corporation to buy your business. Since these insiders already know much (maybe everything) about the business, selling to one or more of them means you probably won't have to put as much work into physically preparing your business for sale, pulling together years of financial and tax data, and explaining all the positive aspects of the business.

Another plus in selling your business to an employee is that you probably know a great deal about the employee's financial status, judgment, and entrepreneurial habits. Working closely with someone each day is bound to give you excellent information about whether that person spends money prudently, pays bills on time, has a stable personal life, and makes good business decisions. This kind of information is particularly important if you're going to receive a promissory note for part of the price.

EXAMPLE: For 15 years, Al has owned Town & Country Footwear, an upscale shoe store in a small city. For the last ten of those years, Ellen has worked alongside him selling shoes and helping to manage the store. When Al goes on a buying trip or takes a vacation, Ellen does an excellent job running the store.

Now, Al, an avid golfer, has a rare opportunity to improve his lifestyle by opening a shoe store in a new shopping plaza located 400 miles away near several expanding golf resorts. Deciding that he can't efficiently own and manage two stores a day's drive apart, Al concludes that to successfully make the move, he needs to sell his existing store. Knowing that Ellen is honest, reliable, and frugal, and that customers like and respect her, Al offers her the first chance to buy the business. Ellen is delighted when she hears about this possibility. But there's a hitch. Although she's carefully saved money over the years, Ellen can only put down 15% of the sale price. Al, who needs money to invest in his new store, prefers 30%. Fortunately, when Ellen's parents step forward and agree to invest 10%, Al is willing to reduce his down payment requirement to 25% and a deal is struck. Ellen will pay Al the remaining 75% of the purchase price over four years in 48 equal installments carrying 7% interest. Al can easily calculate that the income from the store will enable Ellen to meet the note payments and still take a modest but adequate salary for herself, and he's confident that he'll be paid. The sale is concluded within 60 days, and Al is able to depart for greener pastures.

Unfortunately, there can also be a downside to approaching an employee about buying your business. If you can't agree on a fair price or other terms, you may wind up with a disappointed and disgruntled employee—the last thing you need when putting the business on the market. And any key employee you consider to be a possible buyer may also be in a position to sabotage your sale. At the very least, a potential buyer who realizes that an important employee is disaffected or has just quit may be more reluctant to commit.

The fact that this type of problem has the potential to develop doesn't mean you should avoid approaching employees about buying your business. But before you do, think through what may happen if you can't reach an agreement, and act accordingly. For example, if the chances are low that a particular employee will really want to buy the business at a price you expect to receive—or if there's a good possibility you won't be able to come to terms for some other reason—you're probably better off to start by looking elsewhere for buyers.

 Your employees may have more financial resources than you think. Your assumptions about an employee's financial resources can sometimes be off base. For example, unknown to you, an employee with a modest lifestyle may have tucked away money from an inheritance. Or another employee may have meager savings but be willing and able to tap highly solvent family members or friends for help with the down payment. In short, consider the possibility that a worthy person who, based on outward appearances, seems unable to afford your business may actually be a good candidate to do so.

2. Friends and Family Members

Sometimes, a friend or family member will turn out to be the right person to buy your business. Perhaps your niece Molly, who just received her MBA, has a strong entrepreneurial bent—and can raise a $50,000 down payment from the trust fund that her grandma Shirley set up for her. Or maybe your business would be a perfect fit for a close friend who's itching to escape the midmanagement corporate treadmill. Even one of your children— who earlier in life may have disdained the family business—may by now have learned enough about life to think again.

EXAMPLE: Joan and her husband Pete have owned a profitable self-storage facility for 20 years. Now, in their early 60s, they decide they'd like to have more time to travel and get involved in volunteer activities. One afternoon, while enjoying a post-tennis snack with his buddy Chuck, Pete casually mentions that he and Joan plan to sell. By coincidence, Chuck, age 50, has been considering a buyout retirement package offered by his large employer, which is downsizing its operations. Never completely happy working in the corporate environment, Chuck immediately expresses interest in buying what he knows to be a successful business. Soon, a plan begins to crystallize. Chuck decides to accept his employer's buyout package and retire in three months, using part of his lump sum payment from the corporation as a down payment on Joan and Pete's business. Meanwhile, to get some hands-on experience in a business that's new to him, Chuck arranges to come in every Saturday to work at the storage facility. In addition, Joan and Pete agree that they'll be available as consultants and trainers part time for six months after Chuck takes over.

Joan and Pete also own five acres of vacant land adjacent to the self-storage facility. Chuck would like a chance to buy that land as well so that he can eventually build more storage units. But because he doesn't have the cash now, he offers Joan and Pete $10,000 for an option to buy the extra land within five years at $200,000. (The $10,000 is to be applied toward the price of the land if Chuck buys it.) Joan and Pete agree and the deal is done.

You'll be fortunate if a highly qualified friend steps forward to buy your profitable business. But before you rush a deal with someone who is part of your social or family network, carefully consider the downsides of this approach. For example, what will happen to the personal relationship you now enjoy with a close friend if this person turns out to be a poor manager or is lazy, unreliable, or, even worse, dishonest and, as a result, the business does poorly and you don't receive your payments on time? Will you feel free to take legal action to collect what's owed you, even knowing that your perfectly reasonable actions will make things difficult for your friends, spouse, and kids? Might your larger social network even be damaged by any dispute with your former friend as people take sides?

EXAMPLE: For five years, Marge has owned and operated The Kid's Korner, a resale shop for children's clothing. Now pregnant, Marge decides to give up the business so she can be a stay-at-home mom during her child's preschool years. When she mentions her plans to her friends at the monthly meeting of the Tree Town Women's Investment Club, Marge is surprised when Andrea, who has just inherited a tidy sum, expresses an interest in buying the business. At first, Marge is excited and disposed to say yes, since the idea of a quick and easy sale is obviously appealing. But then Marge starts thinking about some problems with selling to Andrea—for example, Andrea has never run any business, is habitually late for meetings, frequently complains that her cleaning woman does a poor job, and puts a high priority on driving a new luxury car. Marge concludes that there is just too much risk that Andrea won't be happy in a business which all but requires that its owner rise before dawn. Not wanting to jeopardize her warm relationship with the members of the Investment Club, or to risk having to resume ownership of the shop should Andrea fail, Marge decides not to follow up on Andrea's expression of interest in The Kid's Korner.

With family members, the fallout from a deal gone sour can obviously have even more wrenching effects. Think about how relatives may behave if you and your feckless cousin end up battling in court. Or consider how you'll feel at a family reunion or a wedding the month after foreclosing on your defaulting nephew's house that was pledged as security for a business loan. The fact that your nephew used business receipts to gamble while running your once highly successful enterprise into the ground, putting your retirement income at risk, may not assuage the hard feelings of your aunt, your uncle, and everyone else on their side of the family.

Again, as with friends, there's no hard-and-fast rule that says you should never sell to a relative. But in addition to carefully assessing the potential buyer's character and experience, it's crucial that you and the friend or family member frankly discuss all the financial issues—and especially the risks—well before you sign a sales contract.

 Keep it professional. If the deal goes forward with a friend or family member, it's absolutely essential that you and the buyer sign a sales contract and all the other papers you'd normally sign if this deal were between strangers. This includes having the buyer sign a promissory note if it's an installment sale. As a practical matter, it also makes sense to insist on a fairly large down payment, preferably in the 30% to 50% range. That way, if trouble arises, you'll be in a position to be a little more patient and relaxed in dealing with it. And to help your friend or family member learn whether he or she will really be happy running your business, it can be a good idea to ask that person to work for you for six months before finalizing the sale.

Also, get an appraisal before you sell to a friend or family member. Seek an appraiser with expertise in your business niche to complete both an objective written appraisal of the business's current value and its prospects. (Chapter 5 discusses how to work with an appraiser.) That way, if your friend or relative later becomes disappointed and tries to claim you charged too much or unloaded damaged goods, you can point to the appraisal and evaluation to show that you acted fairly and honestly.

Get tax advice before selling your business to your children. Perhaps the sale can be integrated with your estate plan for maximum tax savings. Also, a tax pro can help evaluate whether the sale price, the allocation of the price (in an asset sale), or the interest rate (in an installment sale) will pass IRS muster.

3. Customers

Occasionally sales lightning can strike in the form of a good customer who's genuinely attracted to your type of business. Below, in Section B, you'll read about the possibility of selling an established business to a supplier, wholesaler, or a retailer with whom you have a long-time relationship. Here, the focus is on the possibility of selling to an individual customer or client with a genuine interest in what you sell and a dream of opening a similar business. For example, maybe you own a niche business specializing in model building kits for vintage airplanes and ave a dedicated customer who knows as much about the details of model building as you do. Or maybe you rent and repair sail boats and have a customer who not only rents boats from you regularly but likes to come into the back of your shop to watch and even help you install new rigging. Or possibly you own an art print and framing store, a passion shared by a local art teacher who stops by every week to chat and check out new stock. Customers like these may—sometimes without even fully

realizing it—become potential buyers for your business. You'll never know unless you see them as prospects and approach them as such.

Certainly, if a dedicated customer appears to be a possible buyer, and your opening discussions confirm that impression, it's often wise to follow up by offering a fact sheet that summarizes what you're selling and gives an overview of profits and losses for the past several years. If there continues to be mutual interest, you can provide more information, as you would with any other potential purchaser.

EXAMPLE: Laura owns a coffee shop, The Daily Grind. Over a period of a year, Stan, a freelance writer, has become a regular customer, often spending the morning in the shop working away on his laptop while consuming several lattés and a couple of scones. Lately, Laura has observed Stan eyeing the flow of business and has fielded several astute questions about coffee suppliers, popular selling items, and how one gets started in the coffeehouse business. It occurs to Laura, who is ready to sell so as to be able to finally go back to finish her Ph.D., to ask a few questions of her own. When she does, she learns that Stan and his wife Cheryl moved to the area so that Cheryl could begin work as chief of ophthalmology at the big teaching hospital in town. Stan, who is tired of hustling articles for business publications, has concluded that now that Cheryl has a good income, it's his chance to own a business rather than just write about them. Before long, the possibility of Stan's buying out Laura excites both of them. When Stan lines up his parents to put up 25% of his purchase price and cosign a note for the rest and spends three months happily working the espresso machine, Laura becomes convinced that Stan's enthusiasm for the business is more than a temporary latté high. She works out a deal with Stan that allows her to give up the shop and return to school the following September.

B. Strategic Buyers

There are other types of potential buyers out there, including some who may be willing to pay you more than you'd get from an employee, friend, relative, or stranger who is primarily interested in running your business as a standalone operation. Often called strategic buyers, these people typically fall into one of the following three categories:

- a business that's the same as or similar to yours
- a complementary business, or
- a supplier or major customer.

The common thread linking these potential buyers is that their owners will see the acquisition of your business as constituting a logical extension of their own. Or put another way, these people are called strategic buyers because their purchase of your business fits into their larger business strategy. For example, a person who already runs five successful pizza shops in your city may reap significant economy-of-scale benefits by acquiring yours—benefits that wouldn't be available to your cousin who wants to run just your shop.

To identify possible strategic buyers, begin by asking yourself:

- If I were expanding my business rather than selling it, which businesses would I look at for possible purchase?
- Do I have a supplier or major customer who would benefit by owning my business?
- What businesses would be a good fit with mine?

The key, obviously, is to look for synergies that make your business such a logical fit with that of the buyer that acquiring it offers the purchaser a compelling financial advantage. A buyer who realizes that adding your business to his or her existing one makes both more valuable is clearly a good prospect to pay you top dollar. Of course, the buyer needs to be convinced that buying your business makes better financial sense than simply starting one that duplicates yours.

1. Businesses That Are Like Yours

Someone who owns a business that's similar to yours and wants to expand may see various advantages in becoming the owner of yours—for example, it may be less costly, more profitable, and, above all, less risky to pick up a successful existing business than to develop a new location from scratch. In addition, if competition from your business has been keeping a potential purchaser's prices artificially low, buying your enterprise may be a quick way to fatten profit margins. This sounds great, but as with any sales strategy, there's also a downside. Similar businesses are also likely to be competitors—and may be as interested in learning about how yours works as in buying it. This means that you need to take extra precautions before providing information to competitive businesses (as explained in Section C, below).

Let's look more closely at why businesses like yours may be good prospective buyers.

a. The Buyer Can Benefit From Acquiring an Additional Location

Lots of successful business owners who consider the possibility of adding another location pull back when faced with the prospect of having to start from scratch. That's where you come in. By purchasing your business, the buyer doesn't have to find a new space, negotiate a lease, prepare the new space for business, or perform dozens of other worky but essential tasks. And best of all, your successful business comes with a built-in pool of paying customers.

There can be many good economic reasons for a business to add another location—whether it's done by opening a new one or buying a similar business that's already up and running. For one, certain fixed expenses that the buyer is already paying can be spread over a larger enterprise, thus reducing the overhead portion of each product or service sold. For example, a business with $750,000 in annual gross sales may spend $75,000 a year for bookkeeping and administrative services. Buying a business of similar size would produce $1.5 million in annual gross sales—but the $75,000 for bookkeeping and administrative services might only go up to $100,000. Promotional dollars may also go farther as one campaign may draw customers to two locations. And equipment may be used more efficiently. A flower shop may own a delivery truck that's being used only four hours a day. Add a second location and the truck will be used eight hours a days—again cutting the average delivery cost of each flower order and increasing profits.

For retail businesses, adding a second location often allows the business to buy goods at a lower price, since increased volume means it qualifies for a bigger discount. For example, a boat shop that buys and then sells 150 sailboats annually of a particular high-end brand may be eligible for an additional discount if it buys at least 250 units a year, something that would be possible with a second shop.

b. The Buyer Can Instantly Acquire New Customers and Clients

Through your hard work, your business has probably built up a long roster of loyal customers or clients. This can be a very attractive aspect of an existing business. With a good business plan, the buyer should be able to retain most of those customers and clients. And assuming the buyer is already well-established in your field, picking up your customer or client base gives the buyer the opportunity to become a bigger player.

> **EXAMPLE:** George, Peggy, and Alice have a thriving court reporting service, Court Reporter Associates LLC. They get the lion's share of deposition work from Lincoln County attorneys, because over many years these lawyers have come to appreciate the accuracy and timeliness of the company's transcripts. But, after forty years, the three decide it's time for them to retire. They're aware that Statewide Reporting Service LLC, a larger operation in nearby Washington and Jefferson counties, has been gradually expanding. And they've heard through the grapevine that Statewide would love to open an office in Lincoln County, but has held off for fear that competing with Court Reporter Associates would mean low or no profits. George, Peggy, and Alice also know that one of their own employees, Andrew, might be interested in buying the business, but they wisely conclude that Statewide is not only likely to pay more, but can probably put cash on the barrelhead with no need for an installment purchase. So after Alice's initial inquiry to one of Statewide's senior people is greeted warmly, serious discussions ensue. Statewide is particularly pleased that all three owners of Court Reporter Associates agree to stay on for a year's transition period so that current law firm customers have a chance to get used to Statewide. The two businesses agree on price and terms, and a closing takes place within a month.

Sometimes, by acquiring a similar business, a buyer can go beyond merely expanding its base of customers or clients. It can become the leader in a particular market niche. When a business achieves such a leadership role, the vast majority of potential customers or clients automatically will think of that business first when in the market for that type of goods or services. As you might imagine, sales can then grow exponentially.

EXAMPLE: Italia Imports LLC has built a profitable business importing distinctive tile from the Tuscan and Umbrian regions of Italy to the U.S. West Coast. The company's main competitor west of the Mississippi is Tile and Stone Surfaces Inc. So when Antonio, the owner of Italia Imports, decides to sell, he approaches Maria, the owner of Tile and Stone Surfaces. Antonio explains that he can offer not only a warehouse full of unusual tiles (some of which are no longer produced), but can also transfer Italia Imports' exclusive contracts with small producers in Italy plus the extensive roster of building supply and specialty tile retailers that carry its wares. Realizing that if she doesn't purchase Italia, one of several bigger national tile importers is likely to do so, Maria immediately sees the advantages of becoming the biggest importer of high-end Italian tile in the whole western part of the country. Serious negotiations begin.

2. Businesses That Can Benefit From Moving Into a Related Business

There are likely to be many businesses that, while not directly competitive with yours, are involved in a related activity. This possibility is worth paying attention to since, as is true with the other types of strategic buyers discussed above, your business may be more valuable to a related business than it would be to a purely financial buyer. The reasons why a related business might be interested in yours can vary. Your business may provide a way for a buyer to offer a wider range of goods or services to its existing customers. Or, because your customers will begin using the buyer's services or purchasing the buyer's goods, acquiring your business may provide an easy way for the buyer to acquire new customers. And sometimes buying your business will make for an efficient use of the buyer's space or workforce.

Here are a few examples of this complementary relationship between two businesses.

Business #1	Business #2
Alarm system company	Security guard service
Bicycle store	Exercise equipment store
Taxi service	Local delivery service
Upholstery business	Interior decoration service
Poster shop	Picture-framing service
Tree-cutting service	Landscaping business
Women's clothing boutique	Women's shoe store
Restaurant	Catering service

As you've probably already figured out from the match-ups suggested above, once you establish a logical synergy, either business can be the buyer or the seller.

Using synergy as a selling point will usually require some ingenuity on your part. For example, you may see with perfect clarity that a respected catering service is a logical purchaser for your Mediterranean-style restaurant, but that idea may never have occurred to Dan, who owns the best catering service in town. Your marketing job is to create the vision for Dan, being as specific as possible about how two businesses will prosper under the same ownership. For instance, you might point out that the popular seafood specialties upon which Dan built his catering reputation can easily be added to the restaurant menu. And Dan's catering business will certainly benefit from the restaurant's commercial kitchen—which is triple the size of and much more up to date than the cramped kitchen from which Dan currently operates.

3. Commercial Customers and Suppliers

A business you're currently buying from or selling to may also be interested in acquiring your business so as to gain direct access to your customers or sources of supply. Often referred to as vertical integration, the idea is that one business enterprise decides that it's economically efficient to control several levels of the production or distribution system. For example, a car manufacturer engages in vertical integration when it owns its own dealerships. Similarly, a retailer of archery equipment engages in vertical integration when it acquires a small manufacturer of bows and arrows.

To see how this type of synergy can work for small companies, consider two local businesses that have had a long-term and productive relationship. Berkshire Bakehouse, located in low-cost space in an industrial park, produces bread, rolls, bagels, and pastries for a number of commercial clients, including hotels, restaurants, and the locally popular Dora's Deli. Viewed from Berkshire's perspective, Dora's is a customer. Viewed from Dora's perspective, Berkshire is a supplier. Following a vertical integration approach, either can sensibly become a candidate to buy the other's business.

- Suppose Berkshire Bakehouse wants to sell. Phil Berkshire, the owner, might approach Dora, pointing out that Dora's Deli already buys more than one-third of the baked goods Berkshire produces. For starters, this means buying Berkshire's Bakehouse would allow Dora's to enjoy all the profits earned by the baked goods she sells. And perhaps, Phil adds, Dora could use the Berkshire brand, sales contacts, and distribution network to build up her deli business by selling her popular hummus, tabbouleh, and other freshly made products to hotels and restaurants.

- Suppose Dora's Deli wants to sell. Dora could approach Phil, pointing out that there's a large retail demand for Berkshire's products that Berkshire can begin to tap by expanding the bread counter portion of Dora's Deli to become a small bakery outlet. Berkshire can also use the deli as a testing ground to check out the potential market for new products.

One good thing about suppliers or commercial customers is that they already know a lot about your business. A second is that you have a relationship with them. Again, however, these potential buyers may not be actively looking to buy a business and may not even have considered the possibility. So to make headway promoting this type of sale, your job is usually to paint a vivid and detailed picture showing a supplier or commercial customer the advantages of their owning your business.

C. Special Concerns When Approaching Competitors

People with operations similar to yours may have a strong incentive to buy your business and may be willing to pay a good price for it. But they also may use the opportunity to gather information about your business in order to move in on your entrepreneurial turf. The un-happy result: a reduction in your profits, making it harder to sell your business to others. So if you approach direct competitors about the possibility of buying your business, always assume there's a substantial risk that they'll feign interest in your business for the sole purpose of learning more about your client base, your operating methods, and your business plans. In short, it's key to make sure that your competitor's sincerely interested in purchasing your business before you disclose confidential financial information. Here are some ways to protect yourself:

- **Provide only a basic fact sheet about your proposed sale.** See, for example, the sample sales sheet for the bed and breakfast in Section E, below.
- **Before you disclose more information, have the competitor sign a confidentiality agreement, as described in Chapter 10.** Be aware, however, that even a tightly drawn confidentiality agreement can't assure that you'll have legal recourse if the potential buyer breaches the agreement. That's because in some instances it can be difficult to prove that the buyer misappropriated your information instead of legally developing it independently. And in other situations, it may simply not be worth going to court because of the costs involved.
- **Ask for a nonrefundable down payment against the purchase price before disclosing your most confidential**

information, such as customer lists and pricing data. This way, if the buyer turns out to be unreliable, you have at least some money in hand to help offset any damage you may suffer.

⚠️ **If you don't trust a potential buyer, don't gamble.** It's far better to put more time and effort into finding a buyer elsewhere than to risk jeopardizing the financial health of your business by revealing too much too soon to an untrustworthy competitor

D. Marketing Your Business by Word of Mouth

Assuming you've exhausted your A-list of the close-to-home strategic buyers, you'll need to challenge yourself to look further. But before you spend money on ads or agree to work with a pricey business broker to seek out additional prospects, it often makes sense to tap the extended network of people you can reach through free word-of-mouth marketing—unless, of course, you feel it's crucial to keep secret your interest in selling.

Just letting financially savvy friends and business associates know that you're thinking of selling your business is a good way to start. Think about it—you probably have dozens of everyday contacts, each of whom could be the link between you and a buyer. For example:

- At his daughter's soccer game, Ed mentions to Nina (another parent who runs a prominent local business) that he's thinking of putting his vending machine business on the market. Nina, who likes Ed, tells Dave, one of the sales reps who calls on her business, about the opportunity. Dave, who is sick of traveling a three-county territory, calls Ed that night.
- Connie mentions her plan to sell her dry cleaning business to the 15 members of her book club. Edna says that she and her husband, who has just retired from the police force, may be interested.
- While Joe is volunteering for a local beach clean up, he mentions to Bill, another volunteer, that he's preparing his insurance agency for sale. Bill says his neighbor's daughter is moving back to town after a year abroad, and may be in the market for such a business.

True, the word-of-mouth approach is somewhat hit-or-miss. But you can increase your chances of linking up with a potential buyer by carefully targeting who you talk to. Like fishing, it makes all the difference to fish in the right pond with the right bait at the right time. If you plan to sell a bicycle shop, you certainly want to get the word out among people who like bikes, like business, and have the money to buy your shop. This might include talking to the president of the local bike touring club, who is obviously well-positioned to spread the word to any riding enthusiasts who might hanker to be around bicycles full time. Or if you have a profitable business driving seniors to medical appointments, supermarkets, and airports, you might mention your selling plans to the dozen or so midlevel managers at the assisted-living facilities and nursing homes where you regularly pick up your clients. One of them, who has a bit of the entrepreneurial spirit, may leap at the chance to escape the strictures of a large organization and become a business owner.

Since word of mouth is free, you have nothing to lose following this approach, except receiving calls from people whose only qualification to buy a business is in their own mind. To quickly weed these folks out, it's useful to prepare a one-page description of your business mentioning key terms and emphasizing your down payment and credit requirements. Whether or not to state your asking price is a judgment call. Note how the B and B example below hedges on this point.

Of course, if you want to keep secret the fact that your business is for sale, you'll only give the flyer to those whom you can trust to be discreet.

E. Marketing Your Business Through Advertising

There are lots of places to advertise your business for sale. But before you do, you have to be sure you meet two criteria. The first, and most important, is that you're ready to have everyone and his Uncle Ned know that your business is on the market. Even if you follow the common practice of advertising your business without mentioning its name, you can be sure that it will take many knowledgeable readers less than a nanosecond to identify it. And second, you'll want to be sure your ad is going to reach enough potential buyers to justify its cost.

1. Local Papers

For many small local businesses, nothing more is needed than a classified ad in the local newspaper—and perhaps in those serving nearby communities. People looking for a business to buy will likely check the "Businesses for Sale" classification in the paper and will see your ad. One bonus of classified ads in local papers is that the ad may appear in the paper's online edition as well.

In large cities, however, this strategy may be less successful. If you run your ad in a major daily paper, your ad may get lost in the shuffle and you probably won't reach your best prospects. In that situation, a better strategy is often to seek out local business publications, the regional editions of the metropolitan dailies, and community papers serving a specific area of the city. And don't overlook the possibility of advertising in foreign language papers. Immigrants to our country often arrive with extraordinary entrepreneurial zeal and see business ownership as an ideal way to participate in the American dream. And by tapping into extended kinship networks, new Americans are often able to raise the necessary funds. (But think twice before making an installment sale to someone who doesn't have legal status in the U.S. You'll have trouble collecting on the promissory note if the INS requires the buyer to leave the country.)

Whatever the paper you choose for your ad, you're aiming for a small, targeted audience that already knows where to look. For that reason, a classified ad will likely be more effective and appropriate than a larger, more costly display ad. Here are a couple of examples of how your ad might read.

> **TOY STORE.** High-traffic location. Top brands. Established clientele. Good profit history. Down payment under $50,000; balance over five years. Owner will train. Inquiries to P.O. Box 456, Centreville, NY 55555.

> **FULL-SERVICE PRINT SHOP—** photocopies, letterheads, booklets, flyers. Located in flourishing commercial district. Strong earnings. 25% down plus owner financing. Send credentials to Box 789, Daily Herald, 222 Herald Plaza, Sun Center, CA 55555.

Your ad needs to just hit the highlights: type of business, general location, and whether payment terms are available. You could also include a ballpark price (for example, "under $200,000 with $40,000 down payment") to help weed out people who are looking for something a whole lot cheaper. Listing the price isn't necessary and can be counterproductive, because any top price you mention will forever act as a ceiling over what you can ask for.

To try to keep things anonymous at this stage, you can ask readers to reply to a post office box or a box designated for you by the paper's ad department (but again, unless you're in a big metropolitan area, lots of folks will immediately figure out it's your business that's for sale). Or you can route phone calls to an intermediary—a friend or your lawyer, for instance—who won't divulge the name of your business until you're sure a caller is a good prospect. Another option is to ask readers to respond to an anonymous email address.

2. National Papers

You can best reach buyers on a national or regional basis through classified ads in the three main national papers: *The Wall Street Journal, The New York Times,* and *USA Today.* Often an ad in the regional edition covering your extended area will reach the most likely buyers, so there's no reason to spring for a 50-state ad.

3. Business Publications

Publications aimed at business readers may have a limited circulation, but they're useful because they're more targeted than other media. Business publications fall into one of two general categories.

a. General Business Publications

In several metropolitan areas, you'll find weekly or monthly business publications that serve an entire region. And your local chamber of commerce may also put out a publication that accepts advertising. (For a directory of state and local chambers of commerce, go to www.uschamber.com.) These publications can be surprisingly affordable and effective ways to reach possible buyers, since prospective purchasers will likely check them.

b. Trade Publications

You can also effectively reach the national audience calculated to be most interested in your enterprise by advertising in one or more trade publications that serve your industry. You're probably already aware of the specialized publications in your field, but if you're not, go to the reference desk of your local library and ask to see the *SRDS Business Publication Advertising Source*—a directory that lists thousands of trade publications, categorized by industry. To learn more about—and possibly order—this directory, go to www.srds.com. Another reference work is the *Gale Encyclopedia of Associations,* which can lead you to the publications of trade associations. Further information is available at www.galegroup.com. If you prefer to do online research, check http://dir.yahoo.com/business_and_economy/organizations/trade_associations, where you'll find links to a number of trade association sites. When you place an ad in a trade publication, don't expect that the ad will appear immediately. Although the publication may be put out monthly, it quite possibly will have a relatively long lead-in time for ads, such as three months after you place the order.

Some trade organizations put out regional and statewide publications—often in the form of a simple newsletter. These publications can be attractive places to advertise since they reach the businesses in your industry that are closest to where you're located. Also on the plus side, ads here can be dirt cheap, or even free.

4. Websites That List Businesses for Sale

These days, buyers of everything from books and CDs to cars and houses turn to the Internet. It follows that many websites provide places for entrepreneurs to advertise their businesses for sale (and some also have listings for people interested in buying businesses, which you may want to check out). Among the many sites that let you advertise for the sale of your business are:

- bizbuysell.com

For Sale: Gordon Glen Bed and Breakfast

Your Chance to Own a Profitable B & B

We're retiring soon, and are looking to sell our beloved Gordon Glen Bed and Breakfast—a highly successful business that's given us pleasure and profit.

Our B & B is located in a decorator-restored Victorian house in historic Gordon Glen. Set on a wooded and well-landscaped two-acre site, the house contains six spacious guest suites and ample quarters for the owners. The carriage house has been renovated into two additional suites. Local planning and zoning rules allow for the construction of a second outbuilding containing four additional suites.

Our B & B has received a 5-star rating from Metro Guide for five consecutive years. And the respected Romantic Inn Quarterly recently added us to its top 50 list. The food critic for The Daily Tribune called our breakfasts "Outstanding."

But most important: Our suites are already 85% reserved for the next six months on weekends and 50% reserved overall! We bring in tidy earnings year after year, based on our loyal—and expanding—group of guests.

If you like people and a relaxed pace of working, this may be the opportunity you've been looking for. Here are a few basics.

Price: Under $800,000.00. This includes the house and two acres, all furnishings and equipment—and our prized collection of over 200 scrumptious breakfast recipes! (Sorry, our cat Toby isn't included.)

Terms: We prefer a full cash buyout but will consider seller financing with a down payment of least 30% if you're a well-qualified buyer—someone with a strong credit history and who shares our philosophy of B & B hospitality. We'll need to be cashed out within five years, however.

Training: We'll stick around for three months after the sale (or a little longer, if you like) to show you the ropes and introduce you to some of our "regulars."

For a tour and more information, call: Ed and Suzy Swanson at 555-5555.

- businessesforsale.com
- businessbroker.net
- startupjournal.com (operated by *The Wall Street Journal*)
- bizben.com (featuring California businesses)
- bizquest.com
- bizseller.com
- bizforsell.com.

You can use a search feature like Google to find even more sites.

Naturally, some sites will be more effective than others. Select the ones that, in your opinion, will be the easiest for prospective buyers to navigate. It's a plus, too, if all initial communications can be handled through the site to assure confidentiality.

Some sites have listings of business brokers (see Section F, below) and "business wanted" listings—features that may be helpful to you.

5. Direct Mail

A direct mail approach involves putting together a list of prospective buyers— usually no more than 100 or possibly 200 names, and often far less—and mailing each of them a packet of information. Realistically, the odds of successfully selling a business with this approach are long, but very occasionally it works. If you plan to try direct mail, realize that compiling a good list is the key to success. For most—but not all—small businesses, your best targets will be carefully selected local businesses like yours. Start with the Yellow Pages directories for all the communities in your region, and then peruse as many other lists of businesses as possible. For example, see whether your local Chamber of Commerce will sell you a list of its members. These lists often divide businesses into categories, making it easy to identify the most likely prospects. Similarly, national and state trade associations may be able to provide you with the names of their members in your area. And sponsors of a trade show may be willing to share with you or sell you the names of businesses that have had booths at the show and perhaps the names of people who attended.

Since it's better to address your package to the owner rather than just the business, you'll need to do some further digging to figure out who the owner is. You can usually get this information for corporations and LLCs from your state's secretary of state office. Ownership information for partnerships and sole proprietorships should be available from the local office where fictitious business names are registered or business licenses obtained.

Spend some time preparing the materials you send out to be sure they're attractive and readable. In this connection, it often pays to get help from a talented editor and graphic artist. To help assure that the recipient doesn't toss your packet unopened into the recycling bin, use a first-class postage stamp and address each envelope neatly by hand. And, of course, it helps to include a cover letter addressed to a specific person and signed by you. Invite the recipient to call you for further information and possibly to set up a meeting.

Because under even the best of circumstances the response rate to direct mailings can be abysmally low—sometimes just one or two percent—you may also want to plan a follow-up phone call to some of the best prospects.

F. How Business Brokers Can Help Find Buyers

Retaining a broker to sell your business is similar to selling your house through a real estate broker. The broker then takes care of marketing your business, screening prospects, negotiating a deal, and preparing some of the paperwork— all of which can save you considerable time and effort.

But do you really need a broker? Probably not. Almost certainly, with the help of this book and your professional advisers, you'll be able to sell your business yourself. Still, there are situations in which it makes good sense to at least consider using a broker's services, for example:

- Your business is highly specialized or otherwise difficult to market and sell.
- You need to sell quickly and believe that a broker can find a qualified buyer sooner than you can.
- You have limited experience in business matters.
- You can't afford to devote the time and attention that's essential to selling a business on your own.

As you might expect, brokers typically work for a commission based on the sale price of the business—and some may require that you pay a small, nonrefundable fee up front in addition to the commission. The commission rate is negotiable, but it's relatively common for the rate to be set at something like 10% (or more) for a small business sale. The idea of paying a broker $25,000 to help you sell your business for $250,000 may bring you little joy. On the bright side, if a broker is really good and can find the right buyer quickly, that commission may be money well spent. Be aware that if you sign on with a broker and the broker brings you a solvent buyer whom you don't like or don't want to sell to, you'll probably have to pay a commission whether or not you sell to that person.

If you're not inclined to contract with a broker to handle the sale for you because you feel it's too expensive, there's a middle course you might consider, especially if you feel that your marketing skills are deficient. A business broker may be willing to consult with you on marketing issues for a modest hourly fee. This can be a fine way to pick up some marketing tips geared specifically to your business.

And while you're at it, you can also see if the broker is willing to act as an intermediary to receive inquiries about your business—again, for an hourly fee. This can help keep the name of your business confidential until you're ready to disclose it. The broker may also be able to handle the preliminary investigation of the most promising prospects.

For more on finding and working with brokers, including getting piecemeal marketing help, see Chapter 6.

Going Once, Going Twice ... Selling Your Business by Auction

Sometimes, a bidding war is what you need to get the highest price for your business. Especially if there are numerous interested buyers, a broker may suggest conducting a blind auction. Assuming that you agree with this strategy, the broker will contact the best prospects for your business, give them all the pertinent information, and let them bid. Many publishing companies, including some smaller ones, are sold this way. Restaurants, too, are often good candidates for an auction sale.

G. How to Quickly Size Up Prospects

When people respond to an ad, a word-of-mouth campaign, a personal contact, or even a referral from a broker, you need to assess how likely they are to become serious prospects. Most important, this means determining whether the prospective buyer has or can raise the necessary money. Otherwise, you run the risk of wasting valuable time dealing with people who are just curious or who don't have a prayer of financing the purchase of your business. And, especially if you're providing seller financing, you need to judge early on whether the inquirer would be able to make a go of the business so that you don't have to worry about receiving the installment payments. Finally, as emphasized throughout this book, you don't want to share sensitive business information with people who are—or may turn into—competitors.

When you're just starting a dialogue with someone who has responded to your ad or heard about your plans to sell in some other way, you may not be able to get all the answers you need immediately. But with a little effort, you can usually quickly eliminate most of the people who are poor prospects. Here's what you should consider requesting from an inquirer before you give out anything beyond very cursory information about your business:

- **Identification.** Most obviously, you need to know exactly who you're dealing with, so be sure to get the person's full name, address, email, and phone numbers. If you're contacted by a lawyer, business broker, or some other intermediary who refuses to reveal the name of his or her principal, just say no.

- **Employment, career, and educational history.** You're looking for detailed information into what the person is doing now and what he or she has done in the past. To get this it's often simplest to request a resume, just as you might do of a person applying for a key position at your business.

- **Why the person is interested in buying your business.** The reasons why someone is inquiring need to make logical sense to you. If an engineering professor says, "I don't know anything about business, but I like to cook and I've always thought it would be fun to own a restaurant," your antennae should warn you that you may be dealing with a kook. By contrast, if the owner of a small, successful catering company expresses interest, you'd be sensible to keep talking.

- **Preliminary information about financial resources.** How deeply you probe at this stage will turn on what you already know so far about the inquirer. You'll probably want to

require much more information up front from someone who works as a clerk at the local discount store than you would from someone who has just taken early retirement from a good job at a local manufacturing company. Again, the key is to get enough information to eliminate people with inadequate financial resources or skills, and not to try to do the entire sale in a day.

- **References.** If you still feel uncertain about the character or abilities or experience of the person who's inquiring, ask for references from employers, bankers, and business associates. At this early stage, you don't need to check out the person's life history, but you will want to talk to enough people to be reasonably confident he or she is telling a straight story.

Use the screening form below to jot down information on potential buyers.

Where to find the forms. You'll find a copy of the Potential Buyer Information form on the CD-ROM at the back of this book.

After the potential buyer has provided the basic information, and you've concluded from your conversations that there's a reasonable prospect of doing a deal, you'll want to dig deeper. Here are some further sources of information you might consider:

Potential Buyer Information

Name of Potential Buyer: _____

Address: _____

_____

Phone Numbers _____

Email: _____

Current Employment: _____

_____

Past Employment: _____

_____

_____

Education: _____

Business Ownership: _____

_____

Other Business Experience: _____

_____

_____

Reason for Interest in This Business: _____

_____

_____

Possible Cobuyers or Guarantors: _____

Financial Information: _____

_____

_____

References: _____

_____

_____

Comments: _____

_____

_____

_____

_____

_____

- **Going beyond references.** People the buyer names as references are almost sure to paint a positive picture, so, in addition to contacting the named references, you'll want to look further. For more balanced information, you can tap your own extended personal network to find other people who know and, if possible, have done business with the potential buyer. In addition, inquiries to former employers and colleagues may yield a wealth of information—hopefully positive.
- **Bankruptcy history.** You can easily check the federal bankruptcy court in your district to see whether the prospective buyer ever filed for personal or business bankruptcy.
- **Educational background.** If a person's educational or professional background is important in your field, ask for written permission and check with colleges and professional associations.
- **Going online.** Doing a Google search on the prospect may turn up some valuable information. Go to www.google.com and enter the person's name. It's amazing—and a little scary—to see how much stuff is readily available there.

Admittedly, it's a matter of balance. You don't want to be so guarded that you turn away prospects who might turn out to be ideal buyers. At a very early stage, you may even want to trust your intuition. But never trust it too long. Assuming that you proceed to discuss a sale with the inquirer, you'll want to carefully gather additional information before the deal is locked in.

For more on investigating a potential buyer, see Chapter 10.

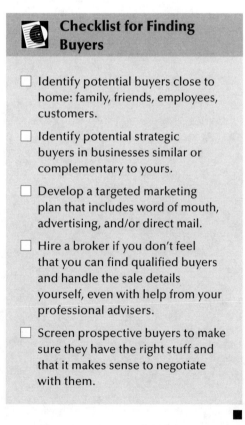

Checklist for Finding Buyers

- ☐ Identify potential buyers close to home: family, friends, employees, customers.

- ☐ Identify potential strategic buyers in businesses similar or complementary to yours.

- ☐ Develop a targeted marketing plan that includes word of mouth, advertising, and/or direct mail.

- ☐ Hire a broker if you don't feel that you can find qualified buyers and handle the sale details yourself, even with help from your professional advisers.

- ☐ Screen prospective buyers to make sure they have the right stuff and that it makes sense to negotiate with them.

Chapter 9

Structuring the Sale

You might think that once you've found a serious prospective buyer for your business and agreed on the sale price, you've accomplished most of your job. Not so. While you've taken a couple of major steps towards selling your business, you're still far from the end of the process. In the sale of all but the tiniest businesses, there are still typically many more core legal and financial issues for you and the buyer to work out and capture in a sales agreement. And until this occurs, you really aren't close to finalizing your sale.

This chapter covers the big five structural issues you and a prospective buyer will typically need to agree on. Before you begin discussions with a buyer, you should have some notion of how you'd like to see these issues resolved. Keep in mind, however, that in the give and take of negotiations, you may not wind up with everything you want.

- **Asset vs. Entity Sale.** Will the buyer be purchasing the assets of your business (its inventory, equipment, and customer lists, for example) or the entity that owns the assets (your corporation or LLC)? As you'll see in Section A, below, the route that you and the buyer choose can have enormous legal, financial, and tax consequences.
- **Lump Sum Payment vs. Installments.** Will the buyer write you a check for the entire sale price at the closing or, instead, make a down payment,

agreeing to pay the balance in installments over a number of years? As explained in Sections B and C, below, the answer to this question will do much to define how simple or complex your sales agreement is. If the buyer is able to pay cash on the barrelhead, you can, of course, leave out a long list of clauses dealing with installment payments and what happens if they're not made. But if your sale is typical, and the buyer will make payments in installments, you'll want to make sure to protect your financial interests. Section D, below, explains how.

- **Retaining Key Employees vs. a Fresh Start for the Buyer.** Will key employees stick around after the sale? Some buyers may see the current staff as an important factor in the decision to acquire your business. If so, you'll want to do your best to work out arrangements to keep them on board. But that won't be a concern if the buyer prefers to start with a clean slate. To learn more about this topic, see Section G, below.
- **A Continuing Relationship With Buyer vs. a Clean Break.** After the sale, will you work for the buyer as an employee or consultant? Staying connected to the business for a few months or even several years gives you a chance to earn additional money. It can also help assure the

buyer that the change in ownership will go smoothly with customers, employees, and other key people, by giving these folks a chance to gradually get used to the new regime. Still, you may prefer to cut all ties to the business so that you're free to move on to another venture or career—or, perhaps, simply to retire. For more information, see Section E, below.

- **Limits on Your Work Life vs. Freedom to Do What You Want After the Sale.** After you sell your business, will there be limits on your being able to do similar work elsewhere? If you plan to retire, go into a different line of work, or make a major life change, you probably won't hesitate to sign a strict noncompete agreement. But if there's a chance you may want to do something even remotely related to the business you're selling, you'll need to be sure any noncompete agreement you sign preserves that right. These issues are covered in Section F, below.

After discussing these big five structural issues, this chapter ends with some tips on how to keep an interested and qualified buyer from drifting away.

Later chapters (Parts 3 and 4 of this book) provide specifics on addressing the basic structural issues in the sales agreement and in related documents such as a promissory note, noncompete agreement, and employment contract.

A. Asset Sale vs. Entity Sale

When you think about selling your business, your first job is to understand exactly what you're selling. Surprisingly, this may not be as obvious as you first imagine. Especially if you built your business from scratch and have never sold or bought a business before, your notion of how a business is structured or even defined for purposes of a sale may not coincide with prevailing legal and commercial concepts. Let's start with the basics. That way, by the time you're ready to negotiate with the buyer and put together your sales agreement, you'll have a good working knowledge of the major ways business sales are structured.

1. A Business Is a Collection of Assets

Almost every business can be viewed as a collection of property we'll call assets— some that you can see and touch, and others that are more abstract. Here are examples of each type of asset.

a. Tangible Assets

Assets you can see and touch are called tangible assets. Here are a few examples:

- cars, trucks, forklifts, and pallet jacks
- computers, copiers, and fax machines
- repair and manufacturing equipment
- counters and other point-of-sale fixtures

- inventory of goods for sale (excluding consignment items), such as clothing, wine, electronic equipment, fishing rods, and so on
- office and other supplies
- desks, furniture, and rugs
- specialized equipment—for example, for a veterinarian's clinic or a tanning salon, and
- cooking and serving equipment (for restaurants).

b.   Intangible Assets

More abstract assets are called intangible. Here are a few examples:

- copyrights and patents
- trademarks (the name of a product or service)
- phone numbers for your business
- business name
- right to occupy leased premises
- trade secrets (confidential recipes, customer lists, business methods)
- accounts receivable
- favorable contracts with suppliers
- business reputation and goodwill, and
- employee relationships, including contracts.

c.   Estimating Your Business Assets

Whether you're selling the assets or the entity, compile a list of all assets—both tangible and intangible. Preparing such a list will help you to more accurately appreciate the value of what you're selling and will be something that the buyer will want to see. And if you'll be

selling the business assets rather than the entity, a basic list can give you a running start on preparing the asset portion of your sales agreement and any related attachments. See Chapter 13 for an idea of how the assets might be treated in a sales agreement for an asset sale.

2.   The Two Ways to Transfer Business Assets

Whatever assets make up your business, there are two basic ways to transfer them to a buyer: You can sell the buyer some or all of the assets themselves (called the asset sale method), or you can sell the buyer the corporation, LLC, or partnership that owns the assets (called the entity sale method). For the sale of most types of businesses, you are legally free to follow either approach. The big exception occurs if you run your business as a sole proprietorship—a one-person business that hasn't been organized as either a corporation or an LLC. Sole proprietors must always treat the sale of their business as a sale of assets.

a.   The Sale of a Sole Proprietorship Is Always an Asset Sale

If you do business as a sole proprietor, by definition you haven't formed a separate business entity such as a corporation or an LLC. It follows, then, that you personally own all the assets and that a sale of your business will always be an asset sale. This is true even though the sales agreement will normally mention your business's name, as well as yours—for example, *Margaret Chen doing business as Sunshine Daycare Center.*

In addition to its assets, your sole proprietorship may have liabilities—the debts your business owes and the legal claims that someone may bring against it. As a sole proprietor, you're personally liable for those liabilities, and selling your business won't automatically relieve you of responsibility for the liabilities you incurred before the sale. You may, however, be able to negotiate a deal in which the buyer agrees to take over and be responsible to pay at least some of the liabilities. Chapter 15 explains how. And if, in addition, your creditors agree to release you from any further responsibility to pay, you'll be completely off the debt hook.

b. The Sale of a Partnership, Corporation, or LLC Can Be Either an Asset Sale or an Entity Sale

If your business isn't a sole proprietorship, it's most likely a partnership, a corporation, or an LLC. A crucial distinction between a sole proprietorship and the other types of businesses is that the law treats a partnership, a corporation, or an LLC as a legal entity separate from its owners. Unlike a sole proprietorship, in which business assets belong directly to the proprietor or owner, when you do business through a partnership, a corporation, or an LLC, the business entity legally owns the assets.

You don't. And this is true even though you may own 100% of the corporate stock or LLC membership interests.

The key fact that the business entity owns the assets means that you have a choice in how you structure the sale of the business: You can structure your sale as either an asset sale or as a sale of the legal entity. In an asset sale, the partnership, corporate, or LLC entity sells its assets to the buyer. By contrast, in an entity sale, the owners sell the entire entity (for example, all the stock in a corporation) to the buyer, in which case the buyer will own the assets (furniture, inventory, intellectual property, and so on) by owning the entity. Certainly compared to an asset sale, where assets are listed and transferred one by one, in an entity sale the buyer has far less opportunity to cherry-pick only the most desirable assets.

If a business entity sells its assets, the buyer doesn't become responsible for the liabilities except to the extent the buyer agrees to do so. In contrast, when a buyer purchases your entity, its liabilities (debts, legal claims against it, and even future lawsuits based on presale conduct) are typically included in the sale and become the responsibility of the buyer. In an entity sale, you (the seller) are not personally responsible for liabilities unless you agree to be.

Or that's the optimistic scenario, anyway. In the real world of business sales, where everything is negotiable, the buyer may bargain to omit some assets from the entity sale (aging equipment, for example) and require that you retain a particular debt or liability (say, the balance owed on a promissory note given to a bank for money loaned to the entity). In short, to accommodate a fussy buyer, you may need to combine some of the major characteristics of an entity sale and an asset sale.

3. How Liabilities Affect the Sale

In addition to having assets, your business may also have liabilities such as debts it owes or possible claims against it that may result in lawsuits. How much your liabilities matter to a buyer will depend in large part on whether the buyer will be acquiring your entity or just its assets. Relevant sales agreement clauses to deal with these liability issues are discussed in Chapter 15. Here's an overview of the differences between asset and entity sales.

a. Entity Sale

A buyer who's thinking of purchasing your entity will be quite interested in learning what the entity's liabilities are. After all, the corporation or LLC that the buyer purchases will need to pay any existing debts and resolve any existing claims. These payments can be a significant financial burden on the business's cash flow. To reduce that burden, the buyer may insist that you pay some or all of the known liabilities

before the closing, and also that you agree to be responsible for any unknown or undisclosed liabilities that pop up later. An alternative route is to factor liabilities into the sale price: You can charge a lower sale price to reflect the fact that the entity will have to spend money on debts that already exist.

b. Asset Sale

A buyer who's thinking of buying the business assets rather than the entity is usually not as concerned about liabilities, which normally don't follow the assets. There are, however, a few exceptions to this general rule—situations in which, in theory, the buyer could become responsible for past liabilities. Fortunately, these exceptions rarely present a serious obstacle to the sale of a small business.

Bulk sales laws. A dwindling number of states have bulk sales laws on their books that apply when you sell the assets of a retail business—a business that sells goods from stock—for example, a store that sells small appliances. In those states, creditors can void the sale if you and the buyer don't give the notices specified in the statute. Giving the notices is filled with legal technicalities and is a big nuisance. If you're in a state with a bulk sales law, there's a simple solution: Just pay off the debts before or at the closing.

Here are the states that still have a bulk sales law:

California	Indiana	Virginia
Georgia	Maryland	Wisconsin

Chapter 20 provides suggestions for complying with bulk sales laws in these states.

Successor liability. Some states also recognize a legal doctrine called successor liability, which applies almost exclusively to manufacturing businesses. Let's say your business manufactures dangerous products. You sell your assets to a buyer and two years later, someone is injured by a product you made. Even though it's an asset sale, the new owner may sometimes be held liable. The courts look at whether the new owner:

- kept the same employees
- kept the same managers
- kept the same product facilities in the same locations
- continued to produce the same product or product line
- used the same business or product name
- used the same business assets
- continued the general business operations, and
- represented itself as the successor to your business.

When most of these factors are present, there's a risk that the buyer will be burdened by liability for the products you made. The buyer may be able to protect against this risk by insurance

Comparison of Mechanics for Asset Sales And Entity Sales		
Entity	**Asset Sale**	**Entity Sale**
Corporation	The corporation sells most or all of its individual assets to the buyer. The corporation normally retains the liabilities.	The shareholders sell their shares of corporate stock to the buyer. The corporation, under its new ownership, continues to own the assets and remains responsible for the existing liabilities.
LLC	The LLC sells most or all of its assets to the buyer. The LLC normally retains the liabilities.	The members sell their LLC membership interests to the buyer. The LLC, under its new ownership, continues to own the assets and remains responsible for the existing liabilities.
Partnership	The partnership sells its assets to the buyer. The partnership normally retains the liabilities.	The partners sell their partnership interests to the buyer. The partnership, under its new ownership, continues to own the assets and remains liable for the existing liabilities.

(which may be expensive) and by asking you to personally indemnify the buyer against liability claims (a topic discussed in Chapter 15). Fortunately, this will be an issue for only a few small businesses being sold, because most small businesses don't manufacture products.

4. Understanding the Tax Consequences of Your Sale

The distinction between an asset sale and an entity sale may at first seem oppressively technical. Either way, the buyer winds up with the assets of your business, so why do you really care how they're transferred? For one thing, there are different liability issues, as discussed in Section 3, above. In addition, the type of sale can make a huge difference in terms of taxes.

Whether you have a corporation, an LLC, or a partnership, there are almost always tax advantages to an entity sale. To understand why, a little background is in order. As you probably know, federal income tax laws provide for several different types of tax rates. In selling your business, the two main ones to consider are the ordinary income rate (which can be as high as 35%) and the long-term capital gain rate (normally, 15%). Naturally, you'd prefer as much of the gain as possible to be taxed at the lower long-term capital gain rate, which typically applies to the gain realized in an entity sale. By contrast, in an asset sale, the gain on at least some

assets will normally be taxed at the ordinary income rate.

In addition, another tax issue is important, especially if your business is organized as a regular corporation (often called a C corporation, after the IRC section which defines it), where both the corporation and its shareholders are subject to federal taxation. Selling the assets of a C corporation exposes you to the hazards of double taxation, which can be financially devastating. By contrast, selling the stock of the C corporation—in other words, an entity sale—results in only one tax bill.

You'll find more detail on the tax consequences of selling your business in Chapter 4. But unless you're unusually savvy about taxes, it will usually make sense to discuss your specific tax situation with a CPA or other tax pro so that you'll know in dollars-and-sense terms the exact tax consequences if you sell your entire business or just its assets.

5. Start by Trying to Sell Your Business Entity—But Be Prepared for Resistance

Unless yours is a sole proprietorship, it's normally best to list your business for sale as a entity. Strategically, this means that even if the buyer successfully negotiates to eliminate a particular asset or liability from the transaction, this will be an exception, not the rule. By contrast, in an asset sale, the buyer is likely to be tempted to regard your list of assets and liabilities as a menu that invites picking and choosing.

Not surprisingly, what's best for you is often not what the buyer wants. Typically, a buyer experienced in business transactions—or who gets advice from a savvy lawyer or accountant—will prefer to buy your business's assets rather than the entity. Here are three key reasons:

- An asset purchase can make it easier for the buyer to acquire only the most valuable assets of the business, leaving the less-desirable ones behind.
- The tax consequences resulting from buying individual assets may be more favorable to the buyer than buying an entity. As explained in Chapter 4, in an asset sale, it's easier for the buyer to start writing off large chunks of the sale price.
- A buyer who purchases a business's assets one at a time usually isn't responsible for the business's liabilities unless the sales agreement specifically says so. There are some exceptions to this rule, including product liability (discussed in Section A3, above) and environmental contamination claims. For example, a buyer who purchases a building full of asbestos may get stuck with the legal responsibility of cleaning up the problem.

If the buyer has more negotiating leverage than you do regarding the structure of the deal, you may wind up with an asset sale. But if your business is well-known in your community or industry, and doing an asset sale means having to laboriously transfer lots of intangible assets (the business name, goodwill, customer lists, supplier relationships, and the like), the buyer may be very willing to buy the entity. This is especially likely to be true where the buyer believes all problems are out in the open. And if your corporation, LLC, or partnership business has a favorable lease or other contract (to supply services on very profitable terms, for example) and that contract can't be assigned to a new entity without the other party's consent, a buyer may have a further incentive to purchase your entire business entity.

EXAMPLE: Excel Products Corporation signs a five-year lease for a building owned by Realty Associates LLC. The lease contains options giving Excel the right to renew the lease for two additional five-year periods at a very moderate increase. As the years pass and the neighborhood becomes far more desirable, Excel's rental rate turns out to be well below the market rate. Four years into the lease, Jean—the owner of Excel—decides to sell the business. For tax reasons and in an effort to avoid any hidden business liabilities, Tom, an interested buyer, first proposes buying Excel Corporation's assets, leaving Jean owning the corporate entity. But Tom changes his mind when he learns that if he buys Excel Corporation, he takes over its favorable lease, but if he buys just Excel's assets, he doesn't. After a thorough investigation that discloses little likelihood of hidden financial or legal claims, Tom agrees to buy the entire corporation. Of course, as an alternative Tom could have offered to buy just Excel's assets while also asking the landlord to separately take over Excel's current lease. But the landlord, who can rent the building for more if Excel leaves, is unlikely to agree unless Tom is willing to pay market rent.

B. Lump Sum Payment vs. Installments

A key element of any negotiation for the sale of a business is how, exactly, the buyer will pay the sale price. The two basic alternatives are for the buyer to pay the whole amount at closing or to make a down payment and then pay you the balance over a number of years.

1. Lump Sum Payment

Ideally, you'd like the buyer to present you with a cashier's check at the closing for the full sale price. Occasionally, this happens, especially if the buyer is a larger company buying you out as a strategic addition to its business. Even individual buyers with deep pockets can sometimes come up with the full payment, as would be the case if the buyer inherited a significant amount of money or received a chunky early retirement buyout. Another possibility is that the buyer has a terrific credit rating and is able to borrow the full purchase price from a commercial lender. Finally, some buyers enjoy the financial backing of a highly solvent parent, relative, or friend, meaning that they, too, can pay everything up front.

But if you find an all-cash buyer, consider yourself lucky. The big reason, of course, is that with the full payment in your pocket, you won't have to worry about what to do if a buyer who has promised to make installment payments doesn't follow through. In addition, getting all your money now, instead of receiving it in many payments over several years, means you'll have far more flexibility when it comes to your future investment or spending plans. Indeed, getting all or most of your money up front is so desirable that in many circumstances it may even be worthwhile to reduce your sale price if it will make such a deal happen.

EXAMPLE: Patti is in discussions with 30-year-old Milton to buy her pet supply business for $400,000. Milton says he'd like to pay $100,000 down and spread the balance over five years. Patti prefers to receive all cash at closing but doesn't think this is likely. But then she thinks about the fact that Milton is usually accompanied to their negotiating meetings by his mother Nora, a successful stockbroker. Realizing that Nora understands investment opportunities and guessing that she's highly motivated to help her son, Patti suggests knocking 8% off the price in return for full cash at closing. Nora immediately interrupts Milton and counters by suggesting a 15% discount. When Patti counters with 10% and Nora asks for 11%, the deal is struck. As Patti had guessed, Nora helps Milton pull this off by agreeing to become a coinvestor in her son's business. Her $252,000 investment together with Milton's $100,000 provides the full discounted sale price of $352,000.

2. Installment Payments

Unfortunately, the typical buyer of a small business won't be able to pay the full sale price at once. Instead, the best you'll be able to work out is a deal in which the buyer makes a down payment at closing and then agrees to pay you the balance, with interest, over a period of several years. The following section will help you decide on appropriate payment terms.

⚠️ **Crafting sensible payment terms may not be enough.** The hard truth is that if you agree to any installment sale—even a conservative plan under which you

receive a substantial down payment and the seller is obligated to pay the balance fairly promptly—you accept considerably more risk than would be the case if you get 100% of the price at closing. To learn strategies that can reduce that risk to the absolute minimum, read Section D, below.

C. How to Structure an Installment Sale

Assuming that you won't find a full-cash buyer, you'll need to understand how to shape your installment sale plan. Here are some suggestions for approaching this key part of a sale. You'll find detailed information on preparing promissory notes in Chapter 19.

1. Aim for a Two-Year or Three-Year Payment Period

Most typically, the promissory note will obligate the buyer to pay the balance of the sales price by making equal monthly payments over two or three years—or perhaps a bit longer. Each payment will consist partly of interest and partly of principal. You usually won't want to accept a payment period longer than five years because the longer the payoff period, the more problems are likely. The amount of each payment is simply what it takes to pay off the entire balance and interest in the time agreed. The calculations are easily arrived at by consulting amortization tables available online (including Nolo's website, www.nolo.com).

⚠️ **Set a realistic payment period.** If you need to have the sale price paid off in a short time, make sure that the business profits will support your payment plan.

EXAMPLE: Tracy has been trying for six months to sell her shoe repair business, when Nelson appears on the scene eager to buy it. Tracy and Nelson agree on a sale price of $150,000, but Nelson is only able to raise a 10% down payment. This would leave $135,000 to be financed under a promissory note that Nelson would give to Tracy at closing. Because Tracy is moving to a more-expensive area, she needs to get all of her money out the business within two or three years. But when she does the math, she realizes that given how much money the business nets each year, it's unlikely that Nelson—who has a family to support—can come up with this much, this soon. Much as she'd like to sell the business to Nelson, she decides it's better to wait until someone else comes along who can make a bigger down payment (thus reducing the monthly installments) and whose family needs aren't as pressing—or perhaps a buyer who can offer excellent security for the debt and maybe even a well-heeled cosigner.

2. Go for as Large a Down Payment as Possible

Insisting on a relatively large down payment (for example, 30%, not 10%) is one of the best ways to assure your sales transaction will be successful. Besides lowering the monthly installment payment (making it more likely that the buyer will be able to pay each month), a buyer who makes a large up front commitment has a clear incentive to work harder to make the business succeed. And a buyer who has more to lose if the business folds is also likely to hang in there longer if for some unforeseen reason the going is initially rougher than expected.

Unfortunately, despite these good reasons to insist on a large down payment, doing so doesn't automatically give you greater assurance that the buyer will make the installment payments as promised. This is particularly likely to be true where an inexperienced businessperson borrows a big chunk of the down payment from a third party. If, for example, to come up with a 40% down payment, Clementine, a naive buyer, borrows all of it from her generous Uncle Clem, she'll have to pay back that loan in addition to making the installment payments she owes you for the business. The obvious problem in this situation is that the business must produce enough profit for Clementine to cover payments on the third-party loan from Clem, plus the money owed to you, plus her own salary.

The down payment doesn't have to consist solely of cash. If the buyer is struggling to raise money for a substantial down payment, there may be other assets available to cover part of it. Maybe the buyer owns a sailboat like one you've been yearning for, a timeshare interest in a prime vacation condo in the Caribbean, or even a serviceable truck. If not encumbered by debt, assets like those could be transferred to you as part of the down payment. Similarly, services can sometimes be used in place of money. For example, a buyer who has home improvement skills that you lack may be willing, as part of the down payment, to repaint your house, build you a deck, or do other needed work in exchange for paying less cash. But if you enter into this type of deal, make sure the work is done to your satisfaction before title to the business is transferred.

3. Always Charge Interest

Since in an installment sale you're extending credit to the buyer, you'll almost surely want to follow the normal commercial practice of charging interest on the unpaid balance, even if you're selling to a family member or long-time employee. Think of it this way: If you received the full sale price at closing, you could invest that money in securities, a money market account, real estate, a certificate of deposit (CD), or even another business, so your capital would earn money for you. Similarly, it's reason-

able to look for interest on any portion of the sale price that's deferred.

Usury laws in many states cap the rate of interest that you can charge an individual (including a sole proprietor). Often, the maximum rate is 10% to 12% per year for individuals. (Institutional credit grantors, such as banks and credit card companies, have pushed through laws allowing them to charge higher rates.) It follows that as a general rule, if you require interest of 10% per year or less, you'll have no usury law problems. But if you wish to charge more, you'll want to check with a lawyer with small business experience.

D. Ten Strategies to Protect Yourself in an Installment Sale

 When to skip ahead. If you'll be receiving all cash at the closing, you can skip this section.

This section covers tried-and-true strategies you can follow in an installment sale to help assure that you'll eventually be paid in full. Using even one or two of these strategies will reduce the inherent risk of not being paid. But there's no reason why you can't protect yourself to the max by combining at least several of the suggested techniques. Think of these measures as a sort of tool chest you can reach into and use as needed. Your job is to pick the tools you need to be sure that the sale of your business really is as safe and secure as reasonably possible.

The specific forms (such as a security agreement) and legal language (including personal guarantee and attorney fee clause in a promissory note) you need to carry out the following strategies are included in Chapter 19.

Strategy #1. Know the Buyer's Credit History

A buyer's credit record is an excellent indicator of how he or she will behave in the future, so it's crucial that you learn all you can about the buyer's credit history and financial resources. A potential buyer who can demonstrate a lifelong history of repaying debts on time, all the time—or even better, of not borrowing frequently in the first place—is a far better risk than is a potential buyer who has a history of late payments, high levels of debt, or, even worse, bankruptcy, business failure, or a real estate foreclosure. You'll find more in Chapter 10 about gathering credit and other key information about the buyer. The point is, however, that in letting someone buy your business on an installment plan, you should put yourself in the same position as a bank that's lending money—that is, you should make it an absolute rule to lend only to highly reliable people. Or put another way, you should just say no to any buyer—including family or friend—whose credit

history is shaky, no matter how anxious you are to sell your business and how convincing the person is about having turned over a new leaf.

Strategy #2. Insist on the Buyer's Personal Guarantee

In many instances, the buyer of your business will be a corporation or an LLC—in some cases, one that's been formed just to acquire and run your enterprise. In this situation, the key thing to understand is that if only a corporation or LLC signs your promissory note obligating itself to make the installment payments, you'll only be able to aim your collection efforts at that legal entity if payments aren't forthcoming. Unfortunately, if the business is failing, this will likely be an exercise in futility, since many small corporations or LLCs will have few assets beyond those of your former business, which the new owners may even be siphoning away from the entity.

To avoid this unhappy result, you'll want to insist on the owner's personal guarantee of the promissory note. This, of course, is exactly what a bank or other commercial lender does on loans to small corporations or LLCs, because it allows a lender to go after the buyer's nonbusiness assets should there be a default in paying the note. If you insist on getting the personal guarantee of the people who own the corporation or LLC, you'll be able to seize their personal assets such as bank accounts and cars if they don't pay as promised.

Strategy #3. Have the Buyer's Spouse Guarantee Payment

It's also wise to seek the personal guarantees of the spouses of the people involved in the purchase—and that's true whether the purchasing entity is a sole proprietorship, partnership, corporation, or LLC. That way, in most states, the spouse's assets as well as property owned jointly by husband and wife will also be available to help pay a judgment if the business defaults.

EXAMPLE: Phyllis agrees to sell her dress boutique to a new one-person LLC formed by Kari: Smart Style Enterprises LLC. It's an installment sale, with a 20% down payment and the rest of the sale price to be paid over a three-year period. A promissory note will be given by Smart Style Enterprises LLC for the unpaid balance and signed by Kari on behalf of the company. But Phyllis also wisely conditions the sale on both Kari and her husband, George, personally guaranteeing the note. Since George has a good job as a radiologist, Phyllis knows that if the LLC has trouble keeping up the payments, she can look to Kari and George for the money. If they don't pay, Phyllis can sue them

as well as the company and get a court judgment against the couple. She has already established that Kari and George own their house and a vacation cabin free and clear (also see Strategy #6, below), and have other investments that could be used to satisfy any judgment. As a result, Phyllis can be reasonably confident that Kari and George won't simply try to walk away from the business if for any reason it does poorly. Having these additional resources available greatly improves the odds that Phyllis ultimately will collect the full amount of the sale price for the business.

Strategy #4. Seek the Guarantee of a Third Party

Sometimes, getting a personal guarantee from the buyer (and even the buyer's spouse, as well) provides you with very little additional protection. Typically this is because the buyer doesn't own real estate or securities or have a well-paying job or other source of income that helps make the guarantee meaningful. Suppose, for example, you're selling to someone who has no valuable personal assets beyond a few bucks in the bank, a five-year-old car, and a rented flat full of thrift shop furniture. If the business fails, the fact that the buyer signed a personal guarantee won't help. In this situation, your best approach is again to follow the approach of commercial lenders and seek the personal guarantee of a third party with lots of assets, such as the buyer's parents, a financially successful friend, or the proverbial rich uncle. Legally, this third party may be called a guarantor or a cosigner. While there are some minor technical differences between them, the legal outcome is normally the same: If the debt isn't paid by the primary signer, the backup signer is on the hook for it.

 Carefully check on the guarantor's financial status and credit history. Never believe a breathless story about how rich and successful a proposed guarantor is without carefully checking to be sure that the guarantor really has pockets deep enough to pay you if the buyer can't. Ask to see a financial statement and order a credit report. Otherwise, two signatures are hardly better than one.

Strategy #5. Keep a Security Interest in the Business

If you've ever financed the purchase of a car, you know that even though you became the car's owner, the bank or other lender could repossess the vehicle if you didn't keep up the payments. That's because, in legal parlance, the lender retained a lien (often called a security interest) on your car until you made all your payments. A similar legal mechanism is available when you sell a business.

To make use of this strategy, your sales agreement should provide that the buyer acquires the business assets subject to your continuing security interest in them. Then, to give legal effect to this provision, at closing, the buyer will sign a security agreement, and you'll prepare what's called a Uniform Commercial Code (UCC) Financing Statement. You'll then file the financing statement with your state's secretary of state (or other designated office) to create a public record that you have a first lien on the business assets should the buyer fail to pay. If later the buyer misses payments or otherwise fails to meet the terms of the security agreement, you can repossess the assets.

But even though it's valuable to have the right to repossess your business if the buyer doesn't pay, realize that taking back business assets will rarely make you personally happy or financially whole. For a variety of lifestyle reasons, you may not want your old business back. And even if you do, the buyer may have made such a huge hash of things that keeping it going is no longer viable.

Strategy #6. Obtain a Security Interest in the Buyer's Real Estate or Other Property

Another highly recommended way to guard against a big loss if a defaulting buyer ruins your business is to demand a security interest in other valuable property the buyer owns, such as a home or other real estate. Typically, this means the buyer gives you a mortgage or deed of trust as security for the amount of the unpaid balance owed for your business, which you cancel only after you've been paid in full.

It's best, of course, to get a first mortgage or deed of trust. If there are no prior liens on the buyer's home, there may be enough equity to pay off your debt. But in the real world, where most people already owe money on their home or other real property, you'll probably be offered a second mortgage or deed of trust. The key here is to understand the amount of equity the buyer has in the property over and above mortgages, home equity loans, and any other liens so you can assess whether a security interest in the property gives you any real protection.

To verify that the buyer owns the real estate and to determine the existence of other indebtednesses, you'll need to require an up-to-date title search and title insurance commitment. Then, following the closing, you'll need to immediately record the mortgage or deed of trust you receive to secure your promissory note at your local land registry or deed office (called the county recorder in some states). A title insurance company can help you with the details and, for a reasonable price, can provide an insurance policy guaranteeing that you have a valid first or second lien on the property. You and the buyer can negotiate about who pays the title insurance premium.

Strategy #7. Use Term Life Insurance as a Backup

What happens if the buyer dies before your note is paid in full? You may have to try collecting the money from the deceased buyer's estate—which can be a legal nightmare, especially if there's not enough money available to pay all creditors. To avoid this problem, consider asking the buyer to take out a term life insurance policy that, in case of death, will provide money to pay off the promissory note. This type of life insurance is relatively inexpensive and it can give you enormous peace of mind. If the buyer should die and the insurance proceeds exceed what's owed on the promissory note, the remaining money will go to the buyer's family—or whomever else the buyer designates as a backup beneficiary.

Strategy #8. Put an Acceleration Clause in the Promissory Note

To additionally protect yourself, insist on including what's called an acceleration clause in the buyer's promissory note. An acceleration clause says that if the buyer fails to make a payment on time, the entire unpaid balance of the debt becomes immediately due.

Including an acceleration clause in the promissory note not only gives you better recourse should the buyer default; it also puts pressure on the buyer to keep up with the payments, since even one missed payment can require the buyer to come up with the entire balance—maybe tens or hundreds of thousands of dollars.

Strategy #9. Include an Attorney Fee Clause in the Promissory Note

Any promissory note the buyer signs will likely have a large balance. It follows that if the buyer defaults, you won't be able to go to small claims court to collect the debt yourself but will need to hire a lawyer to file suit in a formal court. To keep you from unfairly having to bear this substantial cost and to put additional pressure on the seller not to default, you can provide in the promissory note that the buyer will be responsible for all expenses—including court costs and lawyer's fees—needed to collect the note balance. Be aware, however, an attorney fee clause will work only if the buyer is solvent when you move to collect your judgment. If not, the burden of paying your lawyer will still fall entirely on you.

Strategy #10. Use Escrow Arrangements Where Appropriate

When the business you're selling is a corporation or LLC and the buyer has agreed to buy the entity, it's wise to state in the sales agreement that corporate stock certificates or LLC membership certificates won't actually be turned over

to the buyer until the promissory note has been fully paid. To reassure the buyer that he or she will promptly get these documents when all contractual obligations have been met, you and the buyer can agree that your corporate stock certificates or LLC transfer documents will be held by a third party—an escrow agent—until the buyer has made all the payments. If, instead, the buyer defaults, the escrow agent is instructed to return the papers to you.

Here's an example illustrating how to use these ten strategies in tandem.

> **EXAMPLE:** Wendy, a talented and experienced optician, has built a profitable business at an excellent location featuring high-end eyeglass frames and the latest in lightweight lenses. Deciding to retire, she has negotiated to sell the business for $300,000 to Stewart, who recently became a certified optician. Stewart tells Wendy that to limit his personal liability, he is forming a one-person LLC to own the business. He proposes that the LLC pay 20% down and the remaining 80% over a five-year period. As her first step in reducing the risk of extending credit to Stewart, Wendy asks Stewart to prepare a detailed personal financial statement and, using that information, orders his credit report. The good news is that Stewart pays his debts promptly, but Wendy is nevertheless

concerned that his only assets are his home (in which his equity interest is only about $50,000) and $65,000 in mutual funds and bank accounts—most of which Stewart will need to tap for the down payment. Reasonably confident that Stewart has the skill and entrepreneurial drive to succeed in the business, Wendy is willing to sell on the terms he proposes, but only if Stewart takes several additional steps to protect her. First, since the promissory note will be signed by a newly minted LLC with no real assets, Wendy insists that Stewart and his wife Elaine, a veterinarian, personally guarantee the note. Second, Wendy makes

---

Learn to Say "Show Me the Money!"

Because of the high level of nonpayment risk involved, be particularly wary if the buyer proposes to pay for business with stock in another business or via an earn-out arrangement under which the buyer suggests that all or part of the sale price will be determined by how much your business earns in the future under the buyer's ownership. Here's why.

Problems with stock deals. In a stock deal, the buyer might offer to pay you all or part of the purchase price by giving you shares of stock in the buyer's corporation, which might include other businesses or assets the buyer claims are highly valuable. Unless you're approached by an established corporation whose stock is immediately saleable on a public exchange, you'll usually be wise to politely say no. Typically with the stock of a new or obscure corporation, the buyer is trying to engage you in what amounts to a shell game: The buyer ends up with the pea in the form of your business while you end up with an empty shell in the guise of unsaleable stock.

Risks of earn-out arrangements. An earn-out proposal is another equally problematic device under which a sophisticated buyer may propose that the price he or she pays for your business will be at least partially determined by its future earnings. There are a number of risks inherent in this type of transaction, including the fact that the buyer may prove to be a terrible manager, resulting in low earnings. But a more conservatively structured earn-out proposal may make sense if at least these three conditions are met:

- You receive a good price for the business exclusive of the earn-out.
- You stay in day-to-day charge of the business during the earn-out period.
- You receive a substantial additional sum if the business meets sales or growth goals you believe are achievable.

sure that the note includes both an acceleration clause acknowledging that the entire note balance will come due if Stewart is more than ten days late in making a payment, and an attorney fees clause making Stewart responsible for paying any attorney fees and other costs that Wendy incurs in collecting the debt. Third, because Stewart's financial resources are thin, she asks that Stewart's father (whose credit she has also checked) cosign the note. Fourth, she asks Stewart and his wife to give her a second mortgage on their home. Since the home is worth $350,000 and is subject to a first mortgage for $300,000, this means there will be $50,000 of equity available if Stewart defaults on the note to Wendy. Finally, Wendy requires that the new LLC give her a security interest in the business's furniture and equipment and its current and future inventory. That way, Wendy can reclaim the assets of the business if Stewart does poorly and is unable to make timely payments.

E. Doing Future Work for the Business

Assuming that yours is an installment sale, you'll have an important connection to the buyer at least until the last installment payment is safely in your bank. But you may also desire to maintain a more active relationship with the business as a consultant, part-time employee, or adviser. And it's possible that even if you're anxious to move on, the buyer will condition the purchase on your staying in charge—or at least involved—during a transition period which typically might last a year or two. Although you and the buyer can adopt a let's-wait-and-see attitude about the possibility of staying in the business, it's usually a better idea to explicitly make it part of your negotiations.

From your standpoint, there are several advantages to an agreement in which you continue to perform some services for the business after it changes hands. First, you may sensibly want to stay on deck until you're fully paid. Second, unless you have serious health problems or for some other reason no longer want to work, arranging for additional income may seem desirable. Third, you may have strong emotional ties to the business that may make it satisfying to stay involved at least part time.

Continuing to work for the business can even help temper the feeling of loss that you might otherwise feel about selling it. Few businesses succeed to the point that someone else will pay a significant sum to buy them without their original owners giving a damn. And just because the business will no longer be yours doesn't mean you won't get a sense of fulfillment from still staying involved—

in fact, helping the business achieve a successful transition can be very satisfying.

From the buyer's standpoint, it's often desirable to keep a seller active in the business, at least on a part-time basis, for a year or two. Not only will you be available to provide valuable assistance with details of the business operations— such as teaching the new owner the intricacies of the bookkeeping system or how to order the right kinds and amounts of merchandise—but more important, your continuing presence in the business can be reassuring to employees, suppliers, and especially long-time customers who may otherwise be ultra-critical of the new owner. The exception to this general rule is where a buyer believes your business has enjoyed less than a stellar reputation. Such a buyer may want to keep a distance from you, preferring instead to post a sign that proclaims, "Under New Management."

From a legal standpoint, there are two ways that you can arrange to perform future services for the buyer: You can be an employee or an independent contractor.

1. An Employment Relationship

In an employment relationship, you go on—or stay on—the books as a full- or part-time employee with the business paying you either a fixed salary or by the hour. As with any other employee, the business will withhold income tax,

Social Security, and other taxes from your paycheck. And you may also receive benefits, depending on the arrangement you negotiate with the new owner. For example, the business may pay for your health insurance coverage and offer you a paid vacation or sick leave.

If you and the buyer agree that you'll become an employee, it makes sense to sign an employment contract stating what you'll do for the business. This is especially true if you're counting on receiving continuing income. In addition to covering job duties, the contract should also include the amount of time you'll put in, how much you'll be paid, and what benefits (if any) you'll receive. You will also want to cover how long the employment will last—it can be anywhere from a few months to several years—and what happens if you want to leave or the new owner wants to cancel the arrangement before it's run its full term. Or you can sign a contract that doesn't include a date or conditions for termination. This means your employment is "at will" and that the new owner can end it at any time with no need to say why. This may suit you just fine, as it means you, in turn, have no obligation to continue working for an extended period if you don't get along with the owner. Another possibility is to sign a more creative contract with the new owner, one that ties the amount of your future compensation to the success of the business. Let's say, for example, you agree to sell your growing consulting business for $400,000 to a larger consulting firm that wants to move into your market niche. As part of the deal, you also agree to stay on as CEO for two years at a decent salary—plus a very healthy bonus if business growth exceeds the level you projected as part of your sales pitch to the buyer. Under a plan such as this one, you not only are assured of a decent price for your business, but you've built in a major upside that can substantially sweeten the pot. And from the buyer's point of view, you've demonstrated that you're willing to stake considerable future income on trying to walk your optimistic sales talk.

Chapter 21 provides more information on what might go into a written employment contract.

Consider the Effect of Social Security Rules on Your Decision to Continue Working

If you plan to work for the buyer (or another employer) after selling your business, consider how this will affect your Social Security benefits. Timing can be crucial. It's true that you can start drawing Social Security at age 62, but if you're still earning significant money from a job (such as working for the buyer of your business), your benefits will be reduced.

The Social Security picture is usually rosier if you hold off on collecting benefits until you're entitled to full retirement benefits. Beginning with people born in 1938 or later, the age for receiving full benefits will gradually increase from 65 until it reaches 67 for people born after 1959. Once you reach your full retirement age, your Social Security benefits won't be reduced if you receive additional income. In addition, if instead of starting to draw Social Security at age 62 you wait until you reach full retirement age before you start doing so, the amount of your monthly check will be higher.

Taking it one step further, if you keep working beyond your full retirement age and do not draw benefits, the monthly amount you'll ultimately be entitled to receive will continue to increase until you turn 70. True, it will take a number of years to make up for the payments you didn't take earlier, but especially if you have a substantially younger dependent spouse who will likely draw benefits for many years, it may make sense.

Recommended reading on Social Security rules. For more information, check the Social Security Administration's site at www.ssa.gov, and consult *Social Security, Medicare, & Government Pensions,* by Joseph Matthews with Dorothy Matthews Berman (Nolo).

It's possible, of course, that continuing to work for the business and receiving income for your efforts is no big deal—you can take it or leave it. In that case, you can omit a written contract and simply work from week to week. You'll be an at-will employee which, as explained above, means that you or the new owner can end the relationship at any time.

 Get legal advice before signing an employment contract. Employment law can be complex. A lawyer can help assure that the contract fully protects your rights.

2. An Independent Contractor Relationship

In an independent contractor relationship, you're paid by the assignment, typically either on a flat fee or time-metered basis. So, for example, the buyer might agree to pay you a fixed sum for working for three months as a consultant to the business for 20 hours a week. Or the buyer could agree to pay you a flat fee to be available to perform a list of tasks. Or you could be paid X dollars per day for each project you're asked to perform on an as-needed basis.

Unlike an employment relationship, if you're an independent contractor, the business won't withhold taxes from your check. This means that you'll be on your own for paying income taxes and the self-employment tax (which is equal to the employer and employee shares of

Social Security and Medicare taxes). And, unless separately negotiated, you won't receive health insurance, vacation, or other benefits that the business normally provides employees.

a. Complying With IRS Criteria for Independent Contractors

Before agreeing to an independent contractor relationship, an informed buyer will almost certainly want to make sure the IRS won't second-guess the arrangement and later require the buyer to treat you as an employee for employment tax purposes. Because the IRS believes that it stands to receive more money when workers are classified as employees (believing that a significant number of independent contractors fail to pay all the taxes they owe), the IRS may someday challenge the buyer to prove that you really meet the criteria to be considered an independent contractor— for example, that you have a great deal of control over how and where you perform your services. This means the arrangements for your work and how you get paid will typically need to be carefully structured if the buyer is to feel comfortable. Calling you an independent contractor will not, by itself, be enough.

b. Preparing an Independent Contractor Agreement

If you plan to work for the buyer as an independent contractor, it's crucial that you put the details of your agreement in writing so there are no misunderstandings about how much work you'll be assigned and how much you'll later be paid. Chapter 21 contains a sample form that you can use as a starting point in preparing your own independent contractor agreement.

There are several major topics that your independent contractor agreement should cover, including:

- **The services that you agree to perform.** You want to be clear about exactly what you're going to do for the business in the future. For example, if you expect to earn at least $10,000 per year for three years, make sure the agreement calls for you to do work that allows you to bill the business for at least that amount.
- **How much you'll be paid—and when.** Payment may be by the hour, by the day, or by the project. Perhaps your agreement will call for you to submit periodic invoices (a common practice for independent contractors) with the provision that you'll be paid within 10 days after an invoice is sent.
- **The expenses for which you'll be reimbursed.** Depending on the type of work you'll be doing, you may want to provide for reimbursement for necessary expenses. These might include travel, entertainment, communications costs, and supplies.
- **Who will own any intellectual property that you produce.** If you'll be creating copyrighted material or doing innovative work that can form the basis

of a patent or be treated as a trade secret, it will be important to clarify who owns the material.

- **How long the agreement will last.** Typically, you won't want to make a commitment that lasts longer than a few years, though there may be exceptions where a longer arrangement serves your interests.
- **How the agreement can be terminated.** You may want a provision that allows either you or the new owner to end the agreement by giving a certain amount of written notice, such as 60 or 90 days. But if you're counting on receiving income for an extended period, be wary about giving the buyer an easy way to end the deal early.
- **A statement that you're an independent contractor.** This may help the new owner convince the IRS that you're not an employee (which would subject the owner to additional tax obligations). But, as noted above, such a statement will not by itself assure that the IRS will classify you as an independent contractor. The working arrangement must in fact meet the IRS criteria—for example, the business owner can't have too much control over how you perform your duties.
- **Who will pay local, state, and federal taxes on your earnings.** In an independent contractor relationship, this is your responsibility; the

business doesn't withhold taxes from checks it gives you. Mentioning this in your agreement may help establish that you really are not an employee if the IRS or a state agency challenged the buyer about your true status.

- **How any disputes will get resolved.** You can provide for mediation or arbitration as a way to avoid going to court.

EXAMPLE: Clara, a certified commercial real estate appraiser, has built up a profitable appraisal business, Consolidated Appraising. When, after 25 years, Clara is offered both an excellent job teaching appraising at a business school and a contract to write a book on practical real estate appraising, she decides to sell the business to three loyal employees who are also appraisers. As part of the deal, they ask Clara to stay involved with the business part time so as to help maintain Consolidated's strong relationship with several large real estate brokers who send a large chunk of business to Consolidated. This suits Clara fine since, at least while she is working on her book, she'd like to keep her hand in the actual practice of appraising. Therefore, as part of the sale of the business, Clara and the buyers agree that for two years, Clara will be available to consult with them on business

issues and to review their more-difficult appraisals. She'll be paid $125 an hour for her time. She won't be required to provide more than 20 hours of services in any one month and will be able to do the work on her own schedule and mostly from her home office. She'll be guaranteed a minimum payment of $1,250 a month—10 hours worth of time—whether or not she is asked to work that many hours.

 For complete guidance on working as an independent contractor, see *Consultant & Independent Contractor Agreements,* by Stephen Fishman (Nolo). That book and accompanying CD-ROM will lead you and the buyer through the preparation of an independent contractor agreement for virtually any type of situation you're likely to face. It also explains the main differences between being an employee and an independent contractor.

F. Restrictions on What You Do Next: Noncompete Agreements

Anyone who buys your business is likely to want assurance that you won't promptly go into a competing business that will cut into the buyer's income. For example, if you were to sell your successful florist shop, then open a similar business down the street, the buyer would be rightfully be upset. To guard against the possibility of what the buyer will see as unfair competition, you can expect the buyer to ask you to sign an agreement (covenant) not to compete after the business is sold.

 Chapter 16 offers appropriate language for a sales agreement that includes a covenant not to compete. Chapter 21 includes a form and instructions for completing it.

EXAMPLE: Luigi has built a hugely profitable business, Bella Italia Ristorante, by selling pizzas, calzones, lasagna, and other Italian food prepared from old family recipes. Now Rosa is looking to buy the business (including its wonderful recipes), but she's concerned that Luigi may grow bored after a few months in retirement and open another shop in town that would draw away customers from hers. To guard against this, she requests that Luigi agree to a noncompetition clause in the sales contract in which he promises that for three years, he won't own, work in, or invest in any restaurant within 15 miles of Bella Italia Ristorante. Luigi feels this is fair, especially since it's unlikely that he'll ever want to be in the restaurant business again. Rosa and Luigi agree that $1,000 of the sale price will be treated as payment to Luigi for his agreement not to compete.

You may know that in a few states, including California, employers can't legally require that their employees agree not to compete in the future, while in most others, to be enforceable such agreements must be strictly limited by time, geography, and scope. The reason is that judges are leery of restricting someone's right to earn a living. But the situation is different when you sell a business, since the law takes the position that it's legitimate for those buying and selling valuable commercial property to bargain freely over covenants not to compete. So if you do agree to a covenant not to compete, you can assume that it will be legally enforceable.

Before signing a noncompete agreement, consider how much you will be paid for this agreement and how this will restrict you in terms of the following:

- the kind of work you can do and can't do
- the geographical area or where you may work, and
- the length of time the agreement applies.

A buyer may propose a very broad limitation on your future activities, going beyond anything that's reasonably necessary for good protection. If you're planning to retire or go into a completely different line of work, you may not have a problem accepting even unreasonably stringent limitations. But if you have a possible expectation of doing related work—or even the very same work in another part of the country—you'll want to bargain for something less drastic. Fortunately, there's usually a compromise you can work out that will meet your needs and those of the buyer. In the example above, Luigi might feel too restrained if he couldn't be involved in any restaurant for three years. But since Rosa, the buyer of Bella Italia, really only fears that he'll open another Italian place, chances are she'd be willing to accept his covenant not to compete only in this specialty. Accordingly, they could design a covenant not to compete which allows Luigi to enter any type food business where his offerings do not include a list of the twenty most popular Italian dishes.

Your noncompete agreement is a personal commitment you make to the buyer. That promise should be included in or attached to the sales agreement. (See Chapter 16 for appropriate language and Chapter 21 for a sample form.) For your promise to be legally binding, the buyer must pay you something of value in exchange. (In legal parlance, this is known as consideration.) A few dollars will meet this technical legal requirement, which is fine because it's normally in your interest to keep the payment for your covenant as low as you can. The reason is that any payment you receive for a covenant not to compete will be taxed at ordinary income rates. The big exception to this advice occurs if you're selling the assets of a C corporation (or an LLC which has elected corporate tax

treatment). In that situation, to reduce the burden of double taxation, you'll want to be paid as much as possible for the covenant and to reduce the amount attributed to business assets. See Chapter 4 for details about the double taxation issue. And be prepared to negotiate about this until both sides are satisfied.

G. The Future of Key Employees

Potential buyers have varying ideas about what will happen to employees of your business if a sale occurs.

1. Buyer Has No Interest in Keeping Your Employees

Some buyers won't be at all interested in keeping any current employees, preferring instead to bring in their own team or hire from scratch. This is especially likely in a small business that needs only a few workers. Buyers in this case may be thinking of bringing in family members, friends, or workplace colleagues to help run the business, making it counter-productive for you to tout the benefits of keeping key employees in place.

2. Buyer Is Undecided About Keeping Your Employees

Other buyers are primarily interested in your business's name, favorable lease, or other assets. They won't really care if current employees stay on or leave. In that case, your best bet is to simply introduce key employees to the potential buyer and let them size up one another. Then, if there's mutual interest in a continuing relationship, they can work out the details of any future relationship themselves.

3. Buyer Is Very Interested in Keeping Your Employees

By contrast, many potential buyers will be highly interested in making sure that one or more key employees will be staying on after the business is sold. This will be especially likely if you're selling to someone who isn't already running a similar business. In that case, the buyer may hope that a key employee—such as a head chef, chief mechanic, or sales manager—will stick around. One way to offer assurance to a buyer that vital members of the team will still be on board is to sign employment contracts with these workers, guaranteeing them a decent wage for a set period, in exchange for their promise to continue to work for the business for a year or more. In a contract of two or more years, it can make sense to provide for yearly salary increases and a generous bonus at the end of the contract period. This will give the buyer more assurance that your employees will honor the deal. A buyer is particularly likely to be pleased if, in an employment contract, a key employee pledges not to compete with the business for several years after the employment ends.

 Figuring out the noncompete rules in your state can be complicated. In most states, such noncompete promises from employees are legally enforceable if they're reasonable and supported by adequate payment. But in a few states, such as California, noncompete agreements which attempt to bind are not enforceable. You may want to seek advice from a business lawyer in your state.

The mechanics of how the buyer gets the benefit of any employment contracts you sign with your current employee will depend on whether you and the buyer agree on an entity sale or an asset sale. For example, if you sell your corporation or LLC, any preexisting contracts with your employees will automatically be part of the deal, and both the business entity and the contracting employees will continue to be legally bound.

The process is different, however, in an asset sale. Here, the employment contracts won't automatically be transferred to the buyer, so unless you specifically list them in your sales agreement and provide for transferring them to the buyer, you may wind up having to continue to honor the contracts yourself. (Make sure that you and the buyer reach an understanding on this issue early on.)

In addition, your sales agreement should specifically obligate the buyer to honor the employment contracts and indemnify you if for any reason you're ever sued by the covered employees—claiming, for example, that the employee has hasn't been paid in accordance with the contract terms. Remember that employment contracts are legal liabilities—as well as, hopefully, assets—and you want to require the buyer to make all required payments to the employees under all circumstances.

One additional technical detail in an asset sale: At closing, you'll list the employment contracts again in a formal assignment document. (See Chapter 20, for details.) That way, the buyer will have the legal authority to step into your shoes as the employer.

 Plan ahead to make sure employment contracts are assignable. All employment contracts you sign should include language stating that you have the right to transfer the contracts to a new owner. For good measure, this is another good place to include language relieving you of any further financial responsibility to the employees once the contracts have been transferred.

H. Keeping the Buyer Motivated

Before or after you and the buyer negotiate the main terms of the sale—or even while you're doing so—the buyer will want to check out many details of the business and you'll want to check out the buyer as well, as explained in Chapter 10. Throughout the negotiation process, you need to keep the buyer interested in going forward. In fact, you should be aware of this crucial need even if you've signed a letter of intent (as discussed in Chapter 11) or a sales agreement (as covered in Chapters 12 through 18). Indeed, maintaining the buyer's positive attitude about the sale is essential until the closing has been accomplished.

Understand that in most efforts to sell a business, a powerful psychological concern almost always comes into play. For lack of a better term, let's call it buyer's remorse. Even if you've worked hard with the buyer to structure the sale to everyone's satisfaction—and sometimes even after you have a signed sales agreement in hand—your deal can come unraveled for any one of seemingly hundreds of reasons, including death, divorce, and financial reverses. But surely the most common reason that business sales turn sour is that the buyer simply gets cold feet at the last minute and makes up a reason to pull out. Like trying to get a skittish fiancée or fiancé to the altar, it's even possible you'll have to become engaged more than once before you close the deal.

Part of the problem is related to timing. When someone buys a car or a house, the whole transaction is usually completed fairly quickly. The buyer doesn't have a lot of time for a change of heart. Unfortunately, the sale of a business is different in that it usually takes more time, greatly increasing the risk of buyer's remorse setting in.

To counter this exasperating prospect—and to greatly reduce the chances that the buyer will bolt just before the closing—you'll want to be a good psychologist and plan ahead to keep the buyer's enthusiasm up. Ideally, as discussed in Chapter 7, your marketing materials should include a clear business plan that shows how the business will continue to grow and prosper under its new owner. Building on this, you'll want to keep the buyer's eyes focused on your business's excellent future prospects even as you continue to work on—or even haggle over—the many mundane but important contractual details. Especially if a buyer starts showing signs of nervousness or fear (for example, misremembers a term already decided, doesn't return calls as promised, or suddenly becomes unreasonable over an inconsequential issue), you'll need to move quickly to try to reinforce the bright vision you've painted of future growth and profits. Remember, a buyer's burning desire to be an entrepreneur can be blunted by all sorts of fears, many of them irrational.

In short, it's your job to keep the buyer sufficiently excited about the prospects of becoming the owner of your profitable, growing business that his or her fears have no chance to surface.

During the sale process, if you experience any notable achievements—even small ones like a good sales month or favorable mention in the media—make sure the buyer knows about it. Although it may sound corny, you need to be your own best cheerleader.

☑ Checklist for Structuring Your Sale

☐ Reach agreement with the buyer on whether you'll sell the assets or the entity.

☐ Carefully structure any installment plan—for example, by having the buyer's spouse or third party guarantee payment and by keeping a security interest in business.

☐ Aim for a favorable package if you'll continue to work for the company.

☐ Make sure any noncompete agreement isn't unduly restrictive.

☐ Agree on arrangements for what will happen to key employees.

☐ Strive to keep the buyer motivated.

Chapter 10

The Investigation Stage: How Sellers and Buyers Check Each Other Out

Before your discussions with an interested buyer get really serious—and certainly before the two of you sign a sales agreement—the buyer will want to do a lot more than kick the tires and open the hood. Just how extensive the buyer's investigation will be typically depends on both the nature of the business and the characteristics of the buyer. For example, Ben, the savvy owner of the lawn maintenance company across town who is looking to buy your similar business so as to be king of the local turf, may be primarily interested in just three things beyond your routine financial statements: the terms of your major contracts with office complexes and shopping centers, the quantity and quality of your trucks and equipment, and the percentage of your customers who use your services on a month-to-month basis without long-term contracts. Armed with these facts and absent any major negative factors, Ben figures he'll have a pretty good handle on your operation.

By contrast, a newcomer who's interested in buying your bar-and-grill business may want to see piles of financial detail in order to evaluate the potential for profit and growth. Because this person doesn't understand the key business indicators that can predict future profitability, you'll likely be asked to provide three years' worth of monthly financial statements, sales tax records, income tax returns, and a raft of other material. As part of doing this, your job will entail educating the potential buyer about how your bar-and-grill business works.

A buyer's investigation will usually include physical inspections to size up the condition of your business equipment (as in the lawn maintenance example, above) and your business premises. In a retail operation, the buyer will also want to carefully assess the condition of your inventory. Obviously, if the buyer will have to spend money to upgrade the business space, replace old equipment, or acquire up-to-date inventory, this will significantly affect the negotiations over sale price. Not surprisingly, the buyer will also be interested in the growth of your customer base and the loyalty of your customers—whether they're happy and are likely to continue to patronize the business. But physical inspections and evaluations of customer loyalty are just part of the story. More likely, the buyer will focus on your paperwork, such as tax returns and financial statements.

This chapter (Sections A through C), focuses specifically on paperwork buyers will typically want to see and emphasizes the practical and legal importance of providing full and accurate information about your business. Be aware that much of the paperwork you share with a buyer will contain sensitive information. If the sale falls through, this information may give a competitive advantage to a buyer who competes with you now or who may decide to open a competitive new business instead of buying yours. There's often a risk, too, that a prospective buyer will divulge sensitive information to outsiders—again, with the potential that your business could be harmed. To help protect against the misuse of information the buyer acquires during the investigation stage, it's essential that you require that the buyer sign a confidentiality agreement (also called a nondisclosure agreement), as described in Section D, below. In such an agreement, the buyer acknowledges that you'll be revealing valuable proprietary data and promises not to misuse it or share this information with others.

But the buyer isn't the only one who needs to conduct an investigation before signing a sales agreement. It's a two-way street: As a seller, you need to learn more about the buyer. This is especially important if the buyer will make only a down payment on the total sales price, giving you a promissory note to cover the rest—the typical situation when a small business is sold. Clearly, you'll need to be very sure that the buyer has the skill, determination, and integrity it will take to succeed with your business. If you need to count on a check to arrive on time each month, this is a highly critical assessment for a simple reason: If the business fails because the buyer is a subpar businessperson or simply doesn't pay you as promised, you'll likely have to take the business back in a deteriorated condition. To learn the best ways to investigate the buyer's business and personal history in order to be prepared to determine the

buyer's ability to follow through on his or her promises, see Sections E and F, below.

Investigate full-cash buyers, too. While investigating the buyer is critical when you sell your business on an installment basis, it can also play a role in a sale in which you'll receive full payment at closing. Assuming that you've built a decent reputation among employees, customers, and others in your community, you'd hate to have that reputation of goodwill destroyed by a feckless successor. With that in mind, you'll want to take reasonable steps to assure that the buyer is someone who's likely to remain solvent and who'll treat people fairly. Otherwise, your business legacy may be tainted.

A. The Buyer's Investigation of Your Business

You're typical if you currently protect the privacy of your business's accounts, customer lists, and key proprietary information as zealously as you protect the privacy of your personal finances. Just as you probably don't show your personal income tax returns to your brother-in-law, next-door neighbor, or golf partner, chances are excellent that the profit and loss statement of your business is off limits to everyone except your spouse and any partners or investors. So it's absolutely understandable if you're nervous about the prospect of disclosing critical business details to a stranger who may or may not end up buying your business. And this is especially likely to be true if the prospective buyer is a competitor or someone else who, if ill-motivated, could use your confidential information to do you harm. While these concerns are perfectly understandable, sharing important financial and business information is an integral (though not necessarily pleasant) part of every business sale. In fact, the investigation of your business by a prospective buyer is so routine and expected that lawyers and accountants have given it the name due diligence, as in the phrase, "The buyer is doing his due diligence."

But just because you'll need to open your books and business plans to serious prospective purchasers doesn't mean you're required to share sensitive information with everyone who expresses an interest in buying your business. Chapter 8 explains how to evaluate prospective buyers before disclosing confidential business information. For example, you'll want to be extremely careful when dealing with competitors unless you're convinced that they're serious about buying your business and not just fishing for valuable information to help bolster their business or use to open a competing start-up. Indeed, if you have qualms about dealing with any prospective buyer, it's best to just say no to requests to disclose sensitive information.

As part of an investigation conducted by any buyer you're willing to negotiate

with, you'll need to be prepared to produce not only your own internal profit and loss numbers, but also those that you've provided to the IRS, as described in Section C, below. The buyer needs these data to put together a picture of how profitable your business has been—and how profitable it's likely to be under new ownership. What most buyers focus on first is how much money you've made in the last year or two and the trend of your earnings over as many years as possible. The longer-term profits perspective is particularly important, since the buyer is surely aware that it's often possible for a business to manipulate expenses to produce an artificial profit for a year or two (by reducing the number of employees or cutting the amount of new product development, for example), but that it's much harder to pull this off over a three- or five-year period.

Obviously, if your business has been losing money lately, the paperwork you provide may put a damper on the sale. But all may not be lost if you can offer a reassuring explanation that helps the buyer understand that yours is just a temporary downturn. Perhaps, for example, you've recently incurred unusual expenses to greatly expand your product line and it will take a while for sales to catch up. Or maybe you're caught in a short-term economic downdraft that's affecting your whole market segment or geographical community. But if you don't have a reassuring explanation and if the numbers show that your business is truly on the skids, the reality is that you may not be able to sell it right now—or that if you do, you'll be fortunate to get anything more than the value of the business's physical assets.

Turning over raw profit and loss data to a buyer may not do justice to the value of your business. That's why you should consider putting the numbers in perspective for the buyer through a process sometimes called a restatement. Typically this involves removing a number of discretionary expenditures from the expense side of your balance sheet to help the buyer see that your business is actually more profitable than it may at first appear. The salary you're paying yourself or a member of your family, for example, may be higher than what a new owner would need to pay for replacement services. Or you may have expensed several business trips, vehicles, or club memberships that, while legitimate business expenses, weren't essential. Restating your profit and loss statement is explained in greater detail in Chapter 7.

B. Honesty Is the Best Policy: The Importance of Full Disclosure

Acting ethically by giving a buyer full and accurate information about your business should make you feel good—something that's important in every truly successful business transaction. But making an honest presentation of all key facts about your business also has practical value: It's the best way to stay out of legal trouble. To understand why, consider that a buyer who can't make a go of your business may well look around for scapegoats. As the seller, and someone to whom the buyer likely still owes money, you unfortunately are well-positioned to become Scapegoat #1. This means you could find yourself named as a defendant in a lawsuit in which you're charged with fraud and misrepresentation. Or the buyer could simply claim fraud as a reason not to pay you the balance of the purchase price—in effect daring you to initiate legal action. Either way, if you've been less than forthright with the buyer, there's a risk that you'll lose. But by honestly and fully disclosing all material facts about your business—and carefully documenting that you've done so—you'll reduce to the absolute minimum both the risk that you'll end up in court and the risk that the buyer will prevail.

Here are some guidelines to help you stave off a lawsuit by an unhappy buyer and an adverse verdict by a judge or jury:

- Make sure everything you tell a buyer and all the documents and financial materials you provide are as accurate as possible.
- Put all representations about the business in writing so there can be no doubt about what you've told the buyer—and keep a copy

in case questions come up in the future about what you did or didn't disclose.

- Don't duck the tough questions. If the buyer asks you about some detail of the business that you'd prefer to keep out of sight—for example, how bad weather affects customer traffic—prepare a memo that tells it like it is. (And again, be sure to keep a copy.)

- Never tell the buyer that there's money to be made "off the books"— that is, income not reported to the IRS and other taxing authorities. People who say such things run the risk that in any subsequent lawsuit, a judge or jury will brand them as cheats and will find against them on other key issues.

- Just as you should make full written disclosure of any major problems when selling a house, it's an excellent idea to be up front in writing about all significant problems your business faces, especially those the buyer may not be aware of. And be sure you not only keep a copy of your disclosures but can show that the buyer received them.

Consider getting legal advice about disclosures. If you're uncertain about exactly what to disclose and how to phrase the disclosures for maximum protection, your lawyer can guide you through the legal thickets.

Here are some examples of the types of things you should disclose in writing:

- The city plans to tear up the street in front of your business for two months next summer. (See the sample disclosure letter, below.)

- Your main supplier is about to go out of business.

- A big competitor has signed a lease to move in a block away.

- Businesses in your field may suffer as a result of increased competition from similar Internet-based businesses.

Deciding how much to disclose can be ethically, legally, and sometimes even practically challenging. There's no need to tell the buyer that earthquakes, floods, and typhoons happen unless perhaps for some reason your business would be particularly vulnerable if one did. On the other hand, if the leased space the buyer will be taking over from you contains leaky pipes, you'd be wise to note that certain areas will be unsuitable for storing or displaying merchandise.

The sample letter below shows you one way to document disclosures that you make to the buyer. You should make disclosures before rather than after you sign the sales agreement—unless new information surfaces that you didn't know about before.

When in doubt, disclose. No legal expert can give you a complete list of all the disclosures about the external

Sample Disclosure Letter

May 3, 20XX

Linda Simmons
231 Menlo Place
Vinton, Missouri

Dear Linda:

I want to reiterate in writing some things I told you that may affect the operation of the Hanover Square Bookstore in the future:

1. The business owns the HVAC unit. It has failed three times in the last two years and will almost certainly have to be replaced in the next six months.

2. The landlord tells us that next year he'll be renovating the floor above the business. While I think there will be a minimum of noise and dust on the first floor where the store is located, the renovation could be somewhat disruptive.

3. The city will be repaving the street this coming summer. I've been informed that the street will be closed for five days, but the city says the sidewalks will still be accessible during the street closure.

I don't think that any of these things should be a major concern in your consideration of buying the business but you, of course, will need to make your own evaluation.

Please sign a copy of this letter and return it to me so I know you've received it.

Sincerely,

Stan Young
Stan Young
Owner, Hanover Square Bookstore

I acknowledge receiving the above letter.

_____
Linda Simmons

Dated: _____

factors that may affect your business. This doesn't mean you should keep a buttoned lip. Within reason, your best approach is full disclosure. That way if you ever end up in court facing a fraud or misrepresentation lawsuit, you'll be glad if you've followed the Golden Rule of selling a business: Reveal to the buyer all that you'd want to have revealed to you if you were the buyer.

C. Business Information the Buyer Will Want to See

The buyer's investigation of your business will go much more swiftly and smoothly if you anticipate and prepare to meet likely requests. Let's now look at some of the paperwork a buyer will probably ask to see as part of his investigation. If you've followed the advice in Chapter 7 on getting your paperwork in order, you should be in good shape for the buyer's investigation.

1. Tax Returns

Buyers (and the accountants who advise them) almost always ask to see the income tax returns for the business—usually going back at least three years and often five or more. The reason, of course, is that taxpayers have a powerful incentive not only to be accurate in providing numbers, but also to come up with a low bottom line to keep taxes at a minimum. But what's a legitimately low

bottom line for income tax purposes may not represent the true profitability of your business. For example, on your tax return, you may legally deduct certain items from gross income that are discretionary, not essential, expenses to running your business.

Maybe you enjoy travel. If so, you may have your business pay for travel to useful trade shows and conventions that just happen to be held near locations where the fishing or skiing is so terrific you can't help staying over a few extra days. As long as you allocate the cost of air travel and hotel accommodations—for example, between business and pleasure in accordance with IRS guidelines—your deduction of the appropriate portion on your tax return is absolutely legitimate. The buyer, however, may need to be educated that some of your travel expenses can best be looked at as discretionary costs that the buyer can choose to eliminate in order to fatten the bottom line. Assuming there are a number of restated items, your business may be substantially more profitable than it first appeared when only tax returns are reviewed. If the buyer doesn't get the point, his or her accountant surely will.

In Chapter 7, you'll find suggestions for how to prepare a restatement of your tax return figures. In your negotiations with the buyer over how much the business is worth, you should be miles ahead if the buyer sees that the business has provided you valuable perks which, in effect, are a form of additional income for the owner.

If you've kept careful books over the years, your tax returns and the figures in your restatement of tax figures should be consistent with any other business reports you give the buyer, such as your profit and loss statements.

2. Detailed Financial Statements

Financial statements showing income and expenses, especially if they're prepared on a monthly or weekly basis, can help the buyer understand the cash flow of the business. And this in turn can impart confidence to the buyer that your business is well-run. For example, if your records show that the cash flow is uneven—such as is often true for a campus-related business in a college town—the buyer will better understand the need to have enough cash on hand to carry the business through the slow summer months. Among other things, being sure the buyer is prepared (and adequately capitalized) to do this will help assure that you continue to receive payments on the installment note throughout the year, including slow periods. So, as suggested in Chapter 7, get your financial records in good shape early on so you can present the buyer with a well-organized financial history of your operation. It should go without saying that few buyers will be impressed if you hand them a shoebox filled with deposit slips and canceled checks.

3. Your Lease

For many businesses where location isn't critical, the buyer won't care about trying to keep your lease, assuming you even have one. For example, your business may consist of a website headquartered in your converted garage that very profitably sells American antiques from the Revolutionary War period. Or you may be an electrician, plumber, or contractor operating on a month-to-month tenancy from low-cost digs that few customers ever visit.

But if your business is more location-sensitive and you operate under an existing lease—as would normally be true of a restaurant or retail business—the buyer will surely want to closely examine the lease, which will contain essential information such as:

- the length of your tenancy
- whether there are options that allow you or a new owner to renew the lease for additional time periods and, if so, for how long, for how much money, and under what additional circumstances
- the rent
- other tenant costs such as property taxes, insurance premiums, utility bills, and repair and maintenance expenses, and
- landlord and tenant responsibilities.

Beyond these basics, a key issue is almost always whether the lease requires the landlord's consent in order for the buyer to take over and continue to run the business in the same space. This is less likely to be a problem when you're selling the entity rather than the assets. That's because your existing corporation or LLC will continue to be the tenant, which means that there's no assignment of the lease. The entity was the tenant when the lease was signed and will continue to be the tenant after the sale. But some leases to a corporation or LLC do nevertheless require the landlord's consent when the business gets new owners—or perhaps when 50% or more of the ownership interests change hands. If your business is a corporation or an LLC, and your lease doesn't say anything about getting the landlord's consent if someone buys the entity, you don't have to be concerned about whether or not the landlord can object to a change in the ownership of business.

There are a few different ways that a lease may deal with the issue of whether a new business owner can continue as the tenant under the former owner's lease—an issue that's more likely to be of concern in an asset sale than in an entity sale. The following sections discuss the principal types of lease clauses.

Chapter 7 explains how to add value to your lease before negotiating with a specific buyer—for example, by negotiating an extension on a soon-to-expire lease for a few years.

a. Can't Assign Without Landlord's Consent

The lease may simply and clearly say that you can't assign it, or turn the space over to anyone else, without the landlord's written consent. If yours is a tenant-friendly lease, it may go on to say that the landlord won't unreasonably withhold that consent. Even without that language, courts in many states will rule that the landlord must be reasonable. But unfortunately, even a landlord who has an obligation to be reasonable under the lease or according to state law still has a fair measure of discretion. So if a landlord's consent is necessary, it will almost always make sense to talk to the landlord in advance to try to agree on a reasonable standard for approving a new tenant. And if you've lined up a specific buyer, so much the better. Often a landlord will agree to an assignment if the buyer has business credentials strong enough to make it very likely that the rent will be paid promptly and the new owner won't do anything to diminish the value of the property. In some instances, you may want to propose—or be ready to agree to—a small rent increase as a carrot for the landlord to accept the new owner.

EXAMPLE: Tom, a sole proprietor, owns a profitable sports paraphernalia shop located near a PAC 10 football stadium in a building that Tom leases from Franz. Just before putting his business up for sale, Tom exercises an option to renew his lease for an additional five years at a rent of $2,000 a month. Since the rent is 40% below the current market rate, Tom enjoys a good deal. Unfortunately, the lease specifically prohibits an assignment to a new owner without the landlord's consent—and the courts in Tom's state haven't ruled on whether a landlord needs to be reasonable in deciding whether or not to give that consent. A well-financed partnership wants to buy the business from Tom, but the partners are concerned about being able to take over the lease. To encourage the landlord to give his consent to the partnership (which in all respects would be an ideal tenant), Tom arranges a meeting so Franz can meet the partners. At the meeting, Franz quickly realizes that the partnership would make a first-class tenant, and rather than scare the partnership away with a demand for full-market rent, he proposes that the rent be increased to $2,400 a month for the remainder of the lease. This modest increase is acceptable to the partnership in return for Franz's consent to the lease assignment.

b. Can't Assign, Period

The lease may flat out say you can't assign it. In most states, that prohibition is legally binding. The landlord, of course, is free to waive that provision, so it can't hurt to discuss the issue. Again, faced with a responsible new tenant who's ready to take over and perhaps even agree to a modest rent increase, the landlord may say, "Fine, go ahead." If you don't have a specific buyer yet, you can give the landlord a heads-up that you're looking for one and perhaps learn what the landlord's requirements are. Again, in an entity sale, this may not be a concern, since the entity continues to be the tenant and there's no assignment of the lease. But some leases anticipate this situation and state that if 50% or more of the entity ownership changes, the no-assignment clause applies.

c. Nothing Said on the Subject

The lease may not say anything on the subject of whether or not you can assign it to a new tenant. In most states, you'd be free to assign the lease to your buyer. But even then, it's still a good idea to get the landlord involved and hopefully cooperative early in the process.

d. How to Assign Your Lease

In addition to being sure your lease is assignable, you also need to focus on a second important legal issue. This involves studying your lease to see if there's anything in it that releases you from personal responsibility for the rent if a new owner takes over the business. In most states, even those where you have the right to assign the lease, you may still be liable for paying the rent and meeting other obligations under the lease if the new occupant fails to do so. So if the lease doesn't specify that you'll no longer be liable to the landlord in case of an assignment, your safest course of action is to negotiate with the landlord for such a release. Otherwise, it's likely that you'll continue to be on the hook—in effect, guaranteeing to the landlord that the folks who bought your business will keep on paying the rent. See Chapter 17, which explains how you can make the sale contingent on getting the landlord's consent to a lease assignment. The contingency can also refer to the landlord releasing you from personal responsibility once the closing occurs.

 For more on lease clauses and assignments, see *Negotiate the Best Lease for Your Business,* by Janet Portman and Fred Steingold (Nolo).

4. Paperwork Concerning Real Estate Ownership

While most small businesses rent the space they occupy, a significant number own their own building and perhaps even some surrounding land. If that's your situation and you're selling your building along with the business, you will need to prepare detailed paperwork related to the building. Because real estate laws and procedures vary greatly from state

to state (and many business owners establish separate legal entities to own real estate), this book can't provide in-depth information covering the sale of a building or other real estate. You'll need to seek guidance from a lawyer who's had experience with the transfer of real estate in the place where your business is located.

 For an introduction to the legal side of commercial real estate sales, see *A Practical Guide to Real Estate Practice,* by Joshua Stein (ALI-ABA), which you can order at www.ali-aba.org/aliaba/BK12.htm. Another useful resource is *A Practical Guide to Commercial Real Estate Transactions,* by Gregory Stein and others (ABA Publishing), which you can order at www.abanet.org. Also, check with the continuing legal education (CLE) organization in your state for any state-specific publications that may be available.

But regardless of your state, your first job will be to show the buyer clear evidence that you do own the building—usually in the form of a deed, an existing title insurance policy, or a recent title search prepared by a title insurance company. Of course, it's a good idea at this stage to alert the buyer to all mortgages, deeds of trust, or other liens or debts that may presently affect the title. They'll surface shortly anyhow when the title company does a careful search in preparing a "commitment" for a new title insurance policy to be issued in the buyer's name. The commitment is a document that spells out what needs to be done legally to transfer ownership of the building to the buyer. For example, because of the due-on-sale clause in a mortgage or the presence of a lien stemming from a recent lawsuit, you may need to pay off a mortgage loan or other lien at or before closing.

Because of the fear of lawsuits from asbestos, lead, and other environmental hazards, most savvy buyers will also want to see a Phase I environmental study. If you haven't already done so, you might want to order one to expedite your deal. See Chapter 7 for more details on these environmental studies.

5. Other Contracts

A lease for business space is just one type of important contract your business is likely to have. Others may include:

- equipment leases for cars, trucks, computers, phone systems, photocopiers, and machines used for manufacturing or repair
- contracts with suppliers—for example, a contract with a company that supplies chemicals for your dry cleaning business
- contracts to supply goods or services to customers or clients—for example, a contract that requires your heating and cooling company to inspect and maintain a large corporation's HVAC systems, or

- employment contracts with a few key employees.

If contracts such as these exist—and especially if they are important to your business and its operations—the buyer will expect to see them. This is especially true if the buyer is purchasing your entire business entity (and not just its assets) and therefore will be bound by or will receive the benefits of your contracts. Again, full disclosure is essential. Of course, a buyer will be delighted to find that some or perhaps even many of your contracts reflect favorable terms. This would be true if the buyer will inherit an equipment lease with payments well below current market rates, or a contract to provide goods or services to a customer or client for an amount that produces a good profit.

On the other side of the coin, a potential buyer will be dismayed to learn about disadvantageous contracts—for example, one that obligates your business to make hefty payments for equipment that's no longer needed or to provide goods or services to others at a low price. But the fact that you may find a particular contract to be burdensome is never a reason to hide it—just the opposite, because your failure to mention such agreements as part of a sale can often amount to fraud.

This section looks at how the transfer of business contracts works, keeping in mind the distinction between an entity sale and an asset sale. As explained in

Chapter 9 and elsewhere, the buyer acquires the entity itself such as the stock of a corporation or the membership interests in an LLC; the entity continues to own the assets and be responsible for business liabilities. But in an asset sale, all or most business property is transferred to the buyer, who may also assume specific liabilities, while you retain ownership of the empty—or mostly empty—corporate or LLC shell.

a.   Transferring Contracts in an Entity Sale

In the sale of a corporation or an LLC, the contracts usually go along with the business as a matter of law. With no need for separate paperwork, the business entity, albeit under new ownership, gets the benefit of, and bears the burdens of, the contracts the company signed under your ownership. However, there are two situations in which contract may not remain valid in an entity sale:

- The contract itself says that it will be or can be terminated if the corporation or LLC changes ownership. Keep in mind, however, that the law in some states nevertheless requires the other party to the contract to be reasonable in deciding whether or not to deal with your company under new ownership.
- The contract involves the performance of personal services that require special skills, so that it's clear that the contract is tied to the services

of a specific person. For example, if you're an architect and someone hires your LLC to design an office building for them, you're normally not free to transfer the contract to an architect who buys your practice without the consent of the person who retained your services.

EXAMPLE: Marge and Phil are the sole owners and employees of Web Eyes LLC, a small ad agency that writes ads for companies that run websites. They have a two-year contract with Topside Corporation which, for a substantial fee, obligates Marge and Phil to write a series of ads each month for Topside's website. Halfway through the contract, Marge and Phil sell their LLC to Wendy. Topside may decide not to honor the contract now that Wendy is the owner and is writing the ads. Topside signed up to get the special skills of Marge and Phil—and not the unknown skills of an unknown buyer.

While typically there's no legal requirement that the buyer notify vendors, suppliers, and customers that the entity is now under new ownership, it usually makes sense for you and the new owner to give the other parties a heads-up so that the transition is smooth. Especially on major contracts where the other party may be nervous about an unannounced substitution, you'll want to put energy into convincing your suppliers and customers that the new owner is experienced and equipped to honor all existing obligations.

b. Transferring Contracts in an Asset Sale

If you're selling the assets of your business, the basic rule is that there is no automatic legal right to transfer existing contracts to the new owner. In fact, most commercial contracts contain a clause requiring consent before there can be an assignment. So in most situations, you'll not only need to formally transfer each contract by an assignment document, but you'll also need to obtain the written permission of the other party to the transfer. (Chapter 20 explains how.) If the contract doesn't require permission, you're free to transfer it—unless the contract clearly contemplates the rendering of services by a specific person, as in an entity sale, as explained above.

Assuming there's no clause requiring consent to assignment and the contract doesn't involve personal services, you're free to transfer a contract so that the buyer is able to perform it and reap its benefit. For example, you transfer a contract allowing you to purchase services at a favorable price to the buyer. So far, so good, but you also need to know that transferring a contract doesn't automatically relieve your corporation or your LLC from its obligations. The other party may still be able to hold your company liable if something goes wrong in the perfor-

mance of the contract—and even worse, you may still be personally liable if you personally guaranteed performance. Let's say you have a snow removal business that you run as a sole proprietorship—which means you're personally responsible for all business obligations. Let's say, as well, that you have a winter-long contract to remove snow from the walkways and parking areas at Miller Cove Apartments for $3,000. Finally, let's say that in late October, before the first snowfall, you sell your business to Nancy and transfer the Miller Cove contract to her. If Nancy drops the ball and Miller Cove has to hire another contractor in November who charges $5,000 for the season, Miller Cove can sue you for the $2,000 difference. Transferring the contract to Nancy doesn't get you off the hook.

It's important to realize that in an asset sale a buyer is going to want to take over favorable contracts and reject burdensome ones. Fine—now you and the buyer have some negotiating to do. As you should now see, larger problems are likely to develop vis-à-vis third parties. If a contract is favorable to your business, the other party to the contract—such as Miller Cove in the above example—is likely to try to end it as early as possible. Assuming the contract has a no assignment clause, this means Miller Cove probably won't agree to allow the person who purchases your business's assets to take over the contract, unless it is modified to better reflect current business realities.

At any rate, during the investigation stage you'll want to put your hands on, and organize, all existing contracts. You can then analyze the transfer or assignment situation to decide whether you need to contact the other contracting party about keeping the contract in force with a new owner. If you decide that contacting the other party is required or appropriate, it's usually best to start out with a phone call or meeting in which you explain that you are selling your business and you would like to transfer the contract in question to the new owner. If the other party is willing to stick with the new owner and completely release you from any future liability, get it in writing. Usually a letter will do, but the buyer may feel more comfortable with a formal agreement that amends the contract. And, as mentioned above, sometimes negotiation is necessary to make the transfer possible. The other party may say: "I don't mind if Joe takes over the contract, but I want you to remain responsible if he doesn't perform," or "Fine, but Sue will have to agree to pay 10% more."

If a contract is important to the person buying your business, you may need to wheel and deal a bit to keep the contract alive.

6. Information About Accounts Receivable

Lots of businesses conduct important business dealings without formal written documents. This would be the case, for example, if your business ships orders expecting to be paid in 90 days (typically in this situation you may have no more than records of order and shipment). If the buyer expects to receive payment for orders you shipped before closing, the buyer will surely want to review these accounts carefully so as to be reasonably assured payment will be forthcoming.

To facilitate this review, you'll typically need to provide the buyer with information about what is called the "aging" of each account (how long it has previously taken for that customer to pay, such as 30, 60, or 90 days). Where customers reliably pay on time, the buyer normally will be willing to step into your legal shoes. But for accounts that have a history of paying late, or paying only after repeated dunning, you may have to discount the sale price. Or you and the buyer may agree to delete those accounts from the sale entirely rather than negotiate with the seller to accept them at a lower price.

Chapter 14 explains how you can deal with accounts receivable in the sales agreement.

 Collect dicey accounts before you sell. If you have a couple of customers who can be difficult to collect from, make sure their accounts are paid up prior to sale. In an extreme case, you may even want to write off a very old debt and drop the customer. That way, you avoid the prospect of a wormy apple or two causing the buyer to suspect that your entire barrel of accounts receivable is somehow tainted.

7. Corporate or LLC Records

If you're selling the business entity—not just the assets of the business—the buyer and the buyer's lawyer will also want to see your records concerning the entity itself. (For more on why this is true and how sales are typically structured, see Chapter 7.)

a. Sale of a Corporation

Before purchasing the stock of your corporation, the buyer will want to examine your corporate record book, which should contain such things as your original incorporation papers (called articles of incorporation in most states), documents concerning registration of your business names, and any trademarks, bylaws, list of shareholders, minutes of board of directors' meetings, or written documents (called consents) showing legal actions taken by shareholders and directors on paper in the absence of a physical meeting. The buyer may also want to see copies of the annual reports you've filed with the state authorities.

If, like some small business owners, you haven't created any corporate minutes, board resolutions, or written consents to actions taken without a meeting since the day you formed the corporation, you'll have some catching up to do. At the very

least, you should create records of the actions usually taken at annual meetings of shareholders and directors. At a minimum, your shareholders' annual meeting records should document the election of people to serve on the board of directors. Similarly, the board of directors' annual meeting records should document the election of officers. And you should be able to present records of any important corporate decisions customarily taken by the board, such as leasing real property or borrowing money.

Fortunately, there's a perfectly legal and accepted way to create current records for actions that should have been taken at meetings that never took place: Simply prepare current written documents (consents) that ratify (approve) past activities. Let's say, for example, that your corporate shareholders didn't hold an annual shareholders' or directors' meeting for the last three years and didn't sign timely written consents in place of these meetings. To fill in this gap, have your current shareholders sign a "Written Consent in Lieu of Shareholders' Annual Meetings" for the years in question. The written consent might state that your shareholders acknowledge that Joe Brown and Mary White were selected to serve as the corporate directors for 2003, 2004, and 2005 and that the shareholders are ratifying the services of these two as the corporate directors for those years. You'd then put the current date on the written consent. You can prepare a similar written consent for the directors to sign regarding the corporate officers and any other major corporate decisions that you'd like to ratify now.

 Get help to create corporate records. To learn more about corporate records, see *The Corporate Records Handbook: Meetings, Minutes, & Resolutions,* by Anthony Mancuso (Nolo). This book explains the kinds of corporate decisions that should be documented through minutes or written consents and shows you exactly how to do it. And just as important, it shows you how to legally fix holes in your corporate records.

b. Sale of a Limited Liability Company

If you do business as an LLC, you will technically be selling your membership interest. It follows that the buyer will want to see your LLC organizational records. You may or may not have a formal records book that resembles the ones maintained by a corporation; the law allows LLCs to opt for minimal paperwork. But at the very least, you'll need to produce the document that created the entity—called the articles of organization in most states—and a formal operating agreement if there are two or more members of the LLC, and maybe even if you're the only member. And, if your multimember LLC conducts its affairs with the same formality as a corporation, then you'll also need to produce the minutes of membership meetings or written

consents of members for actions taken by the company.

 Get help to create LLC records. For guidance on preparing documents for an LLC, you'll benefit greatly by consulting *Your Limited Liability Company: An Operating Manual,* by Anthony Mancuso (Nolo). It's addressed to LLC owners who'd like to maintain—or create—the same types of entity records as corporations traditionally have done. Scores of examples cover a wide variety of situations.

8. Licenses and Permits

In many localities, all businesses must obtain a basic business license. In addition, many businesses, from restaurants and gun shops to home repair services and hair styling salons, require additional specialized licenses and permits from state and local authorities, and occasionally from the federal government. Some types of licenses can easily and legally be transferred—especially if yours is an entity sale. But others—especially those that are based on your personal skills or training—may be harder to transfer or may not be transferable at all. For example, if your civil engineering firm is a professional corporation, even though you're selling it as an entity, in some states the law may require that each purchasing shareholder have a civil engineer's license. Similarly, if your restaurant and bar is an LLC and you're selling the entity, you may not be able to transfer the license without a liquor board investigation and approval of the new members of the LLC.

If you don't already know, it makes sense to check with the licensing authority for each required license or permit to learn which ones can be transferred and which ones can't. And while you're at it, find out what procedures are needed to make sure the business obtains all necessary licenses under new ownership. Well-informed buyers will probably inquire about your current licenses and permits, if for no other reason than to be sure that as presently operated your business meets minimum governmental requirements for registration. But even if they don't ask, it's wise to offer license information as part of your sales package.

You'd hate for the sale to fall through because, at the last minute, it dawns on the buyer that a license is needed—a license that the buyer may not qualify for. Certainly, if you're going to finance the purchase, you want to know that the buyer will be able to be up and running right from the get-go so that there's money coming in to cover the payments owed to you on the promissory note. So you wouldn't want to sell your pest control business to someone who can't pass the state license exam. To make sure that the buyer is fully aware of the licensing requirements for your business and to help assure a smooth transition of the business, consider preparing a summary of licensing information like the one below.

Sample Licensing Information Summary

To Potential Buyers of Allegro Bar and Grill:

The following is a list of licenses needed to run the business.

Type of License Needed	Expiration Date	Licensing Authority	Is Permission Needed to Transfer?
Beer and wine license	December 31, 20xx	State Alcohol Board	Yes
Liquor license	June 30, 20xx	State Alcohol Board	Yes
Health license	April 30, 20xx	County Health Commission	Reinspection needed. Permits needed for renovations.
Entertainment license	September 30, 20xx	City Police Department	No
Sales tax license	November 30, 20xx	State Revenue Board	No

9. Intellectual Property

Depending on your business, some or even most of its value may reside in its patents, copyrights, trademarks, business names, or trade secrets. These rights are broadly referred to as intellectual property. The buyer—often on the advice of a lawyer specializing in the field—will want to see any documents that confirm ownership of your intellectual property or otherwise relate to it. These documents help the buyer evaluate how secure this intellectual property will be if there's a legal challenge. As a practical matter, if your business has little or no intellectual property, you'll spend little or no time on this detail.

Especially if you are in the publishing or software fields or your key products are protected by patents, the buyer's review may be part of a formal intellectual property audit in which the buyer, with professional help, seeks to put a value on the intellectual property and to size up the risk of potential claims of infringement. The audit may occur in two stages. First, you may be asked for information on how the intellectual property was created and has been protected. This will include copies of copyright, patent, and trademark documents. Then the buyer may dig deeper, reviewing all subsequent registrations, agreements with authors or other creative types, and, especially as regards trade secrets, your security precautions to be sure that secrecy is maintained.

Here's a brief explanation of the various types of intellectual property, and a listing of documents that buyers and their lawyers often ask to see in each category. If your business involves a great deal of intellectual property, you will obviously need more information and possibly legal help to prepare for a sale.

a. Patents

A patent is a document issued by the U.S. Patent and Trademark Office (PTO) that grants a monopoly for a limited period of time on the use and development of an invention (utility patent) or on a design for a useful object (design patent). The utility patent right lasts approximately 17-18 years; the design patent right lasts 14 years. A buyer may want to see:

- all patents granted by the U.S. Patent and Trademarks Office
- all patent applications in process
- all documents pertaining to patent pending status
- employment and independent contractor agreements that might affect patent ownership
- preinvention assignments of rights
- assignments to your company if you acquired the patent from another company or owner
- agreements in which you've licensed other businesses to use your patents, or in which other businesses have licensed you to use theirs, and
- data concerning your supervision of patent rights.

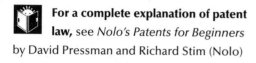

For a complete explanation of patent law, see *Nolo's Patents for Beginners* by David Pressman and Richard Stim (Nolo)

b. Copyrights

A copyright is a legal right granted to the creator of a work of authorship. In a typical small business setting, this can include such things as booklets, brochures, advertising copy, singles, videos, and software. The owner of the copyright can stop others from copying, selling, displaying, performing, or modifying the work for a significant period of time. The copyright in works created after 1977 by individuals usually lasts for the life of the author plus an additional 70 years. The copyright in works created by employees for their employers lasts for 95 years from the date of publication, or 120 years from the date of creation, whichever occurs first. You acquire copyright regardless of whether you register your work with the U.S. Copyright Office. However, there are advantages to the registration process. For one thing, you need to register before you can sue someone for infringement; and by registering early, if you're successful in an infringement lawsuit, you get an award of statutory damages plus your attorney fees and court costs. If your business has copyrights that will be transferred to the buyer as part of the sale, the buyer may ask to see:

- all copyright registrations
- all applications for copyright registrations
- employment and independent contractor agreements that might affect copyright ownership
- copies of the work to see if the copyright notice has been properly included
- assignments from those involved in the creation of the copyrighted material such as an author's assignment of a copyright to the publisher
- agreements in which your business has a license to use someone else's copyrighted material, or in which another business has licensed you to use its copyrighted material, and
- data concerning steps you've taken to prevent infringement and/or to stop those who are infringing on your copyright.

For a full explanation of copyright law and procedure, see *The Copyright Handbook: How to Protect & Use Written Works,* by Stephen Fishman (Nolo).

c. Trademarks and Service Marks

A trademark is a distinctive word, phrase, logo, graphic symbol, or other device that's used to identify the source of a product and to distinguish a manufacturer's or merchant's products from anyone else's. Some examples are Dell computers and Microsoft software. A service mark serves the same function as a trademark,

Business Names and Trademarks

A trade name is the formal name of a business. For example, Ford Motor Company is a trade name. A trade name is used for such things as opening bank accounts, paying taxes, ordering supplies, and filing lawsuits. A trade name can become a trademark or service mark when it's used to identify products or services (for example, a Ford car). Even if you're not sure whether your trade name amounts to a trademark, you should treat it as such for purposes of the sale of your business. In other words, transfer your trade name (and any accompanying goodwill) to the buyer. You should also be prepared to furnish documentation showing that you registered the trade name with the local county clerk or secretary of state.

but for a company's services rather than a particular product—for example, AOL is a service mark for America Online's services. The same law applies to both types of marks. The owner of a trademark or service mark can prevent others from using it in a way that confuses people about the products or services the owner provides or about their origin. As with a copyright, you can register a trademark or service mark with the federal government, but even if you don't, you

have substantial legal rights simply by being the first to use the mark. If you're transferring trademarks as part of the sale of a business, the buyer will want to see:

- examples of how you've used the mark—for example, labels for products or advertisements for services
- applications for federal, state, or international registrations
- registration documents
- assignments, if you've acquired the mark from someone else
- documents indicating steps you have taken to protect the mark, and
- any documents indicating licensing of the mark to third parties.

d. Trade Secrets

A trade secret is any formula, pattern, physical device, idea, process, or compilation of information, or virtually any other information, that (1) isn't generally known or readily ascertainable by your competitors, (2) offers your business an actual or potential economic advantage over others, and (3) you treat in a way that can reasonably be expected to prevent the public or competitors from learning about it. Unlike valuable copyrights and patents, which many businesses don't own, almost every small enterprise owns trade secrets. Lest you consider your business an exception, think of your customer or client list or your roster of suppliers. These lists can be and often are trade secrets, since they are frequently a significant part of what the buyer is paying for. Trade secrets, which are protected by state law, are not registered with any public office. To get a court order barring someone else from improperly using your trade secrets, you need to show the material really is secret and that you've take reasonable precautions to keep it secret. When trade secrets are part of the deal, you should be sure that the buyer has signed a nondisclosure agreement before you discuss or show any trade secret material, as discussed below. The buyer will be interested in seeing:

- any nondisclosure agreements that employees and other people have signed
- any innovations, inventions, or other documents that contain or utilize the trade secret
- assignments, if you've acquired the trade secret from someone else
- any documents regarding licensing of the trade secret to third parties, and
- any other documents you have (such as instructions to employees) that show the steps you've taken to preserve the secrecy of your trade secrets inside and outside your company.

For reasonable steps you can take to safeguard your trade secrets and other sensitive business information, see Section D, below.

 For a complete explanation of trade secret law, see *Nondisclosure Agreements: Protect Your Trade Secrets & More,* by Richard Stim and Stephen Fishman (Nolo).

D. Protecting Sensitive Information With a Confidentiality Agreement

It's understandable if you're cautious—or even slightly paranoid—when you consider releasing confidential information about your business. While it's not the norm, there undoubtedly are dishonest folks out there who may attempt to con you into thinking they're sincere buyers while their real goal is to snoop into your business affairs. It's also true that if a deal to sell your business is going to crystallize, you're going to have to share lots of confidential information with the buyer. No one will pay good money for a supposedly valuable business without carefully investigating how it works. "Trust me!" won't satisfy most buyers, whose response is almost sure to be "Show me."

The question becomes how do you do this with as little risk as possible. Basically, unless you're dealing with a family member, a close friend, or someone else you know well and trust totally, you'll want to hold back information that could provide a potential competitor with a competitive advantage until you've learned as much as possible about the buyer's character and reputation and concluded that they are good. Chapter 8 provides some advice on doing this.

Once you've reasonably concluded that the potential buyer is trustworthy, the next step is to require that person to sign an agreement (called a confidentiality agreement or nondisclosure agreement) pledging to keep your information confidential. This serves two important purposes. First, it drives home the point that what you're giving or showing the buyer is sensitive material that must be treated confidentially. Second, it creates a legal obligation to respect your ownership of the information. In the confidentiality agreement, you want the buyer to agree not to use the sensitive data—and, equally important, not to share it with anyone else except possibly the buyer's professional adviser such as a lawyer or accountant.

There's another concern you may have that can also be dealt with in a confidentiality agreement or in a letter. The issue comes up when a potential buyer is someone who currently competes with you or who may open a competitive business later. You'd like that person to agree not to try to hire away any of your employees. This is important when you realize that long-term employees know so much about your business that their jumping ship could give a competitor a huge advantage.

Your twin goals of keeping information confidential and discouraging buyers from taking away key employees can be accomplished by casting your confidentiality agreement in traditional contract form, but it's equally effective and sometimes less intimidating to a skittish buyer if you use a letter like the one below. You can use this sample confidentiality letter as a starting point in your own deal, editing it as necessary to fit your own situation. If you're especially concerned about confidentiality, it makes sense to have your lawyer review the letter before you present it to the buyer.

 Where to find the forms. You'll find copies of the Confidentiality Letter on the CD-ROM at the back of this book.

By having the buyer or buyers sign a copy of the confidentiality letter and return it to you, the letter becomes a legally binding contract.

 Make a list of what you turn over to or show to the buyer—and attach it to the confidentiality agreement that the buyer signs. As an alternative, you can ask the buyer to give you a signed, itemized receipt for the material you hand over— especially anything that's highly sensitive. That way, if it later becomes necessary to do so, you can establish that the information came from you and not from independent sources, as an unscrupulous buyer may claim. Also, to prevent improper copying

Sample Confidentiality Letter

November , 20XX

Nancy Carr   George McAndrews
2146 Oak Boulevard   616 Tamarack Circle
Granville, SD   Granville, SD

Dear Nancy and George:

As prospective purchasers of the assets of Racafrax Enterprises LLC, you've asked to see information about our finances, customers, suppliers, and trade secrets, as well as proprietary data about our pricing and marketing practices. We are happy to share this information with you, as long as you agree to keep it confidential, as outlined below.

1. You agree that the information we provide to you is valuable and confidential.

2. You agree to maintain the confidentiality of the information we provide to you, though you may share it with your lawyer and accountant for the purpose of evaluating your possible purchase of the business. You will inform these professional advisers that they too must maintain the confidentiality of the information.

3. You agree to use the confidential information only to evaluate your possible purchase of the business and for no other purpose.

4. You agree that you won't contact customers, suppliers, or employees of Racafrax without my prior written permission.

5. You agree that if you and Racafrax do not reach agreement on your purchase of the assets, you will return to us the information we provided to you and all copies and will destroy your notes and summaries.

6. You agree that you won't recruit or hire any Racafrax employees while our discussions about your possible purchase of the business are pending, and for one year afterwards.

If you agree with the above commitments, please sign and return a copy of this letter for our files.

Sincerely yours,

Racafrax Enterprises LLC
By: *Tess Woods*
Tess Woods, Managing Member

We agree to the above terms.

Nancy Carr   *George McAndrews*
Nancy Carr   George McAndrews

Dated: _____   Dated: _____

Confidentiality Agreements Aren't Foolproof

While highly recommended, keep in mind that a confidentiality agreement won't give you anywhere near 100% protection. Here are some reasons why that's so:

- The buyer may use or improperly disclose the information and you may never find out about it.
- Even if you learn that the potential buyer has used or disclosed information you believe belonged to your business, you may not be able to prove in court that the buyer got the information from you and not from some other source.
- Even if you can prove that the information came from you, and that it was disclosed or used improperly, you may not be able to establish in a subsequent lawsuit that as a result your business lost significant business or otherwise suffered significant dollars-and-cents harm.
- A lawsuit can be expensive and the outcome isn't always predictable— meaning that even if a potential buyer misuses your information, you may decide it's not wise to sue the buyer for improper use or disclosure.

In short, although it's always wise to insist on receiving a confidentiality agreement before disclosing sensitive information to any buyer, it's a mistake to believe it will provide anything like full protection.

A confidentiality agreement won't always stop thieves. Just as a bank robber is not stopped by the fact that bank robbery is a federal crime, unscrupulous competitors may sign all sorts of confidentiality documents and nevertheless try to rip you off. And because lawsuits in this area can be expensive to bring and often hard to win (the competitor may succeed in claiming it got the information from other sources), it's a mistake to reveal sensitive information without doing a thorough background check on the buyer. If a prospective buyer who seems too good to be true suddenly appears, your best bet is to slow things down until you have a chance to do a background and reference search. (See Section E, below.) If that doesn't reveal a clean slate, or you just feel uneasy about the buyer's integrity, be prepared to walk away from the negotiations rather than share your business secrets with someone who can harm your business or gain an unfair advantage.

of sensitive material, consider requiring that the buyer's review of confidential information take place at your premises and in your presence. The buyer may be able to memorize a few names from your customer list, for example, but not the entire list.

E. Why and How You Should Check Out the Buyer

Checking out buyers can help you quickly weed out time wasters, kooks, and competitors whose only intention is to mine as much otherwise confidential information as possible. But there are several other compelling reasons why it makes sense for you to look into a buyer's financial resources, business prospects, and reputation for integrity before you sign a sales agreement or share sensitive information. Of course, if the buyer is a friend or relative whom you trust and whose financial status is clear to you, you may understandably decide to omit the normal investigation.

1. Determining the Buyer's Ability to Close the Deal

Like one of the characters in the movie *Jerry Maguire*, your motto should be, "Show me the money!" In this spirit, one early question to a prospective buyer should be, "Do you have the financing it will take to buy my business?" If this seems overly blunt (and of course it

always pays to ask politely), consider that if you were selling your house, you'd be unlikely to spend much time with a buyer who couldn't produce a lender's prequalification letter. A business sale is little different. You don't want to waste time with someone who doesn't quibble about the price but can't come up with the dough.

Obviously, the buyer's ability to bring the necessary money to the closing table is a huge concern if you're selling your business for a lump sum cash payment. But it's just as much a matter of great consequence if—as is more typical—you're selling on an installment basis with, say, a 25% down payment on a $700,000 sale price. You'll still want to be sure that, come closing day, the buyer will be able to produce the $175,000 down payment. You'd hate to sign a contract, take your business off the market, and put time and effort into picking out your ski cabin, only to discover that the buyer can't come up with the money and you need to start all over.

2. Determining the Buyer's Ability to Pay Installments

Even if the buyer can produce the money necessary to make the required down payment, you still must make sure that the buyer is in strong enough financial shape to assure you'll get your installment payments on time. What's more, if you're planning to work for the buyer as an employee or consultant after the closing, you'd like to know that you really will get paid for your services.

If your investigation leaves you with qualms about the buyer's ability to meet all payment commitments following the closing, you can insist on additional protections. These protections might include getting a lien on the buyer's home or having someone who is unquestionably financially solvent guarantee payment of the remainder of the purchase price. These and other protective strategies are outlined in Chapter 9. Your investigation can help you determine how much extra protection you need to make it highly likely that you'll get everything that the buyer promises.

3. Evaluating the Quality of Your Future Relationship With the Buyer

Because it's likely you'll have an ongoing relationship with the buyer after the closing, it's important both to your psyche and pocketbook that you get along. Or put another way, even though the sale of a business is primarily about dollars and cents, it's never wise to ignore the personal characteristics of the buyer. You want to avoid getting into commercial relationships with certain difficult types, including:

- **The Slow Payers.** In an installment sale, where you won't be completely paid for several years, you don't

want to face a situation where it will be like pulling teeth to get the buyer to pay on time each month.

- **The Nickel-and-Dimers.** Similarly, you don't want to sell to a buyer who turns out to be a borderline chiseler who tries to nickel-and-dime you on agreed-upon adjustments to the sale price or, even worse, unfairly deducts chunks of money from installment payments claiming compensation for some imaginary shortcoming in the business.

- **The Outright Crooks.** These are the people who try to buy your business for a small down payment so they can quickly sell off the assets, hide the proceeds, and fade into bankruptcy.

- **The Ethically Challenged.** These folks operate in the gray areas of the law, taking advantage of you at every turn simply because they think they can get away with it.

In short, no matter how good a deal seems on paper initially, if your life is made miserable for months or years by a real jerk, you'll regret the day you agreed to the sale. Life is far too short to enter into a relationship with a problem buyer.

And if as part of your deal you plan to work for the buyer for some months or years as a consultant or employee, you need to figure out early on whether the two of you are compatible. Just as many sellers find it tough to occupy a subordinate role in a business where they once called all the shots, it may not be easy for a buyer to grab the wheel of a business that comes complete with the former owner as back seat driver.

Admittedly, the part of your investigation that aims at evaluating your future relationship with the buyer can be difficult to carry out. The information you're seeking is largely subjective, so that any judgment you arrive at about how this person is likely to behave as owner of your business will be full of guesswork. Perhaps the best you can do is to pay attention to your intuition and try to read between the lines in listening to what others are willing to say about the buyer.

 The buyer's subpar character can tarnish your own reputation. Even though your business comes under new ownership, it's likely that for years after the closing, you'll still be associated with it in the minds of those who know you. Fair or not, the buyer's lack of ethics will, in many people's minds, be confused with yours. Especially if you plan to keep living in your community or working in your field, this is another big reason you should choose as a buyer someone you'll be proud to be associated with.

F. Practical Steps for Evaluating a Buyer

Now that you see how crucial it is for you to know as much as possible about any prospective buyer, how can you efficiently accomplish this? The process normally starts with your requesting a financial statement, career resumé, and other documents from the buyer, and then moving on to additional sources of information, including checking with people who know the buyer.

 If the buyer is a big company, your evaluation efforts may be short and sweet. Such a buyer typically can provide an audited financial statement that contains a wealth of information. The downside is that if you're not used to the language and conventions of the accounting industry, you may have trouble interpreting a complex financial statement. In that case, you can ask your own accountant to explain it to you.

1. Buyer's Financial Statement

You absolutely need to look at the buyer's current financial statement showing what assets the buyer owns and what debts the buyer owes. This is especially important if you'll be extending credit to the buyer by taking back a promissory note for some of the sale price. A bank or other conventional lender would not extend credit without seeing a financial statement—and neither should you.

The assets listed on the buyer's financial statement might include cash in the bank, stocks, bonds, mutual funds, a house, and one or more cars. Debts may include credit card balances, car payments, home mortgages or deeds of trust, and home equity loans or lines of credit. In addition, younger buyers who owe large sums on college loans should also list these.

In addition to the financial statement itself, you'll want evidence that the information is accurate: a bank statement, a recent statement from the buyer's stockbroker, or a deed to the buyer's home. It's also a good idea to peruse the buyer's recent tax returns. The information on the financial statement, coupled with the backup documents the buyer furnishes, should give you valuable insight about the buyer's current financial position and ability to manage money. If the prospective purchaser is already carrying a substantial level of debt, this can tip you off to the need to ask for a more-solvent person to guarantee the buyer's obligations to you—for, example, by signing the promissory note as a guarantor.

If the buyer already owns a business, you'll want to see a financial statement of that business in addition to whatever personal financial statement the buyer gives you. And, of course, if the buyer is a corporation or an LLC, you'll want to review its financial statement as well as the statements of those who will be guaranteeing payment of the promissory note.

 You can use a bank form as a model for a financial statement. If the buyer doesn't have a financial statement already

prepared and doesn't understand how to prepare one, you can pick up a business or mortgage loan application form at the bank where you do business. Part of the form will consist of a financial statement that the buyer can fill in and give to you. That way, you'll wind up with the same information a bank would require in lending money to someone—exactly the information that you need from the buyer.

2. Buyer's Credit History

Lenders who make loans for home or car purchases invariably get a credit report on the borrower. It's logical to get one as well for someone who wants to buy a business. A credit report contains a wealth of information. You can find out, for example, if a prospective buyer has ever filed for bankruptcy or has been:

- late or delinquent in paying bills
- convicted of a crime, or, in many states, even arrested
- involved in a lawsuit, such as a personal injury claim, or
- financially active enough to establish a credit history.

Information covers the past seven to ten years. To run a credit check, you'll need a prospective buyer's name, address, and Social Security number.

For buyers who have been in business before, you can order a credit report about the business from Dun and Bradstreet at www.dnb.com. A local credit bureau should be able to provide a credit report about either a business or an individual. Any of the three national credit reporting services can provide you with a credit report about an individual: Equifax at www.equifax.com, Trans Union at www.tuc.com, or Experian at www.experian.com.

3. Buyer's Career Resumé

Just as people applying for a job routinely present a resumé listing their education and prior work experience and organizational affiliations, a prospective purchaser should be ready to supply similar information. If he or she doesn't, it's appropriate to ask for it. This will not only help you understand more about whether the person is likely to succeed as an owner of your business, but can alert you to key questions you want answered—for example, "What were you doing between 1998 and 2002 when there is a gap in your job history?"

The resumé should contain the names of references and prior business associates. This can help you get started on contacting people who are familiar with the buyer's financial position, work habits, and business ethics.

4. Talking to People Who Know the Buyer

People who have dealt with or observed the buyer can help you understand the buyer's business experience, honesty, and work habits. If these knowledgeable folks are willing to share information with you, it can round out your picture of the buyer. While it's always a good idea to check the buyer's references, it's important to realize that you're likely to receive the names of people who the buyer believes will provide mostly positive feedback. In short, it's also essential to seek out some sources of information about the buyer on your own. You best bet is to find people who have had business dealings with the buyer and who are likely to provide an objective point of view. This can include, for example, the buyer's current and former landlords. In other words, you want to talk to people who have no obvious reason to say only positive things about the buyer. You shouldn't have much trouble finding such folks.

EXAMPLE: Sam is trying to sell his little breakfast restaurant, The Fresh Egg. He is eagerly approached by Maria, who says she used to own a juice bar and would now love to get into the restaurant business. She makes a good first impression when she arrives well-dressed, driving a new Lexus SUV. Sam is less impressed, however, when he sees Maria's financial statement. She has only $1,200 in the bank and no other assets besides her SUV, which she will be paying for over the next three years. She also owes $20,000 in college loans and $5,000 on two credit cards. Sam decides to check some more. After talking with Maria's references—including a college roommate and a member of Maria's former rowing crew—who all say she's terrific, Sam decides to investigate further. Realizing that he has met the landlord of Maria's old juice bar, he calls her and learns that Maria was rarely on time with the rent. When Sam stops by, a nearby store owner says that while Maria's posted hours were 7 a.m. to 6 p.m., she hardly ever opened before 9:30 a.m. and often shut down for a week at a time for vacation. Finally, a city health department inspection report shows that Maria typically had three or more reasonably serious violations whenever routine inspections were made. Although Maria assures Sam that she can borrow the 10% down payment for the restaurant from a boyfriend, Sam wisely decides that extending credit to Maria would be a risky proposition. He tells her that if she's serious about buying the business, she'll need to bring in a guarantor or co-owner who has substantial assets.

5. Buyer's Complaint Record With or Disciplinary Action by Public Agencies

If your business requires a license, you'll want to make sure that the buyer has a currently valid license, as explained in Section C8, above. You'll also want to make sure that this license is in good standing.

This information is often available from licensing agencies—for example, a state agency that licenses auto repair shops or real estate brokers. The licensing authority may also provide any information that's available to the public about any disciplinary action that's been taken against a licensee, as well as consumer complaints. For example, if you're selling your veterinary practice, you'd like to find out if the vet who's offering to buy it has ever been suspended or reprimanded or has a history of extensive complaints from dissatisfied customers. To protect your excellent reputation, you wouldn't want to sell your veterinary practice to someone who has a checkered past.

6. Buyer's Business Plan

A person who is serious about buying your business should have a blueprint for the future that looks ahead to the next three to five years. Be careful about a fly-by-the-seat-of-your-pants buyer who doesn't see the need to create a coherent plan that makes good sense. A buyer without a plan—or with a naïve or silly plan—is unlikely to succeed.

As part of preparing your business for sale, you should have prepared a business plan to demonstrate how the business can continue to thrive after you part with it. (See Chapter 7.) Assuming the plan is realistic (not just a sales gimmick) and the buyer accepts it, you may not need to get a full-scale plan from the buyer. But in all cases you'll want to inquire into what else the buyer plans to do to see if it makes sense. You want to be able to flush out buyers who pretend to accept your plan just to flatter you. Also, it's wise to ask exactly how the buyer expects to run the business and finance your payments in the early months of operation.

 Ask the buyer what happens if things go wrong. Many buyers assume that they'll be making money from the first day they take over and will meet your payments entirely out of that income. Maybe. But it's often no easy task to earn enough to cover payments to you and make a living wage. Also realize that it's certain that the buyer will face a pile of expenses related to the change in ownership, and it's possible that in early days, the net income of the business may be less than expected. Ask the buyer what exactly happens if costs are higher and revenue lower than projected? You want a good answer.

With either an asset sale or an entity sale, the new owner should have enough operating cash to carry the business for at least 90 days—if not longer. Seeing the buyer's business plan, along with information about the buyer's finances, will help you evaluate whether or not the buyer is

likely to stay afloat during the critical early months. Remember, the buyer needs money not only to meet the initial payment to you, but also for riding out the period before income starts arriving faster than bills do.

7. Consulting Court Records on the Buyer

If the buyer comes from your area, check out local court records to find out if he or she has been involved in any lawsuits (though some may show up in a credit report as well). It's relatively easy to check on lawsuits that have been filed in the courts in your county. Simply go to the court clerk's office and inquire. Usually, the clerk will have a computer database or some similar means for looking up the buyer's name. If the buyer comes from another community, see if the local credit bureau can supply the information to you.

If you find that the buyer has been sued a number of times, that should be a caution, if not a stop sign—particularly if the suits were about the buyer's alleged failure to pay bills rather than, say, the buyer's negligent driving. Similarly, finding that a buyer has initiated a number of lawsuits—that is, he or she is the plaintiff rather than the defendant—can also be a go-slow signal. The best way to deal with a buyer who is lawsuit-happy by nature is to suggest that he or she buy someone else's business.

☑ Checklist for Documents Provided for and by Prospective Buyers

Information the Buyer Will Want to See

Here are some of the items a buyer will likely want to see in evaluating your business:

- ☐ Business tax returns
- ☐ Business financial statements
- ☐ Detailed list of assets
- ☐ Details on accounts receivable, debts, and other liabilities
- ☐ Current lease
- ☐ The deed and title insurance policy (if you're selling real estate as part of the deal)
- ☐ Contracts with customers, suppliers, and employers
- ☐ Licenses and permits
- ☐ Documents pertaining to intellectual property.

Information Needed to Evaluate the Buyer

Here are some resources for you to consider seeing when you evaluate a prospective buyer:

- ☐ Financial statement for buyer (and any guarantors)
- ☐ Career resume
- ☐ Credit report for buyer (and any guarantors)
- ☐ References
- ☐ People likely to have objective opinions about buyer
- ☐ Licenses (if required)
- ☐ Business complaint record (if available)
- ☐ Business plan
- ☐ Litigation history

Drafting a Letter of Intent

When, eventually, you and the buyer reach a solid understanding concerning the terms of your deal, you'll need to capture it in a sales agreement, as explained in detail in Part 3 of this book. But sometimes, rather than proceed directly to a binding contract, a seller and buyer decide to sign a preliminary document called a letter of intent. This chapter explains how to prepare a letter of intent and highly recommends that any such letter be nonbinding. Even better, try to skip this step and move as quickly as possible to reach a mutually acceptable final sales agreement.

 Never sign a letter of intent if you have more than one serious suitor. Signing a letter of intent—even a nonbinding one—implies that you hope to reach full agreement and ultimately close with this buyer. If you're serious enough to sign such a letter, don't simultaneously negotiate with others, even if the letter doesn't prohibit it. Unless you clearly tell the preferred buyer in advance that discussions with others will continue to take place (in which case the letter is all but meaningless), you risk an angry confrontation if the buyer learns of your other negotiations. The unhappy result may be that an otherwise viable deal falls apart.

A. Why Use a Letter of Intent?

A letter of intent is an intermediate document that summarizes the main terms that you and the buyer believe will become part a sales agreement. It can be either a legally binding and enforceable commitment to the terms listed in the letter, or simply a nonbinding recap of where you stand in your negotiations.

While using a letter of intent as part of the sale of a small business is relatively uncommon, occasionally a buyer and seller will choose to prepare one. The reasons are varied but usually involve one or both parties' worry as to whether the other is serious about consummating the deal. For example, even at an early stage of negotiations you may find yourself under intense pressure from an eager buyer to get something down in writing and may conclude that the deal may slip away if you don't cooperate. The buyer, in turn, may be pushing for a letter of intent to help reassure a financial supporter that a deal and closing are imminent.

EXAMPLE: Ned owns Green Cab Company LLC, an outfit that operates six cabs in a suburban city. He has been negotiating a sale of the business assets to Lennie, and their deal appears to be falling nicely into place. But Ned and Lennie still have some fine points to work out, including how the sale price will be allocated among the various assets—something that can have important tax consequences for each (as explained in Chapter 4). They also need to agree on the details of Ned's covenant not to compete—its duration and geographical area—as well as how much Ned will be paid for his consulting services during the six months following the sale. Because Lennie is about to go out of town for his daughter's wedding and Ned's tax adviser is tied up with another client's IRS audit, Lennie and Ned won't be able to finalize their deal for at least ten days. Meanwhile, Lennie wants something in writing to show two investors who are helping him come up with the $75,000 down payment. Even though there are some crucial details to be worked out, Ned understands the logic of Lennie's request and prepares a nonbinding letter of intent capturing the high points of the agreement he and Lennie are working on. After both sign this letter, Lennie shows it to his money sources, who assure Lennie he can count on them for the cash he'll need to close the deal.

As a seller, you might want to seek a letter of intent if you've been approached by several potential buyers and would like to tell the lesser candidates that you're close to a deal with your leading choice. You might not want to discourage the others unless you had a relatively firm commitment from the favored candidate.

Another reason why you or the buyer may consider creating a letter of intent is to reduce the chances that the other party will try to introduce new or unpalatable terms just before the closing, when there's enormous momentum to complete the transaction. Although a nonbinding letter has no legal power to prevent this, it may nevertheless be a positive moral force to encourage the other party to hold to the terms of the deal.

B. What to Put in Your Letter of Intent

The items appropriately covered in your letter of intent will depend on the nature of your sale and the key points on which you and the buyer have already agreed. There's no formula that will work for every deal, but below are some points that sellers and buyers will want to consider. Unless you've discussed and agreed on most of these substantive and procedural terms, chances are your negotiations are at such a preliminary stage that it's too soon to even consider preparing a nonbinding letter of intent.

1. Substantive Items

Here are some of the substantive items you might consider covering in a letter of intent:

- the sale price or how it will be determined
- whether the buyer will be buying your business's assets or the corporation, LLC, or other entity itself

- how payment will be made—full sale price at closing or installment payments
- the measures that will protect you in an installment sale, such as your retaining a security interest in the business's assets, getting the buyer's personal guarantee, and possibly obtaining a lien on the buyer's home
- a list of any business assets that are not part of the deal, such as a particular computer or a work of art
- whether some or all accounts receivable will be transferred
- whether liabilities such as bank loans or sums owed on equipment purchases will be transferred as part of the sale or retained by you
- whether liabilities such as the responsibility of paying for warranty repairs on past sales items will be transferred to the buyer
- whether a presale inventory of business property will be conducted and, if so, whether it will be done by the two of you or by an outsider
- whether the buyer will be taking over your current lease
- whether you'll be signing a covenant not to compete that limits your right to do similar work in the future and, if so, an outline of its major terms, and
- any arrangements for you to do future work for the buyer as an employee or consultant.

2. Procedural Items

Here are some of the procedural items you might consider covering in a letter of intent:

- whether you reserve the right to have discussions with other possible buyers or will negotiate exclusively with the person with whom you're signing the letter of intent
- a schedule for completing negotiations and signing a sales agreement, and perhaps the date by which you expect the deal will be closed
- a list of the important issues that remain to be agreed upon
- a description of any further investigation of the business or of your representations about the business that the buyer plans to conduct
- further investigation of the buyer that you plan to conduct, such as looking into the buyer's financial status or prior business experience
- whether you and the buyer will sign nondisclosure agreements to discourage the leaking or misuse of confidential information (though, ideally, you will have already attended to this), and
- whether the letter of intent is binding (something not recommended, for reasons explained in Section C, below).

Customize your letter of intent to meet your needs. Not every item on these lists will apply to your sale—and there may be some points you'd like to include that aren't on either list. That's fine. Your letter of intent should be crafted to closely reflect your transaction and the current state of your negotiations.

C. Why You Should Only Sign a Nonbinding Letter of Intent

Any letter of intent you sign should be of the nonbinding variety. In other words, you should avoid signing a preliminary document that might be treated as a binding contract. Otherwise, you face the possibility that your letter of intent will enmesh you in arguments—and perhaps even litigation—over what exactly you and the buyer have committed yourselves to. Since any letter of intent is by definition going to be less complete than a definitive sales agreement, you risk finding that the general (perhaps even vague) provisions of the letter will later be interpreted by the buyer in ways that surprise and disappoint you. And if a court ultimately agrees with the buyer, you may be stuck with a deal you never intended to agree to. What's more, even if you win in a subsequent court action, you'll have had to cope with a huge, unproductive, and expensive headache.

Think of it this way: No letter of intent will contain crucially important fine-print terms of your sale. For example, you could find yourself legally bound to sell your business to the buyer at the price listed in the letter without the security arrangements needed to give you effective recourse if the buyer doesn't make installment payments on time. While these and other details are customarily included in a sales agreement and in the closing documents referred to in the sales agreement, they may be omitted or glossed over in a more preliminary letter.

 If the buyer insists on a binding letter of intent, get ready to stay up all night. An anxious buyer may want to bind you to the sale as quickly as possible. That's understandable. But instead of signing a binding letter of intent, make the time to promptly negotiate a full and binding sales agreement containing all necessary provisions—even if you and the buyer have to sit up all night to accomplish it. If the buyer doesn't like that approach, suggest signing a nonbinding letter of intent which includes a tight schedule for negotiating the sales agreement which will be binding.

D. Format for a Letter of Intent

A letter of intent is usually just that—a letter (see the sample set out below). You write a "Dear Buyer" letter to the buyer, or receive a "Dear Seller" letter from the buyer. If the person receiving the letter agrees that it accurately states the intent of both of you, he or she signs a copy of the letter and gives or sends the originator a copy that contains both signatures.

There's no legal rule that a letter of intent follow any particular format. Instead of using a letter, your preliminary document can as easily be prepared in the format of a traditional agreement that you both sign. If you follow the more formal approach, your document can be labeled in various ways: Memorandum of Agreement, Memorandum of Understanding, or Preliminary Sales Agreement. The key point is that any document that serves the same purpose as a letter of intent carries with it the same risks, so if you want to avoid legal complications, you need to be sure any document you sign is nonbinding.

If the buyer prepares the letter of intent, it may be ambiguous as to whether or not it's legally binding. There's an easy solution. Before signing, add these words: "This is not a legally binding agreement, but simply a summary of the current status of our discussions. We will only have a legally binding agreement when we both sign a sales agreement."

To help you draft your own letter of intent, here's a sample based on a typical business sale scenario. The seller (Fit for Life LLC) has two stores that sell exercise equipment and a third retail outlet (operating under the name The Long Run) that sells running apparel, including shoes and shorts. Several buyers have expressed an interest in buying The Long Run. One of them, Marvin, seems like the best candidate based on his sterling financial credentials. Still, the negotiations with Marvin have taken longer than Nan and Peter (Fit for Life's owners) anticipated. When Marvin says he needs to delay for a few days while his wife is out of town, Nan and Peter begin to wonder if the deal will really happen or whether they should begin discussions with other potential buyers. Confronting their need to show a definite commitment to the deal, Nan and Peter ask Marvin to sign a nonbinding letter of intent confirming their understanding of the deal. Marvin agrees.

Obviously, you'll have to adapt this sample letter to reflect your own negotiations and style of writing, but do try for a tone that's direct, friendly, and optimistic, and not full of legalisms. Again, the key is to be sure that no one reading this letter can reasonably conclude that you've struck a binding deal. To this end, the opening paragraph of the sample says that it's not a legally binding agreement. And lest there be any doubt, this is repeated near the end of the letter. Whatever else you do, be sure to include that or a similar phrase in your letter of intent so that you don't find yourself unintentionally bound by it.

Fit for Life LLC
123 Sunshine Way
Phoenix, AZ 55555

June 15, 20XX

Marvin Townsend
456 Cactus Road
Phoenix, AZ 55555

Dear Marvin:

This is a letter of intent concerning your proposed purchase of the running apparel business, The Long Run. Our company, Fit for Life LLC, owns The Long Run and is selling it to you. The business you are proposing to buy is located at 789 Southwest Avenue, Smalldale.

This letter of intent is not a legally binding agreement. As we continue to work out the remaining details with you, the terms set out below may change. The purpose of this letter is simply to summarize the results of our discussions so far.

Exclusive Dealing

For the next two months, assuming that Fit for Life hasn't notified you of its intent to withdraw from discussions with you, Fit for Life does not plan to negotiate with any other prospective buyer. Likewise, you do not plan to negotiate for the purchase of any other business.

Terms of the Sale
Sale Price

You (or a corporation or LLC that you may form) will pay $300,000 for the business assets of The Long Run, plus an additional amount reflecting the wholesale value of the merchandise of The Long Run on hand at the time of closing. To determine the value of the merchandise, we will jointly conduct a physical inventory at that time. You will pay the wholesale price for the merchandise that The Long Run acquired in the 90 days preceding closing, and a lesser value for older merchandise as determined to be commercially reasonable by Neil Chang, regional director of the Athletic Apparel Association.

Payment of Sale Price

You will make a down payment of $30,000 at closing. You will sign a promissory note for $270,000 payable in monthly installments of principal and interest (at a 7.0% annual rate). The note will be amortized so that you will make equal monthly payments of principal and interest that will pay off the note in 60 months.

Security for Sale Price

No matter how your business is legally organized, you and your wife will personally sign the promissory note. This means if you form a corporation or LLC to purchase the assets of The Long Run unit from Fit for Life, your business entity will sign the note, and you and your wife will personally guarantee payment. In addition, you will give Fit for Life a security interest in the business assets and a second mortgage on your home for the full amount of the note.

Assets

The assets to be transferred to you include all furnishings and equipment located at The Long Run store (except for the Dell notebook computer on Nan's desk), the merchandise on hand as of the date of closing, the phone number, and the business name, The Long Run. Fit for Life has not registered The Long Run as a trademark but will assign to you all trademark and other legal rights that Fit for Life may have in the name. Fit for Life will keep the accounts receivable as of the date of closing (we only have a few in-house accounts).

Liabilities

At closing or before, Fit for Life will pay all liabilities affecting The Long Run, including the $50,000 debt owed to First Commercial.

The Company Van

The van with the store's logo (The Long Run) on it is leased from VanLease Associates. Fit for Life will arrange to have the lease transferred to you if you will accept responsibility for future lease payments, and if VanLease approves of the transfer. (Or, if you prefer, Fit for Life will keep the van and continue to pay on the lease.)

Real Estate Lease

Fit for Life owns the building where The Long Run is located at 789 Southwest Avenue, Smalldale. As we discussed, Fit for Life is willing to rent it to you under a triple-net lease at $3,000 a month for five years, with an option to renew for five more years for $3,500 a month. If you do decide to rent it, Fit for Life will require a security deposit equal to two months' rent.

Postsale Issues
Competition

Neither Fit for Life, nor either of its co-owners (Nan Ludwig and Peter Sutton), will compete in the sports apparel business in Snow Bird County for five years from the date of closing. The co-owners and Fit for Life company do, however, reserve the right to continue their activities in the exercise equipment business, meaning that Fit for Life and its co-owners could operate a fitness center or a retail shop to sell exercise equipment. You will pay $10,000 to the company and $15,000 each to Nan and Peter for their covenants not to compete.

Consultation

You will retain Nan as an independent contractor to help in the transition of the business for the first six months. You will pay Nan $3,000 a month and she will provide, under your direction, up to 30 hours a month of consultation to you on an as-needed basis. As part of the consulting, Nan will also be available to work with you on the store floor, if you desire. Peter will have no future relationship with the business after the closing.

Items Still to Be Negotiated

Fit for Life still needs to complete its investigation of your financial status, including a credit report and a review of your assets and liabilities. In addition, there are remaining issues to be resolved including how you would be compensated for referring of customers to our exercise equipment store. Your accountant and ours need to help us arrive at an allocation of the purchase price for tax purposes. Other issues may also come up that we will need to address.

Timetable for Negotiations and Closing

We hope that all of us can work out the final details of this nonbinding agreement as soon as reasonably possible. Accordingly, let's try to have a sales agreement ready to sign by July 15. Assuming that this is agreeable to you, we can plan for a closing date of July 31, which would let you fully benefit from the surge in store traffic that typically precedes the Labor Day 10K Run. (By the way, let's talk about cosponsoring that event.) We are available to meet with you on next week on Tuesday afternoon, Wednesday morning, or both to work with you on the final details.

Marvin, we think we've hit the high points of our negotiations for you to purchase the assets of The Long Run from Fit for Life, but because this is a nonbinding agreement, no terms or conditions are final. We have some fine-tuning yet to do and some parts of this proposed deal may change, so we won't have a legally binding contract unless and until we all sign a final sales agreement.

If you agree that we have accurately summarized our discussions, please sign a copy of this letter and return it to us. We think things are moving in the right direction and hope that you do, too.

Sincerely yours,

Nancy Ludwig
_____

Nancy Ludwig
Member/Manager
Fit for Life LLC

Peter Sutton
_____

Peter Sutton
Member/Manager
Fit for Life LLC

Confirmation

I agree with your analysis of where we stand in our negotiations and will work with you to tie up the loose ends so we can have a solid deal.

Marvin Townsend
_____

Marvin Townsend

Dated: June 7 , 20XX

Checklist for a Letter of Intent

☐ Understand the pros and cons of using a letter of intent.

☐ Proceed directly to a sales agreement whenever possible.

☐ If you do use a letter of intent, summarize both substantive and procedural items.

☐ Make sure your letter of intent is not a legally binding contract.

Part 3

Preparing the Sales Agreement

Chapter 12

Preparing the Sales Agreement and Other Legal Documents

The first half of this book explains how to analyze the tax consequences of selling your business, how to prepare and price your business for a sale, where to look for buyers, and what terms to consider in your negotiations. Now it's time to put together the legal documents you'll need to carry out your sale—a topic that's the primary focus of the rest of this book.

This chapter provides an overview of the key documents used in the sale of a business, including the sales agreement, promissory note, and noncompete agreement. It explains why carefully drafted documents are so important to a successful business sale and how to effectively prepare them.

A. Overview of Your Sales Agreement

Once you've found a buyer and struck a deal, it's time to put the terms into a clearly written and legal sales agreement. The sales agreement (or contract) is far and away the most crucial and complex document you'll need, because it alone captures the entire scope of your deal and reflects all of the understanding you've reached with the buyer.

Because this master document dwarfs all others, a full seven chapters are devoted to it. Each chapter presents a series of sales agreement clauses, beginning with the names of the seller and buyer (Clause 1 in Chapter 13) and ending with the signatures (Clause 36 in Chapter 18).

The sales agreement is broken down into 23 basic sections each consisting of one or more clauses. See "Guide to Sales Agreement Clauses," below, for a guide to the different sections of the sales agreement, including which chapter discusses which specific clauses and where to find related documents.

As you review the sales agreement clauses, you'll find that a number of provisions are optional—you can use them or not, depending on what you and the buyer have agreed. This text is clearly labeled "optional." Some clauses are pretty much the same for all sales agreements, except for your specific information, such as the exact sales price. For other clauses, you will choose from several options or craft your own clause, depending on what best fits your circumstances and whether you're selling your assets or your entity. The text of the book will help you choose among options as you read through the following chapters.

Chapters 13 through 18 take you step by step through each clause and explain how to complete it, including the specific legal and financial information you need. The clauses are all on the CD-ROM included in this book for use in assembling your own sales agreement. You'll see that it's easy to delete a clause or add a new one simply by inserting or deleting text and renumbering the rest of the clauses. For example, if you're selling the assets to your business, you will complete Clauses 2 and 3 (explained in Chapter 13), but not Clauses 4 and 5, which apply to entity sales. The next clause for an asset sale would be the Sale Price (Clause 6 in Chapter 14), which you would renumber Clause 4. This may sound confusing, but it will be very clear as you assemble your sales agreement electronically and follow the directions on how to use the CD-ROM in Appendix A. Also, see Appendix B for sample sales agreements that you can use as a model when preparing your own.

 Feel free to innovate. The sales agreement and other documents offered in this book are carefully designed to cover the terms that apply in most business sales—and they provide a great deal of flexibility. But you needn't be a slave to the suggested forms. Ultimately the forms should fit your deal rather than vice versa. You should never shape your deal to fit the forms. So even though the sales agreement and other documents provided here will suffice for many, many sales, in some instances you may need even more flexibility. If so, don't hesitate to delete clauses, add clauses, or modify the suggested wording to reflect your understanding with the buyer. If you follow my recommendation and have a lawyer review the documents before you sign them, you're unlikely to run into any serious problems.

Differences in Sales Agreements for Asset and Entity Sales

As mentioned many times throughout this book, a key point to be negotiated by you and the buyer is whether you'll sell only the assets of your business or the entire entity. (If you don't fully understand this important issue, reread Chapter 9.) Many sales agreement clauses will be identical for an asset or entity sale, and the upcoming chapters specify where you differ. The specific sections where clauses will or may differ between the two types of sales are:

- Identifying the business and what's being sold
- Sale price
- Security for future payment
- Seller's debts and other liabilities
- Seller's representations
- Closing arrangements and documents
- Risk of loss

Appendix B includes sample sales agreements for both asset and entity sales, and the CD-ROM includes separate files for assembling your sales agreement.

Guide to Sales Agreement Clauses

Section and what it covers	Clauses	Where clauses are discussed	Related documents and where to find them
Names	1. Names	Chapter 13, Section A	
Identifying the business and what's being sold	**Asset Sale** 2. Sale of Business Assets (Asset Sale) 3. Assets Being Sold (Asset Sale)	Chapter 13, Section B	Bill of Sale, Assignment of Lease, Assignment of Other Contracts, Assignment of Intellectual Property, and Consent to Sale of Assets: Chapter 20
	Entity Sale 4. Sale of Corporate Stock (Entity Sale—Corporation) 5. Sale of LLC Membership Interest (Entity Sale—LLC)	Chapter 13, Section C	
Sale price	**Asset Sale** 6. Sale Price (Asset Sale)	Chapter 14, Section A	
	7. Price of Inventory (Asset sale) [optional]	Chapter 14, Section B	
	8. Accounts Receivable (Asset Sale) [optional]	Chapter 14, Section C	
	Entity Sale 9. Sale Price (Entity Sale)	Chapter 14, Section D	
	10. Adjustment of Sale Price (Entity Sale) [optional]		
Deposit	11. Deposit [optional]	Chapter 14, Section E	
Payment at closing	12. Payment at Closing	Chapter 14, Section F	
Promissory note	13. Promissory Note [optional]	Chapter 14, Section G	Promissory Note: Chapter 19

Guide to Sales Agreement Clauses (continued)

Section and what it covers	Clauses	Where clauses are discussed	Related documents and where to find them
Security for future payment	**Asset Sale** 14. Security for Payment (Asset Sale) *[optional]*	Chapter 14, Section H	Security Agreements for asset and entity sales, UCC Financing Statement, Escrow Agreement for Stock Certificates, and Escrow Agreement for LLC Transfer Certificates: Chapter 19
	Entity Sale 15. Security for Payment (Entity Sale) *[optional]*	Chapter 14, Section I	
Seller's debts and other liabilities	**Asset Sale** 16. Seller's Debts and Other Liabilities (Asset Sale)	Chapter 15, Section A	Statement Regarding Absence of Creditors: Chapter 20
	Entity Sale 17. Entity's Debts and Other Liabilities (Entity Sale) *[optional]*	Chapter 15, Section B	
Seller's representations	**Asset Sale** 18. Seller's Representations (Asset Sale)	Chapter 15, Section D	
	Entity Sale 19. Seller's Representations (Entity Sale)		
Buyer's representations	20. Buyer's Representations	Chapter 15, Section E	
Covenant not to compete	21. Covenant Not to Compete *[optional]*	Chapter 16, Section A	Covenant Not to Compete: Chapter 21
Future services	22. Future Services *[optional]*	Chapter 16, Section B	Employment Contract and Independent Contractor Agreement: Chapter 21

Guide to Sales Agreement Clauses (continued)

Section and what it covers	Clauses	Where clauses are discussed	Related documents and where to find them
Contingencies	23. Contingency [optional]	Chapter 17, Section A	
Closing arrangements and documents	24. Closing	Chapter 17, Section B	Closing Checklists for Asset and Entity Sales: Chapter 22
	Asset Sale 25. Documents for Transferring Assets		
	Entity Sale 26. Documents for Transferring Entity		
Dispute resolution	27. Disputes [optional]	Chapter 17, Section C	
Risk of loss	28. Risk of Loss (Asset Sale) 29. Risk of Loss (Entity Sale)	Chapter 17, Section D	
Entire agreement	30. Entire Agreement	Chapter 17, Section D	
Modification	31. Modification	Chapter 17, Section D	
Governing law	32. Governing Law	Chapter 17, Section D	
Severability	33. Severability	Chapter 17, Section D	
Notices	34. Notices	Chapter 17, Section D	
Other additional terms	35. Other Additional Terms [optional]	Chapter 17, Section E	
Required signatures	36. Required Signatures	Chapter 18, Section D	

B. Related Legal Documents

Here's an overview of other key legal documents—in addition to the sales agreement—used in the sale of a business and where they appear (complete with instructions) in the rest of the book (Part 4, Chapters 19 through 21). You'll attach most of these documents to your sales agreement, but you won't sign them until the closing—the time when the business actually passes to the buyer. See Section E, below, on how to prepare attachments to your sales agreement. The Sales Agreement Clauses chart indicates how these documents relate to specific clauses in the sales agreement.

1. Documents for Installment Payments

If the buyer will be making a down payment at closing and then paying the rest of the sale price in installments, you'll need documents that firmly commit the buyer to pay you what's owed—and that protect you if the buyer stops paying. These documents (covered in Chapter 19) include a promissory note, security agreement, and UCC Financing Statement. And for good measure, if you're selling your corporation or LLC, you also should consider requiring an escrow agreement under which a third party (escrow agent) takes physical possession of the stock certificates or LLC membership certificates and transfers them to the buyer only after

you're fully paid—a form also discussed in Chapter 19.

2. Documents for Transferring the Assets or the Entity to the Buyer

You'll need to complete documents at the closing to actually transfer your business to the buyer. In an asset sale, you'll need a bill of sale that lists the assets included in the sale—tangible personal property, such as machinery, inventory supplies, and office equipment. In addition, you may need to prepare documents to assign leases and other contracts and to transfer intellectual property such as copyrights, trademarks, and patents. And if you're selling your entity, you'll need to formalize the transfer of your shares of stock or LLC membership interests. Chapter 20 explains all these documents and how to prepare them.

3. Documents Dealing With Non-competition and Working for the Buyer

If you're making a commitment to the buyer not to compete with the business after the closing, you'll need a form to accomplish this, called a covenant not to compete. Likewise, if you'll be working for the buyer after the closing, you'll want to prepare an employment contract or an independent contractor agreement. Chapter 21 provides an overview of these key documents and the main issues you need to consider when preparing them.

4. The Closing Checklist

To assure a smooth closing, you and the buyer should agree on a comprehensive closing checklist as explained in Chapter 22, where you'll also find tips on where and when to hold the closing.

C. Well-Drafted Documents Are Crucial

To make sure you don't end up involved in costly time-consuming legal disputes, you need carefully drafted documents to carry out the sale of your business. The courts are full of lawsuits dealing with ambiguous, incomplete, and even contradictory documents used in business sales. Fortunately, by using well-crafted documents, you can drastically reduce the possibility of legal disputes.

Before moving on to the specifics of assembling your sales agreement and related documents, here's an overview.

1. Comprehensive Documents Avoid Arguments About Who Said What

With a comprehensive sales agreement, promissory note, and other documents such as those recommended in this book, you avoid notoriously unreliable oral agreements, where what's said isn't always what's heard or remembered. By capturing all the details of the deal in a written sales agreement and related documents, you and the buyer can greatly reduce the likelihood of a serious dispute that ends up in court.

2. The Drafting Process Helps You and the Buyer Cover All the Key Issues

In the process of carefully drafting comprehensive documents, you can make sure that all important legal and practical details—including some that you and the buyer may have never even discussed—don't get left out. For example, you and the buyer may not have talked about what will happen if the buyer defaults on the promissory note that represents a significant portion of the purchase price—a point that should always be a major concern for the seller. Or you may not have discussed the mechanics of how the inventory will be valued on the eve of closing.

As part of a careful document-drafting process, any omissions of detail are likely to jump out at you. And, especially if you follow the thorough approach set out in this book, you'll be well-positioned to cover all key points.

3. Well-Drafted Documents Protect Your Interests and Limit Your Liability

You can use your sales agreement to put clear limits on your liability for any claims against the business that may later surface, and you can tailor your representations (statements of fact that the buyer will rely on) and warranties (guarantees to the buyer) to curtail your exposure to the buyer if unforeseen problems should arise—say, an environmental claim involving the business premises. To gain this type of legal protection, however, you'll need to be forthright in what you disclose to the buyer about your business. If instead you distort or hide important information, no prophylactic legal language is likely to protect you.

4. Finely Tuned Documents Can Be a Reference Point If You Have a Dispute

Even when the seller and buyer proceed honestly and in complete good faith, a dispute can later surface over some detail of the sale. If that happens, comprehensive, precisely worded documents can make it easier to resolve the dispute. With those documents in hand, you and the buyer may be able to speedily negotiate a satisfactory solution to the problem. Or, if you can't solve the problem without outside intervention, your written contracts will help contain the problems and the

cost of solving them—whether you take the dispute to mediation, arbitration, or court.

D. Preparing Your Sales Agreement and Related Legal Documents

Now that you understand the many reasons for having clear and comprehensive documents and have a basic overview of what's in the sales agreement and how to draft one, let's consider two important practical concerns:

- Should the first draft come from you or the buyer?
- What role, if any, should your lawyer play in the process?

Check your letter of intent. If you and the buyer have signed a letter of intent (as described in Chapter 11), be sure to consult it as you prepare your sales agreement. It can be a good checklist of the terms that you and the buyer have agreed to in principle.

1. Preparing the First Drafts

Drafting—and, inevitably, redrafting—the sales agreement and other documents requires plenty of mental effort. And, of course, if you hire a lawyer to do the first drafts or to help you with the drafting process, it will cost you serious dollars as well. As a result, you may be tempted to let the buyer or his or her lawyer prepare the first drafts, figuring that you can just review and revise those drafts later in the process. This is a poor approach. Even in a situation where you and the buyer think you've hammered out all important details, the party who does the initial drafts has considerable ability to further shape the deal, maybe even changing key provisions, thus resulting in the need for further negotiations and possibly risking that the sale will fall apart. By contrast, if you do the first drafts, you can be sure that all key points will be covered. If any nitpicking needs to be done, it will be the buyer, not you, who has to employ the fine-toothed comb. An anxious buyer may even hesitate to quibble, which puts you more in control of the ultimate product.

Even though you may be hesitant to draft pages of contract language, keep in mind that by sensibly crafting the first drafts, you often avoid disputes, expedite the process, and may even gain a subtle, strategic advantage. This book, complete with a CD-ROM at the back, does a lot of the work for you.

 If for any reason the buyer creates the first drafts, examine them very carefully. You need to make a word-by-word study of the buyer's drafts to be sure your interests are fully protected, that the terms of the deal (as you understand them) are clearly and accurately stated, and that nothing has been left out. This book will help you do this.

2. Involving a Lawyer

As you know, the legal documents—especially for a business that's worth a substantial sum—need to be done right. For that reason, even if you're a dedicated self-helper, it's usually cost-effective to get at least some help from a business lawyer. (Chapter 6 discusses how to work with a lawyer and other professionals.) Just how much help will depend on a number of factors, including:

- the complexity of your particular deal
- whether or not you've ever bought or sold a business before
- your past experience and comfort level in dealing with legal documents
- how much time you have available to devote to the task of drafting your sales agreement, and
- how important the savings will be if you do some of the drafting yourself.

If your business will sell for a large sum, a business lawyer's fee may take up such a small percentage of the total dollars involved that it's not worth worrying about.

One sensible approach is to create the first drafts yourself, and then have an experienced business lawyer review them before you present them to the buyer. This book will carefully lead you through the drafting process so you'll understand exactly what you're doing and why you're doing it, thus reducing the chances of making a mistake.

Another alternative is to have your lawyer create the sales documents based on the terms you and the buyer have agreed to. If you follow this approach, be careful not to fade (or be pushed) into the background. This is your deal—not the lawyer's—which means that to achieve the result you want, you need to stay in middle of the loop. It follows that before you present any lawyer-drafted documents to the buyer, you need to study them carefully yourself to make sure you understand every word and that they really do capture every nuance of your deal. If for any reason you have doubts or questions, don't hesitate to ask your lawyer to make changes. Fortunately, this task of reviewing the documents, asking questions, and suggesting changes will be infinitely easier for you after you've read the chapters in this part of the book.

It's not your lawyer's sale. Be careful not to let your lawyer hijack your deal by suggesting substantive changes to the deal itself or inserting overly complex or draconian legal provisions. This can happen for a variety of reasons, including the fact that your lawyer is more familiar with larger, more complicated transactions, or unthinkingly pulls a form out of a legal form book or—most unsettling of all—is trying to justify a high fee. In many of these situations, you may wind up with an agreement that's too long, too filled with arcane jargon, too crammed with harsh and unnecessary clauses, or all three. Good

lawyers try to help make deals happen—not destroy them by causing the buyer to panic.

Finally, remember that the buyer's lawyer isn't in the picture to protect you, but to look out for the best interests of the buyer. While this may seem obvious, it bears emphasis, since the buyer's lawyer may be a friendly, fair-minded, and 100% honest individual representing a principled buyer who may even be a friend or family member. That's all well and good, but it doesn't change the fact that the only people who can truly protect your financial interests are you and your own lawyer, if you choose to use one.

You may also want to consult a tax pro at this stage. Ideally, you will have worked out all tax issues early in the game, well before you started the drafting process. But if your sale is especially complex or if you didn't get tax advice early on, it's a good idea to have the documents reviewed by a tax adviser (who may be someone different than your lawyer) to make sure the language will pass IRS muster and that your sale will have the tax consequences that you anticipate.

E. How to Prepare Attachments to Your Sales Agreement

You want your sales agreement to contain all the terms of your contract with the seller, but you don't want it to get bogged down in minutiae. If your purchase involves long detailed lists of assets and liabilities, it's better to put them in attachments to the sales agreement, rather than in the body of the agreement itself. Similarly, you should consider attaching to the sales agreement the main documents that you or the buyer will sign at the closing. As long as the attachment clearly refers to the sales agreement to which it is being attached, this approach is as legal as it is sensible. For example, you can attach the promissory note that the buyer is agreeing to sign or the bill of sale so that later there will be no quibbling over the exact wording of the document.

To effectively attach materials to a contract, simply identify the original document (for example, the sales agreement) and the names of the parties (seller and buyer) and its date. When preparing more than one attachment, label them consecutively—that is, Attachment A, Attachment B, and so on. You can avoid possible confusion by using a heading like the one shown below.

Where to find the forms. You'll find copies of the Attachment to Sales Agreement form on the CD-ROM at the back of the book.

F. Steps in Finalizing Your Sales Agreement and Other Documents

If you've never sold a business before, preparing the documents and then moving toward a closing can seem daunting. These tasks will be manageable, however, if you follow the logical steps outlined below.

1. Do a rough draft of your sales agreement and related documents, using the files on the CD-ROM included with this book. Appendix A explains how to use the CD-ROM.

2. Once you've got a draft sales agreement, print it out. Since you will undoubtedly be making changes along the way, based on your lawyer's review and negotiations with the buyer, be sure to put the

---

Attachment A to the Sales Agreement

Dated: _____

Between _____, Seller,

and _____, Buyer

date and version number on each draft.

3. Have your attorney review your draft and help you craft clauses specific to your sale. You may want to do the first drafts before you get your lawyer involved—this book is designed for that—but you may prefer a different working relationship as explained in Section D2, above.

4. Once you have a rough draft of your sales agreement and other legal documents, you're ready to submit them to the buyer for review. Typically, you may have to negotiate some fine points—and occasionally some major ones as well.

5. After you and the buyer reach full agreement on the wording of the documents, you can both sign the sales agreement following the recommendations in Chapter 18. The other documents (such as the promissory note and noncompete agreement) don't get signed until the closing.

6. The last step is the closing itself—the occasion when final documents are signed and ownership of the business changes hands. The turnover can go amazingly smoothly if you've drafted the necessary papers well in advance and used a closing checklist as recommended in Chapter 22.

Once that is all done, congratulations! You've sold your business!

G. Amending Your Sales Agreement

Once your sales agreement has been signed, it can only be changed if you and the buyer agree to and sign an amendment. A sample of the form you can use to amend your sales agreement after it has been signed is shown below.

Each time you make an amendment, the rest of the terms of the original Sales Agreement and any earlier amendments will remain in effect. If there is a conflict between this amendment and the original sales agreement or any earlier amendment, the terms of the most recent amendment will prevail.

An amendment to a sales agreement should be signed by the same people who signed the agreement itself. As explained in Chapter 18, this can include people other than just you and the buyer. For example, it might include spouses or guarantors.

Here's how to complete this amendment form:

❶ List the amendment number (in consecutive order by date, 1, 2, 3, and so on).

❷ List the seller and buyer names as they appear in the sales agreement.

❸ Fill in the date the sales agreement was signed.

❹ Name the business that you're selling.

❺ Describe in detail the information you want to include in your

Amendment of Sales Agreement

Amendment Number ___❶___

_____❷_____ (Seller)

and _____❷_____ (Buyer)

agree to the following amendment of the Sales Agreement dated ___❸___

concerning :

_____❹_____

_____

_____

_____❺_____

_____

_____

_____

_____

In all other respects, the terms of the original Sales Agreement and any earlier amendments will remain in effect. If there is a conflict between this amendment and the original sales agreement or any earlier amendment, the terms of this amendment will prevail.

_____❻_____

_____

_____

_____

amendment in the space provided. For example, if you are deleting a clause in your agreement, your amendment might read: "Clause [number and name of clause] of the original sales agreement is deleted in its entirety." If you are changing a portion of your agreement—for instance, you are extending the amount of time to remove a contingency—your amendment might say: "Clause [number and name of clause] is amended to extend the time of closing to April 1, 20xx."

6 All parties to the sales agreement should sign and date the amendment; it is not necessary to give the parties' addresses, however, because these are already listed in the sales agreement itself.

⚠️ **Don't use amendments for multiple changes.** Amendments to an existing sales agreement work fine when a couple of items are being changed such as raising or lowering the sales price or removing certain assets from the sale. But if you're changing lots of items in the original sales agreement, amendments can get confusing. Where changes will be extensive, it often makes sense to redo the entire sales agreement to avoid the possibility of confusion.

Who's Selling, Who's Buying— And What's Being Sold

The opening portions of a sales agreement identify the seller and buyer and what you're selling. As explained below, this section of the contract differs for asset and entity sales. All sellers should read Section A for advice on naming the parties in the sales agreement. For advice on identifying what you're selling in an asset sale, read Section B. For relevant terms in an entity sale, see Section C.

A. Naming the Parties

Logically enough, your sales agreement will start off by identifying the seller and buyer—the individuals or businesses (the "parties") who are agreeing to the contract.

A sales agreement can be used by people selling any type of business entity or the assets of a business. Naming the parties can be simple if you're selling a sole proprietorship and the buyer, too, is an individual. In this case, all you need to do is insert your name and the buyer's name. Things can get more complicated if the buyer or seller is a business entity (a partnership, a corporation, or an LLC) rather than an individual. In this case, you'll need to correctly name the business, designate its legal nature, and note the state in which the business is organized. "Format for Names in a Sales Agreement," below, will help you understand how to do this for both asset and entity sales.

Not everyone signing the agreement will be listed as a seller or buyer. For example, when a corporation is a buyer or a seller, the corporate officer who will be signing the agreement on behalf of the corporation won't be named as a seller or buyer. Nor will someone who is signing the agreement as a guarantor or as the spouse of a sole proprietor in a community property state. Chapter 18 explains how to obtain the signature(s) of the person or people with authority to legally bind a business entity that's buying or selling assets or another business entity.

1. Naming the Seller and Buyer in an Asset Sale

In an asset sale, each party (the seller and the buyer) can either be an individual (the operator of a sole proprietorship) or an entity (a partnership, corporation, or LLC).

---

1. Names

_____ (Seller) and

_____ (Buyer) agree to the following sale.

Format for Names in a Sales Agreement

This "Names" chart will help you and the buyer correctly identify the parties at the beginning of the sales agreement. The chart gives the recommended format for completing the Names clause, depending on whether the seller or buyer is a sole proprietor, a business entity, or an individual, and whether the sale is an asset or entity sale. Sections A1 and A2 provide examples for different types of sellers for asset and entity sales, including complicated situations when an entity (rather than an individual) owns the entity being sold.

Status of Seller or Buyer	Identification of Seller or Buyer in an Asset Sale	Identification of Seller or Buyer in an Entity Sale
Sole Proprietor. A one-owner business which is neither a corporation nor an LLC. (When a married couple owns such a business, the business is a partnership, but the couple can file tax returns as a sole proprietorship.)	*Two different styles may be used:* John Smith *[or]* John Smith doing business as Ace Diner *(The second style is preferred if the sole proprietor uses a business name separate from his or her own.)*	Not applicable for a seller; a sole proprietorship is not an entity that can be sold—only its assets can be sold. A buyer who is a sole proprietor can use the same identification format as is used in an asset sale.
Partnership. A business formed by two or more people who haven't created a corporation or an LLC.	Smith & Jones, a Michigan Partnership	A seller or buyer that's a partnership can use the same identification format as is used in an asset sale.
Corporation. A business entity owned by one or more shareholders.	Modern Textiles Inc., a Texas Corporation	A seller or buyer that's a corporation can use the same identification format as is used in an asset sale.
Limited Liability Company (LLC). A business entity owned by one or more members.	Games and Such LLC, a California Limited Liability Company	A seller or buyer that's an LLC can use the same identification format as is used in an asset sale.

Format for Names in a Sales Agreement (continued)

Individual(s). Someone who is not acting on behalf of a business.	(Normally limited to buyers—for example, people buying assets in their own names, intending to later form a corporation or an LLC.) John Smith [or] John Smith and Mary Jones (Individuals who sell the assets of their business will do so as either sole proprietors or partners. See above.)	Individuals who are selling or buying corporate shares, LLC membership interests, or partnership interests can use the same identification format as is used by individuals in an asset sale.

When an entity is selling some or all of its assets to the buyer, you identify the seller by inserting the name of the partnership, corporation, or LLC that's selling the assets. When a sole proprietorship is selling its assets, the business owner (sole proprietor) is named as the seller.

Similarly, when an entity is buying some or all of the assets of a business, you identify the buyer by inserting the name of the partnership, corporation, or LLC that's buying the assets. And when a sole proprietorship is buying assets, the owner of the business that's buying the assets (the sole proprietor) is named as the buyer.

Here are a few examples.

EXAMPLE 1: *Seller Is a Sole Proprietor and Buyer Is a Corporation (Asset Sale)*

1. Names

John Smith (Seller) and Modern Textiles Inc., a Texas Corporation (Buyer) agree to the following sale.

EXAMPLE 2: *Seller Is a Partnership and Buyer Is an LLC (Asset Sale)*

1. Names

Smith and Jones, a Michigan Partnership (Seller) and Games and Such LLC, a California Limited Liability Company (Buyer) agree to the following sale.

⚠ Always include the business's official name to avoid any ambiguity about what entity is involved in the deal. Some corporations and LLCs use a different name (often called a fictitious name) to identify their business to the public. If this is your situation, use your official corporate or LLC name in the sales agreement. So if your Illinois business is New Enterprises Corp., and that corporation does business as Kwik and Klean Laundry, you should name "New Enterprises Corp., an Illinois corporation" as the seller—although it's also okay to say "New Enterprises Corp., an Illinois corporation doing business as Kwik and Klean Laundry." And if you're a sole proprietor who uses a business name separate from your own, do the same.

EXAMPLE 3: *Seller Is a Corporation and Buyer Is a Sole Proprietor (Asset Sale)*

1. Names

Modern Textiles Inc., a Texas Corporation (Seller) and John Smith doing business as Smith's Fabric Center (Buyer) agree to the following sale.

When two or more people or entities are buying the assets of a business, refer to them as Sellers—plural—in the sales agreement. It can get confusing to use the singular Seller to refer to several people or entities.

2. Naming the Seller or Sellers in an Entity Sale

The basic Names clause for an entity sale is the same for an entity and asset sale.

The key difference is how you identify the seller or sellers. Since the entity (corporation, LLC, or partnership) is being sold, it follows that its owners—not the entity itself—are the sellers.

Where small businesses are concerned, identifying the parties in an entity sale is usually simple and straightforward. That's because the entity being sold (such as a corporation or an LLC) is usually owned by one or a few individuals who are selling all of their ownership interests to one or a few other individuals.

The seller or sellers will almost always be either the sole owner of the entity or a small group of owners: the partners in a partnership or the owners of corporate stock or LLC membership interests. In an entity sale, you insert the name(s) of the individual(s) who are selling their shares of corporate stock, their LLC membership interests, or their partnership interests.

When two or more owners (be they people, entities, or both) are selling their interests in an entity, refer to them as Sellers—plural—throughout the sales agreement. This avoids the linguistic awkwardness of using the singular word Seller to cover several people.

Entity sales by partnerships are extremely rare. Also, there's no such thing as an entity sale of a sole proprietorship; the sale of such a business is always an asset sale.

Here are a few examples of how to identify the seller or sellers in an entity sale.

EXAMPLE 1: *Entity Sale of a Corporate Business Owned by Individuals*

If Modern Textiles Inc.—introduced in Example 3 for an asset sale, above—were owned by David Field and Jerry Nestor and they wanted to sell their shares of Modern Textiles stock to a buyer (entity sale), the sellers would be David and Jerry and the Names clause would read as follows:

1. Names

David Field and Jerry Nestor (Sellers) and John Smith doing business as Smith's Fabric Center (Buyer) agree to the following sale.

EXAMPLE 2: *Entity Sale of a Corporate Business Owned by an LLC*

If Modern Textiles Inc. were owned by Kenwood LLC and Kenwood wanted to sell its shares of Modern Textiles to a buyer (an entity sale), the seller would be Kenwood LLC and the Names clause would read as follows:

1. Names

Kenwood LLC (Seller) and John Smith doing business as Smith's Fabric Center (Buyer) agree to the following sale.

Check with your lawyer if you or the buyer have a complicated ownership structure—for example, if another business entity owns the stock of the selling or buying entity or its membership interests. In this situation, the seller or buyer will be the entity that owns the stock or membership interests.

To understand how this works, let's assume an entity sale in which the shares of Aero Corporation are being sold. Let's also assume that Fiddler LLC owns 50% of Aero Corporation, and Joe Doakes owns the other 50%. Here, the sellers would be identified as Fiddler LLC and Joe Doakes.

Remember: A corporation's shareholders can consist of individuals, other corporations, LLCs, and partnerships. Similarly, the members of an LLC can be individuals, other LLCs, corporations, and partnerships. Even some partners in a partnership can be other entities. And on the buyer's side, it's possible that an entity may purchase the entity being sold (for example, Arboretum LLC is purchasing all the shares of Aero Corporation) or that some combination of individuals and entities may buy the ownership interests in the business being sold.

Usually, it's not difficult to sort out who's selling their ownership interests in the entity being sold and who's buying those interests. If you're uncertain, however, you should get advice from a lawyer.

Alternative Format for Naming the Parties in a Sales Agreement (Asset Sale)

The format for naming the parties to a sales agreement discussed above will almost always work well, and it's the one included on the CD-ROM with this book. Just in case you are faced with papers drafted by the buyer's lawyer, you should be aware of a second method that can be appropriate when an entity is selling its assets. This involves having the opening portion of the sales agreement name the owners of the selling entity as well as the entity itself. That is, depending on the entity involved, the Names clause may name the partners in a partnership, the members of an LLC, or the shareholders of a corporation. When this alternative format is used, the identification clause may look like this:

1. Names

Modern Textiles Inc., a Texas Corporation (Seller); Games and Such LLC, a California Limited Liability Company (Buyer); and John Smith and Mary Jones, the shareholders of Modern Textiles Inc. (Shareholders) agree to the following sale.

This alternative is most appropriate when the owners of the selling entity will personally make promises, as would be the case if they guarantee the accuracy of the representations made in the sales agreement. The owners can also accept those responsibilities at the end of the document or in a separate contract (as discussed in Chapter 14). Legally, there's no difference. Either alternative is acceptable.

Similarly, when the buyer is an entity, you can name the individual owners as well as the entity in the opening clause. You might do this, for example, where you and any co-owners of your entity are personally guaranteeing payment of the promissory note or agreeing to be personally responsible for business debts. But, again, signing at the end or in a separate contract protects the seller just as well.

B. Identifying Your Business and What You're Selling in an Asset Sale

When you have an asset sale, the next clause in the sales agreement will identify the type, name, and address of the business in which the assets have been used.

Here's how to fill in this clause.

In the first blank, insert the type of business being sold, such as an automotive supply business.

In the second blank, insert the name the seller's business uses.

In the third blank, fill in the business's complete address (street, city, and state).

Completed, this clause might look the one shown below.

EXAMPLE 1: *Sale of Business With One Location*

2. Sale of Business Assets

Seller is selling to Buyer and Buyer is buying from Seller the assets described below of the restaurant business known as Red's Rite Spot located at 123 Main Street, Berkeley, California.

EXAMPLE 2: *Sale of Business With Several Locations and You're Selling the Assets Used at More Than One Location*

2. Sale of Business Assets

Seller is selling to Buyer and Buyer is buying from Seller the assets described below of the bakery business known as Bagels and Baguettes, located at 456 State Street and 789 North Liberty, Atlanta, Georgia.

1. Why It's Important to Identify the Assets You're Selling

In an asset sale, you should clearly identify the assets you're selling to the buyer, such as:

- goodwill of the business (Option A in Clause 3, Assets Being Sold, below). Goodwill is an intangible asset that may consist of such things as your business's reputation or its loyal customer base.
- the business lease (Option B). If the buyer is going to occupy the same business premises, fill in details on

---

2. Sale of Business Assets (Asset Sale)

Seller is selling to Buyer and Buyer is buying from Seller the assets described below of the _____ business known as _____ located at _____

_____.

the date of the lease, the landlord's name, and the address of the rental property.

- your inventory including any goods you sell at retail (Option C). In an asset sale, you'll transfer ownership of the inventory to the buyer by using a bill of sale, as described in Chapter 20.
- furniture, fixtures, and equipment (Option D). You will itemize these assets on a separate page (an attach-

ment to the sales agreement), rather than in this clause.

- equipment leases such as for phone systems or copiers (Option E).
- contracts with suppliers and contracts with customers that the buyer will be acquiring from you (Option F).
- intellectual property rights, such as copyrights in advertising materials or the trademarked logo of the company (Option G).

Each business is unique, but below is what an asset clause might look like.

---

3. Assets Being Sold (Asset Sale)

The assets being sold consist of:

[*choose all options that apply*]

☐ A. The goodwill of the business, including the current business name and phone number.

☐ B. The lease dated _____ between _____, Seller as Tenant, and _____, Landlord, covering the premises at _____for the time period from _____ to _____.

☐ C. The inventory of goods.

☐ D. The furniture, fixtures, and equipment listed in Attachment _____.

☐ E. The equipment leases listed in Attachment _____.

☐ F. The supply contract with _____ .

☐ G. Intellectual property rights as follows: _____

_____

_____ .

The following assets of the business are excluded from the sale:

_____

_____

_____

_____ .

You can delete those items that don't apply and add those that do, relettering the options as necessary.

At this point, you're just listing the assets you're selling. In Clause 6, Sale Price, discussed in Chapter 14, you'll allocate the sales price among these assets.

Note that accounts receivable are not included in the list of assets in this clause. They are covered separately in Clause 8, discussed in Chapter 14.

You'll notice the reference to attachments in Clause 3, Assets Being Sold. For example, rather than list all the furniture you're selling in the sales agreement itself, I recommend that you list the furniture on a separate sheet that you can attach to the agreement. Chapter 12 explains how to prepare attachments and how they can streamline your sales agreement. Chapter 17 includes a clause (Clause 25, Documents for Transferring Assets) where you specify documents, such as an assignment of the lease, that you (the seller) will deliver to the buyer.

While you may be inclined to simply say in the sales agreement that you're selling all the assets of the business, the buyer will almost certainly want the sales agreement to be more specific. Including a list of assets in the sales agreement can benefit you as well, since it will remove any doubt about exactly which assets are owned by the business and are being sold to the buyer. This is especially important if there are some assets that you or your business entity (corporation or LLC) plan to keep, such as cash, accounts receivable, or even a desk you want to hold on to, or assets that the buyer does not want to buy. Section 2, below, explains how to exclude assets from your sale.

Important chapters to read. There are several chapters you need to read carefully before completing the clause "Assets Being Sold" of the sales agreement.

- Chapter 3 contains a discussion on the importance of clarifying what you'll sell and what you'll keep in an assets sale.
- Chapters 7 and 9 explain the important documents you'll need that are related to assets such as a lease or copyright, and the major types of tangible and intangible assets you may be selling or transferring to the buyer.
- Chapter 10 discusses whether leases and other contracts can or can't be transferred (assigned) to the buyer. (Often, they can't be transferred without the consent of the other party to the contract.) Chapter 10 also discusses the transfer of business licenses, which may be relevant if you are selling a business such as a restaurant or bar.
- Chapter 14 provides information about a business's inventory and accounts receivable.
- Chapter 20 explains how to transfer your assets and the documents you need to do so, including a bill of sale to transfer tangible assets such as furniture and specialized assignments to transfer intangible assets such as a lease or a copyright.

⚠ Contracts not to compete—and agreements to work for the buyer— are not business assets. As discussed in Chapter 4, for tax and other reasons, the total amount of money that the buyer is agreeing to pay you may include several components that are not payments for assets of the business. For example, the total dollars you'll receive from the buyer may include compensation for your agreement not to compete after the assets are transferred and for services you'll perform for the new owner as either a consultant (independent contractor) or as an employee. You should include clauses referring to these contracts in a later part of the sales agreement (See Clauses 21 and 22 in Chapter 16.) You shouldn't do so in the portion of the agreement dealing with the assets being sold. And, as you'll see in Chapter 21, it's usually best to spell out the details of a noncompete agreement or an employment or consulting contract in a separate document that can be an attachment to the sales agreement.

2. Excluding Assets From the Sale

If you and the buyer have agreed that you (or your business) will keep some assets that are or appear to be part of the business, it's smart to list such exclusions in the sales agreement. To avoid disagreements, list even minor items like a cell phone or a wall hanging. In addition to specific physical assets, you may want to exclude other assets

such as cash, accounts receivable, lawsuit claims, tax refund claims, insurance refund claims, and perhaps some business records that will be of no use to the buyer. In some cases, you may want to keep such assets as luxury box seats, event tickets, and club memberships. If you want to exclude specific assets, include a clause like the following at the end of the "Assets Being Sold" clause of your sales agreement.

EXAMPLE: *Exclusion of Certain Assets in Asset Sales*

The following assets of the business are excluded from the sale:

1. The brown, antique wooden desk and bookcase located in the sales office

2. All patents

3. Subscription to The Wall Street Journal

4. The sound system and CD collection

 Don't overlook business insurance policies. Insurance policies are a type of contract. If your insurance agent or broker informs you that your insurance policies can be transferred, and the buyer wishes to assume them, you'll want to include these policies on the asset list. But if insurance can't be assumed, you'll want to be sure the buyer arranges for new policies so there's no gap in coverage. Also, if you'll be retaining a security interest in business property because the buyer will be paying the sale price to you in installments, you'll want to be sure that your name is added to the buyer's insurance as a covered party. (In the security agreement, you can require that the buyer carry insurance that covers both you and the buyer until the sale price has been fully paid. See Chapter 19.) If the buyer gets new insurance, then once the closing takes place, you can cancel your current insurance, in which case you'll probably be entitled to a partial refund of the premium you paid.

C. Identifying the Business and What You're Selling in an Entity Sale

You'll take a different approach if you're selling your business entity rather than its assets. If you sell your corporate, LLC, or partnership entity, you'll be selling your entire ownership interest in the business—that is, your shares of stock or your LLC membership interest. Since the buyer will acquire the corporation or LLC that owns the assets, by definition, everything the corporation or LLC owns will be transferred as part of the sale. In an entity sale, you don't need to identify the assets one by one, and accordingly, the description of what you're selling can be briefer. The sales agreement may say, for example, that you're selling your shares of Acme Corporation or your membership interest in your Boston

Bakery LLC. You can use a clause like one of the following.

For a Corporate Business

> **4. Sale of Corporate Stock (Entity Sale Only—Corporation)**
>
> Seller is selling to Buyer and Buyer is buying from Seller all of the Seller's shares of stock in Modern Textiles Inc., a Texas corporation.

For an LLC Business

> **5. Sale of LLC Membership Interest (Entity Sale Only—LLC)**
>
> Seller is selling to Buyer and Buyer is buying from Seller all of the Seller's membership interests in Digital Services LLC, an Indiana limited liability company.

The point of an entity sale is that the corporation or LLC continues to own the business's assets after the shares or membership interests are transferred to the buyer. It's possible, however, that you and the buyer have agreed that a few assets will not be included in the sale. For example, your corporation may own a computer that you'd like to keep for yourself. If so, you'll need to include language recognizing this. Of course, before the closing, the entity will need to distribute the excluded assets to the entity's owners: the shareholders, LLC members, or partners.

EXAMPLE: *Exclusion of Certain Assets If You're Selling Your Corporation as an Entity Sale:*

Before the closing, Seller will arrange for the corporation to transfer to Seller the ownership of the brown, antique wooden desk and bookcase located in the sales office.

The sales price for an entity sale should not include any payment that you'll receive either now or in the future for your covenant not to compete or for consulting or any other work you agree to perform for the buyer. Unlike an asset sale, in an entity sale, there's no need to allocate the sale price among the assets that the entity owns. That's because you're not selling the assets but, rather, your shares of stock or your LLC membership interest. This means that in the sales agreement, you should omit the asset allocation clause as discussed in Chapter 14. But also make sure that the sales price doesn't include any payment you'll receive for your covenant not to compete or for services you'll render to the buyer. These payments will be dealt with elsewhere in the agreement.

The Sales Price and Terms of Payment

This chapter covers the parts of the sales agreement dealing with the sale price. The first three sections cover issues relevant only in asset sales, including:

- how the sales price is allocated among typical types of assets (Section A)
- issues that come up if the buyer agrees to acquire your inventory of merchandise (Section B), and
- issues that come up if the buyer agrees to acquire your accounts receivable (Section C).

The fourth section (Section D) covers the relevant sale price clauses for an entity sale. As explained below, entity sales don't require you to allocate assets for tax purposes. When you sell your corporate stock, LLC membership interest, or partnership interest in an entity, you're not selling the individual assets. These assets remain the property of the entity. Your sales agreement won't have to allocate the sale price among the assets, nor will you or the buyer have to file IRS Form 8594, *Asset Acquisition Statement*.

This chapter also explains how to develop the sales agreement clauses dealing with how you get paid. These clauses (relevant to both asset and entity sales) cover issues such as:

- whether the buyer will pay a deposit when the sales agreement is signed (Section E)
- how much the buyer will pay you at closing (Section F)

- the terms of the promissory note, if the buyer will be making installment payments after the closing (Section G), and
- arrangements for your getting a security interest in property of the business when the business changes hands—for example, a lien on the business assets or the buyer's home. (Section H covers these arrangements in asset sales, and Section I covers them in entity sales.)

A. Sale Price: Asset Sale

After completing Clause 3 (Assets Being Sold), discussed in Chapter 13, you're now ready to list the total sales price and allocate it among the assets, such as the goodwill or the equipment that you're selling. That's the purpose of the next clause (Sale Price), one of the key clauses in any sales agreement for an asset sale.

1. Allocating the Sale Price

In the first blank, insert the total sale price for the assets. This will be the same figure as the total at the bottom of the column. You'll then allocate this amount among the assets you're selling.

Here's a sample of how the completed Sale Price clause might look. As with all other parts of the sales agreement, you'll need to tailor the language and details of the clause to fit your transaction.

6. Sale Price (Asset Sale)

The sale price for the assets listed in this section is $_____, and is allocated as follows:

[*choose all options that apply*]

☐ A. Goodwill $_____

☐ B. Assignment of Lease $_____

☐ C. Inventory [*List here only if you've agreed on an amount. Otherwise, use Clause 7.*] $_____

☐ D. Accounts Receivable [*List here only if you've agreed on an amount. Otherwise, use Clause 8.*] $_____

☐ E. Furniture, Fixtures, and Equipment $_____

☐ F. Equipment Leases $_____

☐ G. Assignment of Contracts $_____

☐ H. Intellectual Property Rights $_____

Total $_____

a. Proration of Certain Items [*optional*]

The total sale price will be adjusted by prorating rent, taxes, insurance premiums, utility costs, and security deposits as of the date of closing.

b. Inventory [*optional*]

The total sale price will also be adjusted by adding the value of the inventory as covered in Clause 7 (Price of Inventory).

c. Accounts Receivable [*optional*]

The total sale price will also be adjusted by adding the value of the accounts receivable as covered in Clause 8 (Accounts Receivable).

EXAMPLE:

6. Sale Price (Asset Sale)

The sale price for the assets listed in this section is $250,000, and is allocated as follows:

A. Goodwill	$ 100,000
B. Assignment of Lease	$ 5,000
C. Furniture, Fixtures, and Equipment	$ 100,000
D. Assignment of Contracts	$ 40,000
E. Intellectual Property Rights	$ 5,000
Total	$ 250,000

Allocating the sale price among the assets isn't a legal requirement, but it's nevertheless highly recommended for a practical reason: It gives you and the buyer an agreed basis for your income tax computations, reducing the likelihood of hassles with the IRS later on. As explained in Chapter 4, when you sell business assets, some of the gain may be taxed at ordinary income rates and some of the gain may be taxed at long-term capital gain rates, depending on the nature of the assets and the allocation you make. Also, from the buyer's standpoint, allocating the price to different assets can help determine how quickly the buyer can deduct or depreciate the cost of the various assets.

It's crucial that you thoroughly read Chapter 4 and understand how a careful allocation of your sale price into appropriate categories (rather than simply stating a lump sum) can minimize your tax burden. Broadly speaking, in allocating the sale price, your best strategy as the seller is to have as much as possible of the sale price allocated to assets such as goodwill that will generate tax at the long-term capital gain rate.

Completing Form 8594, *Asset Acquisition Statement,* is a highly technical task that is best left to an experienced tax professional. To see why this is so, check out the form and the instructions, which are included in the pdf file on the CD-ROM. By referring to the allocation section of your sales agreement, your tax adviser will find it easy to complete Form 8594 for you. Chances are that you will not be selling any assets that fall into Class I, II, or III (these are cash, securities, and accounts receivable) on the IRS form. Inventory will fall into Class IV and goodwill will be a Class VII item. In all likelihood, the other assets will fall into either Class V (tangible property) or VI (covenant not to compete or other intangible property).

Because what's best for your tax picture won't necessarily be best for the buyer, you may need help from a tax professional to work out a compromise on the allocation figures. This typically involves an adjustment of the sale price to best serve both of your interests. Remember that at tax time, you and the buyer will each have to file IRS Form 8594, *Asset Allocation Statement.* If you agree on the allocation of the sale price and you're reasonable about it, the IRS normally will accept your allocation. A tax professional can also help you make sure that you fill out IRS Form 8594 correctly so that it stands up to scrutiny by the government.

2. Prorations

Because there may be some expenses that you and/or the buyer will owe each other after the closing, it makes sense to address prorations and reimbursements in the sales agreement. Clause 6a does this.

a. When the Buyer Will Owe You Money for Prepaid Expenses

Since bills for business expenses can come due at various times during a given month, and some may even arrive on a quarterly basis, chances are you'll have paid some expenses in advance of the closing date that will benefit the buyer. For example, let's say you close on January 15 and your business has paid rent to the landlord for the whole month of January. Assuming that the buyer will be taking over the lease and staying on in the same space, it's reasonable to expect the buyer to reimburse you for rent for the last half of January. And if upon signing your lease you posted a $2,000 security deposit with the landlord that the landlord will continue to hold, it's reasonable for the buyer to reimburse you for that deposit if it will ultimately be refunded to the buyer at the end of the lease.

Similarly, you may have also paid in advance for property taxes, utilities, or leased equipment such as a photocopier. It is normal business practice for the sales agreement to provide for the buyer to reimburse you for the portion of such payments that covers any time periods after the closing date. The process of splitting these advance payments is called proration. Subsection a of Clause 6 in the sales agreement includes standard language on proration. Usually, by the time the closing rolls around, you'll know the amounts of the prepaid expenses and you can make the adjustments at the closing.

b. When You Will Owe the Buyer Money for Expenses Paid by the Buyer After the Closing

Sometimes, of course, prorations should be made in the opposite direction—that is, you'll owe the buyer for your fair portion of utility and other bills that haven't arrived or aren't due yet, but that partly cover the time when you still owned the business. There are a few ways to handle this:

- If the amounts are insignificant, you may simply agree that the buyer will pay the full cost.
- When the amounts are known at the time of closing, you can handle the proration then by adjusting the sale price in the buyer's favor.

- If you're likely to be owing the buyer money for one or more bills but won't know the exact amount until after closing, you'll need to get something in writing. One option is for the buyer to simply hold back from the first or second installment payment an amount equal to what you end up owing. Or, in an all-cash deal in which you're likely to owe money to the buyer a few months down the road when a certain bill arrives, the buyer might suggest that a portion of the sale price sufficient to cover your obligation be held by a third party (an escrow agent) until the bill arrives. Then part of the money will be used to pay your share of the bill, and the rest will come to you. A lawyer for you or the buyer can be the escrow agent, or it can be anyone else you both select. For example, if you're receiving cash in full when closing the sale of your car wash, the buyer may want you to leave some money with an escrow agent to cover your share of a potentially large water bill when it arrives.

- If the bill is one that the you have been paying regularly for some years, and you have a ballpark figure of what the bill might be and documentation of that to show to the buyer, you can estimate what the bill will be and deduct that amount from the sale price, with an agreement that no adjustments will be made if it is higher or lower. You and the buyer are each taking the risk of losing a few dollars, but you have a sale agreement that's final, with no need for adjustments later.

A lawyer can help you with appropriate wording for the proration part of your sales agreement. The key point here is that it makes sense to address prorations and reimbursements in the sales agreement as we do in Clause 6a.

3. Inventory

Unless you're selling a retail or manufacturing business, you probably won't have inventory to sell. If, however, you do have inventory, there are two ways to deal with it in your sales agreement.

If you and the buyer have agreed on a fixed price for the inventory, you can insert the line item "Inventory" in Clause 6, Sale Price, and specify the price. For example, if you're selling a restaurant and the value of the food on hand at any given time may fluctuate between $2,500 and $3,500, it may be easier to simply allocate $3,000 of the total purchase price to the inventory of food rather than making a physical count on the day of closing. In that case, you won't need to have a separate inventory section in your sales agreement such as discussed below, but you will simply list $3,000 in the line item Inventory.

If you do have inventory but haven't set a price on it yet, you can use the optional inventory language suggested above (Clause 6b), referring to a separate Price of Inventory clause. In this case, you won't include inventory as a line item in the main part of Clause 6.

Section B, below, explains how to complete a separate clause covering inventory in your sales agreement for an asset sale.

4. Accounts Receivable

As with the inventory, if the buyer will be acquiring your accounts receivable, you can deal with this asset in Clause 6 or separately in Clause 8 (discussed in Section C, below). You'll put the accounts receivable as a line item in Clause 6 only if you and the buyer have agreed on an exact amount that the buyer will pay you for these accounts. Otherwise, you'll use the optional wording provided in Clause 6c, above, referring to Clause 8 and an adjustment of the sale price.

5. Payments for Employment or Consultant Services or for a Noncompete Agreement Not Included in Sale Price

As noted in Chapter 13, the sale price of the assets set out above does not include any money you may receive for signing a covenant not to compete or for services you may provide the buyer after the clos-

ing as either a consultant (independent contractor) or an employee. (The same holds true in an entity sale, as explained in Section D, below.) For example, let's say the total amount of money you'll receive as a result of the sale is $500,000, of which $50,000 is for your agreement not to compete in Del Rio County for 36 months and $100,000 is a consultant's fee you'll receive for giving advice to the business for the next 24 months. In that situation, you'll be receiving $350,000 for the assets of the business; that's the amount that should be accounted for in the sale price portion (Clause 6) of the sales agreement. The reason for not including the entire $500,000 is that noncompete agreements or consulting agreements are not assets of a business; you'll need to cover these additional sources of money in another part of the sales agreement with details in separate documents as explained in Chapter 16.

B. Inventory: Asset Sale

If your business doesn't have inventory—or has inventory but won't be transferring it to the buyer—you can skip this section. Also, you can normally skip this section if you're selling your entity rather than its assets—unless yours is one of those rare entity sales in which the sale price of the stock or LLC membership interests is going to be adjusted to reflect fluctuations in the value of the entity's inventory.

If you're selling a retail or manufacturing business or a restaurant, the buyer is likely to be acquiring your inventory as part of the sale. (But do remember that goods you're holding on consignment don't count as inventory.) There are a few ways to deal with this in the sales agreement. If fluctuations in the value of inventory are likely to be small in the days before the closing, you may simply want to fold the inventory into the sale price and allocate a portion of the sale price to it as one more line item, as explained in Section A3, above.

If, however, the value of the inventory is likely to change considerably between the inking of the sales agreement and the closing—or for some other reason it's hard to determine a precise value before closing—you may decide to treat the inventory separately from the sale price for the other assets. In this case you'll need to come up with an inventory clause such as Clause 7, Price of Inventory. Be sure to specify in this clause what you mean by the inventory of goods—for example, clothes or food—and who will do the physical inventory and when. If

---

7. Price of Inventory (Asset Sale) [*optional*]

At closing, in addition to the total sale price listed in Clause 6 above, Buyer will buy the inventory of goods consisting of [merchandise held for sale/parts and supplies/food and beverages] by paying Seller the amount Seller paid for those goods, as shown in the original invoices. A physical count of the goods will be made by [Seller and Buyer] or [*list name of outside inventory company*]. [Seller and Buyer will share equally the cost of having the inventory counted by *list name of outside inventory company*.]

   The count will be made _____ days before closing and will include only unopened and undamaged goods.

a. Price Paid for Inventory [*optional*]

Buyer will pay no more than $_____ for the goods.

b. Minimum Price Paid for Inventory [*optional*]

Buyer will pay at least $_____ for the goods.

c. Minimum Price With a Cap on Maximum Price [*optional*]

Buyer will pay at least $_____ but no more than $_____ for the goods.

considerable inventory is involved—and especially if it was bought at different times and different prices—you and the buyer may prefer not to handle the task yourselves, but to hire an outside company to do the physical counting. In that case, you'll want to specify those arrangements in your sales agreement, including how the cost of counting inventory will be shared.

Sometimes, if the value of the inventory is especially hard to estimate in advance, the buyer may want a cap on how much will be paid for the inventory. By the same token, you may want to state a minimum inventory value. Clause 7, Price of Inventory, includes contractual language (Options a, b, and c) that will let you and the buyer accomplish either or both of these goals. Simply include whatever language applies.

Because a savvy buyer will only be interested in paying for inventory that's readily saleable, the buyer may want to exclude items that are damaged, obsolete, or hard to sell for some other reason. If part of your inventory has problems of this sort, one of your best options is to simplify the deal by running a clearance sale of the undesirable merchandise before closing. Or you could negotiate to sell the distressed portion of your inventory to the buyer at a steep discount, adding language to Clause 7 as shown in the following example.

EXAMPLE:

7. Price of Inventory

At closing, in addition to the total sale price listed in Clause 6 above, Buyer will buy the inventory of goods consisting of merchandise held for sale by paying Seller the amount Seller paid for those goods, as shown in the original invoices. However, the invoice price of goods purchased by Seller more than 12 months before the closing date will be reduced by 75%. A physical count of the goods will be made by Inventory Service Company. Seller and Buyer will share equally the cost of having the inventory counted by Inventory Service Company.

The count will be made two days before closing and will include only unopened and undamaged goods.

C. Dealing With the Purchase of Accounts Receivable: Asset Sale

If your business doesn't have accounts receivable—or has accounts receivable but won't be transferring them to the buyer—you can skip this section. Also, you can normally skip this section if you're selling your entity rather than its assets—unless yours is one of those rare entity sales in which the sale price of the stock or LLC membership interests is going to be adjusted to reflect fluctuations in the value of the accounts receivable.

Among its assets, your business may have accounts receivable (amounts that customers owe your business). There are several ways to handle these accounts:

- **Seller retains and collects the accounts receivable.** The simplest way to handle accounts receivable is for you retain ownership of them and take responsibility for collecting the money owed to your business (Alternative A of Clause 8, Accounts Receivable, below).

- **Buyer collects the accounts and sends the money to seller.** Another common approach is for you to retain ownership of the accounts receivable, but have the buyer collect the accounts in the normal course of business, turning the proceeds over to you (Alternative B, below).

- **Buyer buys the accounts and keeps the amounts collected.** Finally, as part of your sale, you can simply sell to the buyer the accounts that are relatively current—perhaps at a discount, such as 25%, if some will be difficult to collect (Alternative C, below). Here's how these common approaches can be worded for your sales agreement.

---

8. Accounts Receivable (Asset Sale) [*optional*]

[*choose one of the following alternatives and edit according to your situation*]

☐ A. Seller's accounts receivable as of the day of closing will remain Seller's property. Buyer will have no responsibility for collecting those accounts. Seller will have the right to collect those accounts and to keep the amounts received.

☐ B. Seller's accounts receivable as of the day of closing will remain Seller's property. Buyer will use usual reasonable efforts to collect the accounts in the course of its normal billing practices. Within ten days of receiving amounts owed to Seller, Buyer will send those funds to Seller.

☐ C. At closing, Buyer will purchase all of Seller's accounts receivable that are no more than <u>90</u> days old. Buyer will pay Seller the balances owed on these accounts less <u>25</u>%. Buyer will be entitled to keep all sums collected on these accounts. The accounts receivable that Buyer is not buying will remain Seller's property. Buyer will have no responsibility for collecting those accounts. Seller will have the right to collect those accounts and to keep the amounts received.

Make it desirable for the buyer to assume all of your accounts receivable. Rarely will a buyer be willing to pay you the full value of your accounts receivable, since doing so would mean the buyer would be assuming 100% of the risk that all accounts will be paid. Realistically, it's usually fairer to lop off a reasonable percentage of the total amount owed to allow for the difficulty in collecting the more-problematic accounts and the possibility that some won't be collected at all. For example, you might agree that the buyer will pay you 75% of the total amount outstanding on bills that are no more than 90 days old and 60% of the bills more than 90 days old. Although you may be tempted to just hold onto the accounts with the hope of collecting a larger percentage of the total yourself, this is often a poor idea. The fact that you're no longer running the business means you have reduced collection leverage if payment isn't made.

D. Sale Price: Entity Sale

Sections A, B, and C above deal with the sale price clauses in an asset sale. In an entity sale, you will also need to cover the sale price, but the language will differ from that used in an asset sale.

1. No Allocation of Sale Price in Entity Sale

Unlike an asset sale, in an entity sale, there's no need to allocate the sale price among the assets that the entity owns. That's because you're not selling the assets but, rather, your shares of stock or your LLC membership interest. This means that in the sales agreement, you should not include an asset allocation clause such as Clause 6. Instead, the sale price clause for an entity sale would look like the sample below, depending on whether your entity is a corporation or an LLC.

As with the sale price in an asset sale, be sure that the price for an entity sale doesn't include any payment that you'll receive either now or in the future for a covenant not to compete or for consulting or any other work you agree to perform for the buyer. You'll cover these as separate clauses as discussed in Chapter 16.

2. Adjustments to the Sale Price in Entity Sale

If your business has inventory or accounts receivable, fluctuations in the value of those items can influence how much the buyer will be willing to pay for the entity or

---

9. Sale Price (Entity Sale)

The sale price of the [stock/LLC membership interests] is $75,000.

how much you're willing to accept. This can be a concern if there's the possibility of large swings in value between the time the sales agreement is signed and the closing—especially if there's a time gap of more than a few days between signing and closing. In that case, it can make sense to provide for an adjustment to reflect these changes (though such adjustments tend to be less common in an entity sale than in an asset sale). See Sections B and C, above, for a discussion of these issues. An example of a clause you can use in an entity sale is shown below.

You can avoid the issue of adjustments by valuing the inventory and accounts receivable just before signing the sales agreement, factoring those values into the sale price and then moving promptly to close the sale.

E. Deposit

To help make sure the buyer doesn't get cold feet and simply walk away from the sale at the last moment, you may want the buyer to put some money down as a deposit. Then, if the buyer arbitrarily bails

---

10. Adjustment of Sale Price (Entity Sale) [*optional*]

The sale price is based on the <u>corporation</u>'s inventory having a value of $<u>25,000</u> as shown on the original invoices. If at closing the inventory is determined to be worth less or more than that amount, the sale price will be adjusted downward by the amount the inventory is worth less than $<u>25,000</u> or upward by the amount the inventory value exceeds $<u>25,000</u>. Likewise, the sale price is based on the <u>corporation</u> having accounts receivable totaling $<u>10,000</u>. If at closing the accounts receivable are less or more than that amount, the sale price will be adjusted downward by the amount the accounts receivable are less than $<u>10,000</u> or upward by the amount the accounts exceed $<u>10,000</u>.

---

11. Deposit [*optional*]

Buyer will pay Seller a deposit of $<u>5,000</u> when Buyer and Seller sign this contract. This deposit will be applied toward the amount due at closing. Seller will return this deposit to Buyer if the purchase is not completed because Seller does not meet its commitments under this agreement for any reason or if the contingencies in Clause <u>23</u> are not removed. Otherwise, Seller will be entitled to retain the deposit in the event the sale is not completed.

out, you have at least something to show for your efforts. If you and buyer agree that there will be a deposit, this will be paid when you both sign the sales agreement.

If you are collecting a deposit from the buyer, you can use a clause like the one on the preceding page. It will work for either an asset sale or an entity sale. You'll need to fill in the amount of the deposit and any conditions for returning it. The amount of the deposit is a matter for negotiation. You'd like to have a deposit that will adequately compensate you for your time and effort if the buyer, without a good reason, abandons the deal before closing. While you may be able to sue the buyer if the buyer fails to close, chasing an elusive buyer for damages may not be worth it. Your most practical remedy is often to keep the deposit.

The suggested language in Clause 11 lets the buyer get back the deposit if you can't or don't meet your contractual commitments or if contingencies specified in the agreement aren't removed. An example of not meeting your commitments would be if you couldn't or wouldn't transfer to the buyer all of the assets listed in the sales agreement.

Contingencies are covered in Chapter 17. If your sales agreement contains contingencies, the buyer will want protective language along the lines of this suggested deposit clause. Let's say the current lease on your business's space is up in nine months, and you and the buyer have made your deal contingent on the landlord's granting the buyer a five-year extension of the lease. If that extension hasn't been fully worked out with the landlord yet, the buyer may insist on adding a clause in the sales agreement expressly stating that the sale is contingent on the buyer's getting a five-year extension of the lease from the landlord. In that case, the buyer undoubtedly would want to be sure that you returned the deposit if the lease extension couldn't be negotiated.

F. Payment at Closing

How much money changes hands at closing will depend on whether you'll be receiving cash in full or, more likely, only a portion of the purchase price, along with a promissory note for the balance in installments. You can choose one of five alternatives for Clause 12, Payment at Closing, and edit to fit your own situation.

1. Full Payment at Closing (Alternative A)

If the buyer will be paying you cash in full at closing, you can use Alternative A of Clause 12 rather than Alternatives B through E, which refer to installment payments. Note that the suggested language for Alternative A of Clause 12 allows the buyer to pay by cashier's check or wire transfer—either of which gives you far greater protection than accepting the buyer's personal check.

ALTERNATIVE A: *Full Payment at Closing*

> ### 12. Payment at Closing
>
> At closing, Buyer will pay Seller the total amount of the sums referred to in [Clauses 6, 7, and/or 8 [if asset sale] or Clauses 9 and 10 [if entity sale] [less the deposit referred to in Clause 11 [if any]. Payment will be by cashier's check or wire transfer.

ALTERNATIVE B: *Installment Sale—No Adjustment-of-Price Clause for Either Inventory or Accounts Receivable*

> ### 12. Payment at Closing
>
> At closing, Buyer will pay Seller $_____. This payment will be made by cashier's check or wire transfer and, along with Buyer's deposit of $_____, will be applied toward the total sale price of $_____. The balance of the sale price will be paid as described in Clause _____.

ALTERNATIVE C: *Installment Sale—Buyer Is Buying Inventory Under an Adjustment-of-Price Clause*

> ### 12. Payment at Closing
>
> At closing, Buyer will pay Seller $_____plus the value of the inventory as determined under the terms of Clause _____. This payment will be made by a cashier's check or wire transfer and, along with Buyer's deposit of $_____, will be applied toward the total sale price. The balance of the sale price will be paid as described in Clause _____.

ALTERNATIVE D: *Installment Sale—Buyer Is Buying Accounts Receivable Under an Adjustment-of-Price Clause*

> ### 12. Payment at Closing
>
> At closing, Buyer will pay Seller $_____ plus the value of the accounts receivable, as determined under the terms of Clause _____. This payment will be made by a cashier's check or wire transfer and, along with Buyer's deposit of $_____, will be applied toward the total sale price. The balance of the sale price will be paid as described in Clause _____.

ALTERNATIVE E: *Installment Sale—Buyer Is Buying Inventory and Accounts Receivable Under an Adjustment-of-Price Clause*

---

12. Payment at Closing

At closing, Buyer will pay Seller $＿＿＿＿＿＿＿plus the value of the inventory, as determined under the terms of Clause ＿＿＿, and the value of the accounts receivable, as determined under the terms of Clause ＿＿＿. This payment will be made by a cashier's check or wire transfer and, along with Buyer's deposit of $ ＿＿＿＿＿＿＿, will be applied toward the total sale price. The balance of the sale price will be paid as described in Clause ＿＿＿.

---

2. Installment Payment (Alternatives B Through E)

If, as is more typical, the buyer will be paying only a portion of the purchase money at the closing, this, along with any deposit you're holding, will become the down payment, with the balance to be paid in installments. In this case, you can use Alternative B, C, D, or E rather than Alternative A (Full Payment at Closing) and edit it to fit your situation. As noted above, you'll usually want the buyer to pay you either by a cashier's check or the wire transfer of funds into your bank account.

In an installment sale, the exact wording of the Payment at Closing clause depends on whether or not the buyer is acquiring your inventory or accounts receivable. One of the alternatives above (B through E) may meet your needs with or without modification. Or you and the buyer can work out some other formula

for determining how much is to be brought to the closing. That's fine. The key in the Payment at Closing clause is to state unambiguously how the down payment (for an installment plan) will be calculated.

G. Promissory Note

When to skip ahead. Those fortunate sellers who are receiving full payment at closing can skip this section on promissory notes and the following ones on security for future payment.

Unless you're receiving full payment for your business, you'll want the buyer to agree to sign a promissory note at the closing setting out the terms for paying the balance of the sale price. These terms include the amount of each payment, the interest rate, how long the buyer has to pay, and what happens if the buyer fails to make payments. It's best to attach the form for the actual promissory note to the sales agreement, rather than summarizing its main terms in the sales agreement. (Chapter 19 explains how to draft a promissory note and includes a sample note. Carefully read Chapter 19 as well as Chapter 9 before completing the following promissory note clause in your sales agreement.) Some sample language referring to the promissory note is shown below.

Even though the actual promissory note will be an attachment to your sales agreement, you should specify in your sales agreement who will sign the note. The buyer, of course, will sign the note, but maybe you and the buyer have agreed there will be cosigners or guarantors. If so, be sure to include the names of those people (if any) in the promissory note clause. Please see Chapter 19 for information about why it's often wise to insist on having cosigners or guarantors sign the promissory note.

 Use the promissory note only for the sale price balance. Don't use it for any amount owed you for your noncompete agreement. This usually isn't an issue, since the buyer typically pays for the noncompete agreement by a separate check at closing. However, if the buyer will be paying all or part of the noncompete later, I recommend that you use a separate promissory note for this purpose. Doing so can save you king-sized tax and accounting headaches.

---

13. Promissory Note [*optional*]

At closing, Buyer will sign and give to Seller a promissory note for the balance of the sale price. The promissory note will be in the form of Attachment _____. [The following people will sign the promissory note in addition to the Buyer: *list names of others who will sign.*] Each signer will be jointly and individually liable for payment.

---

14. Security for Payment (Asset Sale) [*optional*]

At closing, to secure payment of the promissory note referred to in Clause ___, Buyer will sign a security agreement as shown in Attachment _____, giving Seller a security interest in the assets that Buyer is buying. [In addition, Buyer will give Seller a security interest in *list any other assets, such as a home, that are to be pledged as additional security.*] Seller will have the right to file a UCC Financing Statement with regard to the security pledged.

H. Security for Future Payment: Asset Sale

When a sale involves installment payments, it's advisable to obtain a security interest in the business assets and, if possible, other property belonging to the buyer. That way, if the buyer stops paying, you can take back the business (even though it may be in poor shape by then) and hopefully take possession of other assets as well. But at the very least, you should insist on a security interest in the business assets. If you go this route, your sales agreement clause for an asset sale may look like this. (Section I, below, includes a security interest clause for an entity sale.)

As with a promissory note, it's a good idea that you prepare and attach a security agreement that the buyer will sign, rather than simply describe the main terms of the arrangement in your sales agreement. Chapter 19 provides sample security agreements for asset and entity sales and explains their components. Chapter 19 also explains why it's important to file a Uniform Commercial Code (UCC) Financing Statement as a public record in the appropriate governmental office. At closing, the security agreement will be signed by the person or entity that's buying the assets.

Besides retaining a security interest in the business assets you're selling, sometimes it makes sense to retain a security interest in the lease or even to take a security interest in the buyer's home. If you believe that a lien on the business assets isn't sufficient, see if the buyer will give you a mortgage or deed of trust for the buyer's home as additional security.

Here are some examples of how your sales agreement can address additional security requirements.

EXAMPLE 1: *Security Interest in Business Lease*

If you want to retain a security interest in any lease you're assigning to the buyer so you take back possession of the business space if the buyer doesn't pay as promised, your Security for Payment clause can look like this:

14. Security for Payment

At closing, to secure payment of the promissory note referred to in Clause _____, Buyer will sign a security agreement giving Seller a security interest in the assets that Buyer is buying and <u>the lease that is being assigned to Buyer</u>. Seller will have the right to file a UCC Financing Statement.

Read your lease carefully to make sure it contains nothing that would prevent you from taking back the premises. You may need your landlord's cooperation in amending the lease to remove any such roadblock.

EXAMPLE 2: *Security Interest in the Buyer's House.*

For better security, you may have insisted that the buyer agree that you'll get a mortgage or deed of trust on the buyer's home. If so, you can add language such as this:

14. Security for Payment

At closing, to secure the payment of the promissory note referred to in Clause _____, Buyer will sign a security agreement as shown in Attachment _____, giving Seller a security interest in the assets that Buyer is buying. Buyer will further secure the promissory note by giving Seller a second mortgage (or deed of trust) on the home located at 123 Elm Street, Sarasota, Florida for the loan balance. Buyer will provide to Seller, at Buyer's expense, a title insurance policy insuring the mortgage (or deed of trust). Seller will have the right to file a UCC Financing Statement.

The sample language refers to a second mortgage (or deed of trust) because most homeowners already have a first mortgage on their home. If there's no first mortgage (or deed of trust), simply substitute the word "first" for "second," so that the last part of Clause 14 might look like this:

EXAMPLE:

Buyer will further secure the promissory note referred to in Clause 13 by giving Seller a first mortgage (or deed of trust) on the home located at 123 Elm Street, Sarasota, Florida for the loan balance. Buyer will provide to Seller, at Buyer's expense, a title insurance policy insuring the mortgage (or deed of trust).

As noted in Chapter 19, if there is a first mortgage already in place, the size of the debt which is secured by the mortgage will affect how much equity the owner has in the home. The holder of the first mortgage has first dibs if there's a foreclosure and the home is sold. For example, if the buyer owns a $400,000 home but it's subject to a $320,000 first mortgage (or deed of trust), that leaves only $80,000 worth of equity available to you if you have to foreclose on your second mortgage to pay the debt the buyer owes to you. Depending on how much the buyer owes you, that may or may not be adequate security but, obviously, it's better than nothing.

To give you a valid security interest in the buyer's house, all owners of the house will need to sign the mortgage or deed of trust.

I. Security for Future Payment: Entity Sale

The financing arrangements for the sale of an entity are similar to those for an asset sale. The buyer probably won't pay the entire amount at closing but will make a down payment and then sign a promissory note for the balance. This means you'll want to have the promissory note (which should be signed by the buyer and any cosigners or guarantors) backed up with a security agreement and a UCC Financing Statement that gives you a lien on the entity's assets until the note is fully paid. Chapter 19 provides the necessary forms and instructions.

To make this happen, the sales agreement should provide that at closing, the buyer will cause the entity to give you a security interest in its assets, so that you can take back the assets if the note isn't paid. The entity rather than the buyer needs to sign the security agreement, since the entity rather than buyer will own the assets after the closing. An entity signs documents through its president, managing member, or other authorized person. The clause dealing with this subject might read as shown below.

In an entity sale, you transfer ownership of the entity by endorsing over your stock certificates to the buyer—or, in the case of an LLC, by signing certificates assigning your membership interests to the buyer. As an additional protection, you can have the buyer agree that until the promissory note is fully paid, the shares of stock or the LLC membership interests can't be sold to someone else. And consider asking the buyer to agree that the stock certificates or LLC membership certificates will be held in escrow by a third party and not be delivered to the buyer until the note has been paid in full. If this idea appeals to you, and the buyer agrees, include language (Escrow Arrangements) to this effect at the end of the Security for Payment as shown below.

See Chapter 19 for a sample form of escrow agreement you can attach to your sales agreement language.

---

15. Security for Payment (Entity Sale) [*optional*]

At closing, to secure the payment of the promissory note referred to in Clause _____, Buyer will cause the [corporation / LLC] to sign a security agreement as shown in Attachment _____ giving Seller a security interest in the assets of the [corporation/LLC]. Seller will have the right to file a UCC Financing Statement.

Escrow Arrangements [*optional*]

Until the promissory note referred to in Clause _____ is fully paid, Buyer will not sell the [corporate shares /LLC membership interests]. The certificates representing the [corporate shares/LLC membership interests] will be held in escrow by [*list name of escrow agent*]. At closing, Seller and Buyer will sign an escrow agreement in the form of Attachment _____.

Chapter 15

Dealing With Liabilities and Representations

As a business owner, you're well aware that any business is likely to have at least some liabilities: financial obligations that the business will or may have to pay in the future. Liabilities can take many different forms including, for example, a debt owed to a bank, a phone bill that will come due in 30 days, lease payments on business equipment, salaries owed to employees, or a potential injury claim by someone hurt by a product that your business sold or repaired. One of the main reasons that buyers prefer to acquire the assets of a business rather than the corporate or LLC entity is an understandable desire to avoid as many liabilities as possible. As explained in Chapter 9, in an asset sale, by law the buyer normally doesn't inherit the business's debts and liabilities. These remain solely the obligation of the seller unless the seller and the buyer agree that the buyer will be responsible for some or all of them.

Let's assume—as is usually the case—that you are selling your assets and that your deal with the buyer does not require the buyer to take over any liabilities. You can reassure the buyer on this point by having your asset sale agreement clearly say that you—and not the buyer—will remain responsible for the debts and liabilities of your business. In Section A1 of this chapter, I include sales agreement language to provide this reassurance.

Sometimes, though, as part of the negotiations for the sale of your assets, you and the buyer will contractually agree that the buyer will assume responsibility for certain specific liabilities or types of liabilities. In that case, the asset sale agreement will need to spell out which liabilities the buyer will be taking over. This is covered in Section A2 of this chapter.

An entity sale differs from an asset sale in terms of liabilities. In an entity sale, unless modified by the parties in the sales agreement, the business's liabilities are the sole responsibility of the corporation or LLC being purchased, and they stay with the entity. The shareholders who sell their corporate stock or the LLC members who sell their LLC interests to the buyer are not personally responsible for paying any business debts either during their ownership of the entity or after they transfer the entity to you. (The exceptions to this general rule are covered in the Chapter 3 section on legal liabilities to third parties.) It is possible, however, for an entity sale to be structured so that the selling shareholders or LLC members agree to be responsible for paying certain liabilities of the entity. Section B of this chapter explains how to fine-tune the liabilities clause for an entity sale in order to place this burden on the sellers.

Get legal help when it comes to liabilities. Of all the subjects covered in the sales agreement, the allocation of responsibility for debts and other liabilities may be the most complex and the most likely to require some help from a lawyer. Chapter 6 explains how to find and work with a lawyer.

Other clauses in the sale agreement are also intended to reassure the buyer or the seller. These reassurances are called representations. An example of a representation would be your statement in the sales agreement that the financial information that you've given the buyer is accurate. Representations must be carefully drafted to avoid adverse legal consequences. Sections C, D, and E show how to put together the clauses that contain representations.

A. Liabilities in an Asset Sale

From a legal standpoint, when you sell the assets of your business, you or your corporate or LLC entity or both will remain liable for all preexisting liabilities. This means that normally the buyer won't have to worry about getting stuck for these items. Occasionally, however, a buyer may agree to assume responsibility for some liabilities. This section covers both possibilities. It provides two alternatives (A and B) to a clause on Seller's Debts and Other Liabilities, depending on whether or not the buyer is taking over any liabilities.

1. Buyer Is Not Taking Over any Liabilities in an Asset Sale (Alternative A)

In an asset sale, you and the buyer will most likely agree that at or before closing, you'll pay all debts and claims that you know about and that you'll remain liable for any others that may surface later, such as a delayed bill from a supplier or a customer's demand for a refund for a defective product that you sold. In that situation, you can build a Seller's Debts and Other Liabilities clause by selecting from and possibly modifying Options 1 through 3 in Alternative A of Clause 16, Seller's Debts and Other Liabilities (Asset Sale).

Alternative A of Clause 16 reassures the buyer that you (the seller) will be responsible for all business debts and that the buyer doesn't have to worry about claims by past creditors or about the seizure of business assets to satisfy past debts.

To further reassure the buyer that there won't be any problems with past liabilities, you can include one or more of the following options in Clause 16, Alternative A.

Option 1: Indemnification of Buyer. To help you understand how this indemnification works, let's say that two months after the closing, a bill arrives from a supplier for goods that were sold to your business before the closing. If the supplier tries to collect from the buyer or threatens to seize any of the assets that you sold, this clause obligates you to pay for any legal defense of the claims in addition to paying the debt or judgment. If your business is a corporation or LLC, use the blank space in the Indemnification of Buyer option to fill in your name and those of any other owners. The buyer will probably want this personal assurance as well as the assurance of the entity.

Option 2: Indemnification of Seller. Similarly, it makes sense to include language like that found in the second option of Clause 16, Alternative A. This requires the buyer to protect you from exposure to any debts that arise after the buyer takes over the business. The Indemnification of Seller language is a mirror image of what you undertake to do for past debts.

Option 3: Confirmation of Payment of Debts. This is a practical, commonsense way to deal with the bulk sales law if your business is located in one of the few states that still has such a law on the books: California, Georgia, Maryland, North Carolina, Virginia, or Wisconsin. These laws are explained in Chapter 20. Basically, these laws—which apply only if

---

ALTERNATIVE A: *Buyer Is Not Taking Over any Liabilities in an Asset Sale*

---

16. Seller's Debts and Other Liabilities (Asset Sale)

Buyer is not assuming any of Seller's debts or other liabilities. Seller will pay all debts and other liabilities, whether now known or unknown, that are or may become a lien on the assets being bought by Buyer.

[*choose all options that apply*]

☐ 1. **Indemnification of Buyer.** Seller [and each of Seller's partners/shareholders/ members] will indemnify, defend, and save Buyer harmless from and against all debts and other liabilities arising out of the Seller's ownership or use of the assets before closing.

☐ 2. **Indemnification of Seller.** Buyer [and each of Buyer's partners/ shareholders/members] will indemnify, defend, and save Seller harmless from and against all debts and other liabilities arising out of the Buyer's ownership or use of the assets after closing.

☐ 3. **Confirmation of Payment of Debts.** At closing, Seller will confirm in a Statement Regarding Absence of Creditors (Attachment _____) that Seller has paid all known debts and other liabilities of the business. Buyer and Seller waive compliance with the bulk sales law of the state of _____.

you're selling the assets of a business that sells goods from a stock of merchandise—require creditors to be notified of the sale. The Confirmation of Payment of Debts option lets you and the buyer avoid the cumbersome paperwork that's often required for bulk sales compliance. Most buyers and their lawyers will agree that it adequately protects the buyer from claims of creditors. If you and the buyer do agree to use this option, you'll need to be sure that you pay all known debts either before the closing or out of the closing proceeds. See Chapter 20 for a form you can use for the Statement Regarding Absence of Creditors referred to in the Confirmation of Payment of Debts option of Clause 16, Alternative A.

2. Buyer Is Taking Over Some or all Liabilities in an Asset Sale (Alternative B)

While somewhat unusual, it is possible that in an asset sale the buyer will agree to take responsibility for paying some or all of the debts and liabilities of your business in exchange for an appropriate price reduction. For example, if the assets include a telephone system that you're buying on time and there's still a year's worth of payments to be made, the buyer may agree to take over the monthly payments to the finance company. Or maybe a customer has suffered some minor property damage because a product you installed malfunctioned, but because the

extent of the damage is still not certain, the claim has not been settled. The buyer may be willing to deal with the claim and pay any settlement—within reason—in an attempt to maintain a good relationship with the customer. If you and the buyer agree that the buyer will pay certain debts or be responsible for particular liabilities, you'll need to put appropriate language in the sales agreement.

Alternative B in Clause 16, Seller's Debts and Other Liabilities, can be a starting point when the buyer will be paying some of the bills. See Section 1, above, for the reasoning behind the indemnification language (Options 1 and 2).

You can use a third option (Waiver of Bulk Sales Law Compliance) if your business is located in California, Georgia, Indiana, Maryland, Virginia, or Wisconsin, and you're selling the assets of a retail business—a business that sells goods out of a stock of merchandise. These states still have bulk sales laws, which are intended to protect business creditors. If existing debts are to be paid after the closing, the creditors will need to be notified of the business sale. This is a cumbersome process that can require considerable paperwork, as explained in Chapter 20. A buyer who believes that all bills will be paid on time may not worry about bulk sales compliance. This is especially true if the buyer owes you a large balance and the amounts owed to creditors are relatively small. In that case, the buyer can pay the creditors if necessary on your

ALTERNATIVE B: *Buyer Is Taking Over Liabilities in an Asset Sale*

---

16. Seller's Debts and Other Liabilities (Asset Sale)

Buyer will pay the following debts and other liabilities of the business that arose out of Seller's ownership and use of the assets before the closing: _____
_____
_____ .

Buyer will pay the following debts and other liabilities of the business that arose out of Seller's ownership and use of the assets before the closing: _____
_____
_____ .

Any other debts and liabilities arising out of the Seller's ownership or use of the assets before closing will be paid by [Seller or Buyer].

[*choose all options that apply*]

☐ 1. **Indemnification of Buyer.** Seller [and each of Seller's partners/shareholders/members] will indemnify, defend, and save Buyer harmless from and against all debts and other liabilities that Seller has agreed to pay.

☐ 2. **Indemnification of Seller.** Buyer [and each of Buyer's partners/shareholders/members] will indemnify, defend, and save Seller harmless from and against all debts and other liabilities that Buyer has agreed to pay, and for all debts or liabilities arising out of the Buyer's ownership or use of the assets after closing.

☐ 3. **Waiver of Bulk Sales Law Compliance.** Buyer and Seller waive compliance with the provisions of the bulk sales law of the state of _____ .

---

behalf and deduct from the promissory note balance the amounts you were obligated to pay. The Indemnification of Buyer clause (Option 1) may also ease the buyer's worries on this score. Still, in a state with a bulk sales law, the buyer or buyer's lawyer may insist on strict compliance with the law. If that happens, you won't use Clause Option 3 (Waiver of Bulk Sale Compliance). Instead, you'll need to seek legal advice to make sure that all statutory procedures are followed to the buyer's satisfaction.

B. Liabilities in an Entity Sale

In an entity sale, the liabilities of the business belong to the corporate, LLC, or partnership entity and continue to be the responsibility of that entity after it's transferred to the new owner. Still, as part of the deal, you and any co-owners may agree that you'll personally take care of one or more existing obligations of the entity. If so, you can use a clause such as Clause 17, Entity's Debts and Other Liabilities, to deal with this issue.

Clause 17A (Payment by Seller) commits you to take personal responsibility for payment of a certain debt owed by the entity—for example, $30,000 that the corporation owes to a bank.

You can use a clause such as Clause 17B (Indemnification of Buyer) to reassure the buyer that you've disclosed all known debts of the entity and that you'll be personally responsible for paying any known debts of the entity that you didn't disclose.

Be aware that regardless of what your sales agreement says, you may have committed yourself to be personally liable for some debts of your entity. For example, the bank that lent money to your corporation or LLC probably required you to personally guarantee repayment. Similarly, a company that extended credit to your business for goods or services may have required that same kind of personal guarantee. Unless the lenders or creditors agree to release you, you'll continue to be personally responsible for these debts even after the business changes hands. If the debts are relatively small and the entity seems to be in strong financial shape, the bank or other

---

17. Entity's Debts and Other Liabilities (Entity Sale) [*optional*]

[*choose all options that apply*]

☐ A. **Payment by Seller.** Seller will pay [$_____ of] the $_____ obligation that the [corporation/LLC] owes to [*list name of creditor*].

☐ B. **Indemnification of Buyer.** Seller will indemnify, defend, and save Buyer harmless from and against any other debts and other liabilities of the [corporation/LLC] to the extent that such debts and other liabilities are known to Seller and Seller has failed to disclose them to Buyer.

☐ C. **Buyer's Personal Guarantee of Certain Entity Debt.** Buyer will personally guarantee payment to [*list name of creditor*] of the $_____ which the [corporation/LLC] owes to that creditor and will sign such documents as the creditor requires for that purpose.

creditor may agree to release you from personal liability—although that won't be an easy task. You'll substantially increase your chances of a getting a release if the buyer is financially strong and is willing to be substituted for you on the personal guarantee.

You can use a clause such as Clause 17C (Buyer's Personal Guarantee of Certain Entity Debt) to commit the buyer to personally guarantee payment of a specific entity debt.

C. Representations: What They Are and Why They Matter

The buyer's decision to buy your business will be based not only on his or her own investigation (discussed in Chapter 10) but, equally important, on your statements such as your written and oral statements about the business's past income and expenses. In addition, the buyer will also reasonably assume that certain facts are true—for example, that you or your business entity own the assets you've listed for sale, unless you've indicated otherwise. Similarly, from your perspective—especially if you're selling on an installment basis—your decision to sell your business to a particular buyer will be based to some extent on documents that indicate the buyer's financial position.

Traditionally, buyers and sellers capture these statements and assumptions in a part of the sales agreement called representations or, sometimes, representations and warranties.

Representations. In plain English, a representation is simply a statement of a past or existing fact. Example: "Seller represents that gross sales for the 12 months ending December 31, 2004 were $300,000."

Warranties. A warranty is a promise or guarantee that existing or future facts are or will be true. Example: "Seller warrants that the HVAC unit will be in good condition for the 24 months following the closing."

As you can well imagine, the distinction between a representation and a warranty can get very fuzzy, so legal documents usually use the terms in tandem, as in: "Seller represents and warrants that ...." That way, all the bases are covered— and that's how the suggested clauses approach the subject.

The important point is that representations and warranties clauses in your sales agreement can have serious legal consequences. If it turns out that your statements aren't true and—especially if you were knowingly misleading—you can be responsible to the buyer for financial damages, plus the buyer may be able to undo the sale before or even after the closing. Similarly, the buyer will be responsible to you for the truth of his or her representations and warranties.

The fact that you must normally include representations and warranties in your sales agreement again underlines why it's so crucial that, as discussed in Chapter 10, you provide the buyer with 100% accurate written and oral information. To accomplish this, it's key that you represent only information you personally know about, not things you're pretty sure—or hope—are true. Or put another way, if you have any doubt about any of the key items you list in your representations (for example, that a building is asbestos-free), it's best to include the words "to the best of Seller's knowledge" before that representation.

The next two sections provide suggested clauses you can use to build the part of the sales agreement that addresses representations and warranties.

D. Seller's Representations

The scope and detail of the representations and warranties that the buyer will insist on is going to depend on a number of factors, including:

- **The relative bargaining power of you and the buyer.** Someone who's anxious to buy your business for an attractive price or because it's a great fit with the buyer's existing business may demand little by way of representations. By contrast, someone who's paying top dollar, based on your projection of a rosy future, may expect more extensive statements and guarantees.

- **The buyer's ability to thoroughly investigate your business.** If yours is a small, straightforward business and its finances and assets are relatively easy to understand, the buyer may be content to look at business records, ask a few questions, and require little detail in the representations clause. But if your business is more complex (you own lots of valuable copyrights, for example) and the facts about its finances or operations are more difficult to dig out, the buyer may want you to make much more extensive representations, figuring that you're on the hook—legally and financially—if you make misstatements.

- **The nature of your business operations.** Typically, the buyer likely won't be too demanding if you have a simple service business, like a hair salon. But if your business is more complicated—say, you manufacture, sell, and repair potentially dangerous machinery—you can anticipate that the buyer will expect more from you by way of detailed representations. For example, the buyer may want you to make representations about past and pending product liability claims, workers' compensation claims history, and possible environmental hazards.

When you're selling the assets of a corporation or LLC, don't be surprised if the buyer asks you and the other owners (all the shareholders or members) to personally take responsibility for the representations and warranties. Clause 18, Seller's Representations, provides for this. You'll also need to include appropriate language in the signature portion of the sales agreement, as explained in Chapter 18. While this may be a reasonable request, keep in mind that if the representations turn out to be false or the conditions you're guaranteeing turn out to be different, the buyer can sue you and the other owners personally. And if the buyer's lawsuit is successful, your personal assets are at risk to satisfy the judgment. The buyer may also be able to cancel the deal and get a full refund if a court determines that false information was an essential component of the buyer's decision to complete the deal.

In an asset sale, the clause dealing with the seller's representations may look like Clause 18, shown below (although, of course, you'll need to choose the options that apply to your transaction). A parallel clause for an entity sale (Clause 19) is provided at the end of this section.

Clause 18N—stating that the representations and warranties will survive (last beyond) the closing—emphasizes that two years down the road, if the buyer discovers that you've provided inaccurate information about the business, you can be sued. However, even without this clause, it's very likely that you'll continue

to be liable to the buyer for your statements—at least until the applicable statute of limitations runs out.

In making representations in the sales agreement, there are two good ways to help guard against unintended liability. The first, as mentioned above, is to qualify a statement by prefacing it with the words "to the best of Seller's knowledge." Thiswording appears throughout Clause 18.

The second protective technique is to list any necessary exceptions to your general representation.

EXAMPLE: *Exception to Seller's Representation 18I.*

To the best of Seller's knowledge, the tangible assets are (and at closing will be) in good repair and good operating condition, except for the Excelsior dishwasher and the Concord ice-maker, which are in need of repair.

Depending on the type of entity that's selling the business, the sales agreement should be personally signed by each partner, shareholder, or member of your entity, meaning that you must always be aware of your exposure to personal liability. (See Chapter 18 for advice on the signature portion of the sales agreement.)

Clause 18 will work for an asset sale. It will need to be reworked for an entity sale (Clause 19).

18. Seller's Representations (Asset Sale)

Seller [and each of Seller's partners/shareholders/members] represent(s) and warrant(s) that:

[*choose all options that apply*]

☐ A. Seller owns the assets being sold. At closing, the assets will be free from any claims of others.

☐ B. At closing, Seller will have paid all taxes that have then come due and that affect the business and its assets.

☐ C. To the best of Seller's knowledge, there are no judgments, claims, liens, or proceedings pending against Seller, the business, or the assets being sold, and none will be pending at closing.

☐ D. To the best of Seller's knowledge, the business and financial information in the financial statement dated _____ that Seller has given Buyer is accurate.

☐ E. Until closing, Seller will operate the business in the normal manner and will use its best efforts to maintain the goodwill of suppliers, customers, the landlord, and others having business relationships with Seller.

☐ F. Seller is (and at closing will be) a [corporation/limited liability company] in good standing under the laws of the state of _____ and has (and at closing will have) the authority to perform the obligations contained in this sales agreement.

☐ G. To the best of Seller's knowledge, the assets being sold to Buyer constitute all the assets needed to operate Seller's business.

☐ H. To the best of Seller's knowledge, the current uses of the Seller's business premises are permitted under the applicable zoning laws. To the best of Seller's knowledge, the business premises presently (and at closing will) meet all applicable health, safety, and disabled access requirements and are (and at closing will be) in good repair.

☐ I. To the best of Seller's knowledge, the tangible assets are (and at closing will be) in good repair and good operating condition.

☐ J. To the best of Seller's knowledge, all items in the inventory of merchandise are (and at closing will be) unused and of saleable quality.

☐ K. To the best of Seller's knowledge, Seller is (and at closing will be) in full compliance with all laws, ordinances, or regulations applicable to the operation of the business.

☐ L. To the best of Seller's knowledge, Seller is not (and at closing will not be) in default on any contracts.

☐ M. To the best of Seller's knowledge, Seller is (and at closing will be) in compliance with all environmental laws. To the best of Seller's knowledge, there are (and at closing will be) no hazardous materials on the business premises that may be a source of future liability under the environmental laws.

☐ N. These representations and warranties will survive the closing.

☐ O. Seller [and each of Seller's partners/shareholders/members] will indemnify, defend, and save Buyer harmless from and against any financial loss, legal liability, damage, or expense arising from any breach of the above representations and warranties.

☐ P. The total liability of the Seller [and all of the Seller's partners/shareholders/members] for all breaches of representations and warranties will not exceed $ _____.

19. Seller's Representations (Entity Sale)

Seller(s) represent(s) and warrant(s) that:

[*choose all options that apply*]

☐ A. To the best of Seller(s) knowledge, the entity being sold owns the assets itemized in the list dated _____ At closing, the assets will be free from any claims of others.

☐ B. At closing, the entity being sold will have paid all taxes that have then come due and that affect the business and its assets.

☐ C. To the best of Seller(s) knowledge, there are no judgments, claims, liens, or proceedings pending against the entity or its assets, and none will be pending at closing.

☐ D. To the best of Seller(s) knowledge, the business and financial information concerning the entity in the financial statement dated _____ that Seller(s) has/have given Buyer is accurate.

☐ E. Until closing, the entity will operate the business in the normal manner and will use its best efforts to maintain the goodwill of suppliers, customers, the landlord, and others having business relationships with the entity.

☐ F. The entity is (and at closing will be) a [corporation/limited liability company] in good standing under the laws of the state of _____.

☐ G. To the best of Seller(s) knowledge, the entity owns all the assets needed to operate the entity's business.

☐ H. To the best of Seller(s) knowledge, the current uses of the entity's business premises are permitted under the applicable zoning laws. To the best of Seller(s) knowledge, the business premises presently (and at closing will) meet all applicable health, safety, and disabled access requirements and are (and at closing will be) in good repair.

☐ I. To the best of Seller(s) knowledge, the tangible assets of the entity are (and at closing will be) in good repair and good operating condition.

☐ J. To the best of Seller(s) knowledge, all items in the entity's inventory of merchandise are (and at closing will be) unused and of saleable quality.

☐ K. To the best of Seller(s) knowledge, the entity is (and at closing will be) in full compliance with all laws, ordinances, or regulations applicable to the operation of the business.

☐ L. To the best of Seller(s) knowledge, the entity is not (and at closing will not be) in default on any contracts.

☐ M. To the best of Seller(s) knowledge, the entity is (and at closing will be) in compliance with all environmental laws. To the best of Seller(s) knowledge, there are (and at closing will be) no hazardous materials on the business premises that may be a source of future liability under the environmental laws.

☐ N. The [shares/LLC interests] constitute all of the issued [shares/LLC interests] of the entity. No additional [shares/LLC interests] will be issued before the closing. At closing, the [shares/LLC interests] will be free from any claims of any persons or entities other than Seller(s).

☐ O. These representations and warranties will survive the closing.

☐ P. Seller(s) will indemnify, defend, and save Buyer harmless from and against any financial loss, legal liability, damage, or expense arising from any breach of the above representations and warranties.

☐ Q. The total liability of the Seller(s) for all breaches of representations and warranties will not exceed _____.

E. Buyer's Representations

As the seller, you'll also want to request representations from the buyer. Typically, a seller has fewer unknowns to worry about than a buyer does, so you're likely to require fewer representations.

See Clause 20, Buyer's Representations, for language to include in your sales agreement. This clause can be used for either an asset or entity sale. The only difference is in the first option (A). In an entity sale, you need to insert the words "of the entity" in the first line as noted.

---

20. Buyer's Representations

Buyer represents and warrants that:

[*choose all options that apply*]

☐ A. Buyer has inspected the tangible assets [*insert "of the entity" if an entity sale*] that Buyer is purchasing and the leased premises and has carefully reviewed Seller's representations regarding them. Buyer is satisfied with the physical condition of the tangible assets and the premises.

☐ B. To the best of Buyer's knowledge, the business and financial information in the financial statement dated _____ that Buyer has given Seller is accurate.

☐ C. Buyer is (and at closing will be) a [partnership/corporation/limited liability company] in good standing under the laws of the state of _____ and has (and at closing will have) the authority to perform the obligations contained in this sales agreement.

☐ D. These representations and warranties will survive the closing.

☐ E. Buyer [and each of its partners/shareholder/members] will indemnify, defend, and save Seller harmless from and against any financial loss, legal liability, damage, or expense arising from any breach of the above representations and warranties.

☐ F. The total liability of the Buyer [and all of its partners/shareholder/members] for all breaches of representations and warranties will not exceed $_____.

Chapter 16

Payments for Noncompete and Consultant Deals

I n the course of your negotiations, the buyer may have agreed to pay you for your commitment not to compete with the business after it changes hands. Also, you and the buyer may have agreed that after the closing, the buyer will pay you to work for the business as an employee or consultant (independent contractor). If so, these payments will be in addition to the money the buyer pays you for the assets of your business—or for the business entity itself—and will need to be addressed in the sales agreement.

The best way to do this is to have clauses in your sales agreement saying that separate documents will be signed at closing concerning these arrangements. Then attach to your sales agreement copies of the actual documents, such as an employment agreement, that will be signed at closing. Using separate, attached documents encourages you and the buyer to go into more detail than you might if you simply summarized your understanding in the sales agreement. In addition, you won't have to negotiate further with the buyer about wording after the sales agreement is signed.

This chapter will show you how to draft these clauses. Section A covers sales agreement language regarding your agreement not to compete (sometimes called a covenant not to compete or a noncompete agreement). Section B covers the arrangements for any work you'll be doing for the buyer after the closing, either as an employee or as an independent contractor. The actual documents you will complete and attach to your sales agreement are covered in Chapter 21.

As explained in Chapter 4, the payments you receive for your agreement not to compete and for working for the buyer are taxed at ordinary income rates. To understand exactly how this will affect your own tax picture, it makes sense to consult a tax professional. And to be on the safe side, have a lawyer review the documents that you attach to the sales agreement to make sure you're adequately protected.

A. Agreeing Not to Compete With the Business After the Sale

As discussed earlier in this book (Chapters 3 and 9), many buyers want sellers to agree not to start a competing business or work for a competing company at least for a certain period of time. In exchange, the buyer pays the seller a set amount of money. There's no standard way the amount is arrived at. It can be a nominal $10 or a not-so-trivial $10,000. Logically, you'd want the amount to be relatively high if you were giving up significant opportunities to earn a living. But cutting the other way is the fact you'll pay tax on the payment at ordinary income rates, which are higher than long-term capital gain rates. You might prefer to get a higher sale price for the business (assuming that the extra amount can be assigned to capital gain items) and accept a lower amount for your agreement not to compete. Get advice from a tax professional before negotiating this point with the buyer.

A noncompete agreement can serve two important functions:

- It can allay any anxiety the buyer may have that after the closing, you'll start a new business that competes with the old one or that you'll go to work for a competing business. In both instances, the fear is that you'll divert customers and clients away from the buyer, infringing on the goodwill the buyer had hoped to profit from.

- It can provide tax-planning flexibility for both you and the buyer, as described above. For example, depending on tax considerations, the two of you can agree that you'll be paid a small amount for your covenant not to compete (while at the same time agreeing to a high price for the business assets), or you can agree that you'll receive a substantial sum for your noncompetition agreement (at the same time lowering the price for your business).

Occasionally, your covenant not to compete will be of little concern to the buyer. This may be the case, for example, if you're past retirement age, seriously ill, not likely to reenter the business world, or moving to another part of the country, or if you're selling a business that you recently inherited from your parents and have never participated in. Along the same line, if one of your shareholders or LLC members has always been a passive investor who has had other career interests, the buyer may not insist on a noncompete agreement from that person. In most other situations, however, the buyer will expect to receive a noncompete agreement from you and any other active owners whether you're selling the assets of the business or the entity itself (the corporation or LLC).

Chapter 21 includes a sample noncompete agreement that you can attach to the sales agreement. It explains why it's important to carefully define the type of work and activities that are considered competitive, the geographic location that will be off-limits to you, and for how long the agreement applies.

Sample language (Clause 21) for your sales agreement is shown below. Of course, you won't include this clause if a noncompete agreement is not part of the sale package.

You and the buyer will need to negotiate exactly who will be giving a covenant not to compete. You'll need to insert the names of those people in Clause 21. If your business is a sole proprietorship, it will usually be you, the owner, giving a covenant not to compete—but the buyer may also

---

21. Covenant Not to Compete [*optional*]

At closing, [*insert names of those who will sign a covenant*] will sign and deliver to Buyer a covenant not to compete in the form of Attachment _____, and Buyer will pay [the/each] signer the amounts specified in the attached covenant not to compete.

---

insist on one from your spouse or other family member who is actively involved in running the business. And if your business is a corporation, an LLC, or a partnership, the buyer will expect noncompete agreements from each co-owner and possibly from others (such as family members and even employees) who are closely involved in the operation of the business. There may be different noncompete agreements for different people—that is, restrictions and compensation may differ. In that case, you'll need to attach specific noncompete agreements for each person.

Typically, the buyer pays at closing for each covenant not to compete. If the amount to be paid is substantial, however, you may be willing to accept a promissory note. This would be unusual but if you do agree to a delayed payment, use a separate promissory note rather than the one used for the balance of the sale price. Otherwise, your tax and bookkeeping problems may get out of hand.

A Legally Enforceable Commitment Not to Compete

A buyer who wants your covenant not to compete may be concerned about whether a court will enforce it. The buyer may have heard that some noncompete agreements or covenants are not legally valid. It's true that the law is often suspicious of covenants not to compete signed by employees of a business. This is founded on a fear that the noncompete agreement will interfere with the employee's freedom to earn a living. But when the person signing the covenant is the seller of a business, the law is much less protective. It's assumed that the seller is being adequately compensated for selling the business (even if the covenant itself lists a low dollar figure). You and the buyer should expect that, if you violate the covenant, a court will enforce it as written by issuing an injunction and assessing money damages.

B. Agreeing to Work for the Business After the Sale

As discussed in Chapter 9, the buyer may want you to stay on board for a transition period of several months or maybe even a year or two. This helps the buyer learn the ropes and also can be reassuring to employees, customers, and suppliers. You, too, may have good reasons for wanting to work for the business after it changes hands—for example, you may want the additional income, a more gradual transition out of the income stream that the business has been providing, or some time to adjust to the life change of giving up the business.

Legally, there are two ways you can structure your arrangement to perform future services for the buyer:

- You can be an employee and work full or part time for a fixed salary or on an hourly basis.
- You can be a consultant (independent contractor) to the new business and be paid a flat fee for specific tasks or projects.

Chapter 9 covers the legal issues involved in working as an independent contractor or employee. Read Chapter 9 carefully before you agree to do future work for the new owner. You'll need to decide whether to be an independent contractor or an employee. You'll also need to address the exact job responsibilities, and, of course, your compensation and benefits and termination provisions.

As with a covenant not to complete, you should prepare a separate document covering any future work you agree to do for the buyer—either as an employee or independent contractor—and attach it to the sales agreement. Chapter 21 explains how to do this. It includes sample employment and independent contractor contracts that you can use as a model in preparing your own.

If you will be working for the new owner after the sale, include sample language such as Clause 22, Future Services, in your sales agreement.

In a multiowner business, some owners may work for the buyer, while others may not. In this clause, you'll name only those who are staying on. And since different people may have different duties and compensation, you may need to draft and attach specific contracts

---

22. Future Services [*optional*]

At closing, [*list names of Sellers who will work for Buyer*] and [Buyer/the entity being sold] will sign an [employment/independent contractor] agreement in the form of Attachment _____.

for each. As a further refinement, keep in mind that some sellers may agree to work as employees while others may work as independent contractors. You'll need to adjust this clause to reflect those arrangements.

> **EXAMPLE:** *Some Sellers Will Work as Employees, Others as Independent Contractors*
>
> At closing, Thomas Paley and the entity being sold (Ajax Corporation) will sign an employment agreement in the form of Attachment A, in which Thomas Paley agrees to a term of employment with Ajax Corporation after the closing. Sally Wimple and the entity being sold (Ajax Corporation) will sign an independent contractor agreement in the form of Attachment B, in which Sally Wimple agrees to perform services for Ajax Corporation as an independent contractor after the closing.

A word of explanation about "the entity being sold": Imagine an entity sale in which Carla is buying all the shares of Ajax Corporation stock from Tom and Sally. If Tom and Sally agree to work for the business after the closing, they'll technically be working not for Carla but for Ajax Corporation—the entity being sold. You need to be aware of this distinction between an entity and

its owner when completing this clause and the employment and independent contractor agreements. As recommended in Chapters 9 and 21, you should review the documents with a lawyer to make sure you get it right.

Anyone who's going to sign an employment or independent contractor agreement at the closing should personally sign the sales agreement. (See Chapter 18 for information on the signature portion of the sales agreement.)

Current employees of your business who are not owners will not be involved with the Future Services clause. Normally, in an asset sale, a buyer who wants to keep current employees on the payroll will need to negotiate with each of them separately; the only exception is where an employee has a contract which can be assigned to the buyer—a highly unusual circumstance. If you terminate a contracted employee upon selling the assets of your business, you may or may not be liable for damages, depending on what the contract says.

In an entity sale, current employees will remain on the company's payroll unless the new owner terminates them; existing employment contracts will continue to bind the entity, even after it changes hands.

■

Chapter 17

Other Important Legal Language for the Sales Agreement

Chapters 13 through 16 cover the main clauses you should consider including in your sales agreement, addressing such key topics as the sales price, terms of payment, and covenant not to compete. These clauses make up the guts of a sales contract and, taken by themselves, can constitute a legal and adequate agreement. But to create an optimal agreement, there's more legal ground to cover, including:

- a contingency clause (Section A)
- a reference to closing arrangements and documents (Section B)
- a dispute resolution clause (Section C)
- technical contract clauses, such as how modifications to the contract may be made (Section D), and
- additional optional terms (Section E).

A. Contingency Clause

Your sales agreement may need to include a contingency clause. Similar to a contingency in a contract to sell a house, a contingency in a business sale agreement is an escape valve that lets one party or the other—most often the buyer—cancel the deal if a certain event doesn't occur or a specified condition isn't met. Typically, the sales agreement says that if the buyer uses a contingency to walk away from the deal, that the buyer's deposit will be refunded. (Deposits are covered by Clause 11 in Chapter 14.)

Let's say, for example, that your current store lease runs out in six months. Suppose that you and the buyer are ready to sign a sales agreement, but the buyer (who wants to keep operating from the same location) and the landlord haven't fully negotiated an extension to the lease or substituted a satisfactory new one. The buyer will probably want to be able to cancel the sale if no agreement is reached on the lease. Below is an example of what your contingency clause might look like.

In addition to the lease situation illustrated below, a buyer may want to make the deal contingent on being able to obtain funding or having a liquor

---

23. Contingencies [*optional*]

This sale is contingent on [*fill in*] <u>Buyer and the landlord negotiating and signing a five-year lease satisfactory to Buyer for the premises currently occupied by the business. If the Buyer has not signed such a lease within 30 days from the signing of this agreement, Buyer can cancel this sale by notifying Seller in writing.</u> In that case, Seller will promptly refund Buyer's deposit of $_____. If Buyer does not notify Seller of a cancellation within 35 days of this agreement, the agreement will remain in effect.

license transferred. You, as the seller, may have contingency needs of your own. For example, you may want to cancel the sale if the bank won't release you from personal liability for a loan that your entity took out. There are numerous opportunities for contingency clauses.

Still, keep in mind that in many sales agreements, there are no contingencies at all. But if your sales agreement does require one or more of contingencies, you'll need to customize the wording to fit your deal.

Try to impose relatively short time limits for removal of a contingency—something, perhaps, in the range of 15 to 30 days. That way, if the deal falls through, you can quickly turn to negotiating a new deal with a new buyer. But a deadline doesn't have to be absolute. If you or your current buyer need more time to work on removing a contingency, you can mutually agree to extend the deadline.

Note that the lease example for Clause 23, above, provides for the entire deposit to be returned to the buyer if the buyer cancels the deal based on a sales agreement. You may feel that other arrangements would be more appropriate. For example, your contingency clause might say that the buyer will get back only 50% of the deposit. That way, you have something to show for your time and effort if the sale is aborted.

If you have a contingency clause in your sales agreement and the sale does fall through because a contingency isn't met, it's prudent for you and the buyer to sign a mutual release confirming that the deal is officially dead. This clears the deck for you to move ahead. Your mutual release can look like this.

EXAMPLE:

Mutual Release

Jenny Phillips (Seller) and Horace Madsen (Buyer) cancel the Sales Agreement dated July 10, 20XX for the business known as The Sandwich Shack, located at 654 Archer Road, and release each other from any and all claims with respect to that Agreement. All rights and obligations arising out of the Sales Agreement are null and void.

Buyer has received a refund of the deposit.

You'll need to add signature and date lines to your release, following the format recommended in Chapter 18.

B. Closing Arrangements

At the closing you meet with the buyer to sign and exchange all the documents needed to complete the purchase. This usually occurs within weeks after you sign the sales agreement. You should provide in your sales agreement details as to when and where the closing takes place, using language such as the following.

---

24. Closing

The closing will take place:

Date: August 31, 20XX Time: 9:00 a.m. Location: 654 Archer Road, Chicago

At closing, Buyer [and Buyer's spouse] and Seller [and Seller's spouse] will sign the documents specified in this contract and all other documents reasonably needed to transfer the business assets to Buyer. Buyer will pay Seller the amounts required by this contract and Seller will transfer to Buyer [the business assets/the Seller's stock/the Seller's LLC interests].

Chapter 22 offers suggestions for when and where to hold the closing. Look ahead to those suggestions before completing your own closing clause. As explained in Chapter 22, to help assure an orderly closing, you and the buyer should agree on a customized closing checklist so you know that all the bases will be covered and you won't miss anything at the closing.

Chapter 18 discusses when the seller's or buyer's spouse—and possibly other people—need to sign closing documents. Consult that discussion to see who to specify in this clause in addition to you and the buyer.

1. Documents for Transferring Assets

At the closing of an asset sale, you'll need to sign and give the buyer documents that legally transfer the business assets to the buyer, as well as other documents called for in the sales agreement. These typically include a bill of sale and assignments of the lease, other contracts, and intellectual property. These documents were discussed in Chapter 13 and the forms themselves are included in Chapter 20. Clause 25, Documents for Transferring Assets, below, shows what a typical sales agreement clause covering that subject might look like. Obviously, not all of these options will fit your situation, so edit according to the particular documents you will be providing at closing. Make sure that you list all the documents needed to transfer the assets listed in Clause 3, Assets Being Sold, as discussed in Chapter 13.

Depending on the kind of assets your business owns and will be transferring, there are other documents you may want to list in the last sentence of the transfer-of-assets clause. The sales agreement may describe these assets this way:

25. Documents for Transferring Assets (Asset Sale)

[*choose all options that apply*]

At closing, Seller will deliver to Buyer these signed documents:

☐ A. A bill of sale for the tangible assets being sold, including a warranty of good title.

☐ B. An assignment of the lease at [*fill in property address*], with the landlord's consent.

☐ C. An assignment of the other contracts that are being transferred to Buyer, with the written consent of the other contracting person, if such consent is required.

☐ D. Assignments of all intellectual property contracts, including trademarks, patents, and copyrights, that are part of this purchase.

Seller will also deliver to Buyer at closing all other documents reasonably needed to transfer the business assets to Buyer, including _____
_____.

Transfer of Vehicles

Assignments of the cars and trucks owned by the business, in the form required by the Department of Motor Vehicles.

Transfer of a Liquor License

Assignment of the Class C liquor license owned by the business, in the form required by the Alcoholic Beverages Commission.

Transfer of Real Estate

A warranty deed for the real estate being sold, along with a title insurance policy guaranteeing that Buyer is receiving a marketable title.

2. Documents for Transferring Entity

When you're selling your entity rather than the assets of your business, you'll be transferring your interest in the entity to the buyer. You won't need to worry about transferring individual assets to the buyer. Clause 26, Documents for Transferring Entity, may be appropriate in your sales agreement. Choose the alternative that applies (A or B) and edit according to your situation.

As explained in Chapter 19, if you're selling your entity on an installment payment plan, you and the buyer may agree that the documents transferring ownership will held by a third party—an

A. Documents Delivered to Buyer

---

26. Documents for Transferring Entity (Entity Sale)

At closing, Seller will deliver to Buyer [endorsed stock certificates for the corporation being sold/signed membership certificates transferring all interests in the LLC being sold].

B. Documents Delivered to Escrow Agent

---

26. Documents for Transferring Entity (Entity Sale)

At closing, Seller will deliver to [*list name of escrow agent*] [endorsed stock certificates for the corporation being sold/signed membership certificates transferring all interests in the LLC being sold] in accordance with an Escrow Agreement in the form of Attachment ____.

---

escrow agent—until you've received full payment. In that case, your clause might read like the second alternative (Clause 26B), above.

C. Dispute Resolution Clause

You'd like to believe that once a comprehensive sales agreement has been signed, everything will go smoothly between you and the buyer, but the sad reality is that disputes can arise. These can relate to relatively minor matters such as how to apply your proration formula to a specific bill that arrived after the closing. Or they can be major matters such as a claim by the buyer that you misrepresented key financial information. Ideally, you'd like to be able to negotiate a

settlement of any dispute directly with the buyer. This is usually the quickest, least-costly way to put disagreements behind you and move on. Unfortunately, once you and the buyer become involved in a spat, it can often be difficult to negotiate a mutually agreeable settlement.

It's no secret that when negotiations fail, a lawsuit is usually the worst way to resolve a business problem. Not only is litigation typically expensive, prolonged, and emotionally draining but, worst of all, the results are at least to some degree unpredictable. And if litigation with a buyer takes place before your business changes hands, it can lead to adverse publicity for your company and even cause disclosure of confidential business information. That's why you'll normally want your sales agreement to provide that any disputes be resolved through one of two tried-and-true alternative means:

- **Mediation,** in which you and the buyer try to achieve a voluntary settlement with the help of a neutral third party (the mediator) who uses a highly efficient step-by-step process to help you craft your own solution. As compared to a court fight, mediation is inexpensive, quick, and confidential—and it's effective the vast majority of the time. The mediator doesn't have the power to make decisions, so no resolution will be imposed on you; you and the seller are in control of how to resolve your dispute.

- **Arbitration,** in which you and the buyer empower a neutral third party (the arbitrator) to listen to both sides and arrive at a binding solution in order to resolve the dispute. As with mediation, the process is almost always cheaper and speedier than having a trial, and it's confidential. And, also, just like mediation, there's a minimum of paperwork and formality.

In your sales agreement, you and the buyer can agree that you'll submit any dispute to mediation. Then, if the mediation doesn't lead to a settlement, the dispute will get submitted to arbitration or either party can go directly to court, depending on how your disputes clause is worded. If you choose the arbitration option, the arbitrator will make a final decision that will be enforced by a court, if necessary.

With the following clause, Clause 27, Disputes, you and the buyer can name the mediator and arbitrator now, or agree on them when the need arises. Another possibility is to name an organization such as the American Arbitration Association, which will provide a trained mediator when needed. This disputes clause assumes that you and the buyer will share the cost of the dispute resolution equally and that if the dispute is not resolved within 60 days, you'll either move on to arbitration or go directly to court. In either case, mediation will be attempted first.

If you're not sold on the merits of either mediation or arbitration, and you prefer the traditional route of going to court to deal with problems, do not include Clause 27, Disputes, in your sales agreement.

Resources on mediation and arbitration. For a comprehensive and practical discussion of mediation and other methods of resolving disputes, see *Mediate Don't Litigate: Strategies for Successful Mediation,* by Peter Lovenheim and Lisa Guerin (Nolo). For lists of professional mediators and extensive information on mediation, see the Mediation Information and Resource Center at www.mediate.com. To learn more about arbitration and find an arbitrator, see the American Arbitration Association's website at www.adr.org or the website of the Association for Conflict Resolution at www.acrnet.org.

27. Disputes [*optional*]

If a dispute arises concerning this agreement or the sale, Seller and Buyer will try in good faith to settle it through mediation conducted by [*list name of specific mediator or mediation group*/a mediator to be mutually selected].

Seller and Buyer will share the cost of the mediator equally. Seller and Buyer will cooperate fully with the mediator and will attempt to reach a mutually satisfactory resolution of the dispute.

If the dispute is not resolved within 60 days after it is referred to the mediator, Seller and Buyer agree that

[*choose alternative that applies*]

☐ the dispute will be arbitrated by [*list name of specific arbitrator or arbitration group*/an arbitrator to be mutually selected]. Judgment on the arbitration award may be entered in any court that has jurisdiction over the matter. Costs of arbitration, including lawyers' fees, will be allocated by the arbitrator.

or

☐ either party may take the matter to court.

D. Technical Contract Clauses

If you were to look at a pile of contracts for the sale of a business—or, in fact, for a wide variety of business transactions—you'd find that many of them include a similar set of clauses, usually near the end. Typically, these technical clauses (called "boilerplate") cover such issues as:

- whether the parties intend the contract to be modified in writing only
- how each party will communicate with the other regarding the contract
- what will happen to the rest of the contract if a judge decides that one part of it isn't legal, and

- which state's law will govern the contract.

This section covers the most common technical clauses.

1. Risk of Loss

There's always a possibility that the assets that you're selling will be damaged or destroyed before the closing. You may want to reassure the buyer that if there's a loss, you'll replace the lost or damaged assets or pay for their replacement. If you're following prudent business practices and carrying adequate insurance, that shouldn't be a problem,

A clause to consider using in an asset sale might look like this:

---

28. Risk of Loss (Asset Sale)

Seller will replace or pay for the replacement of any assets that are destroyed or damaged before the closing.

In an entity sale, you can use a slightly different version of this clause:

---

29. Risk of Loss (Entity Sale)

Seller will cause [the corporation/the LLC] being sold to replace or pay for the replacement of any of its assets that are destroyed or damaged before the closing.

---

though should assets be destroyed, you will have to pay for any deductible under your insurance policy.

2. Entire Agreement

Before you sign your agreement, you and the buyer will have discussed and probably negotiated dozens of issues, from the sale price and terms of payment, to how to physically count the inventory and how long you'll work for the buyer as a consultant. Ideally, all the relevant points that you agree on will end up in your contract. But it's also possible that you and the buyer may have talked about additional issues but not reached a conclusion and for that reason left them out of the final agreement. For example, you and the buyer may have talked about the buyer hiring your son to work as a clerk. To avoid the problem

that one of you might later claim that your deal also includes a certain oral agreement, your agreement should say that only what's written in it (not anything else you discussed before) is part of your deal. Although no legal language is absolutely foolproof, including an "Entire Agreement" clause in your sales agreement will go far to prevent the buyer from later successfully claiming in arbitration or court that you agreed to something that's missing from (or conflicts with something in) the contract.

Similarly, you and the buyer may have negotiated your contract by sending letters, emails, faxes, or other written documents back and forth—or may have even written a letter of intent as discussed in Chapter 11 before working on a more formal contract. Again, the purpose of an "entire agreement" clause such as Clause 30 is to prevent those previous writings from being considered part of your contract should either party later try to claim that one or more of them constitutes an inadvertently omitted part of your agreement.

3. Modification

After you've signed your sales agreement but before the closing takes place, you and the buyer may talk about making one or more written changes of its provisions. But you absolutely don't want a casual conversation with the buyer to somehow turn into a modification of your agreement. To prevent this possibility, a "modification" clause such as Clause 31 simply requires that any amendment to the agreement be in writing and signed by both of you.

Chapter 12 explains how to modify a signed sales agreement and includes an amendment form for doing so.

4. Governing Law

Although the chances are small that you and the buyer will end up in court or in arbitration over the sale, it makes sense to designate which state's law will apply to the sale before you get into a dispute. Usually, you and the buyer will be in the same state as the business, so you'll just fill in that state.

While it might take a bit more negotiation, if you and the buyer are located in different states, designating the governing law is more important. Although contract law is very similar from state to state, there can be small but significant differences. If you don't choose which state's law will govern your agreement, you could spend precious time fighting over that issue later instead of attending to the actual dispute. It's usually advantageous for you to have the laws of your home state govern, because this is the law that

---

30. Entire Agreement

This is the entire agreement between the parties. It replaces and supersedes any oral agreements between the parties, as well as any prior writings.

---

31. Modification

This agreement may be modified only by a written amendment signed by both parties.

you and your lawyer will probably be most familiar with. And, of course, using the courts in your own state will be more convenient and less expensive than if you have to travel elsewhere for litigation.

Use Clause 32, Governing Law, to address this issue.

5. Severability

There's always a possibility, however remote, that you'll get into a dispute with the buyer and that a judge or arbitrator will need to interpret your sales agreement. And, once this happens, there's also at least a theoretical possibility that the judge or arbitrator will rule that a provision of your agreement is unenforceable or invalid. If your agreement isn't properly worded, what happens next is iffy. The risk is that some judges or arbitrators, upon discovering an unenforceable or

invalid clause, may void the entire agreement.

To prevent this, Clause 33, Severability, says that if a court or arbitrator finds that any part of your sales agreement is not enforceable, the unenforceable material should simply be discarded (severed), leaving the rest of the agreement intact.

6. Notices

Because you and the buyer may not see each other frequently, it makes sense to formally exchange mailing addresses and agree on how you'll send each other any written communications required by the sales agreement. For example, the buyer may need to send you a notice concerning a bill that you've agreed to pay, and you may need to send the buyer a legal notice, such as a warning that the buyer is in breach of the contract.

---

32. Governing Law

This agreement will be governed by and interpreted under the laws of the state of _____, and any litigation regarding this agreement or its attachments will be brought in the courts of that state.

---

33. Severability

If a court or arbitrator determines that a provision in this agreement is invalid or not enforceable, that determination will affect only that provision. The provision will be modified only to the extent needed to make it valid and enforceable. The rest of the agreement will be unaffected, and all other clauses will remain valid and in force.

Generally, as recommended in Clause 36 in Chapter 18, you'll fill in the respective addresses following the signatures at the end of the sales agreement. A clause like Clause 34, Notices, can be helpful.

This clause applies to notices—not to installment payments. Typically, the address where the buyer is to send you the monthly installment payments can be inserted in the promissory note, and first-class mail will suffice, as explained in Chapter 19.

E. Additional Optional Clauses

For many sales agreements, the clauses discussed above and in the preceding chapters will be all you need. But it's possible that your sale won't fit the typical mold and that you'll need to address some additional issues and terms. Given the reality that there are thousands of different types of businesses, and that every small enterprise is somewhat unique,

no book can present every contractual possibility. So if your sale includes some features not anticipated by the clauses suggested here, you'll need to do some drafting on your own. In most instances, you can simply add sensible language to capture additional needed details, although if the extra material is complicated or lots of money is at stake, you'll be well-advised to work with your lawyer.

There are many kinds of special terms you may need to add to your agreement. For example, perhaps you and the buyer have agreed that for six months following the closing, you'll be able to continue to use your current office within the business premises at no charge. Or maybe you and the buyer have agreed that you and your family will be entitled to a 40% discount on purchases from the buyer over the next five years. Or maybe you'll have the right to buy back certain assets at a discounted price if the buyer should decide to sell the business or its assets. There's no telling what you and the buyer may come up with.

---

34. Notices

All notices must be sent in writing. A notice may be delivered to a person at the address that follows the person's signature or to a new address that the person designates in writing. A notice may be delivered:

A. in person

B. by certified mail, or

C. by overnight courier.

35. Other Additional Terms [*optional*]

[For the first six months following the closing, Buyer will allow Seller to occupy Seller's current office at no charge. Seller will also be allowed to use the telephone and the equipment in the office at no charge.]

Signatures on a Sales Agreement

Don't be surprised if the buyer isn't completely satisfied with your first draft of the sales agreement. Typically, the two of you will have to spend a little time—maybe even a lot of time—discussing and revising the wording. You may go through a number of drafts before you reach a meeting of the minds.

But once you and the buyer have ironed out your differences over substance and language, the sales agreement will, of course, need to be signed before it is legally binding. Usually you and the buyer will sign the agreement several days or weeks before the closing. You can specify the closing date and location in Clause 24 (Closing), which is discussed in Chapter 17. And see Chapter 22, which covers details of the closing, including checklists of other legal documents that may need to be signed to complete the sale.

Signing a sales agreement seems like a simple and obvious task, but it can involve some important legal subtleties which are explained in this chapter. Start by understanding that the signature format will vary, based on whether a person is signing as an individual or on behalf of a business entity. There are also differences based on the type of business entity buying or selling the business.

Chapter 13 explains how to identify the seller and buyer at the beginning of the sales agreement. It points out that the proper naming of the parties will depend on whether you're describing a sole proprietorship, partnership, corporation,

or LLC. To best understand the following discussion of signatures, it will help to review that material.

 In addition to signing the sales agreement, consider some sensible precautions. To keep important clauses from getting lost in the shuffle, make sure you number the pages. Then, you and the buyer should initial each page when you sign the agreement. This is a safeguard against modified pages being inserted —either by accident or as part of a scam.

A. Required Signatures for Sole Proprietors on a Sales Agreement

For a sales agreement to be legally binding, it must be signed by the people who have authority to legally bind the seller and buyer. This section explains who signs for a sole proprietorship. Section B, below, provides an overview of who signs for an entity such as a corporation or an LLC. Section C, below, covers the issue of spouses signing the sales agreement.

If you (the seller) are a sole proprietor and selling your business, you'll sign the sales agreement personally, using the one of the sole proprietor signature formats suggested in Section E, below. In addition, if you're a married sole proprietor and live in a community property state, your spouse should sign as well for the reasons discussed in Section C, below.

If the buyer is a sole proprietor, he or she will sign the sales agreement personally—again, using one of the signature formats suggested in Section E, below. And in some cases, spouses must sign the sales agreement, as discussed in Section C, below.

B. Required Signatures for an Entity on a Sales Agreement

When a seller or a buyer is an entity rather than a person—that is, a seller or buyer is a partnership, corporation, or LLC—things can get more complicated. Basically, the people who have legal authority to bind an entity must sign the sales agreement on behalf of that entity. Who these people might be depends on whether yours is an asset sale or an entity sale. And in some cases, spouses must sign the sales agreement, as discussed in Section C, below.

1. Asset Sale by an Entity

Here's an overview of how to deal with signatures on a sales agreement when your business is a partnership, corporation, or LLC that's selling its assets but the entity isn't being sold.

The buyer will certainly expect the sales agreement to be signed by the person or people who have authority to bind your entity—for example, the president and

secretary of your corporation. But that may not be enough. To be on the safe side, the buyer may want all the partners, shareholders, or LLC members of your entity to sign.

Similarly, if you're selling the assets of your business to a partnership, corporation, or LLC, you'll want to have the agreement signed by the people with authority to bind the buying entity. But also, to avoid problems resulting from dissension among the buyer's owners, you'll wisely ask for the signatures of all partners, shareholders, or members of the buying entity.

2. Sale of an Entity by Its Owners

If you and your co-owners are selling your interests in your entity, each co-owner will sign the sales agreement. No one will sign on behalf of the entity because, in this case, the entity is not the seller. As for the buyer or buyers, these will normally be individuals and they should each sign the sales agreement. However, if another entity is a buyer of your entity, the people with legal authority to bind the buying entity will need to sign—and you'll also prefer to have all owners of the buying entity sign as well.

3. General Guidelines on Who Signs the Sales Agreement for an Entity

Here are some guidelines to help you sort out who is eligible to sign the agreement on behalf of an entity. These guidelines apply when an entity is a seller, a buyer, or a guarantor in either an asset sale or an entity sale.

a. Partnership

The basic rule is that any general partner has the legal power to sign a contract on behalf of a partnership, meaning the other party can rely on just one general partner's signature. The main exception to this rule is where the partners have agreed among themselves in their partnership agreement that only certain partners have the power to sign contracts, or that more than one signature is needed. In that case, and if the other party is informed of this limitation in advance, the assumed authority of each partner to bind the partnership will no longer be in effect. This means, for example, that if you've been informed that only one specific partner has authority to sign on behalf of the partnership or that all partners must sign, your sales agreement won't bind the partnership if you don't follow the partnership's internal rules.

So, if you receive information orally or in writing that the partners have modified the normal rule that any general partner can bind the partnership, your only prudent course is to require all partners to sign the sales agreement.

b. Corporation

A corporation determines which of its officers have the authority to sign agree-

ments on behalf of the business. This is usually stated in the bylaws or a board of directors' resolution. The corporation's president usually is an authorized signer, but other officers may also have the authority.

c. Limited Liability Company (LLC)

In most situations, the same rule that applies to a partnership also applies to an LLC: Any member (owner) can sign on behalf of the LLC. But if the members have agreed that not all members have this power and the other party is told about it, the signature of someone who lacks the authority won't be binding. The exception to this rule is for LLCs where one or more members are given the title of manager. In that situation, only a manager can bind the LLC.

4. Avoid Disputes by Having All Owners Sign the Sales Agreement

So much for the general legal guidelines. To be 100% certain about whether a particular person has the legal power to sign an agreement for the sale of an entity's assets, you'd need to see the entity's organizational records—and, in the case of a corporation, probably its board of directors' resolutions as well. But there's usually a simpler and equally effective way to proceed. Since the selling or buying entity involved in a small business sale will usually have a limited number of owners—partners, shareholders, or LLC members—you can have all of the owners sign the sales agreement to indicate that they approve of the sale and its terms. This heads off any later challenge from an owner who may object to the sale.

If you follow this suggestion and decide to get the signatures of all owners, then in addition to providing a spot for the signature of someone acting on behalf of the entity, you can include an entity owners' approval section like the one shown at the end of Section E, below.

C. A Spouse's Signature on the Sales Agreement

There are a few situations in which it may be prudent to include the signature of a seller's or buyer's spouse on the sales agreement. Let's look at each of them.

1. Signature of Seller's Spouse

If you're married, live in a community property state (listed below in "Community Property Basics"), and are selling the assets of your sole proprietorship, the buyer will almost certainly want to have your spouse cosign the sales agreement. That will eliminate any possibility that your spouse will later claim an interest in the business assets under community property law and prevent the full use of the assets

Community Property Basics

Nine states follow the community property system: Arizona, California, Idaho, Louisiana, Nevada, New Mexico, Texas, Washington, and Wisconsin. In these states, and in the absence of a marriage contract providing otherwise, a married couple's property accumulated after marriage is usually community—or jointly owned—property regardless of the names in which it's held. (Exceptions include property received by inheritance or gift.) This means that a married couple's community property normally includes at least a partial interest in any sole proprietorship business that either spouse owns—even one that was owned by one spouse prior to marriage. Legally, it's also true that in a community property state, if you pay a fair price to purchase business assets from a sole proprietor whose spouse plays no role in running the business, the law doesn't absolutely require that you get the consent of the owner's spouse. Still, because it's almost impossible to determine with certainty how much a business is worth and an uncommitted spouse could always disagree, it's always a good idea in a community property state to require the spouse of a sole proprietor seller to sign the sales agreement and closing documents.

by the buyer. Beyond that, there may be other situations in which you or the buyer will feel more comfortable if your spouse signs the sales agreement, such as if your spouse has a property interest in some of the business assets—or if your spouse has been working closely with you in running your sole proprietorship, creating the impression that your business legally is a partnership rather than a sole proprietorship.

See Section G, below, for suggested language for requiring the signature of a seller's spouse on a sales agreement.

2. Signature of Buyer's Spouse

In an installment sale, the individual buyer or buyers will personally sign the promissory note that covers the balance of the sale price. And if the buyer is an entity, you'll want the co-owners of the entity to personally guarantee the promissory note. But a personal guarantee may be of little value if the signer's spouse has the deep pockets or, in some instances, if the couple's bank accounts and other assets are held in the name of the couple. It follows that you'll be wise to insist that the spouse of the buyer (or, in the case of an entity, the spouses of the owners) sign the promissory note as well. That will assure that their jointly owned property as well as the spouse's paychecks will be on the line if the note payments aren't

made. To avoid any last-minute slip up, you can ask that spouses agree at the end of the sales agreement that they'll cosign the promissory note.

See Section G, below, for suggested language for the signature of a buyer's spouse on a sales agreement.

 Consult a lawyer if you're in the process of getting divorced. You'll need to determine if principles of equitable distribution or community property law in your state give your spouse any rights in the business, the terms of the sale, or the sale proceeds. It may take a domestic relations lawyer to sort this out for you. Because the buyer will certainly want to be reassured on this point, it's best to find out early on whether your spouse can upset the apple cart by refusing to provide a needed signature on the sales agreement. Obviously, if your spouse is a partner in your business or if the buyer will insist on his or her consent anyway, you and your spouse (or his or her lawyer) have some talking to do.

3. Signature Formats

Here is suggested language for the signature of a spouse on a sales agreement.

a. Consent of Seller's Spouse

You can use the following wording when the seller's spouse will be signing:

I am married to the Seller. I consent to the sale described above, and I waive any interest I might otherwise have in the [business assets/entity ownership interests], whether under the community property laws or otherwise.

D. Signature Clause in a Sales Agreement

Now that you understand who must or may sign the sales agreement, it's time to create your own clause. A signature clause you can adapt to fit your particular sale is shown below.

You'll use the phrase "and Seller's spouse" if the seller is a person whose spouse will also be signing the sales agreement. You'll use the phrase "all owners of the selling entity" if the seller is a partnership, corporation, or LLC.

Likewise, you'll use the phrase "and Buyer's spouse" if the buyer is a person and his or her spouse will be signing. And you'll use the phrase "all owners of the buying entity" if the buyer is a partnership, corporation, or LLC.

The optional line about additional signers can be used for situations not fully covered by the main clause, such as when a relative or friend of the buyer will be guaranteeing the promissory note. Normally, however, the add-on line won't be necessary in the Required Signatures clause.

b. Consent of Buyer's Spouse

You can use the following wording when the buyer's spouse will be signing the promissory note in an installment sale:

I am married to [the Buyer/one of the owners of the buying entity/the owner of the buying entity]. In consideration of Seller extending credit to Buyer for the purchase of the [business assets/entity ownership interests] described above, I agree to cosign or personally guarantee the promissory note to be given by Buyer to Seller.

---

36. Required Signatures

This agreement is valid only if signed by Seller [and Seller's spouse/all owners of the selling entity] and Buyer [and Buyer's spouse/all owners of the buying entity].

[optional]

[and by the following additional person/people: .]

E. The Typical Formats for Signing a Sales Agreement

Section D, above, explains how to draft a clause (Clause 36, Required Signatures) listing everyone who must sign your sales agreement before it's a legally binding document. Now you need to finish off the sales agreement by providing a place for everyone to sign. This section covers the formats for signatures and some additional language that may be appropriate when co-owners of an entity, spouses of individuals, or outside guarantors will be signing.

General Signature Format

The elements for the signature section when someone is acting on behalf of a business entity are:

❶ the name of the company

❷ the state where the company is legally established

❸ the type of legal entity

❹ a place for an authorized person to sign on behalf of the company. (Section B, above, explains who is authorized to sign for the company depending on the entity.)

❺ the printed name of the signer

❻ the signer's title

❼ the address of the entity

❽ the date when the person is signing the sales agreement.

For a corporation it would look like this (for a sole proprietor you'll simplify it as set out in "Signature Lines on a Sales Agreement," below):

> ❶ The Coffee Cup Inc.
> ❷ A New York ❸ Corporation
>
> By:_____❹_____
>
> ❺ Alice Appleby
> ❻ President
> ❼ 123 Chesterfield Boulevard
>   White Plains, New York
>
> Dated: ❽_____

Where an individual (such as a shareholder of a corporation) is agreeing to guarantee the accuracy of the representations of a party or agreeing to indemnify the other party (see Section F, below), the signature format can be simplified as follows:

> *Bert Becker*
> _____
> Bert Becker
> 56 Dennison Place
> White Plains, New York
>
> Dated:_____

Signature Lines on a Sales Agreement

This chart shows how you can deal with signatures in a variety of situations. You should include the address of the business or signer as well, as in the "General Signature Format," above.

Individual

John Smith
John Smith

Sole Proprietorship
(Either style can be used)

John Smith
John Smith doing business as Ace's Diner

[or]

Ace's Diner
A Sole Proprietorship

By: *John Smith*
John Smith, Owner

Partnership

Smith & Jones
A Michigan Partnership

By: *Mary Jones*
Mary Jones, Partner

Corporation

Modern Textiles Inc.
A Texas Corporation

By: *Mary Jones*
Mary Jones, President

Limited Liability Company

Games and Such LLC
A California Limited Liability Company

By: *Mary Jones*
Mary Jones, [Member / Manager]

Use these formats on other legal documents as well. The signature formats suggested here for the sales agreement are also appropriate for other documents described in this book (Chapters 19 through 21), such as promissory notes and security agreements.

When an entity is a seller or buyer, you can have the owners of that entity confirm in the signature portion of the agreement that they consent to the sale. Suggested language you can insert immediately before the signatures of the entity's owners is provided below.

1. Owner's Consent When the Seller Is an Entity

When the seller is an entity owned by more than one person, insert the following language before the seller's signature:

> We are all of the Seller's [partners/ shareholders/members]. Each of us approves of and consents to the sale described in the above agreement.

When the seller is a corporation or an LLC owned by just one person, the suggested insertion would read as follows:

> I am the sole [shareholder/member] of the Seller. I approve of and consent to the sale described in the above agreement.

2. Owner's Consent When the Buyer Is an Entity

When the buyer is an entity owned by more than one person, insert the following language before the buyer's signature:

> We are all of the Buyer's [partners/ shareholders/members]. Each of us approves of and consents to the purchase described in the above agreement.

When the buyer is a corporation or an LLC owned by just one person, the suggested insertion would read as follows:

> I am the sole [shareholder/member] of the Buyer. I approve of and consent to the sale described in the above agreement.

This will work if the owners are not intending to accept personal responsibility for commitments contained in the sales agreement—that is, they are preserving their normal immunity from liability for the entity's obligations. If they are intending to accept personal responsibility, I recommend that you use the language suggested in Section F, below.

3. Commitment of Outside Guarantor

In some situations, you might negotiate with the buyer to have someone other than an owner of an entity or a spouse guarantee the promises the buyer is making in an installment sale. You can use the following wording when an outsider will be guaranteeing the buyer's promissory note:

In consideration of Seller extending credit to Buyer for the purchase of the [business assets/entity ownership interests] described above, I agree to cosign or personally guarantee the promissory note to be given by Buyer to Seller.

 Pay close attention to who will be responsible for paying the promissory note debt. Having the owners of the buying corporation or LLC sign a raft of guarantees never hurts, but most important

is to insist that they personally cosign or guarantee the promissory note for the balance of the purchase price. This means if the entity fails to pay in full, the owners are personally liable to do so. The promissory note is discussed in Chapter 19.

F. Accepting Personal Responsibility for Commitments in a Sales Agreement

When the seller or buyer is an individual (or sole proprietor) rather than an entity, that person is automatically liable for the commitments that he or she makes in the sales agreement. It's a different story, however, if the seller or buyer is a corporation, an LLC, or a partnership. In that case, the owners of the entity aren't personally responsible (legally liable) unless one or all of them signs the sales agreement as an individual and specifically agrees to be liable. You and the buyer will be particularly concerned about this legal point if your sales agreement calls for the owners of an entity to accept some personal responsibility for commitments made in the agreement. Let's say that you're selling your assets to a corporation on an installment payment basis. And let's assume, too, that the owners (shareholders) of the buying corporation will be guaranteeing the promissory note that their corporation will be signing. It makes sense for these entity owners not only to indicate that they agree with the purchase of assets, but also that they will sign the promissory note as guarantors—and comply with any other portions of the agreement that are intended to make them personally responsible.

In drafting an appropriate signature section, you'll need to carefully review the clauses of your sales agreement to see exactly what, if any, personal commitments it contemplates.

Your agreement may say, for example, that the owners of the seller's entity will personally:

- indemnify the buyer against certain liabilities (Clause 16, Chapter 15)
- stand behind the seller's representations and warranties (Clause 18, Chapter 15)
- not compete with the buyer (Clause 21, Chapter 16), and
- sign an employment or consulting contract (Clause 22, Chapter 16).

Or your agreement may say, for example, that the owners of the buyer's entity will personally:

- cosign or personally guarantee the promissory note for the balance of the purchase price (Clause 13 Chapter 14),
- indemnify the seller against certain liabilities (Clause 17, Chapter 15), and
- stand behind the buyer's representations and warranties (Clause 20, Chapter 15).

Section E, above, provides language you can use in the signature portion of the sales agreement allowing owners of an entity to confirm that they consent to the sale. The following sections provide additional language you can use to confirm that entity owners not only consent to the sale but also agree to assume personal responsibility. You'll need to modify the language to fit your needs and insert it just before the signature lines for the owner or owners.

1.   Personal Responsibility for a Selling Entity's Commitments

You can adapt the language shown in the two boxes below when owners of a selling entity will be accepting personal responsibility for commitments in a sales agreement.

When the seller is a corporation or an LLC owned by just one person, the beginning of the suggested insertion would read as follows:

I am the sole [shareholder/member] of the selling entity. I approve of and consent to the sale described in the above agreement.

In addition, in consideration of Buyer entering into this agreement with Seller, I agree to: [*insert the rest of the language below*]

We are all of the Seller's [partners/shareholders/members]. Each of us approves of and consents to the sale described in the above agreement.

In addition, in consideration of Buyer entering into this agreement with Seller, each of us agrees to:

1. Indemnify, defend, and save Buyer harmless from and against the debts and other liabilities which, under this agreement, are the responsibility of Seller.

2. Indemnify, defend, and save Buyer harmless from and against any loss, liability damage, or expense arising from any breach of the above representations and warranties made by Seller.

3. Honor the noncompete provisions of this agreement and sign any noncompete document required by this agreement.

4. Honor the [employment/consulting] terms of this agreement and sign any [employment/consulting] document required by this agreement.

2. Personal Responsibility for a Buying Entity's Commitments

You can adapt the following language when owners of a buying entity will be accepting personal responsibility for commitments in a sales agreement.

When the buyer is a corporation or an LLC owned by just one person, the suggested insertion would read as follows:

I am the sole [shareholder/member] of the Buyer. I approve of and consent to the sale described in the above agreement.

In addition, in consideration of Seller entering into this agreement with Buyer, I agree to: [*insert the rest of the language below*]

We are all of the Buyer's [partners/shareholders/members]. Each of us approves of and consents to the purchase described in the above agreement.

In addition, in consideration of Seller entering into this agreement with Buyer, each of us agrees to:

1. Cosign or personally guarantee the promissory note to be given by Buyer to Seller under this agreement.

2. Indemnify, defend, and save Seller harmless from and against the debts and other liabilities which, under this agreement, are the responsibility of Buyer.

3. Indemnify, defend, and save Seller harmless from and against any loss, liability damage, or expense arising from any breach of the above representations and warranties made by Buyer.

G. Signing the Sales Agreement

If you've followed all the information in this book about negotiating and preparing a sales agreement—and you and the buyer are satisfied with the final draft—signing it should be a breeze. But here are few pointers to help you as you enter the home stretch.

1. Timing the Signing

Usually, a seller and buyer sign the sales agreement as soon as all the kinks have been worked out and there's a solid deal. Occasionally, the parties wait to sign until the day of closing. The problem with this second method is that you might spend significant time getting ready to transfer the business, only to learn, at the last minute, that the buyer has had a change of heart. When the outcome is uncertain, you understandably may be reluctant to meticulously prepare for the closing, as recommended in Chapter 22.

I prefer the usual method—signing the sales agreement days or weeks before the closing—because it gives both you and the buyer adequate time to arrange for an orderly transition.

2. Multiple Originals

It makes sense to sign at least two originals of the sales agreement. That way, there's one for you and one for the buyer—and perhaps enough for lawyers, bankers, or anyone else close to the deal who'd like to have an agreement that contains original signatures. By the way, this idea of signing multiple originals applies to many of the documents that will be signed at closing, but not to the promissory note, since the buyer will be uncomfortable with having more than one original in circulation. See the discussion of promissory notes in Chapter 19.

3. Dating the Sales Agreement

While dating an agreement is not a legal requirement, it makes good business and practical sense to do so. The simplest way is to insert a date for each signer, following the name and address information, as shown in the example in Section E, above. This allows people to sign on different dates, which may be the case if several different people need to sign the sales agreement and they can't all be available to do so on the same day.

The agreement will be effective when the last required signature has been obtained.

4. Notaries and Witnesses

There's no practical or legal need to have the signatures on your sales agreement notarized or witnessed. Documents that pertain to real estate ownership—deeds and mortgages, for example—must be notarized. Wills and a few other documents must be signed in the presence of a witness. But very few other legal papers need this level of authentication.

5. Modification

Occasionally, your sales agreement will need to be modified—either just before it gets signed or at some point between signing and the closing. See Chapter 12 for suggestions on how best to accomplish this.

Part 4

Preparing the Promissory Note and Other Sales Documents

Chapter 19

Promissory Notes and Other Installment Documents

When to skip ahead. This chapter covers documents related to installment sales. If you'll be receiving the full sale price up front, you can skip ahead to the next chapter.

Chapters 12 through 18 showed you how to create the sales agreement, the main document involved in the sale of a business. But, as important as the sales agreement is, you'll also need additional documents to carry out the terms of the sales agreement and actually transfer your business to the buyer. Chapters 19 through 21 will help you prepare a dozen documents you're most likely to need, including a promissory note, bill of sale, and assignment of lease. You and the buyer should prepare the sale documents as early in the sales process as possible so that both of you will know in advance the exact wording of the main papers you'll sign at the closing. Chapter 22 explains how to create a closing checklist to reduce the possibility that necessary paperwork may get overlooked.

Because it's likely that you'll sell your business on an installment basis—that is, the buyer will pay for your business over time, rather than in one lump sum payment—this chapter will focus on the four documents you'll need for an installment sale:

- Promissory Note (Section A)
- Security Agreement (Section B)
- UCC Financing Statement (Section C), and
- Escrow Agreement for an Entity Sale (Section D).

The first three documents can be used in either an asset sale or an entity sale. The fourth—the escrow agreement—applies only to an entity sale. These documents will help assure that you'll ultimately receive all the money that you're owed for your business.

 Where to find the forms. You'll find copies of the promissory note, security agreements, UCC Financing Statement and Addendum, and escrow agreements on the CD-ROM at the back of this book.

A. The Promissory Note

Typically, at closing, the buyer makes a down payment and signs a promissory note setting out the terms for paying you the remainder of the sale price. A promissory note says, in effect, "Buyer promises to pay Seller $ plus interest of %" and then it describes how and when the buyer is to make the payments. The promissory note usually covers the following points:

- when the buyer will make installment payments
- the amount of each payment
- what rate of interest the buyer will pay, and

- what happens if the buyer doesn't pay as promised.

To increase the odds that you'll receive all the payments called for in the promissory note, you'll be wise if you negotiate to have your sales agreement provide that the promissory note be guaranteed by the owners of the buyer's legal entity (shareholders or LLC members), the buyers' spouses, and perhaps other people. Assuming that the buyer has agreed to such guarantees, your promissory note should include a place for those guarantors to sign as explained in Section A1b, below.

See Chapter 14, Clause 13, for sales agreement language describing the promissory note. As with other key documents to be signed at closing, the form for the note should be attached to the sales agreement so that the exact wording is known to both you and the buyer well in advance.

1. Understanding Promissory Notes

A promissory note is a binding legal contract. As with all contracts, something of value is exchanged between two parties. In this case, the buyer receives the assets of your business or the ownership of your corporate, LLC, or partnership entity. In exchange, you receive the buyer's promise to pay the balance owed on the sale price—usually with interest—at specified dates. If the buyer doesn't meet

the payment terms, you can sue the buyer and any cosigners or guarantors and get a judgment for the amount owed plus court costs and possibly all or part of your lawyer's fee for obtaining the judgment. With a judgment in hand, you can then collect the money owed from any of the buyer's assets you can find, including bank accounts, securities, vehicles, and even real estate.

a. Interest

The promissory note will state the annual interest rate the buyer will pay on the principal balance. Unless otherwise specified in the note, interest is paid at the end of the borrowing interval—not in advance. So, for example, if the buyer signs the note on January 1 and agrees to make monthly payments that include interest, the February 1 payment will include interest on the balance owed for the month of January.

Because interest rates often move up and down with the health of the economy and rate of inflation, there's no single recommended number. One reasonable approach is to look at the interest you'd receive if, instead of lending the buyer money, you stuck your money in a relatively safe investment such as a mutual fund that specializes in government and high-grade corporate bonds. Then add a premium to that rate to account for the fact that the buyer is a far riskier creditor. For example, if a conservative bond fund pays interest at a rate of 4%, you might want to charge at least 8%. But if bonds are earning 7%, you'd want to charge 10% or more, assuming your state's usury laws allow it.

State usury laws may cap the rate of interest that a lender can charge a borrower—often in the range of 10% to 20%. (Some states let you charge a higher interest rate when you extend credit to a business rather than to an individual, and some impose no limit on loans to an LLC or a corporation.) If you charge more than the rate allowed by your state's usury law, this generally means you can't go to court to collect the excess amount, and you may face other financial penalties. As long as the interest rate doesn't exceed your state's limit, you and the buyer can negotiate any rate that's acceptable to both of you. As a practical matter, you need to check the usury law of your state only if the interest rate you plan to charge exceeds 10%.

Your accountant or bank may be able to tell you your state usury law. Or, to research the law yourself, check your state statutes under the words "usury," "interest," "credit," or "loans."

b. Signers and Guarantors

The buyer will, of course, sign the promissory note, but you and the buyer may agree that others will sign as guarantors to give you extra assurance that the debt will be fully paid. As noted above, a person who signs a note, or guarantees it, is personally liable for repaying it,

meaning that his or her personal assets are at risk if the note isn't paid. So if the buyer is a sole proprietor, he or she will sign the note and be personally liable for paying it. The same is true when the buyer is a partnership and all the partners sign. But if the buyer is a corporation or an LLC, only the entity is liable for repayment—not the shareholders or LLC members who own the entity.

You and the buyer may agree that for additional security, others will sign or guarantee the note. Here is a list of the most likely candidates:

- **The spouse of a person who is signing a note.** That way, you can reach joint or community property of the couple if payment isn't made.
- **The owners of the corporation or LCC that's buying your business.** Unless these shareholders or LLC members personally guarantee the note, they won't be personally responsible for repaying it. Without their guarantee you can only look to the entity and its assets to satisfy the debt.
- **A deep-pocket friend or relative of a signer who's willing to help out.** This is useful if the signer has limited financial means or a checkered credit history.

In Clause 13 (Promissory Note) of your sales agreement (described in Chapter 14), be sure to list the names of everyone who will be required to sign or guarantee the promissory note. Also, see Chapter 9 for additional discussion of these issues.

c. Security Interest

To further assure that the debt the buyer owes you will be fully paid, you and the buyer can agree that you'll retain a security interest (lien) on property of the buyer. This typically consists of a security interest in the assets of the business, using a security agreement and UCC Financing Statement as described below in Sections B and C. By getting a security interest, if the debt isn't paid as promised, you'll be able to take or sell the property that's been pledged as security.

The security agreement and UCC Financing Statement won't work for real estate, however. To have a lien on real estate, the buyer will need to give you a mortgage or deed of trust, which you should then promptly record with the appropriate land records office. A lien on real estate is especially desirable if you're selling a service business that doesn't have much in the way of tangible personal property.

The real estate in which you acquire a security interest doesn't have to be owned or used by the business. It can, for example, be the buyer's home—though, in that case, your lien is likely to take the form of a second mortgage or second deed of trust. Because of variations in state laws and the need to meet subtle technical requirements, you and the buyer should consult a lawyer or title insurance company for guidance on obtaining a valid real estate lien.

See Chapter 14, Clauses 14 and 15 (Security for Payment), for information on how to provide in your sales agreement for the acquisition of a security interest.

Require term life insurance as a backup. Ask the buyer to take out a term life insurance policy that will cover the promissory note in case the buyer dies before paying off the debt. See Chapter 9 for more details on this strategy.

d. Acceleration Clause

The promissory note included in this book contains an acceleration clause. With such a clause in place, if the buyer doesn't make a required payment within a specified number of days after it becomes due, you can immediately demand payment of the entire remaining balance. And if the buyer still doesn't pay, you can promptly sue for the full amount owed. Without an acceleration clause, you'd have to sue the buyer each time an installment payment was missed or wait until all payments were missed and then sue for the full amount. Either choice would be burdensome.

To understand why this legal language can be so valuable, let's look at what happens without an acceleration clause. Assume that under a promissory note with no acceleration clause, the buyer, who is supposed to pay you $1,500 a month, fails to send you a check for two months. Fed up by unreturned phone calls, you decide to go to court. Unfortunately, since the buyer has only missed two payments, you can only sue for the $3,000 that's owed and nothing more. Sure, you'll get a judgment, but what if the buyer pays you the $3,000 and then continues to fall behind on current payments? You may even need to go through the same process again and again. What an annoying and expensive waste of your time and energy, especially if the buyer is badly mismanaging the business in the meantime.

 Require a defaulting buyer to pay for your legal help. I recommend having the promissory note say that the buyer will pay your court costs and lawyer's fees if you have to sue to collect the note. The promissory note included in this chapter has a clause (Collection Costs (Attorney Fees)) that does just that. Since the buyer is likely to understand that costs and legal fees can quickly add up, passing this burden on to the buyer can be a powerful incentive for the buyer—or guarantors—to make the payments on time.

2. Installment Payment Plans

Typically, the buyer will agree to pay you the same amount each month for a specified number of months, with part of each payment going towards interest and the rest to reduce the amount owed (principal). This is the same way most people pay off a home mortgage,

except in this case you'll want a shorter repayment term, such as three to five years. When the buyer makes the last payment, the note's principal and interest are fully paid. In legal and accounting jargon, this type of loan is said to be fully amortized over the period that the payments are made. Amortization calculators, available online and in numerous software packages, can quickly determine how much the buyer must pay each month and for how long, under various payment scenarios.

The promissory note in this book provides for amortized monthly payments. Repayment plans other than the amortization method are also available—though they're used less often because sellers and buyers generally prefer regular monthly payments. See "Alternative Repayment Methods," below, for details.

 When to use a professional. As with other key documents used in the sale of business, it's prudent to have a lawyer or tax professional review the form of the promissory note, especially if the terms of the note are unusual or you're not sure about the legal or tax effect of the language you're using.

3. Promissory Note Form

Here is a sample promissory note form that provides for amortized monthly payments.

Promissory Note
(Amortized Monthly Payments)

1. Names

Buyer: _Georgetown West, Inc., a Florida Corporation_

Seller: _Burgundy Associates LLC, a Florida Limited Liability Company_

2. Promise to Pay

For value received, Buyer promises to pay Seller $ _50,000_ and interest at the yearly rate of _8_ % on the unpaid balance as specified below. Payments will be made to Seller at _123 Center Street, Miami, Florida_ or such other place as Seller may designate.

3. Monthly Installments

Buyer will pay _36_ monthly installments of $ _1,566.82_ each.

4. Date of Installment Payments

Buyer will make an installment payment on the _first_ day of each month beginning _April 1, 20XX_, until the principal and interest have been paid in full, which will be no later than _March 1, 20XX_.

5. Application of Payments

Payments will be applied first to interest and then to principal.

6. Prepayment

Buyer may prepay all or any part of the principal without penalty.

7. Loan Acceleration

If Buyer is more than _30_ days late in making any payment, Seller may declare that the entire balance of unpaid principal is due immediately, together with the interest that has accrued.

8. Security

(a) Buyer agrees that until the principal and interest owed under this promissory note are paid in full, this note will be secured by a security agreement and Uniform Commercial Code Financing Statement giving Seller a security interest in the

equipment, fixtures, inventory, and accounts receivable of the business known as
_____ Gold Star Bakery _____ .

(b) Buyer also agrees that until the principal and interest owed under this
promissory note are paid in full, this note will be secured by a mortgage
covering the real estate commonly known as _____ 345 Wilson Road, _____
___ Miami, Florida _____ and more fully described as follows:
___ Lot 35, Tyler and Williams Subdivision, City of Miami, Dade County, Florida __ .

9. Collection Costs (Attorney Fees)

If Seller prevails in a lawsuit to collect on this note, Buyer will pay Seller's costs and
lawyer's fees in an amount the court finds to be reasonable.

10. Governing Law

This note will be governed by and construed in accordance with the laws of the
state of _____ Florida _____ .

BUYER

__ Andover Enterprises Inc. _____

a __ Florida Corporation _____

By: __ *George Allen* _____

Printed name: ___ George Allen _____

Title: __ President _____

Address: ___ 789 Main Street, Miami, _____

__ Florida _____

Dated: ___ March 1, 20XX _____

Guarantors

We personally guarantee payment of the above note, jointly and severally.

Signature: __ *Jeffery Peterson* _____   Signature: __ *Angie Mason* _____

Printed name: ___ Jeffery Peterson ___   Printed name: __ Angie Mason _____

Address: ___ 678 Elwood Blvd. _____   Address: ___ 234 Arrow Court _____

__ Miami, Florida _____   __ Miami, Florida _____

Dated: ___ March 1, 20XX _____   Dated: ___ March 1, 20XX _____

Alternative Repayment Methods

In certain circumstances, you and the seller may opt for a repayment plan that's different from the typical amortization method. For example, if you're anxious to preserve cash during the early days of taking over the business, you may propose one of the following repayment methods, rather than the amortized monthly payment plan discussed in Section A2:

- **Equal monthly payments—large final balloon payment.** You make equal but relatively modest monthly payments of principal and interest for a set period of time such as three to five years. These payments are not enough to pay off (or fully amortize) the note. Instead, after making the last monthly payment, you must still make one final larger payment, called a balloon payment, to pay off the balance. This type of plan may seem appealing but, after getting used to making relatively modest payments, you may find it hard to suddenly come up with a large payment. Anticipating this, a seller may be reluctant to accept a balloon payment note.

- **Payments of interest only—large final balloon payment of principal.** To keep monthly payments even lower, you pay interest only (no principal) at specified intervals, such as monthly. At the end of the loan term, you make a very large balloon payment to cover the entire principal and any remaining interest. The seller is likely to see this as even chancier and less advisable than a plan of equal monthly payments with a balloon payment.

- **Single payment of principal and interest.** You make no monthly payments but instead pay off the note at a specified date in one payment that includes the entire principal amount and the accrued interest. Most sellers prefer receiving installment payments—and most buyers prefer paying over time, rather than having the balloon payment looming over their heads.

Where to find the forms. You'll find copies of the Promissory Note on the CD-ROM at the back of this book.

Instructions for Promissory Note

Here's how to complete the promissory note with amortized monthly payments.

1. Names

Insert the names and addresses of the buyer (first blank) and seller (second blank). See Chapter 13 for a discussion of how to identify the seller and buyer in the sales agreement and related documents.

2. Promise to Pay

In the first blank, insert the principal amount that's owed. You may have to fill in the amount on the day of closing if the promissory note balance will be affected by price adjustments described in your sales agreement. In the second blank, fill in the annual interest rate. For information on interest rates and usury laws, see Section 1a, above. In the third blank, fill in the address where the buyer is to send payments.

The phrase "For value received" is legal jargon meaning that the buyer has received something from the seller in exchange for the buyer's promise to pay money.

3. Monthly Installments

Insert the number of monthly payments the buyer will make to repay the loan and the amount of each installment. If you know the principal amount, the interest rate, and the number of years that payments will be made, you can consult an amortization calculator or schedule to arrive at the monthly payment. You can use Nolo's Simple Loan Calculator at www.nolo.com or Intuit's *Quicken* program to quickly calculate the amount of each installment.

Computer-generated amortization schedules can also tell what portion of a payment is principal and what portion is interest. At the beginning of the loan repayment period, the interest portion will be relatively high, but it will decline as the buyer continues to make payments.

4. Date of Installment Payments

Insert the day of the month when payments will be made, the date the first payment is due, and the date by which the principal and interest must be repaid in full. For example, if the business is sold on July 15, 2006, you might provide for payments to be made on the 15th of each month, with the first payment due on August 15, 2006.

5. Application of Payments

You don't need to insert anything here. Each payment automatically goes to pay accrued interest first. The rest goes toward the remaining principal.

6. Prepayment

You don't need to insert anything here. This clause allows the buyer to prepay the money owed—that is, pay all or part of the principal in advance. By prepaying, the buyer can cut down on the total amount of interest to be paid.

7. Loan Acceleration

It's typical in a promissory note to provide that if a payment is late by more than a specified number of days, the lender can declare the entire unpaid balance due. As discussed in Section 1d, above, this is called an "acceleration clause." Fill in the number of days after the payment due date that will trigger acceleration. Thirty days is often appropriate.

8. Security

This portion of the promissory note is related to the security (lien) arrangements that you and the buyer have agreed to.

Delete both paragraphs (a) and (b) if the note is unsecured, meaning that you don't have a lien on or security interest in any property.

Retain the first paragraph (a) if the buyer is giving the seller a security interest in business property. Insert the name of the business. You can use one of the Security Agreement forms found in Section B of this chapter, below. Then you should complete a Uniform Commercial Code (UCC) Financing Statement (see Section C, below), which you can record

(file) with the appropriate state or county office. When the buyer pays off the note, you must give the buyer an official discharge of the Financing Statement to file at the same place where the Financing Statement was filed.

Retain the second paragraph (b) if the buyer is giving the seller a lien on real estate. (This topic is discussed in Section 1c, above.) Indicate whether this will be done by a mortgage or deed of trust. (The practice varies from state to state.) Finally, insert the address and the legal description of the real estate as found in the buyer's deed or title insurance policy.

 Have a lawyer prepare the mortgage or deed of trust. Because of the technical intricacies of real estate titles, it's best to have an expert draft the mortgage or deed of trust that will secure the promissory note. After the note is signed, see that the mortgage or deed of trust gets recorded at the appropriate county records office. When the promissory note has been fully paid, you should remove the lien (security interest) by giving the buyer a discharge of the mortgage or deed of trust to be recorded where the original document was recorded.

9. Collection Costs (Attorney Fees)

Nothing needs to be filled in here. This clause requires the buyer to pay the seller's reasonable costs and lawyer's fees if the seller takes the buyer to court to collect on the note and wins the lawsuit.

10. Governing Law

Insert the name of the state where the business is located. For details on this standard clause, see Chapter 17.

11. Signature and Guarantee

Only the buyer and guarantors, if any, sign the promissory note. The seller does not sign it. See Chapter 18 for suggested signature formats for documents such as a promissory note.

As noted above, if the buyer is a sole proprietor or partner and signs the note, the buyer will be personally liable for repaying it. But if the buyer is a corporation or an LLC, the owners of the entity won't be personally liable. That's the reason you may insist on guarantors signing the promissory note. See the discussion of guarantors in Section 1b, above, and also Chapter 14, which covers guarantees by entity owners, spouses, and others.

B. The Security Agreement

In addition to getting the personal promise of the buyer and any guarantors to pay the balance of the sale price, it's a good idea to keep a lien (security interest) on the assets of the business, such as equipment and inventory. This will allow you to take back those assets if the buyer starts to miss the agreed payment dates. You can use a security agreement, like the ones that follow, to retain such a lien. There are two different security agreements in this book—one for an asset sale and one for an entity sale.

These security agreements are separate from your sales agreement, but the sales agreement should refer to them and state generally what your arrangements are. These arrangements are covered in Clause 14 or 15 as described in Chapter 14.

 You can't use a security agreement to place a lien on real estate. For that you'll need a mortgage or deed of trust, and this book does not cover those forms of security. If you're asking the buyer for a lien on real estate, you'll definitely want to see a lawyer for help.

1. Security Agreement Form for Asset Sale

Here is a form of security agreement you can use for an asset sale.

Where to find the forms. You'll find copies of the Security Agreement (Asset Sale) form on the CD-ROM at the back of this book.

Security Agreement for Asset Sale

1. Names and Secured Property

_____Georgetown West Inc., a Florida Corporation_____, Buyer, grants

to __Burgundy Associates LLC, a Florida Limited Liability Company____, Seller, a

continuing security interest in the following property (the "Secured Property"), which consists of:

A. The property listed in Attachment __A__, and

B. Any additional tangible personal property that Buyer now owns or later acquires in connection with Buyer's business, including replacement inventory.

2. Security for Promissory Note

Buyer is granting this security interest to secure performance of a promissory note that Buyer executed on __March 1, 20XX____ as partial payment for certain business assets. The promissory note obligates Buyer to pay Seller $__50,000____ with interest at the rate of __8__% a year, on the terms stated in the promissory note.

3. Financing Statement and Other Documents

Concurrently with the execution of this Security Agreement, Seller will have the right to file a UCC Financing Statement. Buyer will sign any other documents that Seller reasonably requests to protect Seller's security interest in the Secured Property.

4. Use and Care of the Secured Property

Until the promissory note is fully paid, Buyer agrees to:

A. Keep the Secured Property at __456 Charlotte Street, Miami, Florida____ and use it only in the operation of the __Georgetown Donut Shop_____ business.

B. Maintain the Secured Property in good repair.

C. Not sell, transfer, or release the Secured Property unless Seller consents. Buyer may sell inventory in the ordinary course of Buyer's business but will reasonably renew and replenish inventory to keep it at its current level.

D. Pay all taxes on the Secured Property as taxes become due.

E. Insure the Secured Property against normal risks, with an insurance policy that names Buyer and Seller as beneficiaries.

F. Deliver to Seller a copy of the insurance policy insuring the Secured Property and provide to Seller annual proof that Buyer has paid the premiums on the policy.

G. Allow Seller to inspect the Secured Property at any reasonable time.

5. Buyer's Default

If Buyer is more than __ten__ days late in making any payment required by the promissory note or if the Buyer fails to correct any violations of Clause __4__ within __ten__ days of receiving written notice from Seller, Buyer will be in default.

6. Seller's Rights

If Buyer is in default, Seller may exercise the remedies contained in the Uniform Commercial Code for the State of _____Florida_____ and any other remedies legally available to Seller. Seller may, for example:

A. Remove the Secured Property from the place where it is located.

B. Require Buyer to assemble the Secured Property and make it available to Seller at a place designated by Seller that is reasonably convenient to Buyer and Seller.

C. Sell or lease the Secured Property, or otherwise dispose of it.

7. Notice to Buyer

Seller will give Buyer at least __ten__ days' notice of when and where the Secured Property will be sold, leased, or otherwise disposed of. Any notice required here or by statute will be deemed given to Buyer if sent by first-class mail to Buyer at the following address: _____789 Main Street, Miami, Florida_____.

8. Entire Agreement

This is the entire agreement between the parties concerning Seller's security interest in the Secured Property. It replaces and supersedes any and all oral agreements between the parties, as well as any prior writings on that subject.

9. Successors and Assignees

This agreement binds and benefits the heirs, successors, and assignees of the parties.

10. Governing Law

This agreement will be governed by and construed in accordance with the laws of the State of _____Florida_____.

11. Modification

This agreement may be modified only by a written amendment signed by both parties.

12. Waiver

If either party waives any provision of this agreement at any time, that waiver will only be effective for the specific instance and purpose for which that waiver was given. If either party fails to exercise or delays exercising any of its rights or remedies under this agreement, that party retains the right to enforce that term or provision at a later time.

13. Severability

If a court determines that a provision in this agreement is invalid or not enforceable, that determination will affect only that provision. The provision will be modified only to the extent necessary to make it valid and enforceable. The rest of the agreement will be unaffected.

SELLER	BUYER
Burgundy Associates LLC	Georgetown West, Inc.
a Florida Limited Liability Company	a Florida Corporation
By: *Cheryl Jackson*	By: *George Allen*
Printed name: Cheryl Jackson	Printed name: George Allen
Title: Member	Title: President
Address: 123 Center Street, Miami, Florida	Address: 789 Main Street, Miami, Florida
Dated: March 1, 20XX	Dated: March 1, 20XX

Instructions for Security Agreement (Asset Sale)

These instructions are for the security agreement used in an asset sale. If yours is an entity sale, see the special form and instructions in Section B2, below.

1. Names and Secured Property

Insert the names of the buyer (first blank) and seller (second blank). See Chapter 13 for a discussion of how to identify the parties in the sales agreement and related documents.

In the form, "Secured Property" means the property as to which you are obtaining a lien. The language in the form is merely a suggestion. The scope of the property covered by your lien is a matter of negotiation between you and the buyer. As the seller, you'd like the broadest lien you can get, but, at the very least, you should seek a lien on the tangible personal property that the buyer is receiving from you. You can use an attachment like the one suggested for a Bill of Sale (Chapter 20) to list those assets.

With the buyer's agreement, your lien can cover furniture, fixtures, equipment, supplies, inventory, and even accounts receivable. It can cover not only what the buyer receives from you, but also any property that the buyer now owns or later acquires in connection with the business. You can expand the suggested language of the form and the attachment to cover as much ground as the buyer consents to.

A broad description of the "Secured Property" could, for example, look like this in your security agreement:

> All of Buyer's goods, equipment, fixtures, inventory, accounts receivable, and general intangibles, whether now owned by Buyer or acquired later.

2. Security for Promissory Note

In the first blank, fill in the date the buyer is signing the promissory note. Then insert the amount of the promissory note and the interest rate.

3. Financing Statement and Other Documents

You don't need to insert anything in this paragraph. It confirms that you have the right to file a Uniform Commercial Code form (called Form UCC-1) with a governmental agency in your state to let the public know that the business assets are subject to the seller's lien. Anyone checking the public records—a bank's loan department, for example—will learn that the seller has lien on the property described in the notice. Section C, below, includes a sample UCC-1 form.

4. Use and Care of the Secured Property

Fill in the location where the secured property will be kept and the name of the business that will be using it. This paragraph of the security agreement also requires the buyer to keep the secured property in good repair and to retain ownership of it. The buyer also agrees to pay taxes on the secured property and keep it insured.

5. Buyer's Default

This paragraph says that the buyer will be in default (that is, not in compliance with the security agreement) if the buyer doesn't make the required payments or doesn't promptly correct any violation of the requirements listed in the preceding clause. The sample form says the default begins 10 days after the seller sends written notice to the buyer, but you can change this to some other number of days if you wish. When a buyer is in default, you can exercise your rights under Clause 6 (Seller's Rights), including selling the secured property.

6. Seller's Rights

This summarizes your rights under the Uniform Commercial Code if the buyer defaults on the security agreement obligations. Basically, you can seize the secured property and sell it to pay off the buyer's debt.

Fill in the name of the state where the property is located.

7. Notice to Buyer

This clause says that you'll give the buyer at least ten days' notice of when and where the secured property will be sold or otherwise disposed of if the buyer should default. Fill in the address where you should send that notice.

8-13. Standard Clauses

The remainder of the agreement contains standard clauses (technical contract clauses)—most of which are similar to those suggested for inclusion in the sales agreement. See Chapter 17 for an explanation of standard clauses, which deal with such matters as the agreement containing the entire understanding of the parties.

The language about successors and assignees (Clause 9) means that if an individual buyer or seller dies, his or her heirs will be bound by the security agreement but will also get the benefit of its provisions. Similarly, if someone steps into the shoes of either party—whether the party is an individual or entity—those newcomers (successors and assignees) will be bound by and get the benefits of the agreement.

The waiver provision (Clause 12) means that if you don't declare a default immediately if the buyer is late on a payment or two, it won't be held against you. You will still be allowed to declare a default for late payments that occur in the future.

The only thing you'll need to fill in for the standard clauses is the name of the state whose law will apply to the contract in Clause 10.

Signatures

The seller and the buyer will both sign the security agreement. See Chapter 18 for suggested formats for the signature part of documents such as security agreements.

2. Security Agreement Form for Entity Sale

A security agreement for an entity sale will vary slightly from the suggested form shown above for an asset sale. Here's a form you can use as a starting point for your entity sale.

 Where to find the forms. You'll find copies of the Security Agreement (Entity Sale) form on the CD-ROM at the back of this book.

Instructions for Security Agreement (Entity Sale)

These instructions are for the security agreement used in an entity sale. If yours is an asset sale, see the special form and instructions in Section B1, above.

1. Names and Secured Property

In an entity sale (in which you and your co-owner sell your shares of corporate stock or your membership interests in an LLC), you can use a security agreement in addition to the escrow agreement like the one described in Section D, below. If you do so, you'll need to use a slightly different security agreement form from the one provided for asset sales. That's because in an entity sale, the entity rather than the buyer will be granting the security interest to the seller, because the entity and not the buyer will own the assets of the business.

In the opening paragraph, you'll need to insert the names of the entity that's being sold (the corporation or the LLC—for which the form uses the generic term "the Company") and the buyer and the seller. See Chapter 13 for a discussion on how to insert names at the beginning of a document.

In the form, "Secured Property" means the property as to which you are obtaining a lien. The language in the form is merely a suggestion. The scope of the property covered by your lien is a matter of negotiation between you and the buyer. As the seller, you'd like the broadest lien you can get, but, at the very least, you should seek a lien on the tangible personal property owned by the entity at the time ownership of the entity is transferred to the buyer. You can use an attachment like the one suggested for a Bill of Sale (Chapter 20) to list those assets.

With the buyer's agreement, your lien can cover all of the entity's furniture, fixtures, equipment, supplies, inventory, and even accounts receivable. It can also cover any property that the entity acquires later. You can expand the suggested language of the form and the attachment

Security Agreement for Entity Sale

1. Names and Secured Property

Pepper Pots and Pans Inc., a Florida Corporation , the Company, the stock of which has been sold to Mildred Parsons , Buyer, grants to Mitchell Heath , Seller, a continuing security interest in the following property (the "Secured Property"), which consists of:

A. The property listed in Attachment 1 , and

B. Any additional tangible personal property that the Company now owns or later acquires in connection with its business, including replacement inventory.

2. Security for Promissory Note

The Company is granting this security interest to secure performance of a promissory note that Buyer executed on September 1, 20XX as partial payment for the shares of stock of the Company. The promissory note obligates Buyer to pay Seller $ 50,000 with interest at the rate of 8 % a year, on the terms stated in the promissory note.

3. Financing Statement and Other Documents

Concurrently with the execution of this Security Agreement, Seller will have the right to file a UCC Financing Statement. The Company will sign any other documents that Seller reasonably requests to protect Seller's security interest in the Secured Property.

4. Use and Care of the Secured Property

Until the promissory note is fully paid, the Company agrees to:

A. Keep the Secured Property at 1250 West End Avenue, San Jose, California and use it only in the operation of the kitchen supply business.

B. Maintain the Secured Property in good repair.

C. Not sell, transfer, or release the Secured Property unless Seller consents. The Company may sell inventory in the ordinary course of the Company's business but will reasonably renew and replenish inventory to keep it at its current level.

D. Pay all taxes on the Secured Property as taxes become due.

E. Insure the Secured Property against normal risks, with an insurance policy that names the Company and Seller as beneficiaries.

F. Deliver to Seller a copy of the insurance policy insuring the Secured Property and provide to Seller annual proof that the Company has paid the premiums on the policy.

G. Allow Seller to inspect the Secured Property at any reasonable time.

5. Buyer's Default

If Buyer is more than _ten_ days late in making any payment required by the promissory note or if the Company fails to correct any violations of Clause 4 within _ten_ days of receiving written notice from Seller, the Company will be in default.

6. Seller's Rights

If the Company is in default, Seller may exercise the remedies contained in the Uniform Commercial Code for the State of ___California___ and any other remedies legally available to Seller. Seller may, for example:

A. Remove the Secured Property from the place where it is located.

B. Require the Company to assemble the Secured Property and make it available to Seller at a place designated by Seller that is reasonably convenient to the Company and Seller.

C. Sell or lease the Secured Property, or otherwise dispose of it.

7. Notice to the Company

Seller will give the Company at least _ten_ days' notice of when and where the Secured Property will be sold, leased, or otherwise disposed of. Any notice required here or by statute will be deemed given to the Company if sent by first-class mail to the Company at the following address: ___620 Fillmore Circle, San Jose, California___.

8. Entire Agreement

This is the entire agreement between the parties concerning Seller's security interest in the Secured Property. It replaces and supersedes any and all oral agreements between the parties, as well as any prior writings on that subject.

9. Successors and Assignees

This agreement binds and benefits the heirs, successors, and assignees of the parties.

10. Governing Law

This agreement will be governed by and construed in accordance with the laws of the State of _____California_____.

11. Modification

This agreement may be modified only by a written amendment signed by both parties.

12. Waiver

If either party waives any provision of this agreement at any time, that waiver will only be effective for the specific instance and purpose for which that waiver was given. If either party fails to exercise or delays exercising any of its rights or remedies under this agreement, that party retains the right to enforce that term or provision at a later time.

13. Severability

If a court determines that a provision in this agreement is invalid or not enforceable, that determination will affect only that provision. The provision will be modified only to the extent necessary to make it valid and enforceable. The rest of the agreement will be unaffected.

THE COMPANY	**BUYER**
Pepper Pots and Pans Inc.	
a Florida Corporation	a
By: *Charles Pepper*	By: *Mitchell Heath*
Printed name: Charles Pepper	Printed name: Mitchell Heath
Title: President	Title:
Address: 620 Fillmore Circle	Address: 891 South Central Avenue
San Jose, California	San Jose, California
Dated: September 1, 20XX	Dated: September 1, 20XX

to cover as much ground as the buyer consents to.

A broad description of the Secured Property could, for example, look like this in your security agreement:

> All of the Company's goods, equipment, fixtures, inventory, accounts receivable, and general intangibles, whether now owned by the Company or acquired later.

2. Security for Promissory Note

In the first blank, fill in the date the buyer is signing the promissory note. In the next blank, fill in "shares of stock" if the entity is a corporation, or "membership interests" if the entity is an LLC. Then insert the amount of the promissory note and the interest rate.

3-13. Remaining Clauses

See Section B1, above, for a discussion of clauses for a security agreement for an asset sale.

Signatures

The seller and the entity that's being sold will both sign the security agreement. See Chapter 18 for suggested formats for the signature part of a document such as a security agreement.

C. The UCC Financing Statement

The security agreement described in Section B, above, is the buyer's acknowledgment that you have a lien on the business assets until the promissory note is paid in full. But what if, despite that acknowledgment, the buyer sells the business assets to some outsider who doesn't know about the lien? Although the buyer has violated your contract, you're probably out of luck so far as regaining control of the assets is concerned, since the outsider had no knowledge that you still had an ownership interest in the assets.

To avoid that problem, in addition to the security agreement, you should have the buyer sign a UCC Financing Statement, which you'll then file with the appropriate public agency in your state (often a division of the secretary of state's office). The lien then becomes a matter of public record, and any third party is assumed to know of its existence. Think of it this way: The UCC Financing Statement serves the same function as the mortgage or deed of trust on your house, which is filed at a public office and lets everyone know that your lender has a lien on your house. A prudent third party buying business assets will do a UCC lien check, discover your lien, and decline to buy the assets. If the third party fails to do this and acquires the assets, your lien will be legally intact because it's a public record, and you can recover the assets from the third party as long as the buyer of your business still owes you money.

Completing and filing a UCC Financing Statement is simple, because all states now accept the national, standardized form shown below. In almost all states, you can download a blank form and instructions from the website maintained by the secretary of state's office. To locate the website for your state, go to www.statelocalgov.net. In California, for example, you'd wind up at www.ss.ca. gov/business/ucc/ra_9_ucc-1.pdf—and the form on that site should be acceptable in all other states as well. As an alternative, you can phone your secretary of state's office to obtain the form and learn the filing fees.

 Where to find the forms. You'll find copies of the UCC Financing Statement and Addendum and instructions for completing them on the CD-ROM at the back of this book.

You'll want to read the instructions carefully, of course, but here's a summary of how to complete the main items in the form:

- **Boxes A and B.** Put your name and phone number in Box A, and your name and address in Box B.

- **Part 1.** The "Debtor" is the buyer, so use Part 1 to provide information about the buyer. Fill in Box 1a if the buyer is a corporation, an LLC, or a partnership. Fill in Box 1b if the buyer is an individual. Box 1d is for the buyer's tax ID number, which is usually an employer identification number (EIN) for an entity, and either a Social Security number or an EIN for an individual.

- **Part 2.** Fill out Part 2 if there's an additional buyer.

- **Part 3.** The "Secured Party" is the seller, so use Part 3 to provide seller information. If the seller is an entity, fill in Line 3a. Otherwise, fill in Line 3b.

- **Part 4.** This is where you describe the collateral: the assets in which you have a security interest.

- **UCC Financing Statement Addendum.** There's a continuation sheet available (Form UCC 1Ad) if you need to list an additional Debtor or Secured Party or if you need more room to list the collateral or provide special information required in some states.

- **Signatures.** Signatures are no longer required on UCC Financing Statements.

UCC FINANCING STATEMENT
FOLLOW INSTRUCTIONS (front and back) CAREFULLY

A. NAME & PHONE OF CONTACT AT FILER [optional]

Edward Brown   555-123-555

B. SEND ACKNOWLEDGMENT TO: (Name and Address)

Olde Lighting, Inc.

555 Eastern Drive

Berkeley, CA 99999

THE ABOVE SPACE IS FOR FILING OFFICE USE ONLY

1. DEBTOR'S EXACT FULL LEGAL NAME - insert only <u>one</u> debtor name (1a or 1b) - do not abbreviate or combine names

1a. ORGANIZATION'S NAME				
New Lighting, LLC				

OR

1b. INDIVIDUAL'S LAST NAME	FIRST NAME	MIDDLE NAME	SUFFIX

1c. MAILING ADDRESS	CITY	STATE	POSTAL CODE	COUNTRY
555 Jefferson Ave.	Berkeley	CA	99999	USA

1d. TAX ID #: SSN OR EIN	ADD'L INFO RE ORGANIZATION DEBTOR	1e. TYPE OF ORGANIZATION	1f. JURISDICTION OF ORGANIZATION	1g. ORGANIZATIONAL ID #, if any	
38-6666666		LLC	CA		☐ NONE

2. ADDITIONAL DEBTOR'S EXACT FULL LEGAL NAME - insert only <u>one</u> debtor name (2a or 2b) - do not abbreviate or combine names

2a. ORGANIZATION'S NAME				
Olde Lighting, Inc.				

OR

2b. INDIVIDUAL'S LAST NAME	FIRST NAME	MIDDLE NAME	SUFFIX

2c. MAILING ADDRESS	CITY	STATE	POSTAL CODE	COUNTRY
555 Eastern Drive	Berkeley	CA	99999	USA

2d. TAX ID #: SSN OR EIN	ADD'L INFO RE ORGANIZATION DEBTOR	2e. TYPE OF ORGANIZATION	2f. JURISDICTION OF ORGANIZATION	2g. ORGANIZATIONAL ID #, if any	
					☐ NONE

3. SECURED PARTY'S NAME (or NAME of TOTAL ASSIGNEE of ASSIGNOR S/P) - insert only <u>one</u> secured party name (3a or 3b)

3a. ORGANIZATION'S NAME				

OR

3b. INDIVIDUAL'S LAST NAME	FIRST NAME	MIDDLE NAME	SUFFIX

3c. MAILING ADDRESS	CITY	STATE	POSTAL CODE	COUNTRY

4. This FINANCING STATEMENT covers the following collateral:

All furniture, fixtures, equipment, and inventory of Debtor. Also, any tangible personal property (including replacement inventory) that Debtor now owns or later acquires in connection with Debtor's business known as Star Lighting located at 555 Jefferson Ave., Berkeley, CA. Also the proceeds of all insurance policies that now or later cover the secured property.

5. ALTERNATIVE DESIGNATION [if applicable]: ☐ LESSEE/LESSOR ☐ CONSIGNEE/CONSIGNOR ☐ BAILEE/BAILOR ☐ SELLER/BUYER ☐ AG. LIEN ☐ NON-UCC FILING

6. ☐ This FINANCING STATEMENT is to be filed [for record] (or recorded) in the REAL ESTATE RECORDS.   Attach Addendum   [if applicable]   7. Check to REQUEST SEARCH REPORT(S) on Debtor(s) [ADDITIONAL FEE]   [optional]   ☐ All Debtors ☐ Debtor 1 ☐ Debtor 2

8. OPTIONAL FILER REFERENCE DATA

FILING OFFICE COPY — NATIONAL UCC FINANCING STATEMENT (FORM UCC1) (REV. 07/29/98)

D. Escrow Agreement for Entity Sale

There's another technique you should consider using when you're selling the entity (the corporation or LLC) rather than just the business assets. It consists of using an escrow agreement in which a third party—the escrow agent—hangs on to the stock certificates or LLC membership documents until you've been fully paid. As with the techniques discussed above, the purpose of an escrow agreement is to make it easy for you to reclaim ownership of the business entity if the buyer starts to miss payments required by the promissory note. Accordingly, the escrow agreement should state that if the buyer defaults, you get back the transfer documents from the escrow agent.

A real estate title company that routinely performs escrow services will usually be willing to act as the escrow agent for your documents for a modest fee. But you may not need a company to handle the job. You and the buyer are free to choose anyone you feel is trustworthy. If one of you has a lawyer willing to perform the function, that person may be a good choice.

Below are sample escrow agreements you can use in an entity sale. If you're selling corporate shares, use the Escrow Agreement for Stock Certificates form. If you're selling your LLC membership interests, use the Escrow Agreement for LLC Transfer Certificates.

 Where to find the forms. You'll find copies of the two Escrow Agreement forms on CD-ROM at the back of this book.

Instructions for Escrow Agreements for Entity Sale

These instructions apply to both escrow agreements for stock certificates and for LLC transfer certificates.

1. Names

Insert the names of the seller, buyer, and escrow agent. For more information on how to designate the parties at the beginning of an agreement, see Chapter 13.

2. Delivery of Certificates to Escrow Agent

In the first space, insert the name of the company. In the second space, insert the state in which the company was formed. Then, for each certificate being turned over to the escrow agent, list the certificate number and the name of the current owner of the interest represented by the certificate—the person who is selling that interest. This person is referred to as the transferor.

3. Establishment of Escrow

Nothing needs to be inserted in this section. It establishes that the Escrow Agent will serve under the terms of the agreement.

Escrow Agreement for Stock Certificates

1. Names

Theodore Burger _____ (Seller),

Sandra Mason _____ (Buyer), and

Phyllis Chung _____ (Escrow Agent)

agree to the following escrow arrangements.

2. Delivery of Stock Certificates

Seller will deliver to Escrow Agent the following stock certificates for _Enterprise_ _Corporation_ , a(n) _Ohio_ corporation, endorsed in blank for transfer:

Certificate Number	Name of Transferor
101	Theodore Burger

3. Establishment of Escrow

Escrow Agent will accept and hold the stock certificates according to the terms of this agreement.

4. Delivery of Stock Certificates by Escrow Agent as Directed by Buyer and Seller, or by Court Order

Seller and Buyer agree that Buyer will be entitled to receive the stock certificates when all payments have been made to Seller under the promissory note that Buyer signed today in connection with purchase of the business. If Buyer defaults on that note, Seller will be entitled to a return of the stock certificates.

Escrow Agent, however, will not deliver the stock certificates to either Seller or Buyer except as directed by a distribution letter from both, or by a final arbitration award or court order as described below.

If Buyer and Seller furnish a signed distribution letter to Escrow Agent, Escrow Agent will deliver the stock certificates as the letter directs.

Similarly, Escrow Agent will deliver the stock certificates as directed by a final arbitration award or court order that is no longer subject to appeal or stay

After delivery of the stock certificates to the Seller or Buyer, the party not receiving the stock certificates will have no further rights to them.

5. Rights When Buyer Is Not In Default

While the stock certificates are on deposit with Escrow Agent and as long as Buyer is not in default under the promissory note and security agreement signed by Buyer today, Buyer will have the full right to operate the business of the company but may not sell it or encumber its assets.

6. No Judgment to Be Exercised by Escrow Agent

The Escrow Agent will make no independent judgment about whether or not Buyer is in default.

7. Restrictions on Buyer

As long as any of Buyer's obligations stated in the promissory note or security agreement remain unsatisfied, the Buyer will not permit the corporation to participate in a merger or consolidation or to issue any additional shares of stock or grant any stock option.

8. Termination of Escrow

The escrow will end when Escrow Agent no longer holds the stock certificates and the parties have paid Escrow Agent all amounts for which they are responsible. The parties will share equally Escrow Agent's fees.

9. Conduct of Escrow Agent

Escrow Agent will:

A. Not be liable for any action taken by Escrow Agent in good faith and without negligence.

B. Be able to refrain from any action under this agreement if Escrow Agent knows of a disagreement between the parties regarding any material facts or the happening of any event contemplated by this agreement.

10. Additional Documents

The parties will, at the request of any other party, sign any agreements or documents consistent with this agreement that are necessary to consummate the transactions contemplated in this agreement.

11. Notices

Any required or permitted notice will be deemed given to a party if sent by first-class mail to the party at the address following the party's signature.

12. Successors and Assignees

This agreement binds and benefits the heirs, successors, and assignees of the parties.

13. Governing Law

This agreement will be governed by and construed in accordance with the laws of the State of _____Ohio_____.

14. Modification

This agreement may be modified only by a writing signed by all parties.

15. Waiver

If any party waives any provision of this agreement at any time, that waiver will only be effective for the specific instance and purpose for which that waiver was given. If any party fails to exercise or delays exercising any of its rights or remedies under this agreement, that party retains the right to enforce that term or provision at a later time.

16. Severability

If a court determines that any provision of this agreement is invalid or unenforceable, any invalidity or unenforceability will affect only that provision. Such provision may be modified, amended, or limited only to the extent necessary to make it valid and enforceable.

SELLER	**BUYER**
Theodore Burger	_Sandra Mason_
Printed name: __Theodore Burger__	Printed name: __Sandra Mason__
Address: __234 Pepper Pike__	Address: __67 Trenton Road__
__Cleveland, Ohio__	__Cleveland, Ohio__
Dated: __October 2, 20XX__	Dated: __October 2, 20XX__

ESCROW AGENT

Phyllis Chung

Printed name: __Phyllis Chung__

Address: __One Newton Tower__

__Cleveland, Ohio__

Dated: __October 2, 20XX__

Escrow Agreement for LLC Transfer Certificates

1. Names

Theodore Burger _____ (Seller),

Sandra Mason _____ (Buyer), and

Phyllis Chung _____ (Escrow Agent)

agree to the following escrow arrangements.

2. Delivery of LLC Transfer Certificates

Seller will deliver to Escrow Agent the following LLC transfer certificates for

Green Tree LLC _____ , a(n) ___ Ohio _____ limited liability company:

Certificate Number	*Name of Transferor*
101	Theodore Burger

3. Establishment of Escrow

Escrow Agent will accept and hold the LLC transfer certificates according to the terms of this agreement.

4. Delivery of LLC Transfer Certificates by Escrow Agent as Directed by Buyer and Seller, or by Court Order

Seller and Buyer agree that Buyer will be entitled to receive the LLC transfer certificates when all payments have been made to Seller under the promissory note that Buyer signed today in connection with purchase of the business. If Buyer defaults on that note, Seller will be entitled to a return of the transfer certificates.

Escrow Agent, however, will not deliver the transfer certificates to either Seller or Buyer except as directed by a distribution letter from both, or by a final arbitration award or court order as described below.

If Buyer and Seller furnish a signed distribution letter to Escrow Agent, Escrow Agent will deliver the transfer certificates as the letter directs.

Similarly, Escrow Agent will deliver the transfer certificates as directed by a final arbitration award or court order that is no longer subject to appeal or stay.

After delivery of the transfer certificates to the Seller or Buyer, the party not receiving the transfer certificates will have no further rights to them.

5. Rights When Buyer Is Not In Default

While the LLC transfer certificates are on deposit with Escrow Agent and as long as Buyer is not in default under the promissory note and security agreement signed by Buyer today, Buyer will have the full right to operate the business of the company but may not sell it or encumber its assets.

6. No Judgment to Be Exercised by Escrow Agent

The Escrow Agent will make no independent judgment about whether or not Buyer is in default.

7. Restrictions on Buyer

As long as any of Buyer's obligations stated in the promissory note or security agreement remain unsatisfied, the Buyer will not permit the limited liability company to participate in a merger or consolidation, or to issue any additional member or ownership interests, or to grant any option for the purchase of such membership or ownership interests.

8. Termination of Escrow

The escrow will end when Escrow Agent no longer holds the LLC transfer certificates and the parties have paid Escrow Agent all amounts for which they are responsible. The parties will share equally Escrow Agent's fees.

9. Conduct of Escrow Agent

Escrow Agent will:

A. Not be liable for any action taken by Escrow Agent in good faith and without negligence.

B. Be able to refrain from any action under this agreement if Escrow Agent knows of a disagreement between the parties regarding any material facts or the happening of any event contemplated by this agreement.

10. Additional Documents

The parties will, at the request of any other party, sign any agreements or documents consistent with this agreement that are necessary to consummate the transactions contemplated in this agreement.

11. Notices

Any required or permitted notice will be deemed given to a party if sent by first-class mail to the party at the address following the party's signature.

12. Successors and Assignees

This agreement binds and benefits the heirs, successors, and assignees of the parties.

13. Governing Law

This agreement will be governed by and construed in accordance with the laws of the State of _____Ohio_____ .

14. Modification

This agreement may be modified only by a writing signed by all parties.

15. Waiver

If any party waives any provision of this agreement at any time, that waiver will only be effective for the specific instance and purpose for which that waiver was given. If any party fails to exercise or delays exercising any of its rights or remedies under this agreement, that party retains the right to enforce that term or provision at a later time.

16. Severability

If a court determines that any provision of this agreement is invalid or unenforceable, any invalidity or unenforceability will affect only that provision. Such provision may be modified, amended, or limited only to the extent necessary to make it valid and enforceable.

SELLER

Theodore Burger

Printed name: _Theodore Burger_

Address: _234 Pepper Pike_

Cleveland, Ohio

Dated: _October 2, 20XX_

BUYER

Sandra Mason

Printed name: _Sandra Mason_

Address: _67 Trenton Road_

Cleveland, Ohio

Dated: _October 2, 20XX_

ESCROW AGENT

Phyllis Chung

Printed name: _Phyllis Chung_

Address: _One Newton Tower_

Cleveland, Ohio

Dated: _October 2, 20XX_

4. Delivery of Certificates by Escrow Agent

This clause says that the buyer can get the certificates when all payments have been made. Otherwise, the certificates are to be returned to the seller. The escrow agent will only release the certificates as directed in a letter signed by the seller and buyer or in response to a court order or arbitration award. Nothing needs to be inserted in this section.

5. Rights When Buyer Is Not in Default

Even though the buyer does not yet have the certificates, this section gives the buyer the right to operate the business while not in default. The buyer cannot, however, sell the business or have a lien placed on its assets. Nothing needs to be inserted in this section.

6. No Judgment to Be Exercised by Escrow Agent

This section says that the escrow agent will not determine if the buyer is in default. That's up to the parties, a judge, or an arbitrator. Nothing needs to be inserted in this section.

7. Restrictions on Buyer

This section says that until the promissory note is paid the buyer can't allow the company to be part of a merger or consolidation. Also, it can't issue any more ownership interests (stock or LLC memberships) or grant any option for such additional interests. Nothing needs to be filled in here.

8. Termination of Escrow

This section says that the escrow arrangements will end when the escrow agent has delivered the certificates and been paid. The buyer and seller agree to split the escrow agent's fees. Nothing needs to be inserted in this section.

9. Conduct of Escrow Agent

This clause says that the escrow agent can be liable for actions taken negligently or in bad faith, but not otherwise. It also says the escrow agent won't act if the agent knows of a disagreement between the buyer and the seller relating to the escrow arrangements. Nothing needs to be inserted here.

10. Additional Documents

In this section, the parties agree that they'll sign any additional documents that are needed. Nothing needs to be inserted here.

11-16. Standard Clauses

The rest of the sections are standard contract clauses—most of which are explained in Chapter 17. In Clause 13 (Governing Law), you'll need to fill in the state where the business is located.

Signatures

See Chapter 18 for information about how to list the parties in the signature part of a document, such as an escrow agreement.

Chapter 20

Bill of Sale, Lease Assignment, and Other Documents for Transferring Your Business

In this chapter, you'll find the documents you'll need to legally transfer ownership of business assets to the buyer (in an asset sale) or to legally transfer ownership of an entity (in an entity sale). Some of these documents will be mentioned in your sales agreement—especially in Clauses 24, 25, and 26.

The first six sections of this chapter cover the transfer of assets and the documents you need to do this. Because your business may own several different types of assets, you may need to use more than one document to fully accomplish this task, including:

- **Bill of Sale.** You'll normally use a bill of sale to transfer ownership of most tangible assets, such as furniture, equipment, and inventory. See Section A for a sample bill of sale and instructions on how to complete one. Section A also lists property that can't be transferred by a bill of sale, including vehicles and real estate.

- **Statement Regarding Absence of Creditors.** As explained in Chapter 15, a handful of states still have bulk sales laws designed to assure the buyer of some types of retail and wholesale businesses that the assets are free from any claims of your creditors. In Section B, you'll find a practical method to satisfy the buyer's interest in verifying that you complied with any applicable bulk sales provisions.

- **Assignments.** In addition to transferring tangible assets, your business may need to transfer intangible assets, such as leases, employment contracts, and agreements with customers and suppliers, as well as intellectual property, such as trademarks, patents, and copyrights. If so, using a bill of sale won't be sufficient. Specialized contracts—called assignments—are typically used to transfer such property. You'll find examples in Sections C, D, and E.

- **Consent Forms Approving an Entity's Sale of Its Assets.** If your business is a corporation or an LLC, you'll want to document the business entity's approval of the sale of its assets using a formal resolution—a topic dealt with in Section F.

This chapter also includes a discussion (in Section G) of documents you need for transferring ownership of an entity—a corporation or an LLC. This involves transferring the stock or LLC membership interests to the buyer.

Unlike the promissory note and other closing documents covered elsewhere, the documents described in this chapter normally won't be attached to the sales agreement. Instead, for the most part, these documents will be prepared after the sales agreement is signed, and then these documents will be signed at the closing. The only exceptions are the consent documents discussed in Section F; ideally, consent documents should be prepared and signed before the sales agreement is signed.

 Where to find the forms. You'll find copies of the Bill of Sale, Statement Regarding Absence of Creditors, Lease Assignment, and consent forms approving an entity's sale of assets on the CD-ROM at the back of this book. Samples are in the appropriate sections below.

A. Bill of Sale: Asset Sale

 When to skip ahead. If you're selling the stock of a corporation rather than its assets, or you're selling the membership interests in an LLC, you won't need a bill of sale. The entity will continue to own the business assets. You can skip ahead to Section G.

This section explains the various uses of a bill of sale and includes a sample form and instructions for completing it. Basically, the bill of sale is used in an asset sale to transfer ownership of the assets to the buyer. It is used primarily for tangible personal property (business equipment, for example), but in a few instances, it can include some intangible property such as a customer list. Your Sales Agreement, Clause 2, Sale of Business Assets (discussed in Chapter 13), describes the assets you're selling, and Clause 25, Documents for Transferring Assets (discussed in Chapter 17), may

specifically call for you to provide a bill of sale.

1. Transfer of Tangible Property

By definition, in an asset sale, your business will transfer property (assets) to the buyer. You can use a bill of sale to transfer ownership of most types of tangible property, such as:

- furniture
- trade fixtures
- equipment and machinery
- artwork
- inventory
- signs, and
- supplies.

You can also use the bill of sale to transfer ownership of customer lists or the right to a phone number, even though, technically speaking, these constitute intangible property.

2. Transfer of Vehicles

You cannot use a bill of sale to transfer ownership of cars, trucks, airplanes, and, in some states, larger boats, because these vehicles require registration. You'll need to use a state-prescribed form to transfer ownership of vehicles—though there's no harm in also listing vehicles in the bill of sale if the buyer likes having a complete list. In that case, it's a good idea to specify in the bill of sale that you'll also be signing state-required forms to transfer ownership of vehicles.

Check your state department of motor vehicles for the custom and law in your state for transferring ownership of vehicles. To find the website for your state department of motor vehicles, check out your state's home page at www .statelocalgov.net.

3. Transfer of Land and Buildings

Occasionally, an asset sale of a small business will include the sale of real estate owned by the business and used for its operation—for example, the building in which a dry cleaner or print shop is located. You can't use a bill of sale to legally transfer real estate (land and buildings), because a bill of sale works only for tangible personal property. Land and buildings—while they may be tangible—are classified as real property (or real estate) and require special treatment.

The transfer of real estate will require you to sign a deed that you record (file) at a designated county office to make it a matter of public record. And in all likelihood, the buyer will also require you to provide a title insurance policy so it's clear that you're transferring clear title. The buyer may also want to see a recent survey to make sure there aren't any encroachments. And because of understandable concerns about hidden environmental problems, the buyer may require the preparation of at least a Phase I environmental review. (See Chapter 10

for more information about the buyer's investigation of these issues.)

The inclusion of real estate in an asset sale makes the sale more complicated and introduces elements of state law and local procedure that are not covered in depth in this book.

 See a lawyer or a real estate title company for help in transferring buildings and land. Transferring real estate is not difficult, but it is technical in that it typically requires a title search and the preparation and recording of a deed. Unless you have a great deal of experience in local real estate matters, you'll need professional help.

4. Transfer of Business Licenses and Permits

To complete the transfer of your business, you may need to transfer a business license or permit to the buyer or assist the buyer in arranging for such a transfer or even the issuance of a new license or permit. Liquor stores, bars, and restaurants, for example, need licenses issued by a state or local regulatory agency. Since licenses and permits are a matter of state law and local ordinances, and because there's considerable variation from business to business and from place to place, this book provides no forms for this purpose. You and the buyer will need to consult the agencies that issue any necessary licenses and permits for advice on what to do when you're selling your business. If you have trouble navigating the bureaucracy on your own, a lawyer may be able to cut through the red tape. See Chapter 10 for an overview of issues involving the sale of a business that requires a license or permit.

5. Bill of Sale Form

Below is a sample bill of sale form you can use to transfer ownership of the assets of your business to the buyer.

 Where to find the forms. You'll find copies of the Bill of Sale for Business Assets on the CD-ROM at the back of this book.

6. Instructions for Completing a Bill of Sale for Business Assets

Here's how to complete the bill of sale.

1. Names

Insert the names of the seller and buyer as they appear in the sales agreement. See Chapter 13 for a discussion of how to identify the parties in the sales agreement.

2. Acknowledgment of Payment

If the buyer will not owe you part of the sale price after the closing (that is, the buyer is making full payment for your business at the closing), omit the bracketed material dealing with the promissory note and security interest. Otherwise, retain the bracketed material. Chapter 19 covers promissory notes and security agreements.

3. Warranty of Ownership

This clause contains a warranty (guarantee) that the seller owns the assets that are being sold. This assures the buyer that no one else has any rights, such as a partial ownership interest or a security interest, in the assets being transferred. If it later turns out that another person or company does have rights in the property, the buyer can sue the seller for breaching the warranty and can collect money for any damages the buyer suffers as a result.

If the buyer will not be giving you a security interest in the assets, omit the bracketed material dealing with the security interest. Otherwise, retain the bracketed material. Chapter 19 covers security agreements.

4. Signatures

See Chapter 18 for suggested formats for signatures on contracts and other documents. The buyer does not sign the bill of sale. The seller does, and if the seller is a sole proprietorship in a community property state, his or her spouse should also sign. Where an entity is selling its assets and the owners are personally guaranteeing the warranty of Clause 3, they too should sign.

Bill of Sale for Business Assets

1. Names

Burgundy Associates LLC, a Florida Limited Liability Company , Seller, transfers

to   Georgetown West, Inc., a Florida Corporation   , Buyer, full

ownership of the property listed in Attachment   A   to this Bill of Sale.

2. Acknowledgment of Payment

Seller acknowledges receiving payment for this property in the form of a cashier's check [*optional:* and a promissory note secured by a security interest in the property].

3. Warranty of Ownership

Seller warrants that Seller is the legal owner of the property and that the property is free of all liens and encumbrances [*optional:* except for the security interest granted today by Buyer to Seller].

SELLER

Burgundy Associates LLC

a Florida Limited Liability Company

By: *Cheryl Jackson*

Printed name: Cheryl Jackson

Title: Member

Address: 123 Center Street,

Miami, Florida

Dated: February 18, 20XX

7. Attachment to Bill of Sale

Clause 1, Names, refers to a separate attachment for details on the property being transferred. Use a separate sheet (or sheets) of blank paper to list and clearly identify all tangible items being transferred. This attachment then is part of the bill of sale. See Chapter 12 for advice on preparing attachments.

List the names of the seller and buyer on the attachment exactly as they appear in the bill of sale. Next, clearly describe the property you are transferring to the buyer. Your description of the assets should be as detailed as possible. It should include:

- a list of any furniture, fixtures, or equipment (in the case of equipment, it's often appropriate to include make, model, and serial number)
- the amount of and detailed description of any inventory, and
- a full description of any other tangible assets the seller is transferring to the buyer.

Here are a few examples to get you started.

EXAMPLE 1: *Attachment to Bill of Sale Describing Some of the Business Assets of a Small Restaurant*

Attachment A to Bill of Sale
Dated _____

From _____ , Seller,
to _____ , Buyer

1 15-foot Polar Bear walk-in freezer, serial no. 8526422

1 Polar Bear reach-in freezer, serial no. 44986743

1 15-foot Polar Bear walk-in refrigerator, serial no. 883390E

1 Viking gas range, serial no. JUVS4590222

2 Cutlets Select meat slicers, serial nos. JCRO882 and JCR0883

EXAMPLE 2: *Attachment to Bill of Sale Describing Some of the Business Assets of a Small Used Bookstore*

Attachment A to Bill of Sale
Dated _____

From _____ , Seller,
to _____ , Buyer

1. The inventory of books located in the store at 789 Howard Street

2. Two maple desks and chairs

3. Two desk lamps

4. Dell computer system (including printer, monitor, and software)

5. Sony telephone system

6. Panasonic fax machine

7. Office supplies

8. 26 maple book cases

9. Electronic cash register and credit card reader

10. Two window signs

11. Maple counter

12. One forklift

13. Three wall hangings

14. Sixteen wall-mounted photographs and prints

15. Three easy chairs in customer area

16. Two 16' x 20' oriental rugs

17. The customer list

18. All rights to the current phone number of the business

You and the buyer should initial the attachment to the bill of sale.

To make sure the property hasn't deteriorated between the time the parties sign the purchase agreement and the time of closing, the buyer may request making a final inspection of the property just before closing the sale.

B. Bulk Sales Compliance

A handful of states have bulk sales laws that require creditors to be notified of a business sale. (See "States With Bulk Sales Laws," below.) These are designed to prevent sellers from ordering large amounts of goods on credit, selling the business, and leaving the buyer—and the creditors—holding the bag.

Most states that still have a bulk sales law set a specific procedure to be followed to provide the buyer assurance that the seller's creditors have no continuing claims against the assets after they're transferred. Usually, someone selling a business must give the buyer a list (sworn to under penalty of perjury) of all business creditors and the amount each is owed. Then, several days before the sale is closed—the exact number of days is specified in the state law—the buyer must send a notice to creditors so they know the business is changing hands and can arrange to have their claims paid at or before closing. If a proper notice is sent, the buyer knows that, after the closing, purchased goods are free from old claims by creditors of the seller.

Although bulk sales notices are not conceptually difficult, their preparation is governed by fussy state laws, and the notices must be sent (and in some states, published) in very precise ways. In California, for example, a seller needs to notify creditors by (1) filing notice of the sale at the county recorder's office, and (2) publishing notice of the sale in a general circulation newspaper in the county where the assets are located. The filing and publication must be done at least 12 days before the closing. Because the details differ from state to state, you'll need to check the relevant statutes.

Since most states no longer have bulk sales laws, you probably won't have to worry about this topic. And even if you're in a state that hasn't gotten around to repealing its bulk sales law, you may not have a concern, since these laws generally don't apply to service businesses but only to businesses that have an inventory of goods.

States With Bulk Sales Laws

Here is a list of states with bulk sales laws. For details, check your state statutes under "bulk sales" or "Uniform Commercial Code." See Chapter 2 for advice on doing legal research.

California	Maryland
Georgia	Virginia
Indiana	Wisconsin

But if it turns out that your sale is or possibly may be covered, there's a simple, practical way to avoid the cumbersome paperwork that's often required for compliance with a bulk sales statute—and most buyers find it to be an acceptable way to deal with this issue.

Step 1: Provide in your sales agreement that you'll pay all outstanding debts of the business before closing or out of the closing proceeds. (See Chapter 15, Clause 16, Seller's Debts and Other Liabilities, for sales agreement language that requires the seller to pay all outstanding debts.)

Step 2: Pay the debts, as agreed.

Step 3: At closing, sign a statement such as the Statement Regarding Absence of Creditors shown below, and

give it to the buyer. With this assurance, the buyer is less likely to worry about giving notice to creditors to comply with the bulk sales requirements of your state's laws (if any). As noted above, there's some variation from state to state regarding the degree of formality that's needed when a seller verifies in writing at the closing that all debts and liabilities of the business have been paid. But by getting the statement in the form of an affidavit—a written statement signed under oath in the presence of a notary public—you'll meet the formal requirements of every state.

1. Statement Regarding Absence of Creditors Form

Here is a written statement you can give to the buyer verifying that all debts and liabilities of the business have been paid.

 Where to find the forms. You'll find copies of the Statement Regarding Absence of Creditors on the CD-ROM at the back of this book.

2. Instructions for Completing Statement Regarding Absence of Creditors

Here's how to complete the Statement Regarding Absence of Creditors form.

Statement Regarding Absence of Creditors

1. Sale of Business Assets

I make this statement in connection with the sale by ___Burgundy Associates, LLC___
_____, Seller, to _____Georgetown West, Inc._____
_____, Buyer, of the assets of the business known as Georgetown Antiques .

2. No Security Interests

The assets that Seller is transferring to Buyer today by a Bill of Sale are free of all security interests and other liens and encumbrances, except for the security interest granted today by Buyer to Seller.

3. No Creditors

Seller has paid all debts and liabilities of Seller's business. There are no debts or liabilities of the ☒ Seller ☐ Seller's partners ☐ Seller's members ☒ Seller's shareholders that affect Seller's assets or the right of Seller to transfer the assets to Buyer.

4. No Claims

There are no claims or liens either disputed or undisputed against Seller, Seller's assets [*optional:* or the ☐ Seller's partners ☐ Seller's members ☒ Seller's shareholders] that affect Seller's assets or the right of Seller to transfer the assets to Buyer.

5. Indemnification

If, contrary to Clauses 2, 3, or 4 of this Statement there are any security interests or other liens, debts, liabilities, or claims that affect the assets, Seller will immediately remove the encumbrances or liens; pay the debts, liabilities, or claims; and indemnify, defend, hold harmless, and protect Buyer from any loss or liability arising out of such security interest, lien, debt, liability, or claim.

_____Georgetown West, Inc._____

a ___Florida Corporation_____

By: _*John Martin*_____

Printed name: _John Martin_____

Title:____President_____

Address: _456 Crocodile Lane, Boca Raton, FL___

Dated: _6/20/20XX_____

1. Sale of Business Assets

Fill in the name of the seller and the buyer. Chapter 13 offers suggested formats for naming the parties at the beginning of a legal document.

Also, insert the name of the business being sold.

2. No Security Interests

Nothing needs to be inserted here. You are affirming that the assets being sold are not subject to any security interests or other liens.

3. No Creditors

Here you're affirming that all debts and liabilities of the business have been paid. If the business is an entity and not a sole proprietorship, you can also affirm that the owners of the business entity have no debts or liabilities that affect the assets or the right of the seller to transfer the assets. Simply insert one of the indicated choices, depending on the type of entity.

4. No Claims

Here you're affirming that there are no claims against the seller (that's you—if you're a sole proprietor—or your entity) that affect the assets or your right to transfer the assets to the buyer. If your business is an entity and not a sole proprietorship, you can make the same affirmation regarding the owners by inserting one of the indicated choices, depending on the type of entity.

5. Indemnification

Nothing needs to be inserted here. This clause says that if there are any liabilities or claims, the seller will make sure that the buyer won't suffer any loss.

Signatures

If you're a sole proprietor, you'll sign this form. If the seller is an entity, you or another owner will sign on behalf of the entity. Chapter 18 contains suggested formats for the signature portion of a document such as this.

The Statement Regarding Absence of Creditors form should be signed in the presence of a notary public who's authorized to notarize documents in your state.

Notarization

The form contains notarization language that helps protect the buyer against a forgery. The notary will want proof of your identity, such as a driver's license that bears your photo and signature. The notary can help you complete this section of the form and can make any changes needed to comply with local law and practice.

Finding a notary public shouldn't be a problem; many advertise in the Yellow Pages. Banks, real estate offices, title companies, and mail and shipping companies usually have notary services.

Certificate of Acknowledgment of Notary Public

State of _____

County of _____ }ss

On _____, before me, _____

_____,a notary public in and for said state, personally

appeared _____, personally known to me
(or proved to me on the basis of satisfactory evidence) to be the person whose
name is subscribed to the within instrument, and acknowledged to me that he
or she executed the same in his or her authorized capacity and that by his or her
signature on the instrument, the person, or the entity upon behalf of which the
person acted, executed the instrument.

WITNESS my hand and official seal.

_____

Notary Public for the State of _____

[NOTARY SEAL]   My commission expires _____

For legal and ethical reasons, you should always avoid making false statements, but be aware that the stakes are even higher in notarized documents—sometimes called affidavits. Notarized documents are considered to be given under oath. That means that if you knowingly make a false statement in such a document, you can be accused of perjury. Be careful.

C. Assignment of Lease: Asset Sale

Particularly in the sale of a small retail business, restaurant, or service business that caters to a walk-in trade, the buyer will want to continue operating the business at the same location. As part of your deal, you and the buyer may have agreed that you'll assign (transfer) your lease to the buyer. How you document the transfer of your lease rights will depend in large part on whether you're selling your business entity or selling the business assets. This section discusses the transfer of your lease in an assets sale. Section G, below, covers the transfer in an entity sale.

If you're selling the assets of your business and the buyer wants to keep your lease, you'll want to list the lease as an asset in Clause 2 (Sale of Business Assets) of your sales agreement. (See Chapter 13.) Then, at closing, you'll need to assign the lease to the buyer. As discussed in more detail in Chapter 10, this usually means that you need to get the landlord's consent to assign the lease. In Clause 25 (Documents for Transferring Assets) you can list the lease assignment.

You can use the Assignment for Lease form shown below for assigning a lease and getting the landlord's consent. The form basically spells out the fact that the buyer will be taking over the lease and says that the buyer will pay rent and fulfill the other obligations of the seller under the lease.

 Where to find the forms. You'll find copies of the Assignment of Lease on the CD-ROM at the back of this book.

Most of the clauses in this form are self-explanatory. Here's advice on completing some specific clauses.

In Clause 1, Names, insert the names of the seller, the buyer, and the landlord. See Chapter 13 for suggested formats for naming parties at the beginning of a document.

In Clause 2, Assignment, insert the date of your sales agreement, the date of the lease (which you should attach to the assignment), and the address of the premises you lease.

In Clause 3, Effective Date, insert the date that the buyer will take possession of the leased space—probably the date of the closing.

Clause 6, Landlord's Certification, deals with the status of rent payments, the security deposit, and that fact the lease is still in effect. You'll need to fill in the date to which rent is paid and the amount of any security deposit held by the landlord.

Many of the remaining clauses are standard contract clauses as explained in Chapter 17.

For suggested formats for the signature portion of the assignment, see Chapter 18.

D. Assignment of Other Contracts: Asset Sale

A lease may not be the only type of contract that the buyer will take over. Your business may have contracts with customers, suppliers, employees, and service providers that you'll also want to transfer to the buyer as part of the sale. (See the discussion in Chapters 7 and 10.) As with the transfer of a lease, the documentation you need for the transfer of other contracts will depend primarily on whether you're selling the business assets or the entity (the corporation, LLC,

Assignment of Lease

1. Names

This lease assignment is made by ___Frederico Ricci___,
Seller, and ___Hall Morgan___, Buyer,
with the consent of ___Commercial Management LLC___,
Landlord.

2. Assignment

For valuable consideration (as set forth in the Sales Agreement between the parties dated ___January 15, 20XX___), Seller assigns to Buyer all of Seller's rights in the attached lease dated ___May 11, 20XX___, which covers the premises located at ___123 Dolphin Avenue, Portland, Oregon___.

3. Effective Date

This assignment will take effect on ___February 15, 20XX___.

4. Acceptance

Buyer accepts this assignment and assumes the lease and all its terms. From the effective date of this assignment, Buyer will pay the rent to Landlord and will perform all of Seller's other obligations under the lease.

5. Condition of Premises

Buyer has inspected the premises and will accept possession of the premises in as-is condition, subject to Landlord's maintenance obligations under the lease and prevailing law.

6. Landlord's Certification

Landlord certifies that:

A. Seller has paid all rent through ___March 1, 20XX___.

B. Landlord is holding a security deposit of $___5,000___, which Landlord will now hold for Buyer under the lease terms.

C. Seller is not currently in default in performing any obligations under the lease.

D. The lease has not been modified and it remains in full effect as written.

7. Reimbursement

Buyer will immediately reimburse Seller for the security deposit and any rent or other amounts that Seller has paid in advance under the lease for the period following the effective date of this assignment.

8. Landlord's Consent

Landlord consents to this assignment and to Buyer taking over all Seller's rights and obligations under the lease.

9. Release

Landlord releases Seller from liability for the payment of rent and from the performance of all other lease obligations from the effective date of this assignment.

10. Successors and Assignees

This agreement binds and benefits the heirs, successors, and assignees of the parties.

11. Governing Law

This agreement will be governed by and construed in accordance with the laws of the State of _____ Oregon _____.

12. Modification

This agreement may be modified only by a writing signed by the party against whom such modification is sought to be enforced.

13. Waiver

If any party waives any provision of this agreement at any time, that waiver will only be effective for the specific instance and purpose for which that waiver was given. If any party fails to exercise or delays exercising any of its rights or remedies under this agreement, that party retains the right to enforce that term or provision at a later time.

14. Severability

If a court determines that any provision of this agreement is invalid or unenforceable, any invalidity or unenforceability will affect only that provision. Such provision shall be modified, amended, or limited only to the extent necessary to make it valid and enforceable.

SELLER

Frederico Ricci

Printed name: _Frederico Ricci_

Name of business: _D/B/A Ricci Auto_ _Repair_

Address: _123 Dolphin Ave._ _Portland, Oregon_

Dated: _January 22, 20XX_

BUYER

Hal Morgan

Printed name: _Hal Morgan_

Name of business: _D/B/A Hal's Speedy_ _Service_

Address: _345 Central Street_ _Portland, Oregon_

Dated: _January 22, 20XX_

LANDLORD

Commercial Management LLC

a _An Oregon Limited Liability Company_

By: *Sherry Martin*

Printed name: _Sherry Martin_

Title: _Manager_

Address: _One Barclay Plaza_ _Portland, Oregon_

Dated: _January 22, 20XX_

or partnership). This section covers the assignments of contracts other than the lease in an asset sale. Section G, below, covers the topic for entity sales.

When you're selling the assets of your business, it's always appropriate to make a written assignment of your contracts to the buyer, because whoever signed the contract (your entity or you as a sole proprietor) will no longer be involved. But before assigning a contract, you'll need to read it carefully to see whether there are any conditions, such as getting the other party's agreement to the assignment. And you may even find that a contract states that it can't be assigned. In that case, you'll need to see whether the other party is willing to waive that prohibition and allow an assignment anyhow. It's fairly routine to ask for this type of accommodation, but don't be surprised if the other party asks for something in return—for example, if your manufacturing company has signed a contract in which you've agreed to sell widgets to a certain customer at $5.00 a unit and if that contract prohibits assignment, the customer may agree to an assignment if you'll lower the price to $4.50 per unit.

![icon] **Assigning a contract doesn't end your obligations.** Unless a contract contains a rare clause specifically stating that you can assign it without further liability, you or your company will remain liable for performing the obligations you undertook in the contract despite the fact you have assigned the contract to the buyer. In short, if the buyer of your business assets fails to meet the contractual obligations, you or your company are still on the hook. If you're worried about that possibility, consider approaching the other contracting party to seek a release from liability once your buyer takes over. Again, however, the other party may ask you for some concessions in return.

In preparing your sales agreement for an asset sale, you can refer to the contracts being assigned in Clause 2, Sale of Business Assets (see Chapter 13), listing each contract on an attachment if there are more than a few. You can also put the Assignment of Contracts on your list in Clause 25, Documents for Transferring Assets. (See Chapter 17.) Where you need the consent of the other party to the contract being assigned, you make getting that consent a contingency in Clause 23, Contingencies. (See Chapter 17.) The Assignment of Contracts gets signed at the closing.

You can use an Assignment of Contracts form like the one shown below when there's no need to obtain the consent of the other party. If consent is required, you can you use a simple Consent to Assignment of Contract form such as the one shown just after the assignment form.

![icon] **Where to find the forms.** You'll find copies of the Assignment of Contract and Consent to Assignment of Contracts forms on the CD-ROM at the back of this book.

Assignment of Contracts

1. Names

This assignment of contracts is made by ___Frederico Ricci___,
Seller, and ___Hall Morgan___,
Buyer.

2. Assignment

For valuable consideration (as set forth in the Sales Agreement between the parties dated ___January 15, 20XX___, Seller assigns to Buyer all of Seller's rights in the contracts listed in Attachment _A_ to this assignment.

3. Effective Date

This assignment will take effect on ___February 15, 20XX___.

4. Acceptance

Buyer accepts this assignment and assumes the benefits and obligations of the contracts. From the effective date of this assignment, Buyer will meet all of Seller's obligations under the contracts.

5. Successors and Assignees

This agreement binds and benefits the heirs, successors, and assignees of the parties.

6. Governing Law

This agreement will be governed by and construed in accordance with the laws of the State of ___Oregon___.

7. Modification

This agreement may be modified only by a writing signed by the party against whom such modification is sought to be enforced.

8. Waiver

If either party waives any provision of this agreement at any time, that waiver will only be effective for the specific instance and purpose for which that waiver was given. If either party fails to exercise or delays exercising any of its rights or remedies under this agreement, that party retains the right to enforce that term or provision at a later time.

9. Severability

If a court determines that any provision of this agreement is invalid or unenforceable, any invalidity or unenforceability will affect only that provision. Such provision shall be modified, amended, or limited only to the extent necessary to make it valid and enforceable.

SELLER

Frederico Ricci

Printed name: _Frederico Ricci_

Name of business: _D/B/A Ricci Auto_ _Repair Service_

Address: _123 Dolphin Ave._ _Portland, Oregon_

Dated: _January 22, 20XX_

BUYER

Hal Morgan

Printed name: _Hal Morgan_

Name of business: _D/B/A Hal's Speedy_ _Service_

Address: _345 Central Street_ _Portland, Oregon_

Dated: _January 22, 20XX_

Consent to Assignment of Contract

With regard to the ___automotive parts_____

contract dated __May 15, 20XX___ between __Frederico Ricci_____

(Customer) and __Arco Auto Products Inc._____ (Supplier), __Arco_____

_____ consents to Customer's assignment of the contract to

Hal Morgan d/b/a Hal's Speedy Service._____.

__Arco Auto Products Inc._____

a(n) __Oregon Corporation_____

By: __Todd Williams_____

Printed name: __Todd Williams_____

Title: __President_____

Address: __654 Oakdale Street_____

Portland, Oregon_____

Dated: __January 25, 20XX_____

Most of the clauses in the Assignment of Contracts form are self-explanatory. Here's advice on completing some specific clauses.

In Clause 1 (Names), insert the names of the seller and the buyer. See Chapter 13 for suggested formats for naming parties at the beginning of a document.

In Clause 2 (Assignment), insert the date of your sales agreement. Use an attachment to describe each of the contracts that you're assigning to the buyer. See Chapter 12 for information on preparing attachments.

In Clause 3 (Effective Date), insert the date that the assignment take effect— probably the date of the closing.

Many of the remaining clauses are standard contract clauses as explained in Chapter 17.

For suggested formats for the signature portion of the assignment, see Chapter 18.

If you can swing it, adding a sentence such as the following to the consent form would be ideal:

Arco releases Frederico Ricci from all further liability regarding the contract.

E. Assignment of Intellectual Property

As explained in Chapters 7 and 10, your business assets may include intellectual property such as copyrights, patents, trademarks, service marks, and trade secrets that you've agreed will be included in the sale. If you're selling your business assets, you'll need to assign these intellectual property rights to the buyer, using a form like the one included in this book. You should specify in Clause 2 of your sales agreement (Sale of Business Assets; see Chapter 13) that intellectual property is among the assets being sold and then list the specifics in an attachment to your sales agreement. You can list Assignment of Intellectual Property in Clause 25 (Documents for Transferring Assets in Chapter 17) as one of the documents to be signed at closing.

Since most small businesses are likely to have minimal intellectual property among their assets, a simple assignment like the one shown below should suffice.

 Where to find the forms. You'll find copies of the Assignment of Intellectual Property on the CD-ROM at the back of this book.

 Businesses with extensive intellectual property need more specific assignment documents. If the assets you're selling include a significant amount of intellectual property, you'll need to create more specific assignment documents. In that case, consult either *License Your Invention* (for patents and trade secrets) or *Getting Permission* (for copyrights and trademarks), both by Richard Stim (Nolo). It also makes sense to confer with an intellectual property lawyer.

Most of the clauses in the Assignment of Intellectual Property form are self-explanatory. Here's advice on completing some specific clauses.

In Clause 1, Names, insert the names of the seller and buyer. See Chapter 13 for suggested formats for names at the beginning of a document.

In Clause 2, Assignment of Rights, insert the date of your sales agreement.

Note that Clause 4, Additional Documents, refers to an attachment. Use your best efforts to create as complete a list as you can of the intellectual property that you're selling. The Nolo books listed above can provide advice for doing so.

Only the seller signs the assignment. See Chapter 18 for suggested formats for the signature portion of a document, such as an assignment.

The Assignment of Intellectual Property form includes a spot for notarization, which is optional. There is no requirement that copyright, trademark, or patent assignments be notarized. However, many buyers insist on that formality as an assurance that the Seller's signature's is authentic. See Section B, above, for more on notarization.

Assignment of Intellectual Property

1. Names

This Assignment of Intellectual Property is made by _Burgundy Associates LLC,_ _a Florida limited liability company_ , Seller, to _Georgetown West Inc., a_ _Florida Corporation_ , Buyer.

2. Assignment of Rights

For valuable consideration as set forth in the Sales Agreement between the parties dated _February 15, 20XX_ , Seller assigns to Buyer all of Seller's rights, title, and interest in any and all copyrights, patents, trademarks, service marks, trade secrets, and other related proprietary rights (the Intellectual Property) that comprise business assets of Seller, except for any Intellectual Property specifically excluded in the Sales Agreement.

3. Scope of Transferred Rights

This transfer of rights includes, but is not limited to, all registered, unregistered, or pending registrations, derivatives of the Intellectual Property, term extensions, renewals, or foreign rights associated with the Intellectual Property. For any trademark or service mark rights that are being assigned, Seller also transfers to Buyer any goodwill associated with such marks.

4. Additional Documents

Seller has made a good faith effort to list in Attachment 1 the Intellectual Property being transferred. To the extent that Seller has failed to list such Intellectual Property, Seller will cooperate with Buyer to sign further papers to accomplish the transfer of rights. Seller will also cooperate with Buyer in the processing of any Intellectual Property applications, registrations, or prosecutions and will sign any further papers required to evidence this assignment.

Burgundy Associates LLC

a _Florida Limited Liability Company_

By: _Cheryl Jackson_

Printed name: _Cheryl Jackson_

Title: _Member_

Address: _123 Center Street, Miami, Florida_

Dated: _February 22, 20XX_

Transferring the right to use a fictitious name. In an asset sale, if the buyer will be taking over a business name that's not a trademark or service mark, you've probably registered the name as a fictitious or assumed name. In that case, you'll need to check with the state or county office where you registered the name. Chances are they'll have a form you can use to cancel the registration. This should free up the name, making it available for the buyer to pick up using a fresh registration form.

F. Approval of Entity's Sale of Assets

If you operate your business as a corporation and the business entity will be selling its assets (but you'll retain ownership of the entity itself), the sale will need the approval of the board of directors. This is accomplished either by the adoption of a resolution or by having the directors sign a written consent. But that approval may just be one step. When your business is a corporation, an LLC, or a partnership, the legal documents creating your entity may require that before your entity sells all or substantially all of its assets, all the owners—or a specified majority—must consent. The documents in which you'll typically find such a requirement include a corporation's bylaws, an LLC's operating agreement, or a partnership's partnership agreement. Usually you're able to document the authorization to sell the business assets by preparing a simple written consent that's signed by owners of the entity. This avoids the need for a formal meeting where a vote is taken. Sample consent forms are shown below for different types of entities.

Even if unanimous consent isn't required, when your entity is selling its assets, you should have all of the owners sign the sales agreement (as recommended in Chapter 18). This will all but eliminate any possibility of a later dispute if an owner gets cold feet or raises questions about the sale. Following are some written consents that you can use, depending on the kind of entity you have. (If your entity documents don't require unanimous consent of the owners and some of the owners haven't signed the consent, a statute or your entity documents may require you to promptly send a copy of a signed written consent to those owners who have not signed it.) The consent form should be prepared and signed before your entity signs the sales agreement. It will not be attached to the sales agreement but should be kept with your entity's official records.

 For more information on written consents, see *The Corporate Records Handbook, and Your Limited Liability Company,* both by Anthony Mancuso (Nolo).

Directors' Consent to the Corporation's Sale of a Business

We are all of the directors of _____,
a(n) [*list name of state*] corporation. We consent to the corporation's sale of
the [business assets/entity ownership interests] of [*list name of business being*
purchased] on the terms stated in the attached sales agreement.

The corporation's president is authorized to sign the sales agreement on behalf
of the corporation and to take such actions as the president deems necessary or
appropriate to carry out the terms of the sales agreement.

Dated: _____   _____

Printed name: _____   Printed name: _____

Printed name: _____   Printed name: _____

Printed name: _____   Printed name: _____

Printed name: _____   Printed name: _____

Shareholders' Consent to the Corporation's Sale of a Business

We own all of the stock of _____,
a(n) [*list name of state*] corporation. We consent to the corporation's sale of
the [business assets/entity ownership interests] of [*list name of business being*
purchased] on the terms stated in the attached sales agreement.

The corporation's president is authorized to sign the sales agreement on behalf
of the corporation and to take such actions as the president deems necessary or
appropriate to carry out the terms of the sales agreement.

Dated: _____   _____

Printed name: _____   Printed name: _____

Printed name: _____   Printed name: _____

Printed name: _____   Printed name: _____

Printed name: _____   Printed name: _____

LLC Members' Consent to the Company's Sale of a Business

We own all of the membership interests in _____
_____, a(n) [list name of state]
limited liability company. We consent to the company's sale of the [business
assets/entity ownership interests] of [list name of business being purchased] on
the terms stated in the attached sales agreement.

_____ is authorized to sign the
sales agreement on behalf of the company and to take such actions as [ ] he [ ] she
deems necessary or appropriate to carry out the terms of the sales agreement.

Dated: _____   _____

Printed name: _____   Printed name: _____

Printed name: _____   Printed name: _____

Printed name: _____   Printed name: _____

Printed name: _____   Printed name: _____

Partners' Consent to the Partnership's Sale of a Business

We are all of the partners in _____,
a(n) [list name of state] partnership. We consent to the partnership's sale of
the [business assets/entity ownership interests] of [list name of business being
purchased] on the terms stated in the attached sales agreement.

_____ is authorized to sign the sales
agreement on behalf of the partnership and to take such actions as [ ] he [ ] she
deems necessary or appropriate to carry out the terms of the sales agreement.

Dated: _____   _____

Printed name: _____   Printed name: _____

Printed name: _____   Printed name: _____

Printed name: _____   Printed name: _____

Printed name: _____   Printed name: _____

Where to find the forms. You'll find copies of the Directors' Consent to the Corporation's Sale of a Business, Shareholders' Consent to the Corporation's Sale of a Business, LLC Members' Consent to the Company's Sale of a Business, and Partners' Consent to the Partnership's Sale of a Business forms on the CD-ROM at the back of this book.

G. Transferring Your Entity

If you're selling your corporation or LLC as an entity, you'll need to transfer the entity to the buyer at closing. To accomplish this task, you won't use a bill of sale or the other transfer documents that are described above for an asset sale. That's because when you sell your entity, the entity continues to own the assets; transferring the entity gives the new owner full control over those assets. Typically, less paperwork is required to transfer ownership of an entity than to transfer its assets.

In this discussion of transferring ownership of a corporation or LLC, the assumption is that you and all the other owners have signed the sales agreement and that all of you are selling all of your interests in the business to the buyer. This is the situation in the vast majority of small business sales. If this description doesn't apply to your sale, you'll need to carefully check any buy-sell agreement,

shareholders' agreement, or operating agreement to see if there are any limits on the sale of stock or LLC interests. Hopefully, you attended to this critical detail long before you signed the sales agreement to make sure that all necessary parties have consented to the deal.

1. Transferring Ownership of a Corporation

Very likely, when you created your corporation, you issued stock certificates to the owners (shareholders) as evidence of their ownership. If so, look at the back of each certificate, where there should be a transfer clause. You and the other shareholders should sign the back of your certificates in the indicated spot and deliver the certificates to the buyer—or perhaps to an escrow agent to hold until the buyer makes all the required installment payments. It's possible, however, that in your rush to set up your corporation you failed to issue stock certificates; in that case, you can take care of this step before closing. Through a written consent or resolution, your corporation's directors can authorize the issuance of shares and provide for the signing of stock certificates, which can then be transferred to you at the closing.

 For full information on corporate consents and resolutions, see *The Corporate Records Handbook,* by Anthony Mancuso (Nolo).

2. Transferring Ownership of an LLC

Transferring ownership of an LLC is somewhat similar to transferring ownership of a corporation. If your LLC has issued membership certificates that resemble stock certificates, each LLC member can sign the transfer clause. Otherwise, you'll need to prepare a separate document called Assignment of LLC Membership Interests. Whichever method of transfer you use, make sure that the language specifically transfers full economic and membership rights.

 For more on LLC documentation, see *Form Your Own Limited Liability Company* and *Your Limited Liability Company*, both written by Anthony Mancuso (Nolo).

3. After the Transfer

Once ownership of your corporation or LLC has been transferred to the buyer, the buyer is free to select new corporate directors and officers or new LLC managers and to remove the current ones. Still, as part of the changing of the guard, it's appropriate at closing for current officeholders to give their written resignations to the buyer. If you're going to work for the entity after the closing, the arrangements should be covered in an employment agreement or independent

contractor agreement, as described in Chapter 21.

Finally, it's a good idea to change the entity's registered agent. The name and address of a corporation's or an LLC's registered agent are kept on file at the state office where corporations and LLCs are registered. The idea is that there's a specific person authorized to accept notices and lawsuit papers for your business. Chances are that when you set up your corporation or LLC, you named yourself or a co-owner as the company's registered agent. Once you've sold the entity, you'll want to be free of this responsibility. Contact your state's business registration office (usually the secretary of state) for a form to use in changing the registered agent. The form may be available online at the office's website. You can locate the appropriate website by going to www.statelocalgov. net.

H. Assignments in an Entity Sale

Normally, you won't need a separate document to transfer an entity's contracts and intellectual property to the buyer. These rights of the entity stay with the entity, and the buyer will get the benefit of those rights. But let's take a closer look at this subject.

1. Assignment of Lease: Entity Sale

If you're selling your corporation, LLC, or partnership business entity, you usually won't need any special paperwork to give the buyer the benefit of your lease. That's because the entity is already named as the tenant in the lease. But occasionally, a lease will say that if ownership of your entity changes, the landlord's consent is required for the entity to continue to occupy the premises. In that case, of course, you will need to arrange for the landlord to consent in writing. For advice on doing this, see the discussion in Section C, above.

2. Assignment of Other Contracts: Entity Sale

With the sale of an entity (a corporation or an LLC), you ordinarily won't need to make a written assignment of business contracts as you would in an asset sale (as described above in Section D). That's because the contracts are already in the name of the business entity and, after the sale, the corporation or LLC will get the benefit of the contracts—and be bound by the contractual obligations—without any new documents being signed. But there can be an exception in a situation where a contract with the entity contains a clause that says you must get the consent of the other party if the entity is sold. In that case, you'll obviously need to honor that clause by getting the consent, though you won't need to assign the contract, because the entity itself (the corporation or LLC) remains a party to the contract.

Another exception that will require additional written documentation involves the sale of a corporation or an LLC that has a contract which states that a specific person associated with the company will provide future services to the other business. For example, suppose that your ad agency has a contract saying that you'll personally supervise a certain account. If you'll no longer be on the entity's payroll after the business is sold, you and the buyer will need to get the other party's consent to the continuation of the contract. (See Chapter 10, Section C5, for more on the issue of transferring contracts in an entity sale.)

3. Assignment of Intellectual Property: Entity Sale

An assignment isn't normally needed in an entity sale, since the ownership of the intellectual property will remain in the corporation or entity that's being sold.

■

Chapter 21

Documents for Noncompete and Future Work Commitments

When you negotiate for the sale of your business, the discussions will very likely include the question of whether you will continue to have a future working relationship with the business and whether you will make an agreement (covenant) not to compete with the seller after the sale. These topics are covered in detail in Chapters 3 and 9, and this chapter gives you the practical tools to document the agreements you make.

If you agree to sign a noncompete, employment, or independent contractor agreement, you'll then include language in your sales agreement referring to these agreements. Chapter 16 covers the basic functions of noncompete, employment, and independent contractor agreements and includes specific clauses stating that relevant documents will be signed at closing concerning these arrangements, with copies of the actual documents attached to the sales agreement. You may want to go back and reread Chapter 16 now, paying special attention to Clauses 21 (Covenant Not to Compete) and 22 (Future Services).

It's best to prepare any noncompete or future work agreement at the same time that you craft the sales agreement. Then there can be no doubt about what needs to be signed at closing to cover these important topics. These documents can be attachments to the sales agreement. See Chapter 12 for information about attachments.

Section A, below, covers the Covenant Not to Compete. Section B deals with employment contracts, and Section C deals with consulting (independent contractor) contracts.

 Get legal help with noncompete agreements and contracts covering your future work with the business. As with the other important documents discussed in this book, have a lawyer look over all agreements dealing with noncompetition and future services. You may have to live with these documents for years to come, so you want to make sure that they're as clear as possible and can be enforced if need be.

A. Covenant Not to Compete

A buyer may not want to purchase your business unless you agree not to compete with it for a certain period after the sale. A covenant not to compete, also known as a noncompete agreement, usually requires the owners of the business being sold (and sometimes their spouses who work in the business) to refrain from competing against the buyer (typically, for one to three years) in the geographic area where the buyer conducts business. Without a covenant not to compete, the buyer takes the risk that you'll will pocket the buyer's money and open up a competing business down the street, significantly reducing the value of the buyer's purchase.

This chapter explains how to prepare a covenant not to compete and includes a sample agreement.

In working on the covenant, you'll need to consider carefully:

- the kinds of work you can and can't do
- the geographic areas that are off-limits
- the length of time the agreement applies, and
- the payment you'll receive for your covenant.

1. Limits on Your Competitive Activities After the Sale

If you plan to remain active in the same line of work, you'll want to tightly limit any covenant not to compete. For example, you may be willing to agree that for two years after the sale, you won't compete within ten miles of the business location—or perhaps within the same county or state. By contrast, the buyer's suggestion that you sign a five-year commitment prohibiting competitive activities in a ten-state area may be unacceptable to you. Obviously, if you know you're retiring for good, or planning to move to a different part of the country, or entering a completely different line of work, there will be no need to obsess over these details.

But what if your future plans are uncertain? It makes sense to keep open the possibility that you can do some related work that really doesn't threaten the profitability of the business you're selling. For example, if you sell your tile-laying business, you might want to open a showroom that sells imported tile to professional installers. To deal with the possibility that you may wish to do related but essentially noncompetitive work in the future, you must carefully define the type of work that will be off limits. There are two broad ways to do this: One is to narrowly define the work that would constitute prohibited competition. The other is to start with a broad definition of the competitive work that's off-limits but then carve out an exception for the work you may want to do in the future.

To better understand these two approaches, let's look at the case of Len, who is selling his court reporting business to Consolidated Court Reporting LLC. As you may know, court reporters such as Ken generally use their stenographic skills in one or more of the following ways:

- They create a written record (transcript) of trials and other courtroom hearings.
- They create a written record of pretrial discovery depositions in which lawyers question the parties and witnesses who are expected to testify in court.
- They create closed-caption accounts of TV news broadcasts, or real-time transcripts of speeches and lectures—typically displayed on an

auditorium screen, on television, or on notebook computers. This work is intended primarily for the benefit of hearing-impaired people.

Let's now assume that Ken wants to keep open the possibility that after the closing, he can earn money by doing closed-captions and related work. Assuming the buyer is primarily interested in court and other legal-system related parts of Ken's business, the noncompetition language can be approached in two different ways, as illustrated below.

Specifying the Prohibited Competition

For five years following the closing, Seller will not, within Adams County, prepare transcripts of lawsuit depositions, trials, or other legal proceedings.

Under this formulation, Ken is free to do closed-caption and related work—as well as any other type of stenographic work that may become available in the future, as long as it doesn't involve legal proceedings.

Carving Out an Exception

For five years following the closing, Seller will not, within Adams County, provide any court reporting or public stenographic services, except that he may without limitation provide closed-caption accounts for television

programs and real-time transcripts of speeches, lectures, and similar events.

Although this formulation specifically identifies the work Ken can do after closing, it may in fact be a bit more restrictive, because it defines what Ken can do without violating the noncompete agreement but it does not cover other possibilities. In the real world, the difference between the two approaches may be insignificant, but in theory at least, the first approach (specifying the prohibited competitive activities) could possibly open up some additional opportunities for Ken to earn money.

The clause illustrated could be broadened a bit and afford more flexibility to Ken by adding a few more words:

For five years following the closing, Seller will not, within Adams County, provide any court reporting or public stenographic services, except that he may without limitation provide closed-caption accounts for television programs and real-time transcripts of speeches, lectures, and similar events, *and he may provide similar services that are unrelated to specific court cases.*

As in Ken's case, if you're clear about your goals, there are many situations in which the buyer will likely be willing to negotiate so that after the sale you can still earn a living in a related, but not directly competitive, field of work. For example:

- If you're selling a restaurant, the buyer may agree that it will be OK for you to go into the catering business or to work for someone else in the area as a chef.
- Similarly, if you're selling a business that helps companies set up and maintain internal computer networks or intranets, the buyer may have no objection to your operating a business that helps design websites for companies that plan to market products directly to the public or starting a business installing wireless networks in homes, coffee shops, and other locations.
- If you're selling a small manufacturing business, the buyer may have no problem with your owning or working in a service business in the same field, especially if you agree to feature the manufacturer's products.

The point is that you need to think about the type of work you may want to do in the future. Even if the work is somewhat related to the business you're selling and even though you'd be doing it in the same geographical area as that business, it may not cut into the buyer's profits. If so, you need to talk this through with the buyer and then draft noncompete language that clearly lets you do the related work if you choose to—or if, for financial reasons, you discover that you need to.

 If possible, present your future plans as benefiting the buyer. If you want the right to run a business in a closely related field to the one you're selling, the buyer is much more likely to agree to a flexible noncompete agreement that accommodates your plans if you include a few carrots. For example, if you're selling a restaurant but want to open a bakery with a small café, you might propose that your bakery supply bread and pastries to the restaurant at a very favorable price.

2. Covenant Not to Compete Form

A sample Covenant Not to Compete form that you can use as a starting point is shown below.

 Where to find the forms. You'll find copies of the Covenant Not to Compete on the CD-ROM at the back of this book.

3. Instructions for Preparing Your Covenant Not to Compete

Here's how to complete a Covenant Not to Compete form.

1. Names

Fill in your name, the name of your business, and the buyer's name as they appear in the sales agreement.

2. Background

In the first blank, choose the status that best represents your association with the business being sold: owner, if the business is a sole proprietorship; shareholder, if the business is a corporation; or member, if the business is an LLC.

Then indicate whether the buyer is buying the assets or the business entity.

3. Payment

Fill in the amount of money the buyer is paying you for your covenant not to compete. Remember that this payment is separate from the sale price. If you accept a promissory note for all or part of the amount you're owed for your covenant, make it a separate promissory note—not part of the one for the balance of the sale price.

⚠️ **For your promise not to compete to be legally binding, the buyer must pay you something of value in exchange for that promise.** In legal parlance, this is known as consideration. As little as a few dollars will meet this technical requirement. In negotiating the figure, don't lose sight of the tax implications. The payment you receive for your covenant will be taxed at ordinary income tax rates, which are higher than long-term capital gain rates. This means that in many situations, to keep your taxes low, it will be to your advantage to receive a higher amount for the business assets and a

token amount for your covenant. But this is a complicated area of tax law, so check with your tax adviser to see how the tax rules apply to your particular situation. And see Chapter 4 for general information on the tax consequences of selling your business.

4. Noncompetition

Fill in the specific details of your agreement, including the type of business you agree not to participate in and the geographic location (such as a particular metropolitan area) or scope, such as number of miles. You'll need to modify this if miles or geographic scope are not relevant, as might be the case with an Internet business, for example.

In some service or manufacturing businesses, the most effective way to craft a noncompete is to specify certain customers or clients who are off limits. Everyone else is fair game. Say, for example, you're selling your baking company because you plan to devote more time and energy to a restaurant you own. You might agree that if you get back into the baking business in the next five years, you won't sell to the three hotels and 20 food stores that have been your biggest customers in the past, but that you're free to sell to anyone else.

In preparing a noncompete agreement, you need to make sure that the commitment you make isn't so broad or long-lasting that it cuts you off from earning

Covenant Not to Compete

1. Names

I, _____ (Seller)

make this covenant not to compete with the business known as _____

_____ (the Business), which has

been purchased by _____ (Buyer).

2. Background

I have been ☐ an owner ☐ a shareholder ☐ a member of the Business.
Concurrently with my signing of this covenant, the Buyer is buying ☐ the assets
of the business ☐ the business entity.

3. Payment

I make this covenant in consideration of that purchase and of the further payment
of $_____ that I have received from Buyer.

4. Noncompetition

For the next _____ years, I will not directly or indirectly participate in a

_____ business within _____ miles

of the current location of the Business named above. This includes participating
in my own business or acting as a co-owner, director, officer, consultant,
independent contractor, employee, or agent of a competing business.

In particular, I will not:

(a) solicit or attempt to solicit any business or trade from actual or prospective
customers or clients of the Business

(b) employ or attempt to employ any employee of the Business

(c) divert or attempt to divert business away from the Business, or

(d) encourage any independent contractor or consultant to end a relationship
with the Business.

5. Permitted Activities

It will not be a breach of this covenant for me to engage in any of the following
activities: _____

_____

---

6. Breach

I acknowledge and agree that if I breach or threaten to breach any of the terms of this covenant, Buyer and the Business will sustain irreparable harm and will be entitled to obtain an injunction to stop any breach or threatened breach.

7. Governing Law

I agree that this covenant will be governed and construed in accordance with the laws of the State of _____.

Signature: _____

Dated: _____

---

money in ways that don't truly threaten the buyer's income.

Also, in Clause 4 (Noncompetition), indicate the length of the agreement, such as three years. Ordinarily, the buyer will want the seller to agree not to compete for at least one year. Restricting the seller's ability to compete for up to three years is common, but anything more than that is likely to be invalidated by a court unless it's truly necessary to protect the buyer's business, which will be hard to prove.

5. Permitted Activities

Spell out activities you can engage in. If you're selling a bakery, for example, the buyer would probably allow you to work for a company that distributes baking ovens and related equipment. It's part of the baking industry, but your work wouldn't be a competitive threat to the buyer.

Delete this clause if you have no plans to work in a related business and it's highly unlikely you will ever want to.

6. Breach

You do not need to insert anything here. This clause allows the buyer to seek an injunction—an order that someone has to do something or refrain from doing something—against you if you violate the agreement or seem to be about to do so.

7. Governing Law

Usually, you'll fill in the name of the state where the business is located. See Chapter 17 for more information on Governing Law clauses.

Signatures

Only you will sign this covenant. See Chapter 18 for a suggested format to use when signing a document as an individual. Although you'll attach a copy of the covenant to your sales agreement, you won't sign it until the closing.

B. Contract for Employment

If you'll be working for the new owner as an employee, you'll want to prepare an employment contract and attach it to your sales agreement, as discussed in Clause 22, Future Services. (See Chapter 16.) The employment contract gets signed at the closing.

The basic terms of an employment agreement include the job duties, the duration of employment, the payment amount and schedule, benefits (such as health insurance), and termination policy. Chapter 9 explains the legal ins and outs of employment agreements, including

how they compare with working for the new owner as an independent contractor.

The following sample employment contract shows many of the topics that can be addressed in an employment contract.

 It's essential to have a lawyer review your employment contract. There's wide variation in the types of terms that employers and employees agree to, depending on many factors, including the industry and the employee's position. Also, employment law continues to grow ever more complex. As a result, an employment contract needs to be a highly customized document. You want to make sure you don't overlook some subtlety that could cause a problem down the road. Be sure to get solid legal advice before you sign an employment contract.

 Consider getting a personal guarantee. If you'll be signing an employment contract with an entity (a corporation, an LLC, or a partnership), it can make sense to have the owners personally guarantee payment of your wages. A guarantee provision is included at the end of the sample employment contract shown below.

Sample Employment Contract

1. Names

This contract is between Vintage Valley LLC, an Illinois Limited Liability Company, Employer, and Marla Fenby, Employee.

2. Job Duties

Employer hires employee for the position of bookkeeper. Employee agrees to perform the following services for Employer: maintaining of all of Employer's income and expense records and preparation of reports and tax returns in consultation with the Certified Public Accountant retained by Employer.

3. Duration of Employment

The employment will begin on May 1, 20XX, and end on April 30, 20XX, unless terminated sooner as specified in this contract.

4. Compensation

Employer will pay Employee $ 5,000 each month.

5. Other Benefits

Employer will provide the following additional benefits to Employee:

Two weeks' paid vacation each year, and medical and health insurance as described in the Vintage Valley Employee Handbook.

6. Employer's Policies

Employee accepts Employer's policies as contained in the Vintage Valley Employee Handbook, which Employee acknowledges receiving.

7. Termination

If Employee does not satisfactorily perform the job duties described in Paragraph 2 of this contract or substantially violates Employer's policies as set forth in its Employee Handbook, Employer may terminate Employee's employment.

8. Confidential Information

Employee will not disclose or use at any time, except as part of the employment with Employer, any confidential information pertaining to the business of Employer. This includes, but is not limited to, Employer's sales and profit figures; its customer lists; its trade secrets; its relationship with its contractors, customers, or suppliers; and opportunities for new or developing business. Employee acknowledges the unique and confidential nature of this information and the irreparable harm that will be caused to Employer by its unauthorized use or disclosure.

9. Entire Agreement

This contract contains the entire agreement between the parties on the subject of employment. Any amendments require the written agreement of both parties.

10. Governing Law

This agreement will be governed by and construed in accordance with the laws of the State of Illinois.

11. Waiver

If any party waives any provision of this agreement at any time, that waiver will only be effective for the specific instance and purpose for which that waiver was given. If any party fails to exercise or delays exercising any of its rights or remedies under this agreement, that party retains the right to enforce that term or provision at a later time.

12. Severability

If a court determines that any provision of this agreement is invalid or unenforceable, any invalidity or unenforceability will affect only that provision. Such provision may be modified, amended, or limited only to the extent necessary to make it valid and enforceable.

Employer	**Employee**
Vintage Valley LLC	*Marla Fenby*
An Illinois Limited Liability Company	Marla Fenby
By: *Felice Randall*	Address: 678 Morton Blvd.
Felice Randall, Manager	Unit No. 2
Address: 345 Placid Road	Evanston, Illinois
Chicago, Illinois	Dated: April 1, 2006
Dated: April 1, 2006	

Personal Guarantee

In consideration of Employee agreeing to work for Vintage Valley LLC, I personally guarantee performance of all of the Employer's obligations in the above agreement.

Felice Randall

Felice Randall

C. Contract for an Independent Contractor

As part of the negotiations for selling your business, you and the buyer may have agreed that after the closing, you'll work for the buyer as an independent contractor rather than as an employer. If so, you'll want to prepare an independent contractor agreement and attach it to your sales agreement. (See Clause 22, Future Services, in Chapter 16.) You'll sign the independent contractor agreement at the closing of your sale.

The differences between working as an employee and working as an independent contractor are explained in Chapter 9. One key difference is that if you're an independent contractor, the company doesn't withhold income taxes when it pays you. And it's not responsible for withholding or paying any part of the Social Security and Medicare taxes. Taxes are solely your responsibility.

 Recommended reading on independent contractors. For in-depth coverage of this subject, see *Consultant & Independent Contractor Agreements,* by Stephen Fishman (Nolo). The book contains numerous agreements covering different situations.

 Work with a lawyer to develop your independent contract agreement. As with an employment agreement, the law can be complicated. You don't want to leave out anything that can be important to you—or phrase something in a way that can cause big problems later. So make sure to get an experienced lawyer involved in the drafting process.

1. Independent Contractor Agreement Form

A sample Independent Contractor Agreement form that you can use as a starting point is shown below.

 Where to find the forms. You'll find copies of the Independent Contractor Agreement form on the CD-ROM at the back of this book.

2. Instructions for Completing the Independent Contractor Agreement

Here's how to complete the independent contractor agreement.

1. Names

Fill in your name (the Client) and the name of the company hiring you (the Contractor). See Chapter 13 for suggested formats to use in naming the parties at the beginning of an agreement.

2. Services to be Performed

Provide a detailed description of the services you'll be providing.

Independent Contractor Agreement

1. Names

This contract is between _Vintage Valley LLC, an Illinois Limited Liability Company_ ,
Client, and _Marla Fenby_ , Contractor.

2. Services to be Performed

Contractor agrees to perform the following services for Client: _maintaining all of Client's income and expense records and preparation of reports and tax returns in consultation with the Certified Public Accountant retained by Client._ .

3. Time Commitment

Contractor will spend _between 15 and 25 hours per week_ performing the services.

4. Payment

Client will pay Contractor at the rate of $_40 per hour_ .

5. Invoices

Contractor will submit invoices to Client for all services performed.

6. Independent Contractor Status

The parties intend Contractor to be an independent contractor in the performance of the services. Contractor will have the right to control and determine the methods and means of performing the contractual services.

7. Other Clients

Contractor retains the right to perform services for other clients.

8. Assistants

Contractor, at Contractor's expense, may employ assistants as Contractor deems appropriate to carry out this agreement. Contractor will be responsible for paying these assistants, as well as any expense attributable to them including income taxes, unemployment insurance, and Social Security taxes. Contractor will maintain workers' compensation insurance for all of its employees.

9. Equipment and Supplies

A. Contractor, at Contractor's expense, will provide all equipment, tools, and supplies necessary to perform the contractual services, except for the following which will be provided by Client: a computer and bookkeeping software.

B. Contractor will be responsible for all expenses required for the performance of the contractual services, except for the following which will be paid for by Client: stationery and bookkeeping supplies.

10. Local, State, and Federal Taxes

Contractor will pay all income taxes and Social Security and Medicare taxes incurred while performing services under this agreement. Client will not:

- withhold Social Security and Medicare taxes from payments to Contractor or pay such taxes on Contractor's behalf

- make state or federal unemployment compensation contributions on Contractor's behalf, or

- withhold state or federal income tax from payment to Contractor.

11. Intellectual Property

Contractor assigns to Client all patent, copyright, and trade secret rights in anything created or developed by Contractor for Client under this Agreement.

12. Duration of Agreement

This agreement will remain in effect until ___April 30, 20XX___.

13. Entire Agreement

This contract contains the entire agreement between the parties on the subject of services to be rendered by Contractor for Client. Any amendments require the written agreement of both parties.

14. Governing Law

This agreement will be governed by and construed in accordance with the laws of the State of ___Illinois___.

15. Modification

This agreement may be modified only by a written amendment signed by all parties.

16. Waiver

If any party waives any provision of this agreement at any time, that waiver will only be effective for the specific instance and purpose for which that waiver was given. If any party fails to exercise or delays exercising any of its rights or remedies under this agreement, that party retains the right to enforce that term or provision at a later time.

17. Severability

If a court determines that any provision of this agreement is invalid or unenforceable, any invalidity or unenforceability will affect only that provision. Such provision may be modified, amended, or limited only to the extent necessary to make it valid and enforceable.

Client	**Contractor**
Vintage Valley LLC	*Marla Fenby*
An Illinois Limited Liability Company	Marla Fenby
By: *Felice Randall*	678 Morton Blvd.
Felice Randall, Manager	Unit No. 2
345 Placid Road	Evanston, Illinois
Chicago, Illinois	
Dated: April 1, 20XX	Dated: April 1, 20XX

EXAMPLE:

Contractor will advise Client's manager on the ordering of new products and will assist in the placement of products in the store. Contractor will also keep the inventory software updated as needed to meet industry standards.

Basically, you'll insert a plain-English description of the kind of work you'll be doing.

3. Time Commitment

If you're committing yourself to work a certain number of hours or within a certain range of hours, you can supply that information here.

4. Payment

The sample agreement assumes that you'll be paid by the hour. If so, you can insert the hourly rate. If you'll be paid on any other basis, such as a monthly fee or a per-project basis, you can revise the wording to reflect that fact.

5-17. Additional Clauses

You don't need to insert anything in most of clauses 5 through 17. They include statements that:

- You'll give the client invoices for the services performed (Clause 5).
- You'll have independent contractor status (Clause 6).
- You retain the right to work for other people (Clause 7).
- You may hire assistants to help do the work for this client (Clause 8).
- You'll be responsible for your own equipment, tools, and supplies necessary to perform the work and all expenses except where noted (Clause 9).
- You'll be responsible for income, Social Security, and Medicare taxes, and unemployment compensation contributions (Clause 10).
- The client will have all intellectual property rights in what you produce under the agreement—though this language can be modified if that's not what you want (Clause 11).
- The agreement will be in effect until a fixed date (Clause 12).

Clauses 13 through 17 are standard contract clauses and are explained in Chapter 17.

Signatures

You and the client will sign this agreement at the closing. See Chapter 18 for suggested formats for the signature portion of an agreement such as this one.

■

Part 5

Closing the Deal

Preparing for a Smooth Closing

At some point after you and the buyer have signed the sales agreement, you'll need to transfer ownership of the business to the buyer through appropriate legal documents. Usually this involves a meeting—called the closing—at which the buyer pays you the sale price or the agreed down payment. And, if it's an asset sale, the buyer also signs documents such as a promissory note and security agreement. In exchange, to turn ownership over to the buyer, you sign a bill of sale for the business assets—or, in an entity sale, you sign stock certificates or LLC documents. When you walk out the door, you're the former owner of Racafrax Inc., which now has a new boss.

Perhaps surprisingly, you may find that your closing is simultaneously a joyous and bittersweet moment. Even though you're finally wrapping up the sales process and receiving some or all of the money from the sale, you may also be letting go of a business you've built and worked with for years and, in some instances, decades. And, especially when selling coincides with retirement, closing the transaction will represent a major milestone in your life.

In anticipation of what may be an emotional event, it's smart to use the sales agreement to help assure that the closing is conducted efficiently. Your sales agreement can be the starting point for a checklist of the documents that need to be signed at the closing. You can go on to construct a more comprehensive checklist several days before the closing and review it with the buyer. Section A covers the mechanics of conducting a closing. Sections B and C will help you make sure that your checklist is as complete as possible.

Section D introduces you to the possibility of last-minute glitches, and Section E looks ahead to life after the closing.

A. Where and When to Hold the Closing and Who Should Attend

Your sales agreement should say where and when the closing will take place. See Chapter 17, Clause 24, Closing, for suggested language.

This section offers suggestions for setting the date and location of the closing and determining who should be there.

1. Who Attends the Closing

Sometimes, only the seller and the buyer will attend the closing but, often, others need to attend as well. Plan carefully so that all necessary people can be on hand to sign the required papers.

Spouses, for example, may need to attend the closing. Let's say you're married, live in a community property state, and are selling the assets of a sole proprietorship business. In that situation, your spouse should sign the transfer documents. Similarly, it may be necessary for the buyer's spouse to be present to sign documents, such as a promissory note. If spouses or other necessary signers (such as guarantors) won't be able to attend the closing in person, you and the buyer will have to get their signatures in advance or have them sign a power of attorney authorizing someone else to sign papers in their behalf. Under a power of attorney, the person authorized to sign documents is called an agent or, sometimes, an attorney-in-fact.

If you've never sold a business before—and even if you have—your lawyer's presence at the closing can be reassuring to you; it helps you know that you're doing everything correctly.

Chapter 18 discusses the format that individuals and entities should use to sign the sales agreement and other legal documents. Review your sales agreement to see who is committed to signing documents at the closing. Also, look at the documents you've attached to your sales agreement for other indications about who needs to sign at the closing.

2. When to Hold the Closing

It's best to schedule your closing on a weekday, because governmental offices, banks, and title companies are sure to be open and you may need to transact some final business with them on the day of closing. And morning is better than later in the day, because it gives you time to work out problems if something unexpected comes up.

If the last day of a month falls on a weekday, that can be a good time for a closing, since it makes it easier to prorate (divide) expenses, such as rent and taxes. For example, rent is typically due on the first day of a month. By closing on the last day of a month, you and the buyer won't have to fuss over how to allocate a month's rent. But, of course, you want to keep the importance of easy arithmetic in perspective. If you and the buyer are ready to close on the tenth of the month, it won't make sense to hold off for three weeks.

3. Where to Hold the Closing

If you or the buyer are planning to have a lawyer at the closing, you may be inclined to schedule the closing at the lawyer's office, if for no other reason than to avoid the cost of paying the lawyer to travel across town. Usually that's OK, but sometimes there are good reasons to hold the closing at your business place, assuming you have a quiet office large enough to accommodate several people and easy access to computers, copiers, and fax machines. If, for example, you'll be participating in a physical count of the inventory on the day of the closing or for some reason want to have business records at hand, your business place can be the best location.

If no lawyer will be involved in the closing, and your business location is not a good choice, find an alternate place that's quiet, private, and has a computer, printer, copier, and fax so you can easily tweak documents on the spot or, if necessary, even redraft some. Kinko's—the nationwide copy service—has excellent conference room facilities available at many locations. One of these can be an ideal place to close, since any needed business equipment is right there. Some hotel chains as well as many local chambers of commerce offer similar facilities. The cost is usually reasonable.

B. Documents for Transferring Assets

You and the buyer should agree on a customized closing checklist so you know that all the bases are covered. The items on a checklist will vary somewhat from business to business. Many—perhaps most—of them will be addressed in the sales agreement. For example, if you're selling the assets of your business on an installment plan, you'll find that Clause 13 refers to a promissory note and Clause 14 refers to a security agreement and UCC Financing Statement. Both clauses are discussed in Chapter 14. Likewise, if you're planning to work for the new owner after the closing, you'll see that Clause 22, Future Services, discussed in Chapter 16, refers to a consulting agreement or an employment contract. Also, look at Clause 25, Documents for Transferring Assets, in Chapter 17, which lists additional documents that will need to be signed.

Because no two sales are exactly alike, your closing checklist will be unique to your sale. Still, while it helps to see a master list of items that may be required for your closing, such as the Closing Checklist for an Asset Sale, below, remember that no compilation can be exhaustive. If you're selling your entity rather than the assets, see Section C, below, for a similar checklist.

Where to find the forms. You'll find copies of the Closing Checklist for an Asset Sale on the CD-ROM at the back of this book.

Many of the items in the master checklist are covered in detail elsewhere in this book and some items need no explanation, but there are a few that may not be familiar to you.

Insurance Certificates for the Policy Covering Secured Assets. The Security Agreement (discussed in Chapter 19) usually requires that the buyer carry property insurance that protects your interest in the secured assets. At closing, you want to see evidence that such insurance is in place.

Name Change Certificate for Assumed Name. You may have registered an assumed name or fictitious name for your business with a state or local official. If

Closing Checklist for an Asset Sale

[Check all those items that apply to your sale]

Items That Are Relatively Common

☐ Bill of Sale

☐ Cashier's Check

☐ Promissory Note

☐ Security Agreement

☐ UCC Financing Statement

☐ Asset Acquisition Statement (IRS Form 8594)

☐ Consent of Entity Owners to Sale of Assets

☐ Covenant Not to Compete

☐ Employment Contract

☐ Consulting Contract (Independent Contractor Agreement)

☐ Insurance Certificates for the Policy Covering Secured Assets

Items That Are Less Common

☐ Statement Regarding Absence of Creditors

☐ Assignment of Lease

☐ Assignment of Contracts

☐ Assignment of Intellectual Property

☐ Escrow Agreement for Post-Closing Adjustments

☐ Motor Vehicle Transfer Documents

☐ License Transfer Documents

☐ Real Estate Transfer Documents

☐ Title Insurance Commitment

☐ Mortgage or Deed of Trust

☐ Name Change Certificate for Assumed Names

☐ New Signature Cards for Bank Accounts

☐ Name Change Documents for Utility and Tax Bills

☐ Powers of Attorney for Absent Signers

Other Items

☐ Customer Lists

☐ Supplier Lists

☐ Trade Secrets

☐ Keys to Premises

☐ Alarm Codes

☐ Safe Combinations

☐ Computer Access Codes

☐ Keys to File Cabinets

☐ Keys to Vehicles

☐ Owner's Manuals for Equipment

your sales agreement calls for you to transfer the name to the buyer, you'll need to get a form from the registry clerk that you can use to list the buyer as the person or entity entitled to use the name.

New Signature Cards for Bank Accounts. Occasionally, a sales agreement will call for bank accounts to be transferred to the buyer. If so, you'll need to get forms from the bank to remove your name as a signer on the account and to list the buyer or buyer's managers as signers.

Name Change Documents for Utility and Tax Bills. Utility companies and tax officials need to know where to send bills in the future. Find out what documents they need to make the change, and have those documents available at the closing.

C. Documents for Transferring an Entity

As with asset sales, no two entity sales are exactly alike, so your closing checklist will be unique to your sale. The Closing Checklist for an Entity Sale, below, is a compilation of items that may be required for your closing though, understandably, this checklist is not exhaustive. The most common items are listed first, followed by items that are less likely to be on your personalized checklist.

Where to find the forms. You'll find copies of the Closing Checklist for an Entity Sale on the CD-ROM at the back of this book.

A few of the items on the master list may need a bit of explanation.

Corporate or LLC Record Book. Most corporations maintain an official record book (typically in a loose-leaf binder) that contains the articles of incorporation, the corporate bylaws, corporate resolutions and minutes, stock certificate records, and shareholder agreements. An LLC may have a similar record book or may have only a folder containing the articles of organization and the operating agreement. The new owners of the entity will undoubtedly want these records and, of course, are entitled to them. You should retain a photocopy in case legal questions come up later.

New Signature Cards for Bank Accounts. Unless your sales agreement excludes them, entity bank accounts remain the property of the entity. You'll need to get forms from the bank to remove your name as a signer on the account and to list the buyer or buyer's managers as signers.

See Section B, above, for an explanation of insurance certificates.

D. Handling Last-Minute Problems

Rarely is the closing process perfect. Even with the most thorough preparation, it's common for some fine-tuning of the closing documents to occur at the closing table. For example, a tax bill

Closing Checklist for an Entity Sale

[Check all those items that apply to your sale]

Items That Are Relatively Common

☐ Stock Certificates or LLC Membership Certificates

☐ Cashier's Check

☐ Promissory Note

☐ Security Agreement

☐ UCC Financing Statement

☐ Corporate or LLC Record Book

☐ Escrow Agreement for Stock Certificates or LLC Membership Certificates

☐ Change of Registered Agent

☐ Resignation of Directors and Officers

☐ Covenant Not to Compete

☐ Employment Contract

☐ Consulting Contract (Independent Contractor Agreement)

☐ Insurance Certificate for Policy Covering Secured Assets

Items That Are Less Common

☐ Mortgage or Deed of Trust to Secure Payment of Promissory Note

☐ New Signature Cards for Bank Accounts

☐ Powers of Attorney for Absent Signers

☐ Lease

☐ Contracts With Customers and Suppliers

☐ Landlord's Consent If Required by Lease

Other Items

☐ Customer Lists

☐ Supplier Lists

☐ Trade Secrets

☐ Keys to Premises

☐ Alarm Codes

☐ Safe Combinations

☐ Computer Access Codes

☐ Keys to File Cabinets

☐ Keys to Vehicles

☐ Owner's Manuals for Equipment

may not arrive until the last minute; at the closing, you may have to allocate the bill between you and the buyer as required by the sales agreement. Or you may have agreed in the sales contract to pay off some business debts out of the closing proceeds. In that case, the unpaid bills need to be examined, the amounts accounted for, and checks actually written and sent to the creditors. And if the sale price is based in part on the value of the inventory as the day of closing, you may need to make arrangements for the taking of a physical inventory—either right before or sometimes even during the closing.

E. Moving On

So the closing has been completed. You did it: You actually sold your business! You should feel proud that you carried out a complicated task with aplomb. True, no one will give you a trophy and your picture (probably) won't be on the cover of *Time,* but you do have the inner satisfaction of a job well done. And if you're like many another entrepreneur, you may even start thinking about starting the cycle over again by forming or buying another business. Whatever your future holds—whatever your dreams, whether they involve other businesses or not—I wish you well.

■

Appendix A

How to Use the CD-ROM

The asset and entity sales agreements discussed in Chapters 12 through 18 are included on a CD-ROM in the back of the book. This CD-ROM, which can be used with Windows computers, installs files that can be opened, printed, and edited using a word processor or other software. It is *not* a standalone software program. Please read this appendix and the README.TXT file included on the CD-ROM for instructions on using the Forms CD.

How to View the README File

If you do not know how to view the file README.TXT, insert the Forms CD-ROM into your computer's CD-ROM drive and follow these instructions:
- **Windows 9x, 2000, Me, and XP:** (1) On your PC's desktop, double click the My Computer icon; (2) double click the icon for the CD-ROM drive into which the Forms CD-ROM was inserted; (3) double click the file README.TXT.
- **Macintosh:** (1) On your Mac desktop, double click the icon for the CD-ROM that you inserted; (2) double click on the file README.TXT.

While the README file is open, print it out by using the Print command in the File menu.

Note to Mac users: This CD-ROM and its files should also work on Macintosh computers. Please note, however, that Nolo cannot provide technical support for non-Windows users.

Two different kinds of forms are contained on the CD-ROM:
- Word processing (RTF) forms that you can open, complete, print, and save with your word processing program (see Section B, below), and
- Forms from government agencies (PDF) that can be viewed only with Adobe Acrobat Reader 4.0 or higher. (See Section C, below.) Some of these forms have "fill-in" text fields and can be completed using your computer. You will not, however, be able to save the completed forms with the filled-in data. PDF forms without fill-in text fields must be printed out and filled in by hand or with a typewriter.

See the end of this appendix for a list of forms, their file names, and their file formats.

A. Installing the Form Files Onto Your Computer

Before you can do anything with the files on the CD-ROM, you need to install them onto your hard disk. In accordance with U.S. copyright laws, remember that copies of the CD-ROM and its files are for your personal use only.

Insert the Forms CD and do the following.

1. Windows 9x, 2000, Me, and XP Users

Follow the instructions that appear on the screen. (If nothing happens when you insert the Forms CD-ROM, then (1) double click the My Computer icon; (2) double click the icon for the CD-ROM drive into which the Forms CD-ROM was inserted; and (3) double click the file WELCOME.EXE.)

By default, all the files are installed to the \Business Sale Forms folder in the \Program Files folder of your computer. A folder called "Business Sale Forms" is added to the "Programs" folder of the Start menu.

2. Macintosh Users

Step 1: If the "Business Sale Forms CD" window is not open, open it by double clicking the "Business Sale Forms CD" icon.

Step 2: Select the "Business Sale Forms" folder icon.

Step 3: Drag and drop the folder icon onto the icon of your hard disk.

B. Using the Word Processing Files to Create Documents

This section concerns the files for forms that can be opened and edited with your word processing program.

All word processing forms come in rich text format. These files have the extension ".RTF." For example, the form for the Confidentiality Letter discussed in Chapter 10 is on the file Confidentiality. rtf. All forms, their file names, and their file formats are listed at the back of this appendix.

RTF files can be read by most recent word processing programs including all versions of MS Word for Windows and Macintosh, WordPad for Windows, and recent versions of WordPerfect for Windows and Macintosh.

To use a form from the CD to create your documents you must: (1) open a file in your word processor or text editor; (2) edit the form by filling in the required information; (3) print it out; (4) rename and save your revised file.

The following are general instructions. However, each word processor uses different commands to open, format, save, and print documents. Please read your word processor's manual for specific instructions on performing these tasks.

Do not call Nolo's technical support if you have questions on how to use your word processor.

Step 1: Opening a File

There are three ways to open the word processing files included on the CD-ROM after you have installed them onto your computer:

- Windows users can open a file by selecting its "shortcut" as follows: (1) Click the Windows "Start" button; (2) open the "Programs" folder; (3) open the "Business Sale Forms" subfolder; and (4) click on the shortcut to the form you want to work with.
- Both Windows and Macintosh users can open a file directly by double clicking on it. Use My Computer or Windows Explorer (Windows 9x, 2000, Me, or XP) or the Finder (Macintosh) to go to the folder you installed or copied the CD-ROM's files to. Then, double click on the specific file you want to open.
- You can also open a file from within your word processor. To do this, you must first start your word processor. Then, go to the File menu and choose the Open command. This opens a dialog box where you will tell the program (1) the type of file you want to open (*.RTF); and (2) the location and name of the file (you will need to navigate through the directory tree to get to the folder on your hard disk where the CD's files have been installed). If these directions are unclear, you will need to look through the manual for your word processing program—Nolo's technical support department will *not* be able to help you with the use of your word processing program.

Where Are the Files Installed?

Windows Users
- RTF files are installed by default to a folder named \Business Sale Forms in the \Program Files folder of your computer.

Macintosh Users
- RTF files are located in the "Business Sale Forms" folder.

Step 2: Editing Your Document

Fill in the appropriate information according to the instructions and sample agreements in the book. Underlines are used to indicate where you need to enter your information, frequently followed by instructions in brackets. Be sure to delete the underlines and instructions from your edited document. You will also want to make sure that any signature lines in your completed documents appear on a page with at least some text from the document itself. If you do not know how to use your word processor to edit a document, you will need to look through the manual for your word processing program— Nolo's technical support department will *not* be able to help you with the use of your word processing program.

Editing Forms That Have Optional or Alternative Text

Some of the forms have optional or alternate text:

- With optional text, you choose whether to include or exclude the given text.
- With alternative text, you select one alternative to include and exclude the other alternatives.

When editing these forms, we suggest you do the following.

Optional text

If you **don't want** to include optional text, just delete it from your document.

If you **do want** to include optional text, just leave it in your document.

In either case, delete the italicized instructions.

Note: If you choose not to include an optional numbered clause, be sure to renumber all the subsequent clauses after you delete it.

Alternative text

First delete all the alternatives that you do not want to include, then delete the italicized instructions.

Step 3: Printing Out the Document

Use your word processor's or text editor's "Print" command to print out your document. If you do not know how to use your word processor to print a document, you will need to look through the manual for your word processing program—Nolo's technical support department will *not* be able to help you with the use of your word processing program.

Step 4: Saving Your Document

After filling in the form, use the "Save As" command to save and rename the file. Because all the files are "read-only," you will not be able to use the "Save" command. This is for your protection. *If you save the file without renaming it, the underlines that indicate where you need to enter your information will be lost, and you will not be able to create a new document with this file without recopying the original file from the CD-ROM.*

If you do not know how to use your word processor to save a document, you will need to look through the manual for your word processing program—Nolo's technical support department will *not* be able to help you with the use of your word processing program.

C. Using PDF Forms

Electronic copies of useful forms from government agencies are included on the CD-ROM in Adobe Acrobat PDF format. You must have the Adobe Reader installed on your computer to use these forms. Adobe Reader is available for all types of Windows and Macintosh systems. If you don't already have this software, you can download it for free at www .adobe.com.

All forms, their file names, and their file formats are listed at the back of this appendix. These form files were created by government agencies, not by Nolo.

These forms have fill-in text fields. To create your document using these files, you must: (1) open a file; (2) fill in the text fields using either your mouse or the Tab key on your keyboard to navigate from field to field; and (3) print it out.

NOTE: While you can print out your completed form, you will NOT be able to save your completed form to disk.

Step 1: Opening a Form

PDF files, like the word processing files, can be opened one of three ways.

- Windows users can open a file by selecting its "shortcut" as follows: (1) Click the Windows "Start" button; (2) open the "Programs" folder; (3) open the "Business Sale Forms" subfolder; and (4) click on the shortcut to the form you want to work with.
- Both Windows and Macintosh users can open a file directly by double clicking on it. Use My Computer or Windows Explorer (Windows 9x, 2000, Me, or XP) or the Finder (Macintosh) to go to the folder you created and copied the CD-ROM's files to. Then, double click on the specific file you want to open.

- You can also open a PDF file from within Adobe Reader. To do this, you must first start Reader. Then, go to the File menu and choose the Open command. This opens a dialog box where you will tell the program the location and name of the file (you will need to navigate through the directory tree to get to the folder on your hard disk where the CD's files have been installed). If these directions are unclear, you will need to look through Adobe Reader's help—Nolo's technical support department will *not* be able to help you with the use of Adobe Reader.

Where Are the PDF Files Installed?

- **Windows Users:** PDF files are installed by default to a folder named \Business Sale Forms in the \Program Files folder of your computer.
- **Macintosh Users:** PDF files are located in the "Business Sale Forms" folder.

Step 2: Filling in a Form

Use your mouse or the Tab key on your keyboard to navigate from field to field within these forms. Be sure to have all the information you will need to complete a form on hand, because you will not be able to save a copy of the filled-in form to disk. You can, however, print out a completed version.

Step 3: Printing a Form

Choose Print from the Acrobat Reader File menu. This will open the Print dialog box. In the "Print Range" section of the Print dialog box, select the appropriate print range, then click OK.

Forms Included on the CD-ROM

These forms are shown within the chapters of this book and are the Forms CD.

Form	File Name	Chapter
IRS 8594, Asset Acquisition Statement and Instructions	f8594.pdf	3
Confidentiality Letter	Confidentiality.rtf	9
Attachment to Sales Agreement	Attachment.rtf	11
Amendment of Sales Agreement	Amendment.rtf	11
Promissory Note	PromissoryNote.rtf	18
Security Agreement for Asset Sale	AssetSecurity.rtf	18
Security Agreement for Entity Sale	EntitySecurity.rtf	18
UCC Financial Statement and Addendum	ra_9_ucc-1.pdf	18
Escrow Agreement for Stock Certificates	StockEscrow.rtf	18
Escrow Agreement for LLC Transfer Certificates	LLCEscrow.rtf	18
Bill of Sale for Business Assets	BillSale.rtf	19
Statement Regarding Absence of Creditors	CreditorsStatement.rtf	19
Assignment of Lease	LeaseAssignment.rtf	19
Assignment of Contracts	ContractsAssignment.rtf	19
Consent to Assignment of Contract	AssignmentConsent.rtf	19
Assignment of Intellectual Property	IPAssignment.rtf	19
Directors' Consent to the Corporation's Sale of a Business	DirectorConsent.rtf	19
Shareholders' Consent to the Corporation's Sale of a Business	ShareholderConsent.rtf	19

Sales Agreement Clauses

The files of clauses for assembling sales agreements for an asset sale and an entity sale are included on the Forms CD.

Appendix B

Sample Sales Agreements

Sample # 1

Asset Sale of a Restaurant by One Sole Proprietor to Another

Sales Agreement

1. Names

Peter Hanson doing business as Pete's Place (Seller) and Martha Wentworth (Buyer) agree to the following sale.

2. Sale of Business Assets

Seller is selling to Buyer and Buyer is buying from Seller the assets described below of the restaurant business known as Pete's Place located at 234 Morley Circle, Chesterfield, Ohio.

3. Assets Being Sold

The assets being sold consist of:

A. The goodwill of the business, including the current business name and phone number.

B. The lease dated July 1, 2005, between Seller as Tenant, and Property Central LLC, Landlord, covering the premises at 234 Morley Circle, Chesterfield, Ohio for the time period from July 1, 2005 to June 30, 2007.

C. The inventory of food and beverages.

D. The furniture, fixtures, and equipment listed in Attachment A.

E. The equipment leases listed in Attachment B.

F. The supply contract with Western Ohio Provision Company.

G. Intellectual property rights, as follows: rights to all menus and all advertising materials of the business, including all copyrights in those items; the trademarked logo of the business; and the complete recipe file.

The following assets of the business are excluded from the sale:

1. The computer located in the office area.

2. Accounts receivable.

3. The sound system and CD collection.

4. Sale Price

The sale price for the assets listed in this section is $25,000.00 and is allocated as follows:

A. Goodwill	$ 5,000.00
B. Furniture, Fixtures, and Equipment	15,000.00
C. Assignment of Equipment Leases	1,000.00
D. Assignment of Supply Contract	1,500.00
E. Intellectual Property Rights	2,500.00
Total	$ 25,000.00

The total sale price will be adjusted by prorating rent, taxes, insurance premiums, utility costs, and security deposits as of the date of closing.

The total sale price will also be adjusted by adding the value of the inventory as covered in Clause 5.

5. Price of Inventory

At closing, in addition to the total sale price listed in Clause 4 above, Buyer will buy the inventory of food and beverages by paying Seller the amount Seller paid for the food and beverages, as shown in the original invoices. A physical count of the food and beverages will be made by Seller and Buyer one day before closing. Buyer will pay no more than $4,000.00 for the food and beverages.

6. Accounts Receivable

Seller's accounts receivable as of the day of closing will remain Seller's property. Buyer will have no responsibility for collecting those accounts. Seller will have the right to collect those accounts and to keep the amounts received.

7. Deposit

Buyer will pay Seller a deposit of $1,000.00 when Buyer and Seller sign this contract. This deposit will be applied toward the amount due at closing. Seller will return this deposit to Buyer if the purchase is not completed because Seller cannot or does not meet his commitments under this agreement for any reason or if the contingencies in Clause 15 are not removed. Otherwise, Seller will be entitled to retain the deposit in the event the sale is not completed.

8. Payment at Closing

At closing, Buyer will pay Seller 20% of the adjusted sale price. The deposit referred to in Clause 7 will be applied toward the 20% payment. The rest of the closing payment will be made by cashier's check or wire transfer. The balance of the sale price will be paid as described in Clause 9.

9. Promissory Note

At closing, Buyer will sign and give to Seller a promissory note for the balance of the sale price. The promissory note will be in the form of Attachment C. The following person will sign the promissory note along with Buyer: Buyer's husband, Jack Wentworth. Each signer will be jointly and individually liable for payment.

10. Security for Payment

At closing, to secure payment of the promissory note referred to in Clause 9, Buyer will sign a security agreement as shown in Attachment D giving Seller a security interest in the assets that Buyer is buying. Seller will have the right to file a UCC Financing Statement with regard to the security pledged.

Buyer will further secure the promissory note by giving Seller a second mortgage on the home located at 123 Oak Street, Chesterfield, Ohio for the loan balance. Buyer will provide to Seller, at Buyer's expense, a title insurance policy insuring the mortgage.

11. Seller's Debts and Other Liabilities

Buyer is not assuming any of Seller's debts or other liabilities. Seller will pay all debts and other liabilities, whether now known or unknown, that are or may become a lien on the assets being bought by Buyer.

Seller and his wife, Emily Hanson, will indemnify, defend, and save Buyer harmless from and against all debts and other liabilities arising out of the Seller's ownership or use of the assets before closing.

Buyer and her husband, Jack Wentworth, will indemnify, defend, and save Seller harmless from and against all debts and other liabilities arising out of the Buyer's ownership or use of the assets after closing.

At closing, Seller will confirm in a Statement Regarding Absence of Creditors (Attachment E) that Seller has paid all known debts and other liabilities of the business.

12. Seller's Representations

Seller represents and warrants that:

  A. Seller owns the assets being sold. At closing, the assets will be free from any claims of others.

  B. At closing, Seller will have paid all taxes that have then come due and that affect the business and its assets.

C. To the best of Seller's knowledge, there are no judgments, claims, liens, or proceedings pending against Seller, the business, or the assets being sold, and to the best of the seller's knowledge, none will be pending at closing.

D. To the best of Seller's knowledge, the business and financial information in the financial statement dated June 30, 20XX that Seller has given Buyer is accurate.

E. Until closing, Seller will operate the business in the normal manner and will use his best efforts to maintain the goodwill of suppliers, customers, the landlord, and others having business relationships with Seller.

F. To the best of Seller's knowledge, the current uses of the Seller's business premises are permitted under the applicable zoning laws. To the best of Seller's knowledge, the business premises presently (and at closing will) meet all applicable health, safety, and disabled access requirements and are (and at closing will be) in good repair.

G. To the best of Seller's knowledge, the tangible assets are (and at closing will be) in good repair and good operating condition.

These representations and warranties will survive the closing.

Seller and his wife Emily Hanson will indemnify, defend, and save Buyer harmless from and against any financial loss, legal liability, damage, or expense arising from any breach of the above representations and warranties.

13. Buyer's Representations

Buyer represents and warrants that:

A. Buyer has inspected the tangible assets that Buyer is purchasing and the leased premises and has carefully reviewed Seller's representations regarding them. Buyer is satisfied with the physical condition of the tangible assets and the premises.

B. To the best of Seller's knowledge, the business and financial information in the financial statement dated June 30, 20XX that Buyer has given Seller is accurate.

These representations and warranties will survive the closing.

Buyer and her husband Jack Wentworth will indemnify, defend, and save Seller harmless from and against any loss, legal liability, damage, or expense arising from any breach of the above representations and warranties.

14. Covenant Not to Compete

At closing, Seller will sign and deliver to Buyer a covenant not to compete in the form of Attachment F, and Buyer will pay Seller the amounts specified in the attached covenant not to compete.

15. Contingencies

This sale is contingent on Buyer and the landlord negotiating and signing a five-year lease satisfactory to Buyer for the premises currently occupied by the business. If Buyer has not signed such a lease within 15 days from the signing of this agreement, Buyer can cancel this sale by notifying Seller in writing. In that case, Seller will promptly refund the deposit to Buyer. If Buyer does not notify Seller of a cancellation within 20 days from the signing of this agreement, the agreement will remain in effect.

This sale is further contingent on the Ohio Liquor Board's approving a transfer of Seller's liquor license to Buyer. If within 21 days from the signing of this agreement the Board does not approve the transfer, Buyer can cancel this sale by notifying Seller in writing. In that case, Seller will promptly refund the deposit to Buyer. If Buyer does not notify Seller of a cancellation within 23 days from the signing of this agreement, the agreement will remain in effect.

16. Closing

The closing will take place:

> Date: Thursday, September 30, 20XX
> Time: 9:00 a.m.
> Location: The restaurant premises at 234 Morley Circle.

At closing, Buyer and Buyer's husband, Jack Wentworth, and Seller and Seller's wife, Emily Hanson, will sign the documents specified in this contract and all other documents reasonably needed to transfer the business assets to Buyer. Buyer will pay Seller the amounts required by this contract and Seller will transfer the business assets to Buyer.

17. Documents for Transferring Assets

At closing, Seller will deliver to Buyer these signed documents:

> A. A bill of sale for the tangible assets being sold, including a warranty of good title.

B. An assignment of the supply contract with the written consent of the other contracting person, if such consent is required.

C. Assignments of all copyrights that are part of this purchase, and all other intellectual property.

D. Assignment of the Class C liquor license in the form required by the Alcoholic Beverages Commission.

Seller will also deliver to Buyer at closing all other documents reasonably needed to transfer the business assets to Buyer.

18. Disputes

If a dispute arises concerning this agreement or the sale, Seller and Buyer will try in good faith to settle it through mediation conducted by a mediator to be mutually selected. Seller and Buyer will share the cost of the mediator equally. Seller and Buyer will cooperate fully with the mediator and will attempt to reach a mutually satisfactory resolution of the dispute.

If the dispute is not resolved within 60 days after it is referred to the mediator, it will be arbitrated by an arbitrator to be mutually selected. Judgment on the arbitration award may be entered in any court that has jurisdiction over the matter. Costs of arbitration, including lawyers' fees, will be allocated by the arbitrator.

19. Risk of Loss

Seller will replace or pay for the replacement of any assets that are destroyed or damaged before the closing.

20. Entire Agreement

This is the entire agreement between the parties. It replaces and supersedes any oral agreements between the parties, as well as any prior writings.

21. Modification

This agreement may be modified only by a written amendment signed by both parties.

22. Governing Law

This agreement will be governed by and interpreted under the laws of the state of Ohio, and any litigation regarding this agreement or its attachments will be brought in the courts of that state.

23. Severability

If a court or arbitrator determines that a provision in this agreement is invalid or not enforceable, that determination will affect only that provision. The provision will be modified only to the extent needed to make it valid and enforceable. The rest of the agreement will be unaffected.

24. Notices

All notices must be sent in writing. A notice may be delivered to a person at the address that follows the person's signature or to a new address that the person designates in writing. A notice may be delivered:

    A. in person,

    B. by certified mail, or

    C. by overnight courier.

25. Required Signatures

This agreement is valid only if signed by Seller, Buyer, and their respective spouses.

Seller:

_____

Peter Hanson doing business as
Pete's Place
234 Morley Circle
Chesterfield, Ohio

Dated: _____

Buyer:

_____

Martha Wentworth
241 Argo Drive
Chesterfield, Ohio

Dated: _____

Consent of Spouses:

I am married to the Seller. I consent to the sale described above, and I waive any interest in the business assets. I agree to the indemnity provisions of Clauses 11 and 12.

_____

Emily Hanson

I am married to the Buyer. In consideration of Seller extending credit to Buyer for the purchase of the business assets described above, I agree to cosign or personally guarantee the promissory note to be given by Buyer to Seller. I agree to the indemnity provisions of Clauses 11 and 13.

_____

Jack Wentworth

Sample #2

Entity Sale of a Bookstore by the Two Shareholders to an Individual

Sales Agreement

1. Names

Nora Romano and Eileen Nordby (Sellers) and Karl Brandon (Buyer) agree to the following sale.

2. Sale of Corporate Stock

Sellers are selling to Buyer and Buyer is buying from Sellers all of the Sellers' stock of The Reader's Corner Inc., a Pennsylvania corporation.

3. Sale Price

The sale price of the stock is $75,000.

4. Adjustment of Sale Price

The day before the closing, a physical count of the inventory will be made by Inventory Service Associates, with the cost of the count being shared equally by Seller and Buyer. The sale price is based on the corporation's inventory having a wholesale value of $40,000 as shown on the original invoices. If the count discloses that the inventory is worth more or less than that amount, the sale price will be adjusted downward by the amount the inventory is worth less than $40,000 or upward by the amount the inventory value exceeds $40,000.

Likewise, the sale price is also based on the corporation having accounts receivable totaling $10,000. If at closing the accounts receivable are more or less than that amount, the sale price will be adjusted downward by the amount the accounts receivable are less than $10,000 or upward by the amount the accounts exceed $10,000.

5. Corporate Debts and Liabilities

Sellers will pay the $3,000 obligation that the corporation owes to Keystone Cabinetry.

Sellers will indemnify, defend, and save Buyer harmless from and against any other debts and liabilities of the corporation to the extent that such debts and other liabilities are known to Sellers and Sellers have failed to disclose them to Buyer.

6. Deposit

Buyer will pay Sellers a deposit of $5,000 when Buyer and Sellers sign this contract. This deposit will be applied toward the amount due at closing. Sellers will return this deposit to Buyer if the purchase is not completed because Sellers cannot or do not meet their commitments for any reason. Otherwise, Sellers will be entitled to retain the deposit in the event the sale is not completed.

7. Payment at Closing

At closing, Buyer will pay Sellers 20% of the adjusted sale price. The deposit referred to in Clause 6 will be applied toward the 20% payment. The rest of the closing payment will be made by a cashier's check or wire transfer. The balance of the sale price with be paid as described in Clause 8

8. Promissory Note

At closing, Buyer will sign and give to Sellers a promissory note for the balance of the sale price. The promissory note will be in the form of Attachment A. The following person will sign the promissory note in addition to Buyer: Buyer's wife, Felicia Brandon. Each signer will be jointly and individually liable for payment.

9. Security for Payment

At closing, to secure payment of the promissory note, Buyer will cause the corporation to sign a security agreement as shown in Attachment B. Seller will have the right to file a UCC financing statement giving Sellers a security interest in the assets of the corporation.

Buyer will further secure the promissory note by giving Sellers a second mortgage on the home located at 123 Trail Wood Road, Terrance, Pennsylvania. Buyer will provide to Sellers, at Buyer's expense, a title insurance policy insuring the mortgage.

Until the promissory note referred to in Clause 8 is fully paid, Buyer will not sell the corporate shares. The certificates representing the shares will be held in escrow by Pine Trust Company. At closing, Sellers and Buyer will sign an escrow agreement in the form of Attachment C.

10. Lease of Business Premises

Sellers own the building at 345 Allerton, Terrance, Pennsylvania in which the business of the corporation is currently located. At closing, Sellers and Buyer will sign a

Lease with Option to Purchase in the form of Attachment D. Buyer's wife, Felicia Brandon, will cosign the lease.

11. Seller's Representations

Sellers represent and warrant that:

A. The entity is (and at closing will be) a corporation in good standing under the laws of the state of Pennsylvania.

B. The shares being sold constitute all of the issued shares of the entity. No additional shares will be issued before the closing. At closing, the shares will be free from any claims of any persons or entities other than Sellers.

C. At closing, the corporation will have paid all taxes that have then come due and that affect the business and its assets.

D. To the best of Sellers' knowledge, there are no judgments, claims, liens, or proceedings pending against the corporation or its assets being sold except for those already disclosed to Buyer, and to the best of the Sellers' knowledge, there will be no others pending at closing.

E. To the best of Sellers' knowledge, the business and financial information in the financial statement dated June 30, 20XX that Sellers have given Buyer is accurate.

F. Until closing, Sellers will operate the corporation in the normal manner, and will use their best efforts to maintain the good will of suppliers, customers, and others having business relationships with the corporation.

G. To the best of Sellers' knowledge, the current uses of the corporation's business premises are permitted under the applicable zoning laws. To the best of Sellers' knowledge, the premises presently (and at closing will) meet all applicable health, safety, and disabled access requirements and are (and at closing will be) in good repair.

H. To the best of Sellers' knowledge, the tangible assets of the corporation are (and at closing will be) in good repair and good operating condition.

I. To the best of Sellers' knowledge, the corporation is (and at closing will be) in compliance with all environmental laws. To the best of Sellers' knowledge, there are (and at closing will be) no hazardous materials on the business premises that may be a source of future liability under the environmental laws.

These representations and warranties will survive the closing.

Sellers will indemnify, defend, and save Buyer harmless from and against any financial loss, legal liability, damage, or expense arising from any breach of the above representations and warranties.

12. Buyer's Representations

Buyer represents and warrants that:

A. Buyer has inspected the tangible assets of the corporation that Buyer is purchasing and the leased premises and has carefully reviewed Sellers' representations regarding them. Buyer is satisfied with the physical condition of the tangible assets and the premises.

B. To the best of Buyer's knowledge, the business and financial information in the financial statement dated June 30, 20XX that Buyer has given Sellers is accurate.

These representations and warranties will survive the closing.

Buyer and his wife, Felicia Brandon, will indemnify, defend, and save Sellers harmless from and against any financial loss, legal liability, damage, or expense arising from any breach of the above representations and warranties.

13. Covenant Not to Compete

At closing, each Seller will sign and deliver to Buyer a covenant not to compete in the form of Attachment E, and Buyer will pay each Seller the amounts specified in the covenant not to compete.

14. Future Services

At closing, Seller, Nora Romano, and the corporation will sign an employment agreement in the form of Attachment F, and Seller, Karl Brandon, and the corporation will sign an independent contractor (consulting) agreement in the form of Attachment G.

15. Closing

The closing will take place:

Date: Thursday, September 30, 20XX
Time: 9:00 a.m.
Location: The bookstore premises at 345 Allterton

At closing, Buyer and Buyer's wife, Felicia Brandon, and the Sellers will sign the documents specified in this contract and all other documents reasonably needed to transfer the corporate shares assets to Buyer. Buyer will pay Sellers the amounts required by this contract and Sellers will place the share certificates with the escrow agent as provided in Clause 9 above.

16. Closing Documents

At closing, Sellers will deliver to Buyer these signed documents:

A. Stock certificates endorsed in blank, along with the escrow agreement.

B. The Lease With Option to Purchase.

C. The corporate record book.

D. Resignations of corporate officers.

Sellers will also deliver to Buyer at closing all other documents reasonably needed to transfer the entity to Buyer.

17. Disputes

If a dispute arises concerning this agreement or the sale, Sellers and Buyer will try in good faith to settle it through mediation conducted by a mediator to be mutually selected. Seller and Buyer will share the cost of the mediator equally. Sellers and Buyer will cooperate fully with the mediator and will attempt to reach a mutually satisfactory resolution of the dispute.

If the dispute is not resolved within 60 days after it is referred to the mediator, it will be arbitrated by an arbitrator to be mutually selected. Judgment on the arbitration award may be entered in any court that has jurisdiction over the matter. Costs of arbitration, including lawyers' fees, will be allocated by the arbitrator.

18. Risk of Loss

Sellers will replace or pay for the replacement of any corporate assets that are destroyed or damaged before the closing.

19. Entire Agreement

This is the entire agreement between the parties. It replaces and supersedes any oral agreements between the parties, as well as any prior writings.

20. Modification

This agreement may be modified only by a written amendment signed by all parties.

21. Governing Law

This agreement will be governed by and interpreted under the laws of the state of Pennsylvania, and any litigation regarding this agreement or its attachments will be brought in the courts of that state.

22. Severability

If a court or arbitrator determines that a provision in this agreement is invalid or not enforceable, that determination will affect only that provision. The provision will be modified only to the extent needed to make it valid and enforceable. The rest of the agreement will be unaffected.

23. Notices

All notices must be sent in writing. A notice may be delivered to a person at the address that follows the person's signature or to a new address that the person designates in writing. A notice may be delivered:

    A. in person,

    B. by certified mail, or

    C. by overnight courier.

24. Required Signatures

This agreement is valid only if signed by Sellers, the Buyer, and their respective spouses.

Sellers:

_____   _____
Nora Romano   Eileen Nordby
567 Hartley Way   654 McKinley Parkway
Terrance, Pennsylvania   Terrance, Pennsylvania

Dated: _____   Dated: _____

Buyer:

_____
Karl Brandon
351 Barton Pike
Terrance, Pennsylvania

Dated: _____

Consent of Spouses:

I am married to Nora Romano, one of the Sellers. I consent to the sale described above, and I waive any interest in the corporate shares.

_____

Timothy Romano

I am married to Eileen Nordby, one of the Sellers. I consent to the sale described above, and I waive any interest in the corporate shares.

_____

Jeffrey Nordby

I am married to the Buyer. In consideration of Sellers extending credit to Buyer for the purchase of the corporate shares described above, I agree to cosign or personally guarantee the promissory note to be given by Buyer to Sellers and to cosign the lease. I agree to the indemnity provisions of Clause 12.

_____

Felicia Brandon

Sample # 3

Asset Sale of a Landscaping Business by a Single-Owner LLC to a Partnership

Sales Agreement

1. Names

Martin Services LLC, a Colorado Limited Liability Company, doing business as Custom Green (Seller), and Boulder Enterprises, a Colorado Partnership (Buyer), agree to the following sale.

2. Sale of Business Assets

Seller is selling to Buyer and Buyer is buying from Seller the assets described below of the landscaping business known as Custom Green located at 345 Manchester Drive, Boulder, Colorado.

3. Assets Being Sold

The assets being sold consist of:

A. The goodwill of the business, including the business name Custom Green and the company's current phone number.

B. The furniture, fixtures, and equipment listed in Attachment A.

C. The ongoing customer contracts listed in Attachment B.

D. The lease dated September 1, 2005, between Seller as Tenant and Commercial Associates Inc. as Landlord for the premises at 345 Manchester Drive, Boulder, Colorado for the time period from September 1, 2005 to August 30, 2007.

F. Intellectual property rights, as follows: All rights to the copyrighted booklets, "What Every Homeowner Should Know about Landscaping" and "What Every Commercial Property Owner Should Know about Landscaping"; all rights to the patented "Kwik Green-up System" described in Attachment C; and the trademarked logo of the business.

4. Sale Price

The sale price for the assets listed in this section is $200,000.00 and is allocated as follows:

A. Goodwill	$ 50,000.00
B. Furniture, Fixtures, and Equipment	100,000.00
C. Assignment of Equipment Leases	5,000.00
D. Assignment of Supply Contract	35,000.00
E. Intellectual Property Rights	10,000.00
Total	$200,000.00

The total sale price will be adjusted by prorating rent, taxes, insurance premiums, utility costs, and security deposits as of the date of closing.

The total sale price will also be adjusted by adding the value of the accounts receivable as covered in Clause 5.

5. Accounts Receivable

At closing, Buyer will purchase all of Seller's accounts receivable. Buyer will pay Seller the balances owed on these accounts (as jointly determined by Buyer and Seller) less 35%. Buyer will be entitled to keep all sums collected on these accounts.

6. Deposit

Buyer will pay Seller a deposit of $10,000.00 when Buyer and Seller sign this contract. This deposit will be applied toward the amount due at closing. Seller will return this deposit to Buyer if the purchase is not completed because Seller cannot or does not meet its commitments under this agreement for any reason. Otherwise, Seller will be entitled to retain the deposit in the event the sale is not completed.

7. Payment at Closing

At closing, Buyer will pay Seller 30% of the adjusted sale price. The deposit referred to in Clause 6 will be applied toward the 30% payment. The rest of the closing payment will be made by cashier's check or wire transfer. The balance of the sale price will be paid as described in Clause 8.

8. Promissory Note

At closing, Buyer will sign and give to Seller a promissory note for the balance of the sale price. The promissory note will be in the form of Attachment D. The following people will sign the promissory note in addition to Buyer: each partner of Boulder Enterprises along with their spouses. Each signer will be jointly and individually liable for payment.

9. Security for Payment

At closing, to secure the payment of the promissory note, Buyer will sign a security agreement as shown in Attachment E giving Seller a security interest in the assets that Buyer is buying. Seller will have the right to file a UCC financing statement with regard to the security pledged.

10. Seller's Debts and Other Liabilities

Buyer will pay the following debts of the business that arose out of Seller's ownership and use of the assets before the closing:

- The $10,000 balance owed to First Finance Associates for the Durango truck.
- The $5,000 balance owed to First Finance Associates for the tree-trimming machine.

Any other debts and liabilities arising out Seller's ownership or use of the assets before closing will be paid by Seller.

Seller and its owner, Larry T. Martin, will indemnify, defend, and save Buyer harmless from and against all debts and other liabilities that Seller has agreed to pay.

Buyer and each of its partners will indemnify, defend, and save Seller harmless from and against all debts and other liabilities that Buyer has agreed to pay and any debts or liabilities arising out of the Buyer's ownership or use of the assets after closing.

11. Seller's Representations

Seller represents and warrants that:

- A. Seller owns the assets being sold. At closing, the assets will be free from any claims of others.
- B. At closing, Seller will have paid all taxes that have then come due and that affect the business and its assets.
- C. To the best of Seller's knowledge, except for the liens of First Finance Associates in connection with the equipment balance specified in Clause 10, there are no judgments, claims, liens, or proceedings pending against assets

being sold, and to the best of the seller's knowledge, none will be pending at closing.

D. To the best of Seller's knowledge, the business and financial information in the financial statement dated June 30, 20XX that Seller has given Buyer is accurate.

E. Until closing, Seller will operate the business in the normal manner and will use his best efforts to maintain the goodwill of suppliers, customers, the landlord, and others having business relationships with Seller.

F. To the best of Seller's knowledge, the tangible assets are (and at closing will be) in good repair and good operating condition.

G. Seller is (and at closing will be) a limited liability company in good standing under the laws of the state of Colorado and has (and at closing will have) the authority to perform the obligations contained in this sales agreement.

These representations and warranties will survive the closing.

Seller and its owner, Larry T. Martin, indemnify, defend, and save Buyer harmless from and against any financial loss, legal liability, damage, or expense arising from any breach of the above representations and warranties.

12. Buyer's Representations

Buyer represents and warrants that:

A. Buyer has inspected the tangible assets that Buyer is purchasing and the leased premises and has carefully reviewed Seller's representations regarding them. Buyer is satisfied with the physical condition of the tangible assets and the premises.

B. To the best of Buyer's knowledge, the business and financial information in the financial statement dated June 30, 20XX that Buyer has given Seller is accurate.

These representations and warranties will survive the closing.

Buyer and its two partners will indemnify, defend, and save Seller harmless from and against any financial loss, legal liability, damage, or expense arising from any breach of the above representations and warranties.

13. Covenant Not to Compete

Following the closing, Seller will no longer engage in the landscaping business in the state of Colorado. At closing, Larry T. Martin will sign and deliver to Buyer a covenant not to compete in the form of Attachment F, and Buyer will pay him the amounts specified in the covenant.

14. Future Services

At closing, Buyer and Larry T. Martin will sign an independent contractor agreement in the form of Attachment G.

15. Contingencies

This sale is contingent on Seller providing Buyer with written confirmation from the Boulder Parks and Recreation Board that the Centennial Square contract is fully transferable to Buyer. If Seller has not proved such confirmation to Buyer within 15 days from the signing of this agreement, Buyer can cancel this sale by notifying Seller in writing. In that case, Seller will promptly refund the deposit to Buyer. If Buyer does not notify Seller of a cancellation within 20 days from the signing of this agreement, the agreement will remain in effect.

16. Closing

The closing will take place:

Date: Thursday, September 30, 20XX
Time: 9:00 a.m.
Location: The offices of Seller's lawyers (Bryant and Chodak) at 567 Commerce Drive

At closing, Buyer and Buyer's partners, Seller and Seller's owner, Larry T. Martin, will sign the documents specified in this contract and all other documents reasonably needed to transfer the business assets to Buyer. Buyer will pay Seller the amounts required by this contract and Seller will transfer the business assets to Buyer.

17. Documents for Transferring Assets

At closing, Seller will deliver to Buyer these signed documents:

A. A bill of sale for the tangible assets being sold, including a warranty of good title.

B. Motor vehicle transfer documents for all registered vehicles being transferred.

C. An assignment of the customer contracts with the written consent of the other contracting person, if such consent is required.

D. An assignment of the lease at 345 Manchester Drive and of all accounts receivable.

E. Assignments of all copyrights and patents that are part of this purchase and all other intellectual property.

Seller will also deliver to Buyer at closing all other documents reasonably needed to transfer the business assets to Buyer.

18. Disputes

If a dispute arises concerning this agreement or the sale, Seller and Buyer will try in good faith to settle it through mediation conducted by the Boulder Mediation Center.

Seller and Buyer will share the cost of the mediator equally. Seller and Buyer will cooperate fully with the mediator and will attempt to reach a mutually satisfactory resolution of the dispute. If the dispute is not resolved within 60 days after it is referred to the mediator, either party may take the matter to court.

19. Risk of Loss

Seller will replace or pay for the replacement of any assets that are destroyed or damaged before the closing.

20. Entire Agreement

This is the entire agreement between the parties. It replaces and supersedes any oral agreements between the parties, as well as any prior writings.

21. Modification

This agreement may be modified only by a written amendment signed by both parties.

22. Governing Law

This agreement will be governed by and interpreted under the laws of the state of Colorado, and any litigation will be brought in the courts of that state.

23. Severability

If a court or arbitrator determines that a provision in this agreement is invalid or not enforceable, that determination will affect only that provision. The provision will be modified only to the extent needed to make it valid and enforceable. The rest of the agreement will be unaffected.

24. Notices

All notices must be sent in writing. A notice may be delivered to a person at the address that follows the person's signature or to a new address that the person designates in writing. A notice may be delivered:

A. in person,

B. by certified mail, or

C. by overnight courier.

25. Required Signatures

This agreement is valid only if signed by Seller, its owner Larry T. Martin, Buyer, Buyer's partners, and the spouses of each partner.

Seller:

Martin Services LLC
A Colorado Limited Liability Company

By: _____

    Larry T. Martin
    Member
    987 Sky High Avenue
    Boulder, Colorado

Dated: _____

Buyer:

Boulder Enterprises
A Colorado Partnership

By: _____

    Norris Kwan
    Partner
    765 Dexter Avenue
    Boulder, Colorado

Dated: _____

Consent of Seller's Owner:

I am the Seller's sole member. I approve of and consent to the sale described in the above agreement.

In addition, in consideration of Buyer entering into this agreement with Seller, I agree to:

1. Indemnify, defend, and save Buyer harmless from and against the debts and other liabilities which, under this agreement, are the responsibility of Seller.

2. Indemnify, defend, and save Buyer harmless from and against any loss, liability, damage, or expense arising from any breach of the above representations and warranties made by Seller.

3. Sign the noncompete document required by this agreement.

4. Sign and honor the consulting document required by this agreement.

_____

Larry T. Martin

Consent of Buyer's Owners:

We are all of the Buyer's partners. Each of us approves of and consents to the purchase described in the above agreement.

In addition, in consideration of Seller entering into this agreement with Buyer, each of us agrees to:

1. Cosign or personally guarantee the promissory note to be given by Buyer to Seller under this agreement.

2. Indemnify, defend, and save Seller harmless from and against the debts and other liabilities which, under this agreement, are the responsibility of Buyer.

3. Indemnify, defend, and save Seller harmless from and against any loss, liability, damage, or expense arising from any breach of the above representations and warranties made by Buyer.

_____   _____

Norris Kwan   Nina Costanides

Consent of Spouses:

I am married to Larry T. Martin. I consent to the sale described above, and I waive any interest in the business assets, whether under the community property laws or otherwise. I agree to the indemnity provisions of Clauses 10 and 11.

_____

Mindy Martin

I am married to Norris Kwan, one of the Buyer's partners. In consideration of Seller extending credit to Buyer for the purchase of the business assets described above, I agree to cosign or personally guarantee the promissory note to be given by Buyer to Seller.

_____

Estelle Kwan

I am married to Nina Costanides, one of the Buyer's partners. In consideration of Seller extending credit to Buyer for the purchase of the business assets described above, I agree to cosign or personally guarantee the promissory note to be given by Buyer to Seller.

_____

Peter Costanides

Index

A

B

Remember:

Little publishers have big ears.
We really listen to you.

Take 2 Minutes & Give Us Your 2 cents

Your comments make a big difference in the development and revision of Nolo books and software. Please take a few minutes and register your Nolo product—and your comments—with us. Not only will your input make a difference, you'll receive special offers available only to registered owners of Nolo products on our newest books and software. Register now by:

PHONE
1-800-728-3555

FAX
1-800-645-0895

EMAIL
cs@nolo.com

or **MAIL** us
this registration card

- - - - - - - - - - - - - - - - - - fold here - - - - - - - - - - - - - - - - - -

NOLO

Registration Card

NAME _____ DATE _____

ADDRESS _____

CITY _____ STATE _____ ZIP _____

PHONE _____ EMAIL _____

WHERE DID YOU HEAR ABOUT THIS PRODUCT? _____

WHERE DID YOU PURCHASE THIS PRODUCT? _____

DID YOU CONSULT A LAWYER? (PLEASE CIRCLE ONE)   YES   NO   NOT APPLICABLE

DID YOU FIND THIS BOOK HELPFUL?   (VERY)   5   4   3   2   1   (NOT AT ALL)

COMMENTS _____

_____

WAS IT EASY TO USE?   (VERY EASY)   5   4   3   2   1   (VERY DIFFICULT)

We occasionally make our mailing list available to carefully selected companies whose products may be of interest to you.
- ❑ If you do not wish to receive mailings from these companies, please check this box.
- ❑ You can quote me in future Nolo promotional materials.
    Daytime phone number _____.

SELBU 2.0

fold here

- -

Place
stamp here

Nolo
950 Parker Street
Berkeley, CA 94710-9867

Attn: